WEALTH AGAINST COMMONWEALTH

BY

HENRY DEMAREST LLOYD

NEW YORK
HARPER & BROTHERS PUBLISHERS
1894

CONTENTS

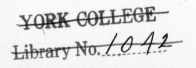

WEALTH AGAINST COMMONWEALTH

CHAPTER I

"THERE ARE NONE"—"THEY ARE LEGION"

NATURE is rich; but everywhere man, the heir of nature, is poor. Never in this happy country or elsewhere—except in the Land of Miracle, where "they did all eat and were filled" —has there been enough of anything for the people. Never since time began have all the sons and daughters of men been all warm, and all filled, and all shod and roofed. Never yet have all the virgins, wise or foolish, been able to fill their lamps with oil.

The world, enriched by thousands of generations of toilers and thinkers, has reached a fertility which can give every human being a plenty undreamed of even in the Utopias. But between this plenty ripening on the boughs of our civilization and the people hungering for it step the "cornerers," the syndicates, trusts, combinations, with the cry of "overproduction"—too much of everything. Holding back the riches of earth, sea, and sky from their fellows who famish and freeze in the dark, they declare to them that there is too much light and warmth and food. They assert the right, for their private profit, to regulate the consumption by the people of the necessaries of life, and to control production, not by the needs of humanity, but by the desires of a few for dividends. The coal syndicate thinks there is too much coal. There is too much iron, too much lumber, too much flour— for this or that syndicate.

1

The majority have never been able to buy enough of anything; but this minority have too much of everything to sell.

Liberty produces wealth, and wealth destroys liberty. "The splendid empire of Charles V.," says Motley, "was erected upon the grave of liberty." Our bignesses, cities, factories, monopolies, fortunes, which are our empires, are the obesities of an age gluttonous beyond its powers of digestion. Mankind are crowding upon each other in the centres, and struggling to keep each other out of the feast set by the new sciences and the new fellowships. Our size has got beyond both our science and our conscience. The vision of the railroad stockholder is not far-sighted enough to see into the office of the General Manager; the people cannot reach across even a ward of a city to rule their rulers; Captains of Industry "do not know" whether the men in the ranks are dying from lack of food and shelter; we cannot clean our cities nor our politics; the locomotive has more man-power than all the ballot-boxes, and mill-wheels wear out the hearts of workers unable to keep up beating time to their whirl. If mankind had gone on pursuing the ideals of the fighter, the time would necessarily have come when there would have been only a few, then only one, and then none left. This is what we are witnessing in the world of livelihoods. Our ideals of livelihood are ideals of mutual deglutition. We are rapidly reaching the stage where in each province only a few are left; that is the key to our times. Beyond the deep is another deep. This era is but a passing phase in the evolution of industrial Cæsars, and these Cæsars will be of a new type—corporate Cæsars.

For those who like the perpetual motion of a debate in which neither of the disputants is looking at the same side of the shield, there are infinite satisfactions in the current controversy as to whether there is any such thing as "monopoly." "There are none," says one side. "They are legion," says the other. "The idea that there can be such a thing is absurd," says one, who with half a dozen associates controls the source, the price, the quality, the quantity of nine-tenths of a great necessary of life. But "There will soon be a trust for every production, and a master to fix the price for every necessity of life," said the Senator who framed the United States Anti-Trust Law. This difference as to facts is due to a difference in the definitions through which the facts are regarded. Those who say "there are none" hold with the Attorney-General of the United States and the decision he quotes from the highest Federal court which has yet passed on this question[1] that no one has a monopoly unless there is a "disability" or "restriction" imposed by law on all who would compete. A syndicate that had succeeded in bottling for sale all the air of the earth would not have a monopoly in this view, unless there were on the statute-books a law forbidding every one else from selling air. No others could get air to sell; the people could not get air to breathe, but there would be no monopoly because there is no "legal restriction" on breathing or selling the atmosphere.

Excepting in the manufacture of postage-stamps, gold dollars, and a few other such cases of a "legal restriction," there are no monopolies according to this definition. It excludes the whole body of facts which the people include in their definition, and dismisses a great public question by a mere play on words. The other side of the shield was described by Judge Barrett, of the Supreme Court of New York. A monopoly he declared to be "any combination the tendency of which is to prevent competition in its broad and general sense, and to control and thus at will enhance prices to the detriment of the public. . . . Nor need it be permanent or complete. It is enough that it may be even temporarily and partially successful. The question in the end is, Does it inevitably tend to public injury?"[2]

Those who insist that "there are none" are the fortunate ones who came up to the shield on its golden side. But common usage agrees with the language of Judge Barrett, because

---

[1] Annual Report Attorney-General of the United States, 1893.

[2] People of the State of New York *vs.* The North River Sugar Refining Company. Supreme Court of New York—at Circuit (January 9, 1889). New York Senate Trusts, 1889, p. 278.

it exactly fits a fact which presses on common people heavily, and will grow heavier before it grows lighter.

The committee of Congress investigating trusts in 1889 did not report any list of these combinations to control markets, "for the reason that new ones are constantly forming, and that old ones are constantly extending their relations so as to cover new branches of the business and invade new territories."

It is true that such a list, like a dictionary, would begin to be wrong the moment it began to appear. But though only an instantaneous photograph of the whirlwind, it would give an idea, to be gained in no other way, of a movement shadowing two hemispheres. In an incredible number of the necessaries and luxuries of life, from meat to tombstones, some inner circle of the "fittest" has sought, and very often obtained, the sweet power which Judge Barrett found the sugar trust had: It "can close every refinery at will, close some and open others, limit the purchases of raw material (thus jeopardizing, and in a considerable degree controlling, its production), artificially limit the production of refined sugar, enhance the price to enrich themselves and their associates at the public expense, and depress the price when necessary to crush out and impoverish a foolhardy rival."

Corners are "acute" attacks of that which combinations exhibit as chronic. First a corner, then a pool, then a trust, has often been the genesis. The last stage, when the trust throws off the forms of combination and returns to the simpler dress of corporations, is already well along. Some of the "sympathetical co-operations" on record have no doubt ceased to exist. But that they should have been attempted is one of the signs of the time, and these attempts are repeated again and again until success is reached.

The line of development is from local to national, and from national to international. The amount of capital changes continually with the recrystallizations in progress. Not less than five hundred million dollars is in the coal combination, which our evidence shows to have flourished twenty-two years; that in oil has nearly if not quite two hundred millions; and the other combinations in which its members are leaders foot up hundreds of millions more. Hundreds of millions of dollars are united in the railroads and elevators of the Northwest against the wheat-growers. In cattle and meat there are not less than one hundred millions; in whiskey, thirty-five millions; and in beer a great deal more than that; in sugar, seventy-five millions; in leather, over a hundred millions; in gas, hundreds of millions. At this writing a union is being negotiated of all the piano-makers in the United States, to have a capital of fifty millions. Quite beyond ordinary comprehension is the magnitude of the syndicates, if there is more than one, which are going from city to city, consolidating all the gas-works, electric-lighting companies, street-railways in each into single properties, and consolidating these into vast estates for central corporations of capitalists, controlling from metropolitan offices the transportation of the people of scores of cities. Such a syndicate negotiating in December, 1892, for the control of the street-railways of Brooklyn, was said by the New York *Times,* " on absolute authority, to have subscribed $23,-000,000 towards that end, before a single move had been made or a price set on a single share of stock." It was in the same hands as those busy later in gathering together the coal-mines of Nova Scotia and putting them under American control. There are in round numbers ten thousand millions of dollars claiming dividends and interest in the railroads of the United States. Every year they are more closely pooled. The public saw them marshalled, as by one hand, in the maintenance of the high passenger rates to the World's Fair in the summer of 1893.

Many thousands of millions of dollars are represented in these centralizations. It is a vast sum, and yet is but a minority of our wealth.

Laws against these combinations have been passed by Congress and by many of the States. There have been prosecutions under them by the State and Federal governments. The laws and the lawsuits have alike been futile.

In a few cases names and form of organization have been changed, in consequence of legal pursuit. The whiskey, sugar, and oil trusts had to hang out new signs. But the thing itself, the will and the power to control markets, livelihoods, and liberties, and the toleration of this by the public—this remains unimpaired; in truth, facilitated by the greater secrecy and compactness which have been the only results of the appeal to law.

The Attorney-General of the national government gives a large part of his annual report for 1893 to showing "what small basis there is for the popular impression" "that the aim and effect of this statute" (the Anti-Trust Law) "are to prohibit and prevent those aggregations of capital which are so common at the present day, and which sometimes are on so large a scale as to practically control all the branches of an extensive industry." This executive says of the action of the "co-ordinate" Legislature: "It would not be useful, even if it were possible, to ascertain the precise purposes of the framers of the statute." He is the officer charged with the duty of directing the prosecutions to enforce the law; but he declares that since, among other reasons, "all ownership of property is a monopoly, . . . any literal application of the provisions of the statute is out of the question." Nothing has been accomplished by all these appeals to the legislatures and the courts, except to prove that the evil lies deeper than any public sentiment or public intelligence yet existent, and is stronger than any public power yet at call.

What we call Monopoly is Business at the end of its journey. The concentration of wealth, the wiping out of the middle classes, are other names for it. To get it is, in the world of affairs, the chief end of man.

There are no solitary truths, Goethe says, and monopoly—as the greatest business fact of our civilization, which gives to business what other ages gave to war and religion—is our greatest social, political, and moral fact.

The men and women who do the work of the world have the right to the floor. Everywhere they are rising to "a point of information." They want to know how our labor and the gifts of nature are being ordered by those whom our ideals and consent have made Captains of Industry over us; how it is that we, who profess the religion of the Golden Rule and the political economy of service for service, come to divide our produce into incalculable power and pleasure for a few, and partial existence for the many who are the fountains of these powers and pleasures. This book is an attempt to help the people answer these questions. It has been quarried out of official records, and it is a venture in realism in the world of realities. Decisions of courts and of special tribunals like the Interstate Commerce Commission, verdicts of juries in civil and criminal cases, reports of committees of the State Legislatures and of Congress, oath-sworn testimony given in legal proceedings and in official inquiries, corrected by rebutting testimony and by cross-examination—such are the sources of information.

One important exception is in the description of the operations of a great international combination in England, Germany, Holland, and elsewhere in Europe; this has had to be made from unofficial material. The people there are neither economically nor politically developed to the point we have reached in America, of using the legislative investigation and the powers of the courts to defend livelihoods and market rights, and enforce the social responsibilities of industrial power. Full and exact references are given throughout for the guidance of the investigator. The language of witnesses, judges, and official reports has been repeated verbatim, except for the avoidance of the surplusage and reduplication usual in such literature, and that, to permit the use of the dialogue form, the construction has been changed from the third person to the first in quotations from evidence. With these qualifications, wherever quotation marks have been used, the transcription is word for word. Evidence from such sources is more exact, circumstantial, and accurate than that upon which the mass of historical literature is founded.

To give the full and official history of numbers of these

combinations, which are nearly identical in inspiration, method, and result, would be repetition. Only one of them, therefore, has been treated in full—the oil trust. It is the most successful of all the attempts to put gifts of nature, entire industries, and world markets under one hat. Its originators claim this precedence. It was, one of its spokesmen says, "the parent of the trust system." [1] It is the best illustration of a movement which is itself but an illustration of the spirit of the age.

[1] *Combinations,* by S. C. T. Dodd, p. 19.

CHAPTER II

CUT OFF FROM FIRE

ROME banished those who had been found to be public enemies by forbidding every one to give them fire and water. That was done by all to a few. In America it is done by a few to all. A small number of men are obtaining the power to forbid any but themselves to supply the people with fire in nearly every form known to modern life and industry, from matches to locomotives and electricity. They control our hard coal and much of the soft,[1] and stoves, furnaces, and steam and hot-water heaters; the governors on steam-boilers and the boilers; gas and gas-fixtures; natural gas and gas-pipes; electric lighting, and all the appurtenances. You cannot free

[1] References:

1. Investigation by the Senate of Pennsylvania into the Anthracite Coal Difficulties, 1871.

2. Morris Run Coal Company vs. The Barclay Coal Company. Pennsylvania State Reports, Vol. 68, p. 173.

3. Report on the Coal Combination. New York Assembly Committee on Railroads, 1878.

4. Labor Troubles in Anthracite Regions, 1887–1888. House of Representatives, 50th Congress, Second Session. Report No. 4147.

5. New York Senate Investigation of the Coal Combination, 1892.

6. Alleged Coal Combination. House of Representatives, 52d Congress, 2d Session. Report No. 2278. January 18, 1893.

7. Coxe Brothers & Co. vs. The Lehigh Valley Railroad Company, before the Interstate Commerce Commission. Report and Opinion of the Commission.

8. John C. Haddock vs. Delaware, Lackawanna and Western Railroad Company, before the Interstate Commerce Commission, 1890.

9. Hocking Valley Investigation. General Assembly of Ohio, 1885.

10. Trusts or Pools. Investigation by Legislature of Ohio, 1889.

11. Alleged Combinations in Manufactures, Trade, etc. Dominion House of Commons, 1888.

yourself by changing from electricity to gas, or from the gas of the city to the gas of the fields. If you fly from kerosene to candles, you are still under the ban.

The report adopted by the National Association of Stove Manufacturers, at the Thirteenth Annual Convention, 1884, said: "While it is true that iron is a dollar or two lower than last year, and that the cost of labor has also been reduced, your committee is confident that there is not a manufacturer present who can truthfully say he can afford to reduce the price of his goods." "It is a chronic case," the President said in 1888, "of too many stoves, and not enough people to buy them."

The match company, by whose consent all the fires in the United States and Canada are lighted, was organized, as stated, by the Supreme Court of Michigan, for the purpose of controlling the manufacture and trade. Thirty-one manufacturers, owning substantially all the factories where matches were made in the United States, either went into the combination, or were purchased by the match company, and out of this number all were closed except about thirteen.

One of the company, who has been a conspicuous candidate for a nomination to the presidency of the United States, testified that the price of matches was kept up to pay the large sums of money expended to exclude others from the match business, remove competition, buy up machinery and patents, and purchase other match factories. This was told in a suit between two stockholders on a question of their relative rights; but the court, of its own motion, declared the combination illegal, and took notice of the public interests involved.[1]

"Such a vast combination is a menace to the public," said the court. "It is no answer to say that this monopoly has, in fact, reduced the price of friction-matches. That policy may have been necessary to crush competition. The fact exists that it rests in the discretion of this company at any time to raise the price to an exorbitant degree." "Indeed, it is doubtful if free government can long exist in a country where such

---

[1] Richardson *vs.* Buhl *et al.* Michigan State Reports, vol. lxxvii., p. 632.

enormous amounts of money are allowed to be accumulated in the vaults of corporations, to be used at discretion in controlling the property and business of the country against the interest of the public and that of the people, for the personal gain and aggrandizement of a few individuals."

Within the last thirty years, 95 per cent. of the anthracite coal of America—practically the entire supply, it was reported by Congress in 1893—has passed from the ownership of private citizens, many thousands in number, into the possession of the railroads controlling the highways of the coal-fields.

These railroads have been undergoing a similar process of consolidation, and are now the property of eight great corporations. This surrender of their property by the individual coal-mine owners is a continuing process, in operation at this moment, for the complete extinction of the "individual" and the independents in this field. It is destined, according to the report of Congress of 1893,[1] to end "in the entire absorption . . . of the entire anthracite coal-fields and collieries by . . . the common carriers."

Anthracite coal is geographically a natural monopoly contained in three contiguous fields which, if laid close together, would not cover more than eight miles by sixty. But bituminous coal, although scattered in exhaustless measures all over the continent, is being similarly appropriated by the railroads, and its area is being similarly limited artificially by their interference.

"Railroad syndicates," says the investigation of 1888,[2] "are buying all the best bituminous coal lands along their lines in Missouri, Kansas, Colorado, Arkansas, Tennessee, Alabama, and other Western States and Territories, no doubt with a view of levying tribute upon the people's fuel and the industrial fires of the country."

Canada remains unannexed politically, but its best coal deposits have become a part of the United States. In 1892 a syndicate of American capitalists obtained the control of the

---

[1] Page ii.   [2] Page xxii.

principal bituminous coal-mines of Nova Scotia. Among them were men connected both with the anthracite pool and with the combination which seeks control of the oil market of Canada and of the United States.

The process of consolidation is shown by official and judicial investigations to have been in progress in the bituminous fields at least as far back as 1871, with the same purposes, methods, and results as in the anthracite fields, though more slowly, on account of the greater number and vastness of the deposits. From Pennsylvania to the Pacific coast these are narrowed to the territory along the railroads, and narrowed there again to the mines owned or favored by the railroad managers.

The investigations by Congress in 1888 and 1893 both state that the railroads of the country are similarly becoming the owners of our iron and timber lands, and both call upon the people to save themselves. A new law of industry is rising into view. Ownership of the highways ends in ownership of everything and everybody that must use the highways.

The railroads compel private owners to sell them their mines or all the product by refusing to supply cars for their business, and by charging rates for the transportation of coal so high that every one but themselves loses money on every ton sent to market. When the railroads elect to have the output large, they furnish many cars; when they elect to have the output small, they furnish few cars; and when they elect that there shall be no output whatever, they furnish no cars.

One of the few surviving independent coal producers, who is losing heavily on every ton he sends to market, but keeps on in the hope that the law will give him redress, was asked by a committee of Congress why he did not sell out and give up the business? He was willing, he said, to abide the time when his rights on the railroad could be judicially determined. There was another reason. "It might be considered a very sentimental one. I have spent, sir, considerable time and a large amount of energy and skill in building up my business, and I rather like to continue it."

"In other words, you don't want to be forced to sell out?"

" No, sir ; I don't want to be forced to sell my product, any more than I want to be forced to sell my collieries." [1]

Though coal is an article of commerce greater in volume than any other natural product in the United States carried on railroads, amounting to not less than 130,000,000 tons a year ; and though the appliances for its transportation have been improved, and the cost cheapened every year, so that it can be handled with less cost and risk than almost any other class of freight, the startling fact appears in the litigations before the Interstate Commerce Commission and the investigations by Congress, that anthracite freight rates have been advanced instead of being decreased, are higher now than they were in 1879, and that coal is made by these confederated railroads to pay rates vastly higher than the average of all other high and low class freight, nearly double the rate on wheat or cotton. These high freight rates serve the double purpose of seeming to justify the high price of coal, and of killing off year by year the independent coal-producers. What the railroad coal-miner pays for freight returns to its other self, the railroad. What the independent coal-producer pays goes also to the railroad, his competitor. " This excess over just and reasonable rates of transportation constitutes an available fund by which they (the railroads) are enabled to crush out the competition of independent coal-producers." [2]

By these means, as Congress found in 1888,[3] the railroad managers have forced the independent miners to sell to them or their friends at the price they chose to pay. They were the only possible buyers, because only they were sure of a supply of cars, and of freight rates at which they could live.

The private operators thus being frozen out are able, as the investigation by the New York Legislature in 1878 showed, to produce coal more economically than the great companies, because not burdened with extravagant salaries, royalties, and

[1] Coal Combination, Congress, 1893. Testimony of John C. Haddock, pp. 242–261.

[2] Same, p. iv. [3] Report, p. xlv.

leases, interest on fictitious bonded debts, and dividends on false capitalization of watered stock. By the laws of supply and demand they would compete out the unwieldy corporations, but these administer a superior political economy in their supply and demand of cars and freight rates. ● The unfittest, economically, survives.

"The railroad companies engaged in mining and transporting coal are practically in a combination to control the output and fix the price. . . . They have a practical monopoly of the production, the transportation, and sale of anthracite coal."[1] This has been the finding in all the investigations for twenty years. "More than one, if not all, of the anthracite monopolies," Congress reported in 1888, "run several of their mines in the name of private operators to quiet the general clamor against carrying companies having a monopoly of mining also."

The anthracite collieries of Pennsylvania could now produce 50,000,000 tons a year. The railroads restrict them to 40,000,000 or 41,000,000 tons,[2] nine or ten million tons less than they could furnish to ward off the frosts of winter and to speed the wheels of the world, and this creation of artificial winter has been in progress from the beginning of the combination.

In the ten months between February and November, 1892, the price of coal in the East, as investigated by Congress in 1893,[3] was advanced by the coal railroads as much as $1.25 and $1.35 a ton on the kinds used by house-keepers, and the combinations, the report of Congress says, "exercise even a more baleful influence on the production and transportation of coal for the Western market." The extortion in the price fixed by the coal railroads was found by Congress, in 1888, to be an average of one dollar a ton—"considerably more than a dollar a ton"—on all consumed in the United States, or $39,000,000 in that year, and now $40,000,000 to $41,000,000 a year. The same investigation found that be-

---

[1] Coal Combination, Congress, 1893, pp. iii., iv., vi.   [2] Same, p. i.

[3] Same, p. v.

tween 1873 and 1886 $200,000,000 more than a fair market price was taken from the public by this combination.[1]

This in anthracite alone. How many hundreds, perhaps thousands, of millions more have been taken by the railroads which control the bituminous coal - fields from Pennsylvania to the Pacific, there are no adjudicated means of estimating.

By the same power which has crushed out the independent coal - miner, the retailer in the cities has been reduced from a free man to an instrument to despoil his neighbors— with whom he is often a fellow-victim—for the benefit of absentee capitalists; he is hounded by detectives; by threats of cutting off his supply, is made a compulsory member of a secret oath - bound society to "maintain prices." "Combinations exist," says the Canadian report, "among coal-dealers in Toronto, Ottawa, Montreal, and London. Detectives are employed and the dealers placed under surveillance. . . . Oaths of fidelity to the constitution and rules are required not only of the members, but also of their salesmen, and the oaths in the cases of these employés are made in some instances retroactive as well as prospective. All violations of oaths are adjudicated upon by the executive committee referred to, the penalties being heavy fines or expulsion. . . . In accordance with arrangements made with the American coal - dealers, those who were in default in membership, either from inability to pay fines or from other causes, were prevented from purchasing coal in the United States."[2]

The retailer dare not tell his wrongs even in the committee-rooms of Congress. "Your committee," says the report of 1893 to Congress, "experienced great difficulty in obtaining testimony from retail coal-dealers, who apparently labor under fears of injury to their business in case they should appear and give evidence."

"During the first forty years," Congress reported in 1888, "the mines were worked by individuals, just as are farms. The hundreds of employers were in active competition with

---

[1] Report, pp. xiv., xv., xlix.
[2] Combinations, Canadian Parliament, 1888, pp. 5, 6, 7.

each other for labor. The fundamental law of supply and demand alike governed all parties. As to engagement, employer and employé stood upon a common level of equality and manhood. Skill and industry upon the part of the miner assured to him steady work, fair wages, honest measurement, and humane treatment. Should these be denied by one employer, many other employers were ready to give them. The miner had the same freedom as to engagement, the same reward for faithful service, and protection against injustice that the farm-hand possesses because of the competition between farmers employing hands. . . . This virtual combination of all employers into one syndicate has practically abolished competition between them as to wages; and gradually, but inexorably, the workmen have found themselves encoiled as by an anaconda until now they are powerless." [1]

There was an investigation of the coal combination by the Pennsylvania Legislature in 1871, the testimony taken in which showed that when, after a thirty days' strike by the men, a number of private coal-mine owners acceded to their terms, and wished to reopen their mines and send coal again to market, the railroads, by which alone they could get to market, raised their freights, as their men were still on strike, to three times the previous figures. These great corporations had determined not to yield to their men, and as they were mine-owners and coal-sellers as well as carriers, they refused to take coal for their competitors. . . . The result was that the price of coal was doubled, rising to $12 a ton; the resumption by the private mine-owners was stopped; and they, the workmen, and the consumer were all delivered over to the tender mercies of the six great companies. [2]

The coal companies in the anthracite regions keep thousands of surplus laborers on hand to underbid each other for employment and for submission to all exactions; hold them purposely ignorant when the mines are to be worked and when

[1] Report, p. lxx.
[2] Investigation by the Senate of Pennsylvania into the Anthracite Coal Difficulties, 1871.

closed, so that they cannot seek employment elsewhere; bind them as tenants by compulsion in the companies' houses, so that rent shall run against them, whether wages run on or not, and under leases by which they can be turned out with their wives and children on the mountain-side in midwinter if they strike; compel them to fill cars of larger capacity than agreed upon; make them buy their powder and other working outfit of the companies at an enormous advance on the cost; compel them to buy coal of the company at the company's price, and in many cases to buy a fixed quantity, more than they need; compel them to employ the doctor named by the company, and to pay him whether sick or well; "pluck" them at the company's stores, so that when pay-day comes around the company owes the men nothing, there being authentic cases where "sober, hard-working miners toiled for years or even a lifetime without having been able to draw a single dollar, or but a few dollars, in actual cash," in "debt until the day they died;" refuse to fix the wages in advance, but pay them upon some hocus-pocus sliding scale, varying with the selling price in New York, which the railroad slides to suit itself; and, most extraordinary of all, refuse to let the miners know the prices on which their living slides—a fraud, says the report of Congress, "on its face." [1]

The companies dock the miners' output arbitrarily for slate and other impurities, and so can take from their men five to fifty tons more in every hundred than they pay for. [2]

In order to keep the miners disciplined and the coal-market under-supplied, the railroads restrict work so that the miners often have to live for a month on what they can earn in six or eight days; and these restrictions are enforced upon their miners by withholding cars from them to fill, as upon competitors by withholding cars to go to market. [3]

Labor organizations are forbidden, and the men intentionally provoked to strike, to affect the coal-market.

The laboring population of the coal regions, finally, is kept

[1] Report, pp. lxx., and following.   [2] Same, p. lxxvi.   [3] Same, p. lxxvii.

2

"down" by special policemen enrolled under special laws, and often in violation of law, by the railroads and coal and iron companies practically when and in what numbers these companies choose. These coal and iron policemen are practically without responsibility to any one but their employers, are armed as the corporations see fit with army revolvers, or Winchester rifles, or both, are made detectives by statute, and not required to wear their shields. They provoke the people to riot, and then shoot them legally.[1]

" By the percentage of wages," says the report of Congress, " by false measurements, by rents, stores, and other methods, the workman is virtually a chattel of the operator." It says, to summarize: " The carrier drives out both operator and owner, obtains the property, works the mine, 'disciplines' the miner, lowers wages by the importation of Huns and Italians, restricts the output, and advances the price of coal to the public. It is enabled to commit such wrongs upon individuals and the public by virtue of exercising absolute control of a public highway."[2]

The people of Pennsylvania, in 1873, adopted a new Constitution. To put an end to the consolidation of all the anthracite coal lands into the hands of the railroads, this Constitution forbade common carriers to mine or manufacture articles for transportation over their lines, or to buy land except for carrying purposes. These provisions of the Constitution have been disobeyed "defiantly." " The railroads have defiantly gone on acquiring title to hundreds of thousands of acres of coal, as well as of neighboring agricultural lands." They have been "aggressively pursuing the joint business of carrying and mining coal." So far from quitting it, they " have increased their mining operations by extracting bituminous as well as anthracite."[3]

Instead of enacting "appropriate legislation," as commanded by the new Constitution, to effectuate its prohibitions, the Legislature has passed laws to nullify the Constitution by pre-

---

[1] Report, pp. ix., xciv., and following.   [2] Same, p. xlv.   [3] Same, p. xiii.

venting forever any escheat to the State of the immense area of lands unlawfully held by the railroads. Every effort breaking down to meet the evil by State action, failure was finally confessed by the passage in 1878, by the Pennsylvania Legislature, of a joint resolution asking Congress to legislate " for equity in the rates of freight."

In 1887 Congress passed the Interstate Commerce Law, and established the Interstate Commerce Commission to enforce justice on the railway highways. The independent mine-owners of Pennsylvania appealed to it. Two years and a half were consumed in the proceedings. The Commission decided that the rates the railroad charged were unjust and unreasonable, and ordered them reduced.[1] But the decision has remained unenforced, and cannot be enforced. The railroads treat the Commission with the same contumely they visit on the Constitution of Pennsylvania, and two years after the decision Congress in 1893 found their rates to be 50 cents a ton higher than what the Commission had declared to be just and equitable.[2] The Interstate Commerce Law provides for the imprisonment in the penitentiary of those guilty of the crimes it covers. But the only conviction had under it has been of a shipper for discriminating against a railroad.

---

[1] Coxe case before Interstate Commerce Commission, Coal Combination, Congress, 1893, p. 183.

[2] Same, p. v.

CHAPTER III

PROHIBITION THAT PROHIBITS

THAT which governments have not yet been equal to has been accomplished by the private co-operation of a few citizens. They decree at their pleasure that in this town or that State no one shall manufacture alcohol, and they enforce the decree. Theirs is the only prohibition that prohibits.

From the famous whiskey ring of 1874 to the pool of 1881 and the trust of 1887, and from the abandonment of that "trust" dress and the reorganization into one corporation in 1890 down to the present, this private regulation of the liquor traffic has gone on. It is a regulation of a good deal more than the liquor traffic. Through its control of alcohol it is a power over the arts and sciences, the manufacture and the preparation of medicines, and a power over politics. More than one chapter of our history exhibits the government itself holding to these rectifiers relations suggestive of anything but rectification. The report of the investigation by Congress in 1893 notes the fact that on the strength of a rumor that the internal - revenue tax was to be increased by Congress, the Trust raised its prices 25 cents a gallon. This would amount to a profit of $12,500,000 on its yearly output.

By February, 1888, all the important distilleries in the Northern States—nearly eighty—were in the Trust, excepting two, the larger of which was in Chicago. The cases of these irreconcilable competitors were set for consideration, according to the *Chicago Tribune's* report, at a private meeting of the trustees February 3d. In April the Chicago distillery firm published the fact that they had caught a spy of the Trust in their works. He had given them a confession in writing. In September it was discovered that the valve of a vat in this distillery had been tampered with in such a way as to have caused an explosion had it not been found out in time. The next month its owners made known that they had been offered and refused $1,000,000 from the Trust for their works. In December the country was startled by the news that this distillery had been the scene of an awful explosion of dynamite. All the buildings in the neighborhood were shaken and many panes of glass were broken. A jagged hole about three feet square was torn in the roof. There were 15,000 barrels of whiskey stored under the roof that was torn open, and if these had been ignited a terrible fire would have been added to the effect of the explosion. A package of dynamite which had failed to explode, though the fuse had been lighted, was found on the premises by the Chicago police.

The Chicago representative of the whiskey combination ridiculed the idea that the Trust had had anything to do with this. "Such a thing," he said, "is contrary to the genius of a trust."

The wholesale liquor-dealers threatened, at a conference in 1890 with the president of the Trust, to manufacture for themselves, to escape the advance which had been made in the price of high-wines. The president said, as reported in the *Wine and Spirit Gazette:*

"I do not believe there is a spirits distillery in the country that you can buy. We own nearly all of them, and have at present seventy-eight idle distilleries."

February 11, 1891, the explosion of December, 1888, was recalled by the unexpected arrest of the secretary of the combination in Chicago by the United States authorities. The Grand Jury of Cook County found an indictment, February 17th, against the prisoner. April 20th he was indicted by the Federal Grand Jury. The crime of which he was charged was attempting to bribe a government gauger to blow up the troublesome distillery. The gauger whom the secretary endeavored to enlist had been loyal to his trust, the government, and had made known to his superiors the offer and purpose of the bribe.

If the explosion had been carried out 150 men at work in the distillery would have been destroyed. The evidence given Congress afterwards tended to show that part of the plan was that the bribed gauger who was to set and explode the infernal-machine was not to be allowed to survive to claim his reward and perhaps repent and tell. The fuse was fixed so that the explosion would be instantaneous instead of giving the time promised him to get out of the way.

In a statement to the press, February 15th, the president of the Trust said, as the result of a conference of the trustees:

"We have unanimously agreed to stand by the secretary."

Early in June rumors were in circulation in New York that the Chicago independent had sold out; and soon after the confirmation of the report, with full details, was authoritatively published.

June 8th the judge of the United States Court in Chicago quashed the Federal indictment, on the ground that it is not a crime under any of the United States laws for an internal-revenue officer to set fire to a distillery of his own volition and impulse, and that it is not a crime against the United States for another person to bribe him to do such an act. He held that the offender could be punished only through the State courts. The United States had property in the distillery to the extent of $800,000 due for taxes, which was a legal lien on the property; but the United States District Attorney and the judge could find no Federal law under which, for the gauger to destroy this property of the United States, or for the Whiskey Trust to bribe him to do so, it was a crime. When the indictments framed by the State Attorney of Chicago came before the State courts, three of the four were found defective and were quashed. The Chicago correspondent of the New York *World* telegraphed that he had been told by the State Attorney, at the time the Federal proceedings were quashed, that of his four indictments he relied most upon that for conspiracy; "but in court yesterday the State

Attorney let the charge of conspiracy fall to the ground because, as he said, there was not evidence enough to secure a conviction."

"We haven't the evidence of the gauger; I don't know where he is," the State Attorney said.

But this witness declared in a public letter in February, 1893, "Myself and others with positive evidence were always ready to testify, and I have the facts to-day."

The judge of the State court held the motion to quash until July, and then announced that he would make no decision until August. He withheld his ruling until October. Then he held the secretary for trial on two counts, charging conspiracy to bribe the gauger and destroy the independent distillery; but remarked "informally," the newspapers said, that conviction would be difficult.

When the case was called March 22, 1892, a delay was granted "until next Monday," to enable the prisoner's counsel to read the "bill of particulars" to find out what he was charged with. The secretary did not trouble himself to attend court. His case was not heard of again until June 24th, when he was released on a nolle prosequi entered by the State Attorney because the evidence was insufficient, and became a free man. That was the end.

Owing to this success of State and United States attorneys in being unsuccessful, the people have never had an opportunity of hearing in court the evidence on which the Government acted in making the arrest, and on which the grand juries found the indictments. But the gauger through whom the secretary of the Trust had attempted to execute his plans was called as a witness before the Committee of Congress which investigated the Trust in 1893, and he told again the story of the infernal-machine. It was as follows, in his own words, omitting names and unnecessary details:

"I was United States internal-revenue gauger from 1879 until after Mr. Cleveland's election, and I was reappointed in 1889, and have been continuously since that time. Late in December, 1890, I received a letter from the secretary of the

whiskey combination at Peoria, telling me that he would
like to meet me at the Grand Pacific Hotel on New-year's
Day. I met him. He said, 'You may be able to do considerable good here; not only for us, but of considerable advantage to yourself. Your $1500 a year is nothing to what you
would get by helping us. You can get $10,000 by assisting
us in this thing; in fact, to make matters right, you could
get in three months $25,000.'" The gauger reported this to
his superiors, who told him to go on. "Be particular, and
after every interview with him make a note of everything
that passes between you while it is fresh in your mind." "I
did that," the witness continued, "and I have the original
notes in my pocket. There are the original notes," exhibiting
them to the committee. "They have never left my possession. I have kept them on my person right along." After
some correspondence and another interview, he met the secretary again January 25th. "Now," said the latter, "I can give
you something which, if put under a cistern, will in three or
four hours go off, and no person know what it was or who did
it, and all the trouble that has been caused us will be stopped
at once, the sufferings of many people stopped, and no loss to
those folks, as they are well insured." "When I recovered
from my surprise I asked if it was an explosive. He replied,
'No; a simple but effective thing which would shoot a ball
into a tub through the bottom. You will have $10,000 for
your work of placing this under a cistern of high-proof, either
alcohol or spirits, or what is better than cash, 200 shares of
stock.' I asked at what they sold. He said, 'Forty-seven, but
it would be up ten points at once,' and I could profit by the
raise. 'This will raise a big row.' 'Yes,' he said, 'one cistern
well caught, all would go, and it would be right into the warehouse and stop everything at once. It is the most effective
way to help us and make a clean job, and you having access
to all parts of the distillery and unsuspected is why you could
do it so easily.' He had then, in room 35, powder and four
steel elongated balls, solid, turned, and with long points. The
principal article, however, was a kind of yellowish liquid,

which when exposed to sixty-five degrees temperature would produce a flame caused by evaporation. I remarked that there was probably no hurry about this thing, and he said, 'The sooner the better; you may be ordered away from here, and I am come all prepared; everything is ready to load, and that can be done quickly.'"

The gauger reported all this to his superior and told him that "I proposed to take the infernal apparatus." His superior said, "Of course." "I then returned to Grand Pacific, room 35; found loading just completed and much material scattered about, oakum in can saturated slightly with kerosene and alcohol to give good start. The secretary said that three fuses were attached to the gun, one of which would go off under water. He had one steel shell which had been shot through three inches of wood in experimenting. He showed me particularly how to place can; to feel underneath for timbers; put it where ball will enter tub. Also, that in stopping over to meet the president of the combination to-morrow he would have a chance to buy up stock reasonably before our work caused the raise. He expected to buy 1000 shares. Friday, the 30th of January, I rather anticipated a visit from the secretary at my hotel, but I received a letter from him instead of a visit, and Judge Hart, the solicitor of the Internal-Revenue Department, who was there in Chicago, when he read the letter thought that the evidence was certainly conclusive." On Sunday, the 8th, the gauger surrendered the box containing the infernal-machine, which was sealed, to a high official who had come on from New York. "The reason why he came on is that the authorities would not believe my testimony. They did not think it was possible a gentleman in the secretary's position would undertake so heinous a crime, and they did not know but what I was a crank. On Monday, the 9th, I was instructed to write a letter. The thing was to arrest in a proper way. The next day I received a despatch: 'Will be at Pacific to-morrow (Wednesday) morning.'

"Wednesday morning the secretary was arrested, as he was about to enter the hotel, by a deputy marshal, and conducted

to the Marshal's office in the Government building. There
was a bottle of this composition found in his grip. He had
told me it would go off in three or four hours. I was in the
anteroom of the city grand jury after the chemist had given
his testimony. The chemist said that it was his opinion it
would have or might have gone off in three seconds. Fire
would cause the shooting of the ball, and the ball making a
hole in the tub—alcohol or high-proof spirits—coming down,
of course all would have gone up. It could not have helped it,
and the explosion would have followed at once, not from the
machine, but from the contents of the cistern. They are
very explosive indeed, alcohol and high-proof spirits." [1]

What the Government authorities thought of all this is
shown in a letter which is spread upon the records of the
Treasury Department. It is addressed by the Commissioner
of Internal Revenue to the gauger. After thanking him for
his "highly commendable" conduct in relation to the bribe
the Commissioner says to Mr. Thomas S. Dewar :

"While your rejection of the offer was just what was expected from
you, considering your official and personal standing, yet I realize that
you have done more than simply reject the offer. You so conducted the
affair as to place the guilty party, it is hoped, in a position in which he
will be punished for this violation of law. The proposition was not only
to attempt to corrupt an honest officer of the Government, but was to
induce you, by the offer of a large sum of money, to commit a most heinous and inhuman act."

No attempt was made by the representatives of the Trust
before the committee to deny this testimony. They simply
disclaimed any responsibility for what their associate and
employé had done. "Whatever there was in that," testified
the president of the Whiskey Trust, "was with the former
secretary of this company, if there be anything of it." [2]

The Trust increased the number of plants under its control
from "nearly eighty" to eighty-one or eighty-two, the num-

---

[1] Whiskey Trust Investigation. Committee on the Judiciary Report, March 1,
1893. 52d Congress, 2d Session, House of Representatives, Report No. 2601, p. 16
and following.   [2] Same testimony, p. 28.

ber reported by the investigation of Congress in 1893. Its annual production was then 50,000,000 gallons; about 7,500,-000 gallons of it alcohol, 42,500,000 spirits. It is evident, says the report, that the company will soon have within its grasp the entire trade, and be able to dictate prices to consumers at pleasure.

"How do you account for spirits going up and corn going down at the same time in two or three instances?" the treasurer was asked.

"Simply because the distillers were getting in a position whereby they ran less than their capacity."[1]

The experience of mankind has always found, as Lord Coke pointed out, that monopoly adulterates.

The report of Congress states that unquestionably the largest part of the product of the combination finds its way into the open markets in the form of "compounded"—or artificial—bourbon and rye whiskeys, brandies, rums, gins, cordials. The testimony establishes the fact that about one half of the whiskey consumed in the country is of this compound product. These compounded liquors are supplied from the drugstores to the sick as medicine. One of the expert witnesses summoned to explain the process of this adulteration appeared before the committee with two demijohns, one containing pure alcohol and the other spirits, and a number of bottles containing essential oils, essences, etc., with which he proposed to make some experiments. "The basis here, this white product, is what is known as 'spirits' in the trade. With the use of these essential oils and essences now before you any kind of imitation liquor can be produced at almost a moment's notice. My first experiment will be with Jamaica rum. I put a drop of Jamaica-rum essence into this white spirits, a few drops of coloring matter, and some sugar syrup. Try of it and smell of it. Does it smell like rum and taste like it? If they want to make it cheaper, they reduce it with water. I will reduce it with water, and you will now notice

---

[1] Whiskey Trust Investigation, Congress, 1893, p. 62.

that the bead has disappeared from it. I will reproduce the bead by the use of bead oil. I put one drop in, and here is the result. Now, using rye-whiskey essence instead of Jamaica-rum essence, I will flavor this spirits. I will now put some prune juice into it to tone it. I will put some raisin oil in it to age it, and I will now commence to color it. This first exhibit" (holding it up before the committee) "is about the color of one-year-old whiskey that has been properly bonded. I will now color it so it will imitate a two-year-old whiskey. This is about the three-year-old now" (exhibiting it). "I will now give this the color of ' velvet whiskey,' which is sold as high as $4 a gallon " (exhibiting it). " The present price of spirits, to-day, I think, is $1.30 a gallon. The utilization of any of these essential oils and essences and coloring matter to make the transfer does not exceed a cost of one and a half cents a gallon. I am prepared to make imitations of any of these liquors at any time with this spirits basis—all the different whiskeys, Scotch and Irish whiskeys, the foreign gins and rums and brandies, after-dinner cordials and liqueurs. These materials as you have them exhibited before you of essential oils and essences are part and parcel of the stock in trade of every man in the United States of America who has got a rectifying license as a wholesale liquor dealer. . . . They are very generally and extensively in use throughout our entire country, in every hamlet and village, in all the branches of trade, the wholesale liquor dealer, the grocer having a liquor dealer's license, and retail druggists. . . . When a doctor prescribes French brandy, he expects to get a production which is a distillation of wine made from the grape. In that imitation brandy made from spirits and cognac oil he gets a crude product of corn, defeating entirely his purpose in the prescription. The same applies to gin, rum, and other articles wherever the imitations are found." [1]

Some of the substances named by witnesses as occurring in the oils and essences used for this adulteration are sulphuric

----

[1] Whiskey Trust Investigation, Congress, 1893, pp. 14, 15.

acid, prussic acid, fusel oil, creosote, nitro-benzol—all poisons, and some of them so virulent that a teaspoonful would kill.

"I have been warned when in the employ of these people not to take the crude material into my mouth," said one of the witnesses. Another witness denied that there was any danger in the infinitesimal portions used of the flavoring matter.

"The only result," said one of the members of the committee, "of the testimony and hearing of the committee will be to educate the public to the Trust methods. It will have no effect on the Trust."

CHAPTER IV

" SQUARE EATERS "

"By Heaven, square eaters, more meat I say !"
—*Beaumont and Fletcher.*

A DELEGATE to one of the millers' national conventions said, "We want cheaper wheat and dearer flour."

The Canadian Parliament reports that "the Biscuit Association," which had been in existence six years, had kept up the prices of its products, "although the prices of the ingredients used have in that time very materially decreased."

An Associated Press despatch from Chicago announced that at "a joint meeting of all the cracker bakers between Pittsburg and the Rocky Mountains, held this morning, it was unanimously agreed to advance the price of crackers."

A "Bread Union" has been formed in London for the amalgamation of concerns controlling hundreds of shops. Its chairman instructed the stockholders that by concentrating a large number of shops under one management in any district it could "quickly stifle the opposition of any small unprincipled trader bent on reducing prices for competition purposes." The Dominion Parliament, in condemning the Grocers' Guild as "obnoxious to the public interest in limiting competition, in enhancing prices," pointed out that "no reasonable excuse exists for many of its arbitrary acts and agreements. The wholesale grocery trade had been for many years in a flourishing condition; failures were almost unknown."

But though prosperous the grocers formed this guild, admitting some, proscribing others, and established by private legislation the profits they desired. The profits were "afterwards increased, and in no instance lowered, though values generally had fallen."

At Minneapolis, the seat of the greatest flour-manufacturing industry in the world, the elevators and railroads have united against the wheat-growers in a way which does much to realize the dream of the miller, of "cheaper wheat and dearer flour." A committee of the Minnesota legislature investigated this combination in 1892. The majority stopped short of reporting that it fixed the prices of wheat, but admitted that some of the testimony tended that way, and that the evidence "would seem to establish" that one of the most powerful railroads had done so, and "had attempted to coerce compliance with its requirements in the matter of prices by threats to embarrass the business of local buyers."[1] A report from a minority of the same committee was more outspoken. It summarizes the evidence, which shows that the railroads and the elevator companies united to enforce a uniform price for wheat. This price was six and a quarter cents below what it should be. All the railroads adjusted their freight rates to the artificial "list-price," and though rivals, they all charged the same rates. The elevator companies, owning an aggregate of fifteen hundred elevators, had a common agent who sent word daily, by telegram and letter, to all wheat-buyers as to the price to be paid the farmers. The report calculates the amount thereby taken from the wheat-growers by the elevators at from four to five millions of dollars a year.

The findings of this report were ratified by the adoption of its suggestions for a remedy. "There is," it said, "no agency but the State itself adequate to protect, now, the producer of wheat in Minnesota and the Northwest from the influence of this combine." It therefore recommended the erection and operation of elevators by the State. This was approved by the Legislature and by the Governor, appropriations were made, and the officials of the State went forward with the plan until the Supreme Court of the State stopped them on the ground of "unconstitutionality."

[1] Report of the Investigating Committee appointed by the Legislature of Minnesota of 1891, to determine whether wheat was taken without inspection from a public elevator in Duluth. April 7, 1892, p. 11.

That which we see the national associations of winter-wheat millers and spring-wheat millers, and the fish, and the egg, and the fruit, and the salt, and the preserves, and other combinations reaching out to do for a "free breakfast table," to put the "square meal" out of the reach of the "square eater," has been achieved to the last detail in sugar and meat. Every half-cent up or down in the price of sugar makes a loss or gain to the sugar combination at the rate of $20,000,000 a year. When it was capitalized for $50,000,000 it paid dividends of $5,000,000 a year. The value of the refineries in the combination was put by the New York Legislative Investigation of 1891 at $7,000,000.

The Hon. Wm. Wilson, of the committee of Congress investigating trusts in 1888, and the framer of the tariff bill of 1893, in a public communication quoted figures showing that this Trust had a surplus of $10,000,000 at the end of 1888, after paying its 10 per cent. dividend. The profits for the next five and a half months were $13,000,000. This surplus of one year and net profits of less than half a year together amount to $23,000,000, nearly half the then nominal capital, and several times more than the real value of all the concerns, as given above. These profits so conservative a paper as the New York *Daily Commercial Bulletin* called "plunder," and it reaffirmed that epithet when called to account. Stock was issued for this "fabulous valuation" of $50,000,000, put on this $7,000,000 of original value, and was made one of the specialties of the stock market.

"There has been an enormous and widespread speculation in the certificates of the trust," says the report of the New York Senate. "It was plainly one of the chief purposes of the trust to provide for the issue of these certificates, affording thereby an opportunity for great speculation in them, obviously to the advantage of the persons managing the trust. The issue of $50,000,000 certificates was amply sufficient for a speculation of many hundreds of millions of dollars." [1]

---

[1] Trusts, New York Senate, 1891, pp. 9, 11.

Since this investigation by the New York Legislature, the Sugar Trust has been reorganized into a single corporation. The capital of this is $75,000,000, all " water," since the value of the plants is fully covered by the bonds to the amount of $10,000,000. The actual value of the refineries in the Trust, excluding those which have been closed or dismantled, was investigated by the New York *World*, January 8, 1894, and put at $7,740,000. On this actual value of $7,740,000 in operation the Trust paid in regular and extra dividends in 1893 no less than $10,875,000, and acknowledged that there was in addition a surplus of $5,000,000 in the treasury. This was in addition to the interest on the $10,000,000 of bonds.

When a farmer sells a steer, a lamb, or a hog, and the housekeeper buys a chop or roast, they enter a market which for the whole continent, and for all kinds of cattle and meats, is controlled by the combination of packers at Chicago known as "the Big Four." [1] This had its origin in the "evening" arrangement, made in 1873 by the railroads with preferred shippers, on the ostensible ground that these shippers could equalize or even the cattle traffic of the roads. They received $15 as "a commission" on every car-load of cattle shipped from the West to New York, no matter by whom shipped, whether they shipped it or had anything to do with it or not. The commission was later reduced to $10. They soon became large shippers of cattle; and with these margins in their favor "evening" was not difficult business. [2] By 1878 the dressed-beef business had become important. As the Evener Combine had concentrated the cattle trade at Chicago, the dressed-beef interest necessarily had its home at the same place. It is a curious fact that the Evener Combine ceased about the time the dressed-beef interest began its phenomenal career. [3]

The committee appointed by the United States Senate to investigate the condition of the meat and cattle markets fixed

[1] Meat Products, United States Senate, 51st Congress, 1st Session, Report No. 829, 1890, p. 2.

[2] New York Assembly, " Hepburn Report," 1879, p. 70.

[3] Meat Products, United States Senate, 1890, p. 3.

3

upon St. Louis, Mo., and November 20, 1888, as the time and place of meeting, because the International Cattle Range Association and the Butchers' National Protective Association assembled at the same time and place. It was supposed that prominent members of these associations would avail themselves of the opportunity to appear before the committee. Some of them did testify frankly, but the presence of antagonistic influences, especially in the International Cattle Range Association, immediately became apparent, and industrious efforts were made to prevent the inquiries of the committee from affecting injuriously the dressed-beef interest at Chicago. The committee found that under the influence of the combination the price of cattle had gone down heavily. For instance: In January, 1884, the best grade of beef cattle sold at Chicago for $7.15 per hundred pounds, and in January, 1889, for $5.40; Northwestern range and Texas cattle sold in January, 1884, at $5.60, and in January, 1889, at $3.75; Texas and Indian cattle sold in 1884 at $4.75, the price declining to $2.50 in December, 1889. These are the highest Chicago prices for the months named.

"So far has the centralizing process continued that for all practical purposes," the report says, "the market of that city dominates absolutely the price of beef cattle in the whole country. Kansas City, St. Louis, Omaha, Cincinnati, and Pittsburg are subsidiary to the Chicago market, and their prices are regulated and fixed by the great market on the lake."[1] This great business is practically in the hands of four establishments at Chicago. The largest houses have a capacity for slaughtering 3,500 cattle, 3,000 sheep, and 12,000 hogs every ten hours. When the Senate committee visited Chicago, it was found impossible to obtain the frank and full testimony of either the commission men doing business at the Union Stock Yards, or of the employés of the packing and dressed-beef houses. The former testified reluctantly, and were unquestionably under some sort of constraint as to their public

[1] Meat Products, United States Senate, 1890, pp. 1, 2.

declarations. In private they stated to the members of the committee that a combination certainly existed between the "Big Four;" but when put on the stand as witnesses they shuffled and prevaricated to such a degree as, in many cases, to excite commiseration. The committee reported that the overwhelming weight of testimony from witnesses of the highest character, and from all parts of the West, is to the effect that cattle-owners going with their cattle to the Chicago and Kansas City markets find no competition among buyers, and if they refuse to take the first bid are generally forced to accept a lower one.

As to the effect upon retailers, local butchers, and consumers, it was admitted by the biggest of the Big Four "that they combined to fix the price of beef to the purchaser and consumer, so as to keep up the cost in their own interest." [1] They combined in opening shops and underselling the butchers of cattle at places all over the country, in order to force them to buy dressed meat. They combined in refusing to sell any meat to butchers at Washington, D. C., because the butchers had bid against them for contracts to supply with meats the Government institutions in the District of Columbia.

The compulsion put upon local butchers is illustrated in the S—— case. The following telegram was sent from the office of one of the combination at Chicago to an agent in Pennsylvania: "Cannot allow S—— to continue killing live cattle. If he will not stop, make other arrangements, and make prices so can get his trade."

S—— was a local butcher. He testified that he was approached by the agent with a proposition that he should sell dressed beef. He refused, and was then informed that he would be broken up in business. Notwithstanding this threat, he continued to butcher, and made his purchases of cattle at Buffalo. From the time of his refusal to sell dressed beef as proposed, he could not buy any meat from Chicago, and could not get any cars from the Erie Railroad to ship his cattle from

---

[1] Meat Products, United States Senate, 1890, p. 6.

Buffalo. He was boycotted for his refusal to discontinue killing cattle.[1] One of the combination, when testifying to this
matter, disclaimed responsibility for the despatch, but stated
that he did not think a butcher should be permitted to kill
cattle and at the same time sell dressed beef. "He could
not serve both interests."   "We have no hesitation in stating
as our conclusion, from all the facts," says the report, "that a
combination exists at Chicago between the principal dressed-
beef and packing houses, which controls the market and fixes
the price of beef cattle in their own interest."

When pork is cheap, less beef is eaten. Beef monopoly
must therefore widen into pork monopoly. This has happened. There is a combination between the pork-packers at
Chicago and the large beef-packers. It began in 1886. The
existence of such an arrangement was admitted by its most
important member; and it is found to have seriously affected
the prices of beef cattle, both to the producer and consumer.
It was shown that one of the companies of the Big Four made
in 1889 profits equal to 29 per cent. on its capital stock—
which may, or may not, have been paid in—and this was not
the largest of the companies. As to the idea that other capitalists might enter into competition with those now in possession, the report says: "The enormous capital of the great
houses now dominating the market, which each year becomes
larger, enables them to buy off all rivals."

The favoritism on the highways, in which this power had
its origin in 1873, has continued throughout to be its main
stay. The railroads give rates to the dressed-beef men which
they refuse to shippers of cattle, even though they ship by the
train-load—"an unjust and indefensible discrimination by the
railroads against the shipper of live cattle." The report says:
"This is the spirit and controlling idea of the great monopolies which dominate the country. . . . No one factor has been
more potent and active in effecting an entire revolution in the
methods of marketing the meat supply of the United States

---

[1] Meat Products, United States Senate, 1890, Testimony, pp. 464, 465.

than the railway transportation." [1]   There have been discriminations by the common carriers of the ocean as well as by the
railroads.   The steamship companies exclude all other shippers, by selling all their capacity to the members of the beef
combine, sometimes for months in advance.   It is useless for
any other shipper to apply.

Property is monopoly, the Attorney-General of the United
States says.   Those who own the bread, meat, sugar, salt, can
fix the price at which they will sell.   They can refuse to sell.
It is to these fellow-men we must pray, " Give us this day
our daily bread."   And when we have broken bread for the
last time, we can get entrance to our " long home" only by
paying "exorbitant" toll for our shrouds and our coffins to
the "Undertakers'" and the "National Burial Case" associations. [2]

---

[1] Meat Products, United States Senate, 1890.
[2] Trusts, New York Senate, 1888.   Combinations, Canadian Parliament, 1888.

CHAPTER V

STRIKING OIL

IT was an American idea to "strike oil." Those who knew it as the "slime" of Genesis, or used it to stick together the bricks of the Tower of Babel, or knelt to it in the fire temples, were content to take it as it rose, the easy gift of nature, oozing forth on brook or spring. But the American struck it.

The world, going into partial eclipse on account of the failing supply of whale oil, had its lamps all ready for the new light, and industries beyond number needed only an expansion of the supply.

De Witt Clinton, with the same genius that gave us the Erie Canal, suggested as early as 1814 the use of petroleum for light. Reichenbach, the great German chemist, predicted in 1830 that petroleum would yield an illuminating oil equal to the finest. Inventors and money-makers kept up close with scientific investigators in France, Great Britain, and America.

As early as 1845 the manufacture of coal-oil, both for light and other purposes, had become important in France. Selligue had made himself master of the secrets of petroleum. His name, says one of his chroniclers, "must forever remain inseparably connected with that of the manufacture of light from oil, and to his researches few have been able to add."[1]

The name of this genius and benefactor of humanity has remained almost unknown, except within a small scientific world. He was a member of the French Academy, and almost every year between 1834 and 1848 he came to it with some new dis-

---

[1] F. H. Storer, *American Journal of Science*, vol. xxx., 1860.

covery. On one occasion he reminds his associates that he holds a patent, granted in 1832, for making illuminating oil from coal, and declares that the business can be developed to any extent which commerce or the arts may require. By 1845 he had unlocked nearly every one of the hidden places in which this extraordinary product has stored its wonders. He found out how to make illuminating oil, illuminating gas, lubricating oil, colors, paraffine for candles, fertilizers, solvents for resin for painters, healing washes, chemicals. He had three refineries in operation in the Department Saône-et-Loire, as described in the report of a committee of the French Academy in 1840. He exhibited his oils in the London Exhibition of 1851, and twelve years before, in the Parisian Industrial Exhibition of 1839, he had crude and refined oils and paraffine to show. "Among the most important objects of the exhibition," said its German historian, Von Hermann, "if they can be prepared economically." This Selligue accomplished. Between 1837 and 1843 he refined more than 4,000,000 pounds of oil, and 50 per cent. of his product was good illuminating oil.

Before 1850, the Scotch had succeeded in getting petroleum, called shale oil, out of bituminous coal, had found how to refine it, and had perfected lamps in which it would burn. Joshua Merrill, the pioneer of oil refining in this country, with his partners, successfully refined petroleum at Waltham, Mass., where they established themselves in 1853. The American manufacturers were making kerosene as early as 1856 from Scotch coal,[1] imported at a cost of $20 to $25 a ton, and getting experts like Silliman to analyze petroleum, in the hope that somehow a supply of it might be got. By 1860 there were sixty-four of these manufactories in the United States. "A crowd of obscure inventors," says Felix Foucon, in the *Revue des Deux Mondes*, "with unremitting labors perfected the lamp—when it was premature to dream that illumination by mineral oil should become universal." All

---

[1] Petroleum and Its Products, by S. F. Peckham, U. S. Census, 1885, p. 159.

was ready, as the eminent English geologist, Binney, said, "for the start of the vast American petroleum trade." It was not a lack of knowledge, but a lack of petroleum, that hampered the American manufacturer before 1860.[1] The market, the capital, the consumer, the skilled labor, the inventions, and science were all waiting for "Colonel" Drake.

With Drake's success in "striking oil" came to an end the period, lasting thousands of years, of fire temples, sweep and bucket, Seneca oil; and came to an end, also, the Arcadian simplicity of the old times—old though so recent—in which Professor Silliman could say, "It is not monopolized by any one, but is carried away freely by all who care to collect it."

The oil age begins characteristically. As soon as Drake's well had made known its precious contents, horses began running, and telegrams flying, and money passing to get possession of the oil lands for the few who knew from those who did not know. The primitive days when "it was not monopolized by any one" were over. Thousands of derricks rose all over the territory, and oil scouts pushed with their compasses through the forests of the wilderness in all directions. Wells were bored all over Europe, as well as America, wherever traces of oil showed themselves, sometimes so close together that when one was pumped it would suck air from the other.

As soon as the petroleum began to flow out of the ground, refineries started up at every available place. They were built near the wells, as at Titusville and Oil City, and near the centres of transportation, such as Pittsburg and Buffalo, and near the points of export, as Philadelphia, Baltimore, New York. Numbers of little establishments appeared on the Jersey flats opposite New York.

There was plenty of oil for every one; at one time in 1862 it was only ten cents a barrel. The means of refining it had long before been found by science and were open to all; and even poor men building little stills could year by year add on

---

[1] Petroleum and Its Products, by S. F. Peckham, U. S. Census, 1885, p. 160.

to their works, increase their capital, and acquire the self-confidence and independence of successful men. The business was one of the most attractive possible to capital. " There is no handsomer business than this is," said one of the great merchants of New York. " You can buy the (crude) oil one week, and sell it the next week refined, and you can imagine the quantity of business that can be done." Men who understood the business, he said, " if they had not the capital could get all of the money they wanted." [1]

Whatever new processes and contrivances were needed the fertile American mind set about supplying. To carry the oil in bulk on the railroads tubs on flat cars were first used; but it was not long before the tub was made of iron instead of wood, and, laid on its side instead of bottom, became the tank of the cylinder car now so familiar.

The fluid which lubricates so many other things on their way through the world is easily made to slip itself along to market. General S. D. Karns was the author,[2] in 1860, of the first suggestion of a pipe line. He planned only for oil to run down hill. Then Hutchinson, the inventor of the Hutchinson rotary pump, saw that oil could be forced through by pressure, and the idea of the pipe line was complete. The first successful pipe line, put down by Samuel Van Syckel,[3] of Titusville, in 1865, from Pithole to Miller's Farm, four miles, has grown into a net-work of thousands of miles, running through the streets of towns, across fields and door-yards, under and over and beside roads, with trunk lines which extend from the oil regions to Pittsburg, Cleveland, Buffalo, Baltimore, New York, Williamsport, Chicago, and the Ohio River.

There was a free market for the oil as it came out of the wells and out of the refineries, and free competition between buyers and sellers, producers and consumers, manufacturers and traders. Industries auxiliary to the main ones flourished.

[1] Testimony of Simon Bernheimer, New York Assembly " Hepburn " Report, 1879, p. 3549 and following.

[2] Petroleum and Its Products, by S. F. Peckham, U. S. Census, 1885, p. 93.

[3] Same, p. 93.

Everywhere the scene was of expanding prosperity, with, of course, the inevitable percentage of ill-luck and miscalculation; but with the balance, on the whole, of such happy growth as freedom and the bounty of nature have always yielded when in partnership. The valleys of Pennsylvania changed into busy towns and oil fields. The highways were crowded, labor was well employed at good wages, new industries were starting up on all sides, and everything betokened the permanent creation of a new prosperity for the whole community, like that which came to California and the world with the discovery of gold.

But shadows of sunset began to creep over the field in its morning time, and the strange spectacle came of widespread ruin in an industry prospering by great leaps. Wherever men moved to discover oil lands, to dig wells, to build refineries or pipe lines, to buy and sell the oil, or to move it to market, a blight fell upon them.

The oil age began in 1860. As early as 1865 strange perturbations were felt, showing that some undiscovered body was pulling the others out of their regular orbits.

Before the panic of 1873—days of buoyant general prosperity, with no commercial revulsion for a cause—the citizens of this industry began to suffer a wholesale loss of property and business among the refineries in New York, Pittsburg, Cleveland, and elsewhere, the wells of the oil valleys, and the markets at home and abroad.

To the building of refineries succeeded the spectacle—a strange one for so new a business—of the abandonment and dismantling of refineries by the score. The market for oil, crude and refined, which had been a natural one, began to move erratically, by incalculable influences. It went down when it should have gone up according to all the known facts of the situation, and went up when it should have gone down. This sort of experience, defying ordinary calculations and virtues, made business men gamblers.

"We began speculating in the hope that there would be a change some time or other for the better," testified one who had gone into the business among the first, and with ample capital and expert skill.[1]

The fright among the people was proportionate to the work they had done and the value of what they were losing. Since the first well was sunk the wilderness had become a busy region, teeming with activity and endowed with wealth. In ten years the business had sprung up from nothing to a net product of 6,000,000 barrels of oil a year, using a capital of $200,000,000 and supporting a population of 60,000 people. The people were drilling one hundred new wells per month, at an average cost of $6000 each. They had devised the forms, and provided the financial institutions needed in a new business. They invented many new and ingenious mechanical contrivances. They had built up towns and cities, with schools, churches, lyceums, theatres, libraries, boards of trade. There were nine daily and eighteen weekly newspapers published in the region and supported by it. All this had been created in ten years, at a cost of untold millions in experiments and failures, and the more precious cost of sacrifice, suffering, toil, and life.

The ripe fruit of all this wonderful development the men of the oil country saw being snatched away from them.[2]

More than once during these lean years, as more than once later, the public alarm went to the verge of violent outbreak. This ruinous prosperity brought stolid Pennsylvania within sight of civil war in 1872, which was the principal subject before the Pennsylvania Legislature of that year, and forced Congress to make an official investigation.

The New York Legislature followed Congress and the Pennsylvania Legislature with an investigation in 1873.

" There was great popular excitement. . . . It raged like a violent fever," was the description it heard of the state of things in Pennsylvania.[3]

There were panics in oil speculation, bank failures, defalca-

---

[1] Testimony, Trusts, Congress, 1888, p. 214.

[2] Titusville *Morning Herald*, March 20, 1872.

[3] Testimony, Erie Investigation, New York Assembly, 1873, p. 418.

tions.   Many committed suicide.   Hundreds were driven into bankruptcy and insane asylums.

Where every one else failed, out of this havoc and social disorder one little group of half a dozen men were rising to the power and wealth which have become the marvel of the world.   The first of them came tardily into the field about 1862.   He started a little refinery in Cleveland, hundreds of miles from the oil wells.   The sixty and more manufacturers who had been able to plant themselves before 1860, when they had to distil coal into petroleum before they could refine petroleum into kerosene, had been multiplied into hundreds by the arrival of petroleum ready made from below.   Some of the richest and most successful business men of the country had preceded him and were flourishing.[1]   He had been a book-keeper, and then a partner, in a very small country-produce store in Cleveland.   As described by his counsel some years later, he was a "man of brains and energy without money." With him were his brother and an English mechanic.   The mechanic was bought out later, as all the expert skill needed could be got for wages, which were cheaper than dividends.[2] Two or three years later another partner was added, who began life as "a clerk in a country store,"[3] and had been in salt and lumber in the West.   A young man, who had been in the oil region only eleven years, and for two of the eleven had been errand-boy and bookkeeper in a mixed oil and merchandise business,[4] a lawyer, a railroad man, a cotton broker, a farm laborer who had become refiner, were admit-ted at various times into the ruling coterie.

The revolution which revolved all the freemen of this in-dustry down a vortex had no sooner begun than the public began to show its agitation through every organ.   The specta-

---

[1] Testimony of Simon Bernheimer, New York Assembly. "Hepburn" Report, 1879, p. 3548.

[2] Testimony, Freight Discriminations, Ohio House of Representatives, 1879, pp. 184–5.

[3] Testimony, Trusts, Congress, 1888, p. 304.

[4] Testimony, Pennsylvania Tax Case, 1883, p. 486.

cle of a few men at the centre of things, in offices rich with plate glass and velvet plush, singing a siren song which drew all their competitors to bankruptcy or insanity or other forms of "co-operation," did not progress, as it might have done a hundred years ago, unnoticed save by those who were the immediate sufferers. The new democracy began questioning the new wealth. Town meetings, organizations of trades and special interests, grand juries, committees of State legislatures and of the United States Senate and House of Representatives, the civil and criminal courts, have been in almost constant action and inquiry since and because.

It was before the Committee of Commerce of the National House of Representatives in 1872 that the first authentic evidence was obtained of the cause of the singular ruin which was overwhelming so fair a field. This investigation in 1872 was suppressed after it had gone a little way. Congress said, Investigate. Another power said, Don't investigate. But it was not stopped until the people had found out that they and the production, refining, and transportation of their oil—the whole oil industry, not alone of the valleys where the petroleum was found, but of the districts where it was manufactured, and the markets where it was bought and sold, and the ports from which it was shipped abroad—had been made the subject of a secret "contract" [1] between certain citizens. The high contracting parties to this treaty for the disposal of an industrial province were, on one side, all the great railroad companies, without whose services the oil, crude or refined, could not be moved to refineries, markets, or ports of shipment on river, lake, or ocean. On the other side was a body of thirteen men, "not one of whom lived in the oil regions, or was an owner of oil wells or oil lands," who had associated themselves for the control of the oil business under the winning name of the South Improvement Company. [2]

---

[1] This contract is printed in full in Exhibits, New York Assembly "Hepburn" Report, 1879, pp. 418–51, and Trust Report, Congress, 1888, pp. 357–61.

[2] Trusts, Congress, 1888, p. 353.

By this contract the railroads had agreed with this company of citizens as follows :

1. To double freight rates.

2. Not to charge them the increase.

3. To give them the increase collected from all competitors.

4. To make any other changes of rates necessary to guarantee their success in business.

5. To destroy their competitors by high freight rates.

6. To spy out the details of their competitors' business.

The increase in rates in some cases was to be more than double.[1] These higher rates were to be ostensibly charged to all shippers, including the thirteen members of the South Improvement Company; but that fraternity only did not have to pay them really. All, or nearly all, the increase it paid was to be paid back again—a " rebate." [2] The increase paid by every one else—" on all transported by other parties "— was not paid back. It was to be kept, but not by the railroads. These were to hand that, too, over to the South Improvement Company.

This secret arrangement made the actual rate of the South Improvement Company much lower—sometimes half, sometimes less than half, what all others paid. The railroad officials were not to collect these enhanced freight rates from the unsuspecting subjects of this " contract " to turn them into the treasury of the railroads. They were to give them over to the gentlemen who called themselves "South Improvement Company." The " principle " was that the railroad was not to get the benefit of the additional charge it made to the people. No matter how high the railroads put the rates to the community, not the railroads, but the Improvement Company, was to get the gain. The railroads bound themselves to charge every one else the highest nominal rates mentioned. " They shall not be less," was the stipulation. They might be more up to any point; but less they must not be.[3]

The rate for carrying petroleum to Cleveland to be refined

---

[1] Art. 2, sec. 3.   [2] Art. 2, sec. 4.   [3] Art. 2, sec. 5.

was to be advanced, for instance, to 80 cents a barrel. When paid by the South Improvement Company, 40 cents of the 80 were to be refunded to it; when paid by any one else, the 40 cents were not merely not to be refunded, but to be paid over to his competitor, this aspiring self-improvement company.[1] The charge on refined oil to Boston was increased to $3.07; and, in the same way, the South Improvement Company was to get back a rebate of $1.32 on every barrel it sent to Boston, and on every barrel any one else sent. The South Improvement Company was to receive sums ranging from 40 cents to $1.32, and averaging a dollar a barrel on all shipments, whether made by itself or by others. This would give the company an income of a dollar a day on every one of the 18,000 barrels then being produced daily, whether its members drilled for it, or piped it, or stored it, or refined it, or not.

To pay money to the railroads for them to pay back was seen to be a waste of time, and it was agreed that the South Improvement Company for its members should deduct from the ostensible rate the amount to be refunded, and pay the railroads only the difference. Simplification could not go further. The South Improvement Company was not even to be put to the inconvenience of waiting for the railroads to collect and render to it the tribute exacted for its benefit from all the other shippers. It was given the right to figure out for its members what the tribute would amount to, and pay it to them out of the money they owed the railroads for freight, and then pay the railroad what was left, if there was any left.[2] The railroads agreed to supply them with all the information needed for thus figuring out the amount of this tribute, and to spy out for them besides other important details of their competitors' business. They agreed to make reports every day to the South Improvement Company of all the shipments by other persons, with full particulars as to how much was shipped, who shipped, and to whom, and so on.[3]

[1] Art. 2, Sec. 4. [2] The same. [3] Art. 2, Sec. 8.

The detective agency thus established by the railroads to spy out the business of a whole trade was to send its reports "daily to the principal office" of the thirteen gentlemen. If the railroads, forgetting their obligations to the thirteen disciples, made any reduction in any manner to anybody else, the company, as soon as it was found out, could deduct the same amount from its secret rate.[1] If the open rate to the public went down, the secret rate was to go down as much. For the looks of things, it was stipulated that any one else who could furnish an equal amount of transportation should have the same rates;[2] but the possibility that any one should ever be able to furnish an equal amount of transportation was fully taken care of in another section clinching it all.

The railway managers, made kings of the road by the grant to them of the sovereign powers of the State, covenanted, in order to make their friends kings of light, that they would "maintain the business" of the South Improvement Company "against loss or injury by competition," so that it should be "a remunerative" and "a full and regular business," and pledged themselves to put the rates of freight up or down, as might be "necessary to overcome such competition."[3] Contracts to this effect, giving the South Improvement Company the sole right for five years to do business between the oil wells and the rest of the world, were made with it by the Erie, the New York Central, the Lake Shore and Michigan Southern, the Pennsylvania, the Atlantic and Great Western, and their connections, thus controlling the industry north, south, east, west, and abroad. The contracts in every case bound all the roads owned or leased by the railroads concerned.[4] The contracts were duly signed, sealed, and delivered. On the oil business of that year, as one of the members of the committee of Congress figured out from the testimony, the railroad managers could collect an increase of $7,500,000 in freights, of which they were to hand over to the South Im-

---

[1] Art. 2, Sec. 5.   [2] Art. 3.   [3] Art. 4.
[4] Exhibits, New York Assembly "Hepburn" Report, pp. 418–51.

provement Company $6,000,000, and pay into the treasury of their employers—the railways—only $1,500,000.

The contract was signed for the New York Central and Hudson River Railroad by its vice-president, but this agreement to kill off a whole trade was too little or too usual to make any impression on his mind. When publicly interrogated about it he could not remember having seen or signed it.[1]

"The effect of this contract," the vice-president of the Erie Railway Company was asked, "would have been a complete monopoly in the oil-carrying trade?"

"Yes, sir; a complete monopoly."[2]

Of the thirteen members of the South Improvement Company which was to be given this "complete monopoly," ten were found later to be active members of the oil trust. They were then seeking that control of the light of the world which it has obtained. Among these ten were the president, vice-president, treasurer, secretary, and a majority of the directors of the oil trust into which the improvement company afterwards passed by transmigration. Any closer connection there could not be. One was the other.

The ablest and most painstaking investigation which has ever been had in this country into the management of the railroads found and officially reported to the same effect:

"The controlling spirits of both organizations being the same."[3]

The freight rates were raised as agreed and without notice. Rumors had been heard of what was coming. The public would not believe anything so incredible. But the oil regions were electrified by the news, February 26, that telegrams had been sent from railroad headquarters to their freight agents advising them of new rates, to take effect immediately, making the cost of shipping oil as much again as it had been. The popular excitement which broke out on the same day and

---

[1] New York Assembly "Hepburn" Report, 1879, p. 1566.

[2] Testimony, Erie Investigation, New York Assembly, 1873, p. 300.

[3] New York Assembly "Hepburn" Report, 1879, p. 42.

"raged like a violent fever" became a national sensation. The Titusville *Morning Herald* of March 20, 1872, announces that "the railroads to the oil regions have already put up their New York freight from $1.25 to $2.84, an advance of over one hundred per cent." Asked what reason the railroads gave for increasing their rates, a shipper said, "They gave no reason; they telegraphed the local roads to put up the rates immediately." This advance, the superintendents of the railroads told complaining shippers, had been made under the direction of the South Improvement Company, and they had been instructed to make their monthly collections of oil freights from that concern.

The evidence even seems to show that the South Improvement Company was so anxious for the dance of death to begin that it got the freight agents by personal influence to order the increased rates before the time agreed upon with the higher officials. Strenuous efforts were made to have the public believe that the contracts, though sealed, signed, delivered, and put into effect, as the advance in rates most practically demonstrated, had really not been put into effect. The quibbles with which the president of the South Improvement Company sought to give that impossible color to the affair before the committee of Congress drew upon him more than one stinging rebuke from the chairman of the committee.

"During your whole examination there has not been a direct answer given to a question." "I wish to say to you," said the chairman, "that such equivocation is unworthy of you."

The plea needs no answer, but if it did, the language of the railroad men themselves supplies one that cannot be bettered. To the representatives of the people, who had telegraphed them for information "at once, as the excitement is intense, and we fear violence and destruction of property," General McClellan, of the Atlantic and Great Western, replied that the contract was "cancelled;" President Clark, of the Lake Shore, that it was "formally abrogated and cancelled;" Chairman Homer Ramsdell, of the Erie, that it was "abrogated;" Vice-president Thomas Scott, of the Pennsylvania Railroad, that it was "terminated officially;"[1] Vice-president Vanderbilt, of the New York Central and Hudson River Railroad, that it was "cancelled with all the railroads."

Contracts that were not complete and in force would not need to be "cancelled" and "abrogated" and "terminated." These announcements were backed up by a telegram from the future head of the oil trust then incubating, in which he said of his company: "This company holds no contracts with the railroad companies."[2] But in 1879 its secretary, called upon by the Ohio Legislature to produce the contracts the company had with the railroads, showed, among others, one covering the very date of this denial in 1872.[3]

Before Congress the South Improvement Company sought to shelter themselves behind the plea that "their calculation was to get all the refineries in the country into the company. There was no difference made, as far as we were concerned, in favor of or against any refinery; they were all to come in alike."

How they "were all to be taken in" the contract itself showed. It bound the South Improvement Company "to expend large sums of money in the purchase of works for refining," and one of the reasons given by the railroads for making the contract was "to encourage the outlay." Upon what footing buyer and seller would meet in these purchases when the buyer had a secret arrangement like this with the owners of the sole way to and from wells, refineries, and markets, one does not need to be "a business man" to see. The would-be owners had a power to pry the property of the real owners out of their hands.

One of the Cleveland manufacturers who had sold was asked why he did so by the New York Legislature. They had been very prosperous, he said; their profits had been $30,000 to $45,000 a year; but their prosperity had come to a sudden stop.[4]

[1] New York Assembly "Hepburn" Report, 1879, Exhibits, p. 418.
[2] Report of the Executive Committee of the Petroleum Producers' Union, 1872, p. 23.　　[3] Testimony, Ohio House of Representatives, 1879, p. 257.
[4] Testimony, New York Assembly "Hepburn" Report, 1879, p. 2525.

"From the time that it was well understood in the trade that the South Improvement Company had . . . . grappled the entire transportation of oil from the West to the seaboard . . . . we were all kind of paralyzed, perfectly paralyzed; we could not operate. . . . . The South Improvement Company, or some one representing them, had a drawback of a dollar, sometimes seventy cents, sometimes more, sometimes less, and we were working against that difference."[1]

It was a difference, he said, which destroyed their business.

He went to the officials of the Erie and of the New York Central to try to get freight rates that would permit him to continue in business. "I got no satisfaction at all," he said; "I am too good a friend of yours," said the representative of the New York Central, "to advise you to have anything further to do with this oil trade."

"Do you pretend that you won't carry for me at as cheap a rate as you will carry for anybody else?"

"I am but human," the freight agent replied.

He saw the man who was then busily organizing the South Improvement Company. He was non-committal. "I got no satisfaction, except 'You better sell, you better get clear.' Kind of *sub rosa :* 'Better sell out, no help for it.'"

His firm was outside the charmed circle, and had to choose between selling and dying. Last of all, he had an interview with the president of the all-conquering oil company, in relation to the purchase of their works. "He was the only party that would buy. He offered me fifty cents on the dollar, on the construction account, and we sold out. . . . . He made this expression, I remember: 'I have ways of making money that you know nothing of.'"

For the works, which were producing $30,000 to $45,000 a year profit, and which they considered worth $150,000, they received $65,000.

"Did you ascertain in the trade," he was asked, "what was the average rate that was paid for refineries?"

---

[1] Testimony, New York Assembly "Hepburn" Report, 1879, p. 2527.

" That was about the figure. . . . . Fifty cents on the dollar."

" It was that or nothing, was it not ?"

" That or nothing."

The freight rates had been raised in February. This sale followed in three weeks.

" I would not have sold out," he told the Legislature, " if I could have got a fair show with the railways. My business, instead of being an enterprise to buy and sell, became degraded into running after the railways and getting an equal chance with others." [1]

" The only party that would buy " gave his explanation a few years later of the centralization of this business.

" Some time in the year 1872," he swore, " when the refining business of the city of Cleveland was in the hands of a number of small refiners, and was unproductive of profit,[2] it was deemed advisable by many of the persons engaged therein, for the sake of economy, to concentrate the business, and associate their joint capital therein. The state of the business was such at that time that it could not be retained profitably at the city of Cleveland, by reason of the fact that points nearer the oil regions were enjoying privileges not shared by refiners at Cleveland, and could produce refined oil at a much less rate than could be done at this point. It was a well-understood fact at that time among refiners that some arrangement would have to be made to economize and concentrate the business, or ruinous losses would not only occur to the refiners themselves, but ultimately Cleveland, as a point of refining oil, would have to be abandoned. At that time those most prominently engaged in the business here consulted together, and as a result thereof several of the refiners conveyed " to his company, then as always the centre of the centralization, " their refineries, and had the option, in pay therefor, to take stock " in this company, " at par, or to take cash." This company, he continued, " had no agency in creating this state of things which made that change in the refining business neces-

---

[1] Testimony, New York Assembly " Hepburn " Report, 1879, pp. 2525–35.

[2] See ch. xxxii. for " the state of the business " " unproductive of profit."

sary at that time, but the same was the natural result of the trade, nor did it in the negotiations which followed use any undue or unfair means, but in all cases, to the general satisfaction of those whose refineries were acquired, the full value thereof, either in stock or cash, was paid as the parties preferred." [1]

The producers were not to fare any better than the refiners. The president of the South Improvement Company said to a representative of the oil regions substantially: "We want you producers to make out a correct statement of the average production of each well, and the exact cost per barrel to produce the oil. Then we propose to allow you a fair price for the oil."

Within forty - eight hours after the freight rates were raised, according to programme, "the entire business of the oil regions," the Titusville *Herald*, March 20, 1872, reported, "became paralyzed. Oil went down to a point seventy cents below the cost of production. The boring of new wells is suspended, existing wells were shut down. The business in Cleveland stopped almost altogether. Thousands of men were thrown out of work."

The people rose. Their uprising and its justification were described to the Pennsylvania Constitutional Convention of 1873 by a brilliant "anti-monopolist," "a rising lawyer" of Franklin, Venango Co. The principal subject to which he called the attention of his fellow - members was the South Improvement Company, and the light it threw on the problems of livelihood and liberty. Quoting the decision of the Pennsylvania Supreme Court in the Sanford case,[2] he said:

"That is the law in Pennsylvania to-day. But in spite of this decision, and in spite of the law, we well know that almost every railroad in this State has been in the habit, and is to-day in the habit, of granting special privileges to individuals, to companies in which the directors of such railroads are interested, to particular business, and to particular localities. We well know that it is their habit to break down certain localities, and

[1] Standard Oil Company *vs.* W. C. Scofield *et al.* Court of Common Pleas, Cuyahoga County, O. Affidavit of the President of the Standard Oil Company.
[2] 11 Harris.

build up others, to break down certain men in business and to build up others, to monopolize certain business themselves by means of the numerous corporations which they own and control, and all this in spite of the law, in defiance of the law.

"The South Improvement Company's scheme would give that corporation the monopoly of the entire oil business of this State, amounting to $20,000,000 a year. That corporation was created by the Pennsylvania Legislature along with at least twenty others, under the name of improvement companies, within a few years past, all of which corporations contain the names as original corporators of men who may be found in and about the office of the Pennsylvania Railroad Company, in Philadelphia, when not lobbying at Harrisburg. The railroads took but one of those charters which they got from the Legislature, and by means of that struck a deadly blow at one of the greatest interests of the State. Their scheme was contrary to law, but before the legal remedy could have been applied, the oil business would have lain prostrate at their feet, had it not been prevented by an uprising of the people, by the threatenings of a mob, if you please, by threatening to destroy property, and by actually commencing to destroy the property of the railroad company, and had the companies not cancelled the contract which Scott and Vanderbilt and others had entered into, I venture to say there would not have been one mile of railroad track left in the County of Venango—the people had come to that pitch of desperation. . . . Unless we can give the people a remedy for this evil of discriminations in freight, they will sooner or later take the remedy into their own hands." [1]

Soon after this attorney for the people was promoted from the poor pay of patriotism to a salary equal to that of the President of the United States, and to the place of counsel for the principal members of the combination, whose inwardness he had descried with such hawk-eye powers of vision. Later, as their counsel, he drafted the famous trust agreement of 1882.

The South Improvement Company was formed January 2d. The agreement with the railroads was evidently already worked out in its principal details, for the complicated contracts were formally signed, sealed, and delivered January 18th. The agreed increase of freights went into effect February 26th. The pacific insurrection of the people began

[1] Debates of the Constitutional Convention of Pennsylvania, 1873, v. 3, pp. 522-3.

with an impromptu mass-meeting at Titusville the next day,
February 27th. Influential delegations, or committees, on
transportation, legislation, conference with press, pipe lines,
arresting of drilling, etc., were set to work by the organization
thus spontaneously formed by the people. A complete embargo was placed on sales of oil at any price to the men who
had made the hateful bargain with the railroads. The oil
country was divided into sixteen districts, in each of which
the producers elected a local committee, and over all these
was an executive committee composed of representatives
from the local committees—one from each. No oil was sold
to be used within any district except to those buyers whom
the local committee recommended; no oil was sold to be
exported or refined outside the district, except to such buyers
as the executive committee permitted. One cent a barrel was
paid by each producer into a general fund for the expenses
of the organization.

Steps were taken to form a company with a capital of
$1,000,000, subscribed by the producers, to advance money, on
the security of their oil, to those producers who did not want
to sell.

Able lawyers were employed and sent with the committees
to all the important capitals—Harrisburg, Washington, the
offices of the railway companies. The flow of oil was checked,
the activities of the oil world brought near a stop.

Monday, March 15th, by the influence of the Washington
committee, a resolution was introduced into the House of
Representatives by Representative Scofield, ordering an investigation of the South Improvement Company. Immediately upon this the frightened participants cancelled the contracts. By the 26th of March the representatives of the
people had secured a pledge in writing from the five great
railroads concerned of "perfect equality," and "no rebates,
drawbacks, or other arrangements," in favor of any one thereafter. March 30th, Congress began the investigation which
brought to light the evidence of the contracts, and meanwhile
the committees on legislation and pipe lines were securing

from the Pennsylvania Legislature the repeal of the South Improvement Company charter, and the passage of a "so-called" Free Pipe Line law, discovered afterwards to be worthless on account of amendments shrewdly inserted by the enemy.

It was an uprising of the people, passionate but intelligent and irresistible, if the virtue of the members held good. Until April 9th the non-intercourse policy was stiffly and successfully maintained. But by that time one man had been found among the people who was willing to betray the movement. This man, in consideration of an extra price, violating his producer's pledge, sold to some of those concerned in the South Improvement Company a large quantity of oil, as they at once took pains to let the people know. The seller hoped to ship it quietly, but, of course, the object in buying and paying this additional price was to have it shipped openly, and the members of the South Improvement Company insisted that it should be done so.[1]

This treachery had the effect planned. Every one became suspicious that his neighbor would be the next deserter, and would get the price he would like to have for himself. To prevent a stampede, the leaders called a mass-meeting. Reports were made to it of what had been done in Congress, the Legislature, and the other railway offices; the telegrams already referred to were read affirming the cancellation of the contracts. Amid manifestations of tumultuous approbation and delight the embargo on the sale of oil was declared raised.

"We do what we must," says Emerson, "and call it by the best name possible." The people, as every day since has shown, grasped the shell of victory to find within the kernel of defeat.

The committee of Congress noticed when the contracts were afterwards shown to it, that though they had been so widely declared to be "cancelled," they had not been cancelled, but were as fresh—seals, stamps, signatures and all—as

---

[1] Testimony, New York Assembly "Hepburn" Report, 1879, p. 2766.

the day they were made. This little circumstance is descriptive of the whole proceeding. Both parties to this scheme to give the use of the highways as a privilege to a few, and through this privilege to make the pursuit of livelihood a privilege, theirs exclusively—the railroad officials on one side, and their beneficiaries of the South Improvement Company on the other—were resolute in their determination to carry out their purpose. All that follows of this story is but the recital of the sleuth-like tenacity with which this trail of fabulous wealth has been followed.

The chorus of cancellation from the railroads came from those who had meant never to cancel, really. In their negotiations with the representatives of the people they had contested to the last the abandonment of the scheme. "Their friendliness" to it "was so apparent," the Committee of the Producers reported, "that we could expect little consideration at their hands,"[1] and the committee became satisfied that the railroads had made a new contract among themselves like that of the South Improvement Company, and to take its place. Its head frankly avowed before the Investigating Committee of Congress their intention of going ahead with the plan. "They are all convinced that, sooner or later, it will be necessary to organize upon the basis on which the South Improvement Company was organized, including both producers and refiners."

This conviction has been faithfully lived up to. Under the name of the South Improvement Company the arrangement was ostentatiously abandoned, because to persist in it meant civil war in the oil country as the rising young anti-monopolist lawyer pointed out in the Constitutional Convention. Mark Twain, in describing the labors of the missionaries in the Sandwich Islands, says they were so successful that the vices of the natives no longer exist in name—only in reality. As every page will show, this contract no longer exists in name—only in reality. In the oil world, and in every

[1] Report of Executive Committee of the Petroleum Producers' Union, 1872.

other important department of our industrial life—in food, fuel, shelter, clothing, transportation,[1] this contract, in its various new shapes, has been kept steadily at work gerrymandering the livelihoods of the people.

The men who had organized the South Improvement Company paid the public revolt the deference of denial, though not of desistance. The company had got a charter, organized under it, collected twenty per cent. of the subscription for stock, made contracts with the railroads, held meetings of the directors, who approved of the contracts and had received the benefits of the increase of freights made in pursuance of the agreement. This was shown by the testimony of its own officers.[2]

But "the company never did a dollar's worth of business," the Secretary of the Light of the World told Congress,[3] and "there was never the slightest connection between the South Improvement Company and the Standard Oil Company," the president of the latter and the principal member of both said in an interview in the New York *World*, of March 29, 1890. "The South Improvement Company died in embryo. It was never completely organized, and never did any business. It was partly born, died, and was buried in 1872," etc.

Still later, before a committee of the Legislature of New York, in 1888, he was asked about "the Southern Improvement Company."

"There was such a company?"

"I have heard of such a company."

"Were you not in it?"

"I was not."[4]

So help me God!

At almost the moment of this denial in New York, an associate in this and all his other kindred enterprises, asked before Congress who made up the South Improvement Com-

[1] See ch. xxxiii.
[2] Report Executive Committee Petroleum Producers' Union, 1872.
[3] Trusts, Congress, 1888, p. 290.
[4] Testimony, Trusts, New York Senate, 1888, p. 420.

pany, named as among them the principal members of the
great oil company, and most conspicuous of them all was the
name of this denier.[1]

The efficiency with which this "partly born" innocent
lived his little hour, "not doing a dollar's worth of business,"
was told in a summary phrase by one of the managers of the
Pennsylvania Railroad, describing the condition of the oil
business in 1873 :[2]

"All other of our largest customers had failed."

When the people of the oil regions made peace after their
uprising it was, as they say, with "full assurance from the
Washington committee that the throwing off the restrictions
from trade will not embarrass their investigation (by Congress),
but that the Sub-Committee of Commerce will, nevertheless,
continue, as the principle involved, and not this particular case
alone, is the object of the investigation." [3]

The Committee of Commerce did not "continue." The
principal witness, who had negotiated the contracts by which
the railroads gave over the business of the oil regions to a few,
refused in effect, beyond producing copies of the contract, to
be a witness. Permission was given by the Committee of Congress during its first zeal to the Committee of Producers from
Pennsylvania to copy the testimony as it was taken, but no
official record of its discoveries exists. This transcript was
published by the producers, and copies are possessed by a few
fortunate collectors. The committee did not report, and in
the archives of the national Capitol no scrap of the evidence
taken is to be found. All has vanished into the bottomless
darkness in which the monopoly of light loves to dwell.

---

[1] Testimony, Trusts, Congress, 1888, p. 289.

[2] Testimony, Commonwealth of Pennsylvania *vs.* Pennsylvania Railroad Company *et al.*, 1879, p. 707.

[3] Report Executive Committee Petroleum Producers' Union, 1872.

CHAPTER VI

"NOT TO EXCEED HALF"

Notwithstanding the ceremonial treaty of equal rights on the railroads to all, which had been secured by the uprising of the people against the South Improvement Company in 1872, the independents, one after the other, continued to be side-tracked by an unseen power. Four years later, on the 20th of July, 1876, their only two important survivors in Cleveland, frightened by the high death-rate of the business, and by a deepening pressure on themselves, answered a summons to come to the palace of the President of the Light of the World. The contract which was then made was afterwards produced in court.[1] It was called an "Agreement for an Adventure," in something like "the merry sport" in which the good Antonio gave a bond for a pound of his flesh.

A few years after this "adventure" with his competitors and his efforts to have them closed by the courts, the President was asked if his trust had sought in any way to diminish the production of refineries in competition with it.

"Oh no, sir," he replied.

"Nothing of the kind?"

"Oh no, sir."[2]

He was asked the question again, and again the denial was repeated.

"Done nothing of the sort?"

"Not at all."

[1] Exhibit A, Answer of Defendants, Case of Standard Oil Company *vs.* W. C. Scofield *et al.*, Cleveland, 1880.

[2] Testimony, Trusts, New York Senate, 1888, p. 385.

But now he said, You must bind yourselves for ten years to refine only 85,000 barrels of oil a year.[1]

They had refined 120,000 barrels the year before, and could have done 180,000, and were growing up with the country. "The prospects were much better for the future."[2]

But they agreed.

You must give me and my associates all the profits you make during this period above $35,000 a year, until we too have got $35,000 a year out of your business, and we will guarantee you $35,000 a year, if we let you run.

They had made $41,000 the year before, but they agreed.

You must divide with "us," after each has got $35,000 a year, all the additional profits.

They had to put into this "adventure" all their buildings and machinery, valued at $61,760.42, all their time and attention, and $10,000 in cash, while their conquerors put in only $10,000 cash and no plant and no time. But they agreed to this demand for "half."

You must stop refining altogether, and let us take out our $10,000 whenever we send you notice that through competition, or a decrease or change in the production of petroleum, Cleveland can "barely compete" with other places. You must sell the kerosene you manufacture, and buy the petroleum you make it of at the prices we fix.

The combination could make the business unprofitable whenever it chose, and under the previous stipulation could close them up at its own pleasure, until the ten years had rolled by. But they agreed.

You must resume again after any such suspension, and let us take half the profits whenever we give you notice. You must let us enter or withdraw, throw our $10,000 in or out, suspend or resume, again and again, as we choose! They agreed.

You must make us monthly reports of all your transactions. You must not enlarge nor contract your works without our consent. They agreed.

[1] Exhibit A, Answer of Defendants, Case of Standard Oil Company *vs.* W. C. Scofield *et al.*, Cleveland, 1880, Section 7.   [2] Affidavits of the defendants.

You must not go into the manufacture of petroleum, nor any other new business anywhere else in the world during this adventure! You must ship your products by such routes as we direct! They agreed.

You must keep this adventure secret. Our name must not appear, and even if you all die, you must agree that we may continue the business in your name, or any other name we choose.

"The firm name," as their counsel pointed out, "was to be kept up even when the members were mouldering in their graves. But the public were to understand that the business of that firm, as it had been conducted in the lifetime of those men, was still being carried on."

You are to be thus tied up for ten years, limited at the best to half the profit on half your capacity, with a right in us to close you up altogether, or to close and resume whenever we choose, with no right in you to start or stop or withdraw. But we are to be left free, in our own refineries, to refine all the oil the market will take, and keep all the profit, and enlarge our works and extend our business.

And, finally, you must put your hand and seal to a statement that you do this to "reconcile interests that have seemed to conflict" and "equalize the business," and that this agreement gives you your "due proportion thereof."

This "free contract" two of the three men who were to make it knew nothing of until their consent was demanded.

One of the partners had secretly been won over. Through him all preliminary negotiations had been conducted.

"I was not consulted," testified one of the other two, until after the contract was "all drawn and prepared," and at first he refused to sign it. The plan was concocted "secretly and unknown to me."

"I was at first opposed to the arrangement," declared the other.[1]

But this was not all the contract. The President, who, as

---

[1] Affidavits of the defendants.

he testified, "conducted most of the negotiations," and "had been familiar with the dealings thereunder," supplemented the written documents with oral instructions: [1]

You must not seem to be prosperous. You must not put on style,[2] he cautioned them; above all, you must not drive fast horses or have fine rigs; you must not even let your wives know of this arrangement.[3]

A false account was opened on the books to conceal the nature and origin of this transaction from their own book-keepers. In the name of that account false and fictitious checks were drawn, bills made out, balances struck. A box was taken out at the Cleveland post-office—box 125—in the name of an imaginary "Mr. G. A. Mason," and through this box the correspondence of the "adventure" was carried on. Each of the three parties to the "adventure" continued to march and fight under its own flag as before. All possible pains were taken to conceal the fact that they had ceased competition with each other. They kept up every appearance to the public of being actively engaged in competitive business. The inevitable spy appears in this scene as in every other in the play. The "reconciler," to enforce the provisions that the "reconcilees" should not engage in business elsewhere, extended a system of espionage over them, and followed their movements, and kept watch what they did with their money, and made oath to the courts of the results of these "inquiries and investigations." The espionage continued after this.

A year or two after this contract had been broken by the help of the courts, the then secretary of the great oil company, through an intermediary, approached the book-keeper of the firm which had been freed from the trust.

"Would you not like to make some money?"

"He inclined to let him believe he did want to make some money," his employer afterwards told Congress. "He came and told me about it. I requested that he continue and find out what information they wanted. He was to have had so

---

[1] Affidavits of the defendants.　　　　[2] Same.　　　　[3] Same.

much per year, but he was to have been paid a down payment; he got $25."

"What service was he to render for that?"

"I have a memorandum. There were so many things he was to do that I cannot carry it in my head."

"One of the questions was, ' What was the result of last year's business?' The other was, 'A transcript of the daily shipments, with net prices received from the same; what is the cost for manufacturing outside of the crude; the kind of gasoline and naphtha made, and the net prices received for the same; what they do with tar and the percentages of the same; what per cent. of water white and what per cent. of Michigan water white; how much oil exported last year?' This information, as fast as received, to be mailed to Box 164, Cleveland post-office. . . . He (the book-keeper) made an affidavit of it, and I took the money back myself personally." [1]

When orders came in for more oil than the limit put upon them, the "reconcilees," asserting their commercial manhood, went on refining to supply the demands of the public instead of the commands of the clique. They contended that they were not bound by the limitation, and in this were afterwards upheld by the court; but, meanwhile, they were called to account and frightened into another "reconciliation." He was present, the chief reconciler told the court, at the interview in which they "agreed to diminish their manufacture . . . to bring the entire amount within the terms" of the contract.

But again they began to refine to supply the needs of the people evidenced by the market demand. Then their supply of crude was shut off. Their suzerain owned the pipe line to Cleveland. When its escaping victims got around that difficulty, it took its "contract" to the courts.

To shut these competitors down to half their capacity, and to reconcile and equalize interests by taking half of all they made on that was merely an incident, collateral to the grander plan, the vaster "adventure," of getting all the profits

---

[1] Testimony, Trusts, Congress, 1888, p. 547.

of that greater field out of which these competitors were barred altogether. Such contracts as these, its counsel said, were made with refiners all over the country. The chief profit of the adventure lay, not in the divided profits of the picayune business it let the vassals do, but in the undivided profits of the empire kept for itself. Why should the reconciler hurry with expensive lawyers into court for a summary injunction to prevent a "reconcilee" from making more oil, when the reconciler, who toiled not nor spun, was to get half of the gain of $2.05 on every barrel of it? Why, but that every "co-operative" barrel so made would displace in the markets a barrel, all the profits of which went to it.

The "reconcilees" were called into court. A judge was asked to issue an injunction forbidding them to depart from the strict letter of the contract.

They have been refining more than 85,000 barrels of oil a year, was the complaint.

They "threaten to distil crude petroleum without regard to quantity."[1] They are "parties in rebellion," said the lawyers. The judge said, No. This is a contract in restraint of trade, and released those who were in its toils.

The immediate effect of this "equalization" was an advance in the rates of profit. The year before the independent refiners had made a profit of only 34 cents a barrel.[2]

The first year of the "adventure" the profits jumped up to $2.52 a barrel. The dividends rose from $41,000 to $222,047, while the production fell from 120,000 to 88,085 barrels. For the four years the average profit was $2.05 a barrel, or 500 per cent. advance. The lowest profit was $1.37.

" Refined oil advanced to an average of $8 per barrel for that year " (1876), says the counsel of the trust.[3]

These great winnings were made in the depth of the depression following the panic of 1873.

While a world-compelling decline not only of prices but

---

[1] Petition for Relief and Injunction, Standard Oil Company *vs.* W. C. Scofield *et al.*, etc.   [2] Affidavits of the defendants.

[3] *Combinations*, etc., S. C. T. Dodd, p. 25.

of profits, was in progress, the authors of this arrangement kept up kerosene to a point at which $630,691 was made in four years out of an investment of $81,000, half of which went to those who put in $10,000 and their power over freight agents.

This "adventure," as was said by the Hon. Stanley Matthews, who appeared as counsel for the victimized refiners, was better than a gold-mine. It was a mint. Without giving any personal supervision or any time, without any expenditure except the insignificant investment of $10,000, made as a mere stalking-horse, these men took a share of the profits of "the party of the second part," which is not to be calculated by ordinary percentage, but by multiplications, over and over again, every year, of the money they put in it.

By reducing the volume of business one-half, by increasing the profit from 34 cents a barrel to $2.05, the reconcilers pocketed $315,345.58 in four years, on an investment of $10,000, with no work. This was the fact. The theory with which the fact was hidden from the people is given to the New York Legislature in 1888. The principle on which the trust did business, its president said, was:

"At a limited profit; a very small profit on an extremely large volume of business."[1]

When its secretary was before Congress, he was asked about the operations of himself and his associates in these years, 1876, 1877, of wonderful profits. He had been participating during that time in not only this profit of $2.05 a barrel, but in divided profits rising to $3,000,000 in a year on $3,000,000 of capital, and in undivided profits which rolled up $3,500,000 of capital into $70,000,000 in five years. But he said:

"The business during those years was so very close as to leave scarcely any margin of profit under the most advantageous circumstances."[2]

The effect on the consumer appears from the statement

[1] Testimony, Trusts, New York Senate, 1888, p. 422.
[2] Testimony, Trusts, Congress, 1888, p. 772.

in this case of one of the best-known producers and refiners
in the oil regions, one intimately associated with the members
of the combination.   He showed that oil which was selling at
twenty cents a gallon retail could be sold at a large profit at
twelve cents a gallon.

As to the effect on the working-man, the demand for labor
declined, wages went down, and the number of unemployed
increased.

When there was competition in Cleveland the great company could not afford to have its skilled workmen idle, because they would seek employment with the other refineries;
but now, having the refining business all in its own hands,
when it was temporarily to its advantage to refine oil in Pittsburg, Oil City, or other points, in preference to Cleveland,
it could with impunity let its hands remain idle in Cleveland,
knowing that when it wanted them it could easily secure them,
as there are no other refineries in Cleveland to employ them,
and "that has been a very serious injury to workingmen." [1]

There was no pretence that the design of this contract was
not to make oil scarce—*i.e.*, dear.

In the affidavit which was made in support of the injunction the principal reconciler showed that his company had
restricted itself as much as it restricted these competitors.
He urged as the reason why the contract had been made and
why the courts should sustain it, that "the capacity of all the
refineries in the United States is more than sufficient to supply the markets of the world, and if all the refineries were run
to their full capacity they would refine at least twice as much
oil as the markets of the world require; that this difference
between the capacity of refineries and the demands of the
market has existed for at least seven years past, and during
that period the refineries" of his company "have not been
run to . . . . exceed one-half of their capacity."

When these surviving independents of Cleveland were
forced into this adventure, in 1876, the source of the power

---

[1] Affidavit of Levi T. Scofield.

which could compel "free" citizens in this age of individual-
ism to execute such a bond was not known. The appalling
mortality among the independents showed that something
was seriously wrong. There was something, however, in this
"Agreement for an Adventure" which pointed straight to it.
That was a clause which guaranteed those who became vassals
that they should have the same freight rates and get back the
same rebates as the monopoly.[1] "Had the monopoly the
power," said the Hon. Stanley Matthews, "to procure freights
on better and more advantageous terms than the rest of the
public engaged in the same business? . . . And if they had
such power, how did it get it? . . . If this or any other corporation is allowed to exalt itself in this way and by these
means above competition, it is also exalted above the law."

The great lawyer, who soon afterwards became a justice of
the Supreme Court of the United States, could not answer
the questions he raised. The facts were hidden in secret contracts with the railroads. As regards Cleveland, they did not
come out until five years later, in 1885. It then became an
adjudicated fact that in 1875, the year before this "Agreement for an Adventure," the Lake Shore Railroad had made
a contract with the oil combination to drive these very
competitors and all others out of business, just as the same
road had done for the South Improvement Company in 1872.
When they escaped from their "reconciler," they brought this
railroad and the contract into court. The case was fought up
to the Supreme Court.

That tribunal found that the Lake Shore road had contracted with this company to carry its products ten cents per
barrel cheaper than for any other customers. It showed that
this made a difference to the victims of the "Adventure"
equal to more than 21 per cent. a year on their capital.

"The understanding," the court said, "was to keep the price
down for the favored customers, but *up* for all the others,
and the inevitable tendency and effect of this contract was to

---

[1] Exhibit A, etc., Section 12.

enable the Standard Oil Company to establish and maintain an overshadowing monopoly, to ruin all other operators, and drive them out of business." The course of the railroad the court declared to be one of "active participation in the unlawful purposes" of the oil company. The Lake Shore was to have all its business out of Cleveland, but, a competing railroad being built, the Lake Shore made a contract to give this new line a part of the plum, to induce it to unite in the policy of keeping freights *down* for the favored customer, and *up* for all others. When the President of the trust was asked afterwards by the New York Legislature if there had been no arrangement by which it got its transportation cheaper than others could, he replied, "No, sir." And later he reiterated that in their arrangements for freight there was "nothing peculiar."[1]

But the Supreme Court of Ohio, in describing this arrangement, diversify the staid rhetoric of their legal deliverance with the unaffected exclamation:

"How peculiar!"

They declared the contract between the two railroads "void," and "not only contrary to a sound public policy, but to the lax demands of the commercial honesty and ordinary methods of business." They also pronounced the contract between the railroad and the oil company as "made to build up a monopoly," and as "unlawful."[2]

The great lawyer, we have said, could not answer the questions he asked. The facts, we have said, were hidden in a secret contract. And yet the answers to the questions, the facts, had been all brought to the verge of disclosure by the investigation by Congress early in the same year, 1876.

Although the investigation, in consequence of the "I object" of the Hon. Henry B. Payne, of Cleveland,[3] had been referred to the Committee of Commerce, and though the railroad and oil clique men would not answer, and the committee would not press them, there was a volunteer witness from

---

[1] Testimony, Trusts, New York Senate, 1888, pp. 388, 421.

[2] Scofield *et al. vs.* Lake Shore and Michigan Southern Railway Company, 43 Ohio State Report, p. 571.   [3] See ch. xxvii.

Cleveland, who began to upset all the plans to smother. This willing witness was a Cleveland refiner, a shrewd man, as would easily be believed by those who knew that he was the brother of an organizer of the oil combination. He, too, had been a member of it, but for some reasons was now "out," and was one of the swimmers who felt themselves being drawn down. He betook himself for relief to Congress. He dodged no subpœnas, but, going before the Committee of Commerce, he began to tell more fully than any other witness had ever done, or had ever been able to do, the story of the relations between the combination and the railroads, which he knew of his personal knowledge. When he began talking in this free way to the public authorities, his former associates saw that they had underestimated his abilities as a refiner. They began to feel that it might be well to make some concessions to this particular brother, though not to the Brotherhood of Man.

The investigation was summarily suspended,[1] and his testimony was spirited away. With the only power that could have interfered thus silenced, the surviving independents were corralled as we have described. This was done two short months after the first move was made, May 16th, for the investigation which might have saved the independents at Cleveland and elsewhere from the duress which drove men to death or adventures of reconciliation.

All over the oil regions the combination has followed this policy of "not to exceed half."[2]

Nineteen pages of the testimony of a member in the suit begun by the Commonwealth of Pennsylvania are taken up with the operations of one of its constituent companies in the purchase or leasing of competing refineries, many of which were shut down or pulled down.

This witness could name only one refinery out of the score of independent concerns once flourishing in Pittsburg, which was not under its control.[3]

---

[1] See ch. xxvii.   [2] See Testimony, Trusts, Congress, 1888, p. 800.
[3] Commonwealth of Pennsylvania *vs.* Pennsylvania Railroad *et al.*, 1879, Testimony, p. 472.

"Dismantled," was the monotonous refrain of many of his answers to the questions as to what had been done with the refineries thus got under control. Asked why these works had been thus dismantled or shut down, he explained it variously as due to unfavorable location or worn-out machinery or some such disadvantage.

If these works were so badly situated and so illy fitted for the business and so old, why did it purchase them? "Can you give good commercial reasons why it would buy all unprofitable junk?" he was asked.[1]

"I cannot give any reason why they bought the works," was the helpless answer.

From the beginning to the end the language used by the founders of the combination proves scarcity to have been their object. "There is a large number of refineries in the country —a great deal larger than is required for the manufacture of the oil produced in the country, or for the wants of the consumers in Europe and America," said one of the principal members in 1872.[2]

This is almost identical with the language used in 1880 in the effort to enjoin Cleveland refiners who "threatened to distil."

In 1887 we will see the same power putting its hand and seal to an agreement to enforce the doctrine that there was too much oil in the earth.

In 1872 there were more refineries than were needed for the oil; in 1887 there was too much oil. The progression is significant. And down to the present pool with the Scotch refiners we will see the same men enforcing abroad, year by year, the same gospel of want.[3]

"The producers in America are quite alive to the wisdom of not producing too much paraffine, and are already adopting measures to restrict it," said the chairman at the annual meeting of one of the principal Scotch companies.[4]

---

[1] Commonwealth of Pennsylvania, 1879, Testimony, p. 490.
[2] Report Executive Committee Petroleum Producers' Union, 1872.
[3] See ch. xxxi.   [4] Glasgow *Herald*, June 16, 1892.

CHAPTER VII

"YOU ARE NOT TO REFINE"

IN the obituary column of the Cleveland *Herald*, of June 6, 1874, was given the news of the death of one of the pioneer manufacturers of Cleveland. He began the refining of petroleum in that city in 1860, several years before any of those who afterwards became the sovereigns of the business had left their railroad platforms, book-keeping stools, and lawyers' desks. He was married in the same year, and from that time until his death, in 1874, gave his whole life to his refinery and his family, and was successful with both. The *Herald* said of him editorially:

"He was well known in Cleveland and elsewhere as a business man of high character. He was a prominent member of the First Presbyterian Church, was at one time President of the Young Men's Christian Association, and was active in all enterprises of a religious and benevolent character. He was about forty years of age, and leaves a wife and three children."

His enterprise had been "very profitable," his wife said afterwards in court, in narrating how she and her children fared after the death of the husband, father, and bread-winner. "My husband devoted his entire energies and life to the business from about 1860 to the time of his death, and had acquired through his name a large patronage. My husband went into debt just before his death," she continued, "for the first time in his life. For the interest of my fatherless children, as well as myself, I thought it my duty to continue the business. I took $75,000 of the $100,000 of stock, and continued from that time, 1874, until November, 1878, making handsome profits, during perhaps the hardest business years of the time since my husband had begun." [1]

The business received from her the most thorough and faithful attention, and she maintained the prosperity her husband had founded by making a profit of about $25,000 a year.

A representative of one of the oil combination came to her, she continued, "with a proposition that I should sell to them." This agent was "a brother manufacturer," who, but a short time before in a conference with her, had agreed that in view of the dangers which seemed to threaten them, he and she should mutually watch out for each other, and that no arrangement should be made by either without letting the other know. The next she saw of her ally he pounced upon her in her office with the news that he was in the oil combination, that the head of it had told him he meant to have control of the refining business if it took him ten years, but he hoped to have it in two. He went on to warm the woman's heart by the declaration that since he had become acquainted with the secrets of the organization he wondered that he and she had been able to hold out so long. After which preliminaries he proposed that she, too, should sell to it. With sagacity and spirit she declined point-blank to have any negotiation with him.

She declined to deal with subordinates, and said she did not want to sell. The principal then called upon her at her residence. This was in 1878, and these were dark days for "outside" refiners. One by one they were sinking out of sight, and slipping under the yoke like the victims of the "reconciliation" and "equalization" described in the last chapter.

For six years word had been passing from one frightened lip to another that they were all destined for the maw or the morgue, and the fulfilment of the word had been appalling. He knew the members of the oil combination, one of the best-known veterans of the oil region testified in this case, naming them; "I have heard some of them say, in substance,

[1] Affidavit, Oct. 18, 1880, Case of Standard Oil Company *vs.* W. C. Scofield *et al.*, Cleveland, 1880.

' that they intended to wipe out all the refineries in the country except their own, and to control the entire refining business of the United States.' "

"The big fish are going to eat the little fish," one of the big fish told a neighbor and competitor. When one of the little fish said he "would not sell and was not afraid," he was told, "You may not be afraid to have your head cut off, but your body will suffer!"

The woman was brave with love and enthusiasm for the memory of her husband and the future of her children. She had had a great success, but she knew the sea she was swimming. She saw strong men going down on every side. She herself afterwards told in court of her great anxiety as she would hear of one refinery after another surrendering, feeling sure that that would eventually be the fate of her company.

All that the witnesses just quoted had reported, all that was said of the same tenor by the witnesses before Congress in 1876, and much more, had been filling the hearts of the business men of Cleveland, Pittsburg, Titusville, New York, with a reign of terror ever since 1872. It was with a full realization of all this that she went down to her parlor to receive the great man of commerce, who passes the contribution-box for widows' mites outside the church as well as within. This gentleman was in her house in pursuance, practically, of his own motion. She did not want to sell; the suggestion of a sale had come from the other side. "I told him," the widow said to the judge, "that I realized that my company was entirely in the power" of his company. "All I can do," I said to him, "is to appeal to your honor as a gentleman, and to your sympathy, to do the best with me that you can. I beg of you to consider your wife in my position, left with this business and with fatherless children, and with a large indebtedness that my husband had just contracted for the first time in his life. I felt that I could not do without the income arising from this business, and I have taken it up and gone on, and been successful in the hardest years since my husband commenced." "I am aware," he replied, "of what

you have done. My wife could never have accomplished so
much." She had become alarmed, the woman of business
resumed, because his company was "getting control of all
the refineries in the country."

He promised, with tears in his eyes, that he would stand by
her. It should never be said, he cried, that he had wronged
the widow of his fellow-refiner. "He agreed that I might
retain whatever amount of stock I desired. He seemed to
want only the control. I thought his feelings were such that
I could trust him, and that he would deal honorably with me."
This was the last she saw of him. He promised to come to
see her during the negotiations, but did not do so. He promised to assist and advise her, but did not do so. He declined
to conduct the negotiations with her in person as she requested, "stating to her," he said, in giving his version of the
affair to the court, " that I knew nothing about her business
or the mechanical appliances used in the same, and that I
could not pursue any negotiations with her with reference to
the same; but that if, after reflection, she desired to do so, some
of our people familiar with the lubricating-oil business would
take up the question with her. . . . When she responded, ex-
pressing her fears about the future of the business, stating
that she could not get cars to transport sufficient oil, and other
similar remarks, I stated to her that though we were using
our cars, and required them in our own business, yet we would
loan her any number she required, or do anything else in reason to assist her, and I saw no reason why she could not
prosecute her business just as successfully in the future as
in the past." This assurance to his widow-competitor that
he would let her have cars was, of itself, enough to justify all
her alarm, and show that there was no hope for her but in
making the best surrender possible. It was proof positive
that he did control the transportation, that the well-defined report that no one but he and his could get their business
done by the railroad was true. Permission to go upon the
highways by the favor of a competitor is too thin a plank
for even a woman to be got to walk. Withdrawing from

direct connection, but managing the affair to the end as he testifies, he sent back to her the agent she had refused to talk with.

Negotiations were accordingly resumed perforce with this agent. He submitted to his principals a statement in her behalf of the value of the property, but did not waste time over the form of letting her see it, or consulting with her before submitting it in her name.

This statement she never authorized, never heard of, and never read until it was produced in court against her.[1]

One interesting feature of the contract which was the subject of the "adventure" described in the chapter "Not to Exceed Half" was repeated here. The representative who "took up this matter" with the widow carried on his bargaining in great part with the minor stockholders, one of whom claimed afterwards that all he had done was under her directions, and "to her entire satisfaction." But she was entirely unaware of either her "directions" or her "satisfaction." "He never had the slightest authority from me to represent me in any way in the sale."[2]

Another of the minor stockholders also busied himself in representing her without her knowledge. On behalf of the widow agents were making figures, though she knew nothing of their agency or the figures. By these combined efforts a sale was finally concluded at figures which, though she owned seven-tenths of the property, she had never authorized, and were far below the only figures she had given as those she was willing to take.

Compelled to deal with a subordinate against her will, fearing to remain in so hazardous an occupation, and yet needing for her children the income it brought her, this woman manufacturer's position was most harassing. All through, as her cashier and treasurer told the court, she was dissatisfied, felt that she was compelled to sell though she wanted to retain her property.

---

[1] Affidavit, Nov. 17, 1880. [2] Affidavit, Nov. 30, 1880.

"In my hearing," her confidential clerk said, "she declared she sold because she was compelled to do so."

She told her fellow-stockholders that she had been informed by the agent who was dealing with her, that if they did not sell out it would only be a question of time before they would be forced to sell out, as he intended to place oil like that made by her company in the hands of all their agents, to undersell them and close them out. This decided them to sell.

"Inasmuch as the managers of the Standard Oil Company appeared to have made up their minds to obtain this property, and not to give them the chance they had before in competition," the stockholders, as one of them testified, "concluded it better to sell the property at such price as they could then get, rather than to run the risk of a still greater loss in the future, not one of the stockholders desiring to part with the property at all, but rather choosing with fair competition to retain their interest in the property."[1]

She had made 15 per cent. in the last six months, and, aside from these threats, the business looked prosperous, for the orders were becoming more numerous every day. But the widow could refuse to sell only by braving threats which had broken more than two out of three of all the men about her. She put upon the property a price warranted by its income, $200,000, which was adopted by the directors of the company in a formal motion authorizing a sale at that figure. But in her name a proposition was made by the agent to sell for $71,000. "I never heard of the figure of $71,000," she says, "and cannot imagine where it originated. The only proposition that was ever made was that of $200,000." What the stock was worth in her estimation and that of her employés who had inside knowledge is seen in the evidence of her confidential clerk. Though he was her nephew also, he had with difficulty, he says, bought stock at par.

She had refused to sell at par to others. Now the only offer she could get was $60,000 for the works and good-will, the

---

[1] Affidavit, May 1, 1880.

purchasers paying in addition the cash value of the material in stock, and at that price she had to let them go. She asked to be allowed to remain an owner to the extent of $15,000 in the business into which she and her husband had built their lives. "No outsider can have any interest in this concern," was the reply. The combination "has dallied as long as it will over this matter," its agent continued. "It must be settled up to-day or go."

The power of this business to produce a profit of $25,000 a year was worth almost $400,000, according to the valuations maintained for the stock of the oil trust on the New York Stock Exchange by the men who bought out the widow. One hundred dollars in oil trust stock producing $12 a year has sold as high as $185. If $12 a year was worth $185, $25,000 a year was worth nearly $400,000. It was part of the agreement that the oil company should go on as before. "It was particularly enjoined," testified the cashier and treasurer, "that the sale should be kept a profound secret." [1] It was intended that the company should go on as before as far as the public was concerned. The purchasers agreed to continue to employ the hands already at work, but stipulated that not a word should be said to any one of them to reveal that the company was not as independent as it had been. [2]

"And you are not to engage in the refining business," is the concluding phrase of an agreement between the oil combination and a once competitor whom it had forced to sell out in 1876. [3]

"You are not to engage in refining," the same power said in 1877 to the Pennsylvania Railroad, and now to this widow: You must sign this bond not to go into business again for ten years.

The bond is given in full in the record of the case. It put the widow under a forfeit of five thousand dollars for ten years, that—

---

[1] See chapter "Not to Exceed Half."   [2] Affidavit, May 1, 1880.
[3] Commonwealth of Pennsylvania *vs.* Pennsylvania Railroad Company *et al.*, Testimony, p. 751.

"I will not directly, or indirectly, in any way, either alone or in company with any person, or as a share-holder in any corporation, engage in or in any way concern myself or allow knowingly any capital or moneys to be employed in the business or trade of refining, manufacturing, producing, piping, or dealing in petroleum, or any of its products, within the county of Cuyahoga, and State of Ohio, nor at any other place whatsoever." [1]

Their secret of success, the president swore in this very case, is "the very large volume" of purchases, "long continuance in the business," "experience," "knowledge of all the avenues of trade," "skill of experienced employés," and so forth. But with all this they did not dare leave this middle-aged woman free to challenge them again on the field of competition. The purchase was made in the name of three members of the great oil company, and it was paid for by the check of that concern.

Of these men one was among the "trustees" indicted and tried in 1885 for complicity in the plot to blow up a rival refinery, but let go by the judge.

At the time the sale was concluded the widow refiner declared, "The obtaining of her stock was no better than stealing." When the papers were brought to her to sign she "hesitated," and said, "It is like signing my death-warrant. I believe it will prove my death-warrant." "The promises made by the president," she testifies, "were none of them fulfilled."

Being only a woman, and not understanding "business," for all her brilliant success in stepping into her husband's place, and doing the double work of home-maker and bread-winner, the widow could not restrain herself from giving a most uncommercial piece of her mind to those who had got possession of her property for a sum which they would recover out of its profits in two or three years. She sent the following letter:

"November 11, 1878, Monday Morning.

"Sir,—When you left me at the time of our interview the other morning, after promising me so much, you said you had simply dropped the remarks you had for my thought. I can assure you I have thought much and long as I have waited and watched daily to see you fulfil those promises, and it is impossible for me to tell you how utterly astonished I am at the

[1] Exhibit A, Affidavit, October 18, 1880.

course you have pursued with me. Were it not for the knowledge I have that there is a God in heaven, and that you will be compelled to give an account for all the deeds done here, and there, in the presence of my husband, will have to confess whether you have wronged me and his fatherless children or not—were it not for this knowledge I could not endure it for a moment, the fact that a man, possessed of the millions that you are, will permit to be taken from a widow a business that had been the hard life work and pride of herself and husband, one that was paying the handsome profit of nearly twenty-five thousand dollars per annum, and give me in return what a paltry sum, that will net me less than three thousand dollars ; and it is done in a manner that says, Take this or we will crush you out. And when, on account of the sacred associations connected with the business, and also the family name it bears, I plead that I may be permitted to retain a slight interest (you having promised the same at our interview), you then, in your cold, heartless manner, send me word that no outsider can hold a dollar's worth of stock in that concern. It seems strange to be called an outsider in a business that has been almost entirely our own and built up at the *cost* it has to ourselves. It is impossible for us to find language to express our perfect indignation at such proceedings. We do not envy you in the least when this is made known in all its detail to the public. One of your own number admits that it is a great *moral* wrong, but says as long as you can cover the points legally you think you are all right. I doubt, myself, very much the legality of all these things. But do not forget, my dear sir, that God will judge us morally, not legally, and should you offer him your entire monopoly, it will not make it any easier for you. I should not feel that I had done my entire duty unless, before I close, I drop a remark for your thoughts. In my poor way I have tried, by my life and example, with all those I have come in contact with in a business way, to persuade them to a higher, purer, and better life. I think there is no place in the world that one has such opportunities to work for good or evil as in a business life. I cannot tell you the sorrow it has caused me to have one of those in whom I have had the greatest hopes tell me, within the last few days, that it was enough to drive *honest* men away from the Church of God, when professing Christians do as you have done by me."

In reply to this she received a letter in which her charge that her business had been taken from her was repelled as "a most grievous wrong," and "a great injustice." She was reminded that two years before she had consulted with the writer and another member of the oil combination "as to selling out your interest, at which time you were desirous of selling at *considerably less price*, and upon time, than you have now received in cash, and which sale you would have been glad to have closed if you could have obtained satisfactory

6

security for the deferred payments. As to the price paid for the property, it is certainly three times greater than the cost at which we could now construct equal or better facilities."

The letter concluded with an offer to return the works upon the return of the money, or, if she preferred, to sell her one hundred, or two hundred, or three hundred shares of the stock at the price that had been paid her. These propositions were left open to her for three days.

The "cost of the works" is not the standard of value in such transactions. Six millions of dollars, according to a member of the committee of Congress which investigated the oil trust in 1888, is the value of the "works" on which they issued $90,000,000 of stock, which sold in the stock market at a valuation of $160,000,000.

The offer to sell back the refinery was like the offer to let her have cars. To accept it was to pass openly and consciously into slavery. Two years before, when she was weak with grief, inexperience, and the fear that she might not succeed in her gallant task of paying her husband's debts and saving the livelihood of the children, she had thought of selling out at a sacrifice. They knew this because she had asked their advice, and now cheapened her down by reference to the valuation of that moment of despair. All the life energies of herself and her husband, the various advantages of position, the benefit of their pioneership since 1860, and of having established a place in so lucrative a business, all the good-will of customers, all the elements that contributed to the ability to earn the nearly $25,000 a year she was making, were brushed out of the bargain by the mere assertion of a figure at which it was alleged better works could be built. By the time the offer was made she had, moreover, put the sum she had received into such investments, she told the court, as she had been able to find, and the money to accept the offer was no longer in her hands. Indignant with these thoughts, and the massacred troop of hopes and ambitions that her brave heart had given birth to, she threw the letter into the fire, where it curled up into flames like those from which a Dives once begged for a drop of water. She never reappeared in the world of business, where she had found no chivalry to help a woman save her home, her husband's life-work, and her children. But when the men who had divided her property among them invoked the assistance of the law to complete the "equalization" told of in the previous chapter, she went into court and told her story to save her friends from ruin. There, under the gathering dust of years, this incident has remained buried in the document-room of the Court of Common Pleas of Cuyahoga County, until now brought forth to give the people a glimpse into what the real things are which our professors of market philosophy cover with their glittering generalities about the cost of production and the survival of the fittest.

This episode and that of the "Agreement for an Adventure" in the preceding chapter have been written up by the author from the original papers on file in the Court of Common Pleas at Cleveland, which he visited for that purpose in 1891. Certified copies of the documents were procured from the clerk of the court. Lately, the astounding fact was ascertained that all the documents except two or three formal pleadings were gone from the records of the court. But for these certified copies there would now be no authentic record of these cases. This disappearance bears a strong likeness to the suppression of the investigation by the Committee of Commerce of Congress in 1872, and the theft of the testimony taken by the House Committee of Commerce [1] in 1876, and the mutilation of the transcript submitted to Congress in 1888 of the evidence taken in the Buffalo Explosion Case. [2]

[1] See ch. xxvii.   [2] See ch. xviii. and following.

CHAPTER VIII

" no !"

THERE has never been any real break in the plans revealed, "partly born," "and buried" in 1872. From then till now, in 1893, every fact that has come to the surface has shown them in full career. If they were buried, it was as seed is— for a larger crop of the same thing.

The people had made peace, in 1872, on the pledge of "perfect equality" on the highways. Hardly had they got back to their work when they began to feel the pinch of privilege again. The Pennsylvania road alone is credited with any attempt to keep faith, and that only "for some months." "Gradually," as a committee of the people wrote to the managers of the Pennsylvania Railroad, "the persons constituting the South Improvement Company were placed by the roads in as favorable a position as to rates and facilities as had been stipulated in the original contract with that company." [1]

As soon as pipe lines were proved practicable they were built as rapidly as pipes and men to put them in the ground could be had, but there was some lubricant by which they kept constantly slipping into bankruptcy.

They were "frozen out," as one of their builders said, "summer as well as winter."

By 1874, twenty pipe lines had been laid in the oil country. Eighty per cent. of them died off in that and the following year.[2] The mere pipes did not die, they are there yet; but the ownership of the many who had built them died.

There were conservatives in the field to whom competition

[1] Trusts, Congress, 1888, p. 363.
[2] Testimony, New York Assembly "Hepburn" Report, 1879, p. 1693.

was as distasteful as to the socialists. To "overcome such competition," and to insure them "a full and regular" and "remunerative business" in pipe lines, in the language of the South Improvement Company contract, all that was needed was to put into operation the machinery of that contract which no longer existed—in name. The decease of the name was not an insuperable obstacle.

In exact reproduction of the plan of 1872, the railroads, in October, 1874, advanced rates to the general ruin, but to the pool of lines owned by their old friends of the South Improvement Company they paid back a large rebate. That those who had such a railroad Lord Bountiful to fill their pockets should grow rich fast was a matter of course.[1]

Getting this refund they got all the business. Oil, like other things, follows the line of least resistance, and will not flow through pipes where it has to pay when it can run free and get something to boot. Nobody could afford to buy oil except those who were in this deal. They could go into the market, and out of these bonuses could bid higher than any one else. They "could overbid in the producing regions, and undersell in the markets of the world." [2]

This was not all. In the circular which announced the bounty to the pet pipes there was another surprise. It showed that the roads had agreed to carry crude oil to their friends' refineries at Pittsburg and Cleveland without charge from the wells, and to charge them no more for carrying back refined oil to the seaboard for export than was charged to refineries next door to the wells and hundreds of miles nearer the market. "Outside" refiners who had put themselves near the wells and the seaboard were to be denied the benefit of their business sagacity. The Cleveland refiners, whose location was superior only for the Western trade, were to be forced into a position of unnatural equality in the foreign trade. In short, the railroads undertook to pay, instead of being paid, for what they carried for these friends, and

[1] Rutter Circular, Trusts, Congress, 1888, p. 363.
[2] New York Assembly "Hepburn" Report, 1879, p. 44.

force them into an equality with manufacturers who had builded better than they.

Evidently they who had contrived all this had their despondent moments, when they feared that its full beneficence would not be understood by a public unfamiliar with the "science of transportation."

To the new rules was attached an explanation which asserted the right of the railroads to prevent persons and localities from enjoying the advantage of any facility they may possess, no matter how "real."

"You will observe that under this system the rate is even and fair to all parties, preventing one locality taking advantage of its neighbor by reason of some alleged or real facility it may possess." [1]

Meanwhile good society was shuddering at its reformers, and declaring that they meant to stop competition and "divide up property."

"Do you do that in any business except oil?" the most distinguished railroad man of that day was asked. "Do you carry a raw product to a place 150 miles distant and back again to another point like that without charge, so as to put them on an equality?"

To which he replied—it was he who could not remember that he had ever seen the South Improvement Company contract he signed in 1872—"I don't know." [2]

"Could any more flagrant violation of every principle of railroad economy and natural justice be imagined than this?" the report of the New York Legislature asks. [3]

An expert introduced by the railroads defended this arrangement. He insisted that all pipe lines had a chance to enter the pool and get the same refund. [4] But a witness from the pipe-line country, who was brought to New York to testify to the relations of the railroads and the oil combination, let out the truth.

[1] Rutter Circular, Trusts, Congress, 1888, p. 363.
[2] Testimony, New York Assembly "Hepburn" Report, 1879, p. 1596.
[3] Same, Report, p. 43.   [4] Same, Testimony, p. 3429.

"Why didn't they go into the pool?" he was asked, in reference to one of the most important pipe lines.

"Because they were not allowed to. They wanted to freeze them out. They were shut out from the market practically." [1]

For these enterprises, as they failed one after the other, there was but one buyer—the group of gentlemen who called themselves the South Improvement Company in 1872, but now in the field of pipe-line activity had taken the name of United Pipe Line, since known as the National Transit Company, and then and now a part of the oil trust.

"The United Pipe Line bought up the pipes as they became bankrupt one after another," testified the same friendly witness.[2]

Then came a great railroad war in 1877. A fierce onslaught was made on the Pennsylvania Railroad by all the other trunk lines.

In this affair, as in all dynastic wars, the public knew really nothing about what was being done or why. The newspapers were filled with the smoke of the battles of the railroad kings; but the newspapers did not tell, for they did not then know, that the railroads were but tools of conquest in the hands of greater men.

The cause of the trouble was that the managers of the Pennsylvania Railroad had begun to reach out for the control of the oil trade. They had joined in the agreement in 1872 to give it to the oil combination, but now they wanted it for themselves. Through a mistletoe corporation — the Empire Transportation Company — they set to work building up a great business in oil cars, pipe lines, refineries.

"We like competition; we like our competitors; we are neighbors and friends, and have been all these years," the president of the oil trust testified to the New York Legislature,[3] but he served notice upon this competitor to abandon the field.[4] He and his associates determined to do more than compel the great railroad to cease its competition. They

---

[1] Testimony, New York Assembly "Hepburn" Report, 1879, pp. 2792–95.
[2] Same, p. 2795.   [3] Testimony, Trusts, New York Senate, 1888, p. 445.
[4] Testimony, Commonwealth of Pennsylvania *vs.* Pennsylvania Railroad *et al.*, 1879, p. 670.

determined to possess themselves of its entire oil outfit, though it was the greatest corporation then in America. This, the boldest stroke yet attempted, could be done only with the help of the other trunk lines, and that was got.

The ruling officials of the New York Central, the Erie, the Baltimore and Ohio, the Lehigh Valley, the Reading, the Atlantic and Great Western, the Lake Shore railroads, and their connections, were made to believe, or pretended to believe, that it was their duty to make an attack upon the Pennsylvania Railroad to force it to surrender.[1] "A demand," says the New York Legislative Committee of 1879, "which they" —the railroads—"joined hands with the Standard Oil Company and proceeded to enforce by a war of rates, which terminated successfully in October of that year" (1877).[2]

The war was very bitter. Oil was carried at eight cents a barrel less than nothing by the Pennsylvania.[3] How low the rates were made by the railroads on the other side is not known. The Pennsylvania was the first to sue for peace. Twice its vice-president "went to Canossa," which was Cleveland. It got peace and absolution only by selling its refineries and pipe lines and mortgaging its oil-cars to the oil combination. It "was left without the control of a foot of pipe line to gather, a tank to receive, or a still to refine a barrel of petroleum, and without the ability to secure the transportation of one, except at the will of men who live and whose interests lie in Ohio and New York."[4]

It was only seven years since the buyers had organized with a capital of $1,000,000. Now they were able to give their check for over $3,000,000 for this one purchase. "I was surprised," said Mr. Vanderbilt to the New York Legislative Committee of 1878, speaking of this transaction, "at the amount of ready cash they were able to provide." They

[1] Testimony of A. J. Cassatt, Commonwealth of Pennsylvania vs. Pennsylvania Railroad et al., 1879, pp. 666, 669, 671.

[2] New York Assembly "Hepburn" Report, 1879, p. 44.

[3] Testimony, Commonwealth of Pennsylvania, etc., 1879, p. 665.

[4] Appeal to the Executive of Pennsylvania, Trusts, Congress, 1888, p. 354.

secured, in addition to the valuable pipe lines, oil cars, and refineries in New York and Pennsylvania, the more valuable pledge given by the Pennsylvania Railroad that it would never again enter the field of competition in refining, and also a contract giving the oil combination one-tenth of all the oil freights received by the Pennsylvania Railroad, whether from the combination or its competitors—an arrangement it succeeded in making as well with the New York Central, Lake Shore, and other railroads.[1]

One of the earliest members of the oil combination was present at the meeting to consummate this purchase. Something over $3,000,000 of his and his associates' cash changed hands. The meeting was important enough to command the presence of a brigade of lawyers for the great corporations, and of the president, vice-president, and several directors of the Pennsylvania Railroad, and, representing the Poor Man's Light, the vice-president, the secretary, and five of the leading members of the combination, besides himself.[2]

But when asked in court about it he could not remember any such meeting. Finally, he recalled " being at a meeting," but he could not remember when it was, or who was there, or what it was for, or whether any money was paid.[3]

Three years later this transaction having been quoted against the combination in a way likely to affect the decision of a case in court,[4] the treasurer denied it likewise. " It is not true as stated .... directly or indirectly...."[5]

Eight years later, when the exigencies of this suit of 1880, in Cleveland, had passed away, and a new exigency demanded a "revised version," the secretary of the combination told Congress that it was true.[6]

"The pleasures of memory " are evidently for poets, not for such millionaires. That appears to be the only indulgence they cannot afford.

---

[1] Testimony, Commonwealth of Pennsylvania *vs.* Pennsylvania Railroad *et al.*, 1879, p. 735.   [2] Same, p. 672.   [3] Same, p. 460.   [4] See ch. vi.
[5] Standard Oil Company *vs.* W. C. Scofield *et al.* Affidavit of the treasurer of the Standard.   [6] Testimony, Trusts, Congress, 1888, pp. 771–72.

The managers of the Pennsylvania road went back with the zeal of backsliders reconverted to their yoke in the service of the men who had given them this terrific whipping. They sent word to the independent refiners, whom they had secured as shippers by the pledge of 1872 of equal treatment, that equal rates and facilities could be given no longer. The producers and refiners did not sit down dumb under the death sentence. They begged for audience of their masters, masters of them because masters of the highway.

The third vice - president, the official in charge of the freight business, was sent to meet them.

"As you know," they began by reminding him, "we have been for the past year the largest shippers of petroleum the Pennsylvania Railroad has had."

He acknowledged it.

"Shall we, after the 1st of May, have as low a rate of freight as anybody else?" they then asked.

"No," he said; "after the 1st of May we shall give the Standard Oil Company lower rates than to you."

"How much discrimination will we have to submit to?" the poor "outsiders" asked.

"I decline to tell you," was the reply.

"How much business must we bring your road to get as good rates as the combination?" they then asked, and again—

"I decline to tell you," was the only answer they got.

"If we will ship as much, will you give us as low freight rates?"

"No."

"We have been shipping over the Pennsylvania Railroad a year," they persisted, "why can we not continue?"

"It would make them mad; they are the only people who can make peace between the railroads."

"I think," said he, "you ought to fix it up with them. I am going over there this afternoon to talk with those people about this matter, and," he continued, "you will all be happy, and everything will work along very smoothly."

"We gave him very distinctly to understand that we did

not propose to enter into any 'fix up' where we would lose our identity, or sell out, or be under anybody else's thumb; we are willing to pay as high a rate of freight as anybody, and we want it as low as anybody has it," they told him.

But the reply to all of it was, " You cannot have the same rate of freight."

As the magnate of the railroad seemed to be determined not to permit them to move to market along his rails, one of the independents referred to a plan for a new pipe line then under consideration by them, the Equitable, as perhaps promising them the relief he refused.

"Lay all the pipe lines you like," the vice-president retorted, with feeling, " and we will buy them up for old iron."

The independents appealed from the third vice-president to the president; they had to beg repeatedly for a hearing before they got it. They came together in the June following, the independents coming on from New York for the purpose. Since their interview with the third vice-president rates had been advanced upon them, and not only that, but when they had oil ready to ship at those high freight rates, the railroad on one pretext or another refused them cars. One of them had contracts to deliver oil from his refinery in New York to go abroad. When he ordered the cars that were needed to take the crude oil to New York to be refined they were refused him. The ships lay idle at the docks, charging him heavy damages for every day of delay; at the wells his oil was running on the ground.

" You had better go and arrange with the Standard Oil Company; I don't want to get into any trouble with them," the president said. " If you are business men, you will make an arrangement with them. I will do all in my power to bring it about."

" We will never take our freight rates from them," they replied; "we are not willing to enter into any such arrangement."

" Why don't you go to the other roads ?" the president asked his suppliants.

"We have done so. It's of no use. On the New York Central the cars are owned by the combination, and the Erie is in a like position. We have been shippers on the Pennsylvania Railroad a long, long while, and you ought to take care of us and give us all the cars we need. We are suffering very greatly for the want of them. Can we have the same rate that other shippers get?"

"No."

"If we ship the same amount of oil?"

"No."

"If you have not cars enough, will you, if we build cars, haul them?"

"No. You will not have any peace or prosperity," continued the president, "until you make terms with the combination."

Like the third vice-president he offered to intercede with them to get transportation over his own road for his own customers. Like men they refused the offer.

"We were, of course, very indignant," one of them said, in relating this experience in court.[1]

A little later a rich and expert refiner, who had sold out in 1876, made up his mind to try again. The Pennsylvania road had a new president by this time, but the old "no" was still in force.

"When I was compelled to succumb I thought it was only temporarily, that the time would come when I could go into the business I was devoted to. I was in love with the business. I took a run across the water; I was tired and discouraged and used up in 1878, and was gone three or four months. I came back ready for work, and had the plan, specifications and estimates made for a refinery that would handle ten thousand barrels of oil in a day. I selected a site near three railroads and a river; I would have spent about five hundred thousand

---

[1] For the full report of these remarkable interviews with the President and Third Vice-President of the Pennsylvania Railroad see Testimony, Investigation Pennsylvania Secretary of Internal Affairs, 1878, pp. 47 *et seq.*, 60 *et seq.*; Testimony, Commonwealth of Pennsylvania *vs.* Pennsylvania Railroad *et al.*, 1879, pp. 160 *et seq.*, 204 *et seq.*, 237 *et seq.*

dollars, and probably a couple of hundred thousand more. I believed the time had arrived when the Pennsylvania Railroad would see their true interest as common carriers, and the interest of their stockholders, and the business interest of the City of Philadelphia. I called on the President of the Pennsylvania Railroad ; I laid the plans before him, and told him I wanted to build a refinery of ten thousand barrels' capacity a day. I was almost on my knees begging him to allow me to do that.

" ' What is it you want ?' he said.

" ' Simply to be put upon an equality with everybody else— especially the Standard Oil Company. I want you to agree with me that you will give me transportation of crude oil as low as you give it to anybody else for ten years, and then I will give you a written assurance that I will do this refining of ten thousand barrels of oil a day for ten years. Is not that an honest position for us to be in ? I as a manufacturer, you the president of a railroad.'

" ' I cannot go into any such agreement.'

" I saw the third vice-president. He said, in his frank way, ' That is not practicable, and you know the reason why.' " [1]

After their interviews with the President and Vice-President of the Pennsylvania Railroad, these outsiders went to the officials of the other roads, only to hear the same " No !" from all. [2]

At one time, to get oil to carry out their contracts and fill the vessels which were waiting at the docks and charging them damages for the delay, these refiners telegraphed to the oil regions offering the producers there ten cents above the market price if they could get oil to them over any of the roads to New York. They answered they could not get the cars, and none of them accepted the offer. [3]

All the roads—as in 1872—were in league to " overcome " them.

[1] Testimony, Trusts, Congress, 1888, pp. 225-26.

[2] Testimony, Investigation, Pennsylvania Secretary of Internal Affairs, 1878, pp. 49, 59 ; Testimony, New York Assembly " Hepburn " Report, 1879, pp. 710, 3548-56 ; Exhibits, same, p. 176 ; Testimony, Commonwealth of Pennsylvania *vs.* Pennsylvania Railroad *et al.*, 1879, p. 247.

[3] Testimony, New York Assembly " Hepburn " Report, p. 712.

Thus, at a time when the entire movement of oil was at the rate of only 25,000 or 30,000 barrels a day, and the roads had cars enough to move 60,000 barrels a day, these independent refiners found themselves shut completely off from the highway.[1] The Pennsylvania Railroad, the New York Central, the Erie, and their branches and connections in and out of the oil regions, east and west, were as entirely closed to them as if a foreign enemy had seized the country and laid an embargo on their business—which was, indeed, just what had happened. The only difference between that kind of invasion and what had really come was, that "the dear people," as the president of the trust called them,[2] would have known they were in the hands of an enemy if he had come beating his drums loud enough, and firing off his two-thousand pounders often enough, and pricking them deep enough with his bayonets; but their wits are not yet up to knowing him when he comes among them disguised as an American citizen, although they see property destroyed and life lost and liberty thrown wherever he moves.

There was enough virtue in Pennsylvania to begin a suit in the name of the State against the men who were using its franchises for such purposes, though there was not enough to push it to a decision. The Third Vice-President of the Pennsylvania Railroad, when examined as a witness in this suit, confirmed these statements about the interviews with himself and the president of the road in every particular about which he was questioned.

"We stated to the outside refiners that we would make lower rates to the Standard Oil Company than they got; we declined to allow them to put cars of their own on the road."[3]

His evidence fills seventy-six pages, closely printed, in the report of testimony. It was clear, full, and candid; remark-

[1] Testimony, New York Assembly "Hepburn" Report, 1879, p. 720.

[2] Testimony, Trusts, New York Senate, 1888, p. 445.

[3] Testimony, Commonwealth of Pennsylvania *vs.* Pennsylvania Railroad *et al.*, 1879, pp. 725–26.

ably so, considering that it supplied officially from the company's own records the facts, item by item, which proved that the management of the Pennsylvania Railroad had violated the Constitution of Pennsylvania and the common law, and had taken many millions of dollars from the people and from the corporation which employed them, and secretly, and for no consideration, had given them to strangers.

This testimony is so important that it was reprinted substantially in full both by the "Hepburn" committee of the New York Legislature in 1879 [1] and the Trust Investigating Committee of Congress in 1888. [2] As instances, it showed that in one case where the rate to the public was $1.15, this favored shipper was charged only 38 cents. In another case the trade generally had to pay $1.40 a barrel on crude petroleum, but the oil combination paid 88½ cents.

"And then the refined rate was 80 cents ?"

"80 cents net to the Standard."

"And to all others ?"

"$1.44½."

"But there were no other outside shippers," he pleaded—how could there be ?

There was only one important member in Pennsylvania of the oil combination who could be caught with a subpœna. At his first appearance in court, on the witness stand, he took lofty ground.

"I decline to answer." [3]

Put on the stand again, he was asked :

"Were you allowed a rebate amounting to 64½ cents per barrel ?"

"No, sir ; not to my knowledge." [4]

Put on the third time and compelled to produce his books, he had to read aloud in court the entries showing the payment he had thus denied under oath.

"There was a total allowance of 64½ cents per barrel." [5]

---

[1] Exhibits, pp. 453–514.   [2] Testimony, pp. 174–207.
[3] Testimony, Commonwealth of Pennsylvania *vs.* Pennsylvania Railroad *et al.*, 1879, p. 11.   [4] Same, p. 352.   [5] Same, p. 510.

And then he shut up again—but too late ; and to all other questions about his rebates said, gloomily, " I decline to answer."

When the president of the oil trust was asked afterwards by the New York Legislature if some company or companies embraced within it had not enjoyed from railroads more favorable freight rates than outside refineries, he replied :

" I do not recall anything of that kind."

" You have heard of such things ?"

" I have heard much in the papers about it." [1]

But at the time these rates were being made, one of his principal associates admitted that the president was the person who attended to the freight rates.[2] This was also put beyond a doubt in the Ohio investigation by the evidence of his first partner in the little oil refinery at Cleveland which had grown so great, he who had furnished the only mechanical and refining knowledge it had started with, and who had, until within a year, been a fellow-stockholder and director.

" Do these contracts contain anything of the nature that would discriminate against the small refiners of the State ?"

" I think they did. . . . Up to the time I left the company the open rate was $1.40 to the seaboard. They "—the oil combination—" ship for 80 cents. . . . The president told me it was the rate at that time." [3]

With every known avenue to the sea thus closed to them it certainly looked as if all was up with the " outsiders." But the men, who had too much American spunk to buy peace with dishonor by consenting to a " fix-up " under compulsion, had the wit to find out a loop-hole of temporary escape. They built tank boats for the canal, and thus succeeded in getting 200,000 barrels of oil to New York that summer before the canal closed.[4]

[1] Testimony, Trusts, New York Senate, 1888, p. 420.

[2] Testimony, Commonwealth of Pennsylvania *vs.* Pennsylvania Railroad *et al.*, 1879, p. 374.

[3] Testimony, Discriminations in Freight Rates, Ohio House of Representatives, 1879, pp. 181–85.

[4] Testimony, New York Assembly " Hepburn " Report, 1879, p. 800.

Since then all chance of escape by the canal has been cut off. The railroads made a war of freight rates against it, and the only canal that connected the oil regions with the Erie canal route to the sea was dried up, and turned into a way for a railroad by a special act of the New York Legislature. The railroad so built has ever since been managed as one of the most diligent promoters of the policy of excluding the common people from the oil business.

According to the funeral notices given out by the railroad officials and the members of the South Improvement Company this concern was dead, but in the quaint phrase of the producers it was really alive and hard at work, but "with a new suit of clothes and no name." These interviews between the independent refiners and the railroad officials of the three trunk lines form one of the most extraordinary scenes which have taken place between a government and its subjects since the era of modern democratic liberty.

The railway officials are, in the world of the highway, the government. They hold their supreme power to tax commerce, and to open and close the highways, solely and altogether by grant of the State, and under the law of the common carrier. It is only by the exercise of the sovereign power of eminent domain to take the property of a private individual by force, without his consent, for public use—never for any other than public use—and only by the grant of the right to cross city streets and country roads that the railroads come into existence at all. This says nothing of the actual cash given to the railroad projectors by the government, which, in New York State alone, amounts to upwards of $40,000,000.[1]

The independent refiners represent the people, claiming of the highway department of their government those equal rights which all citizens have as a birthright, and the government informs these citizens that their rights on the highways have been given as a private estate to certain friends of the

[1] Exhibits, New York Assembly "Hepburn" Report, 1879, pp. 238–45.

7

ruling administration, much as William the Conqueror would give this rich abbey or that fertile manor to one of his pets.

"We have no franchise that is not open to all," say the "trustees." "It is a free open market." "There is nothing peculiar to our companies." "It is as free as air."

In truth they have had no less a franchise than, as in 1872, the excluding possession of all the great trunk-lines out of the oil country, and all their connections east and west, and this franchise has since widened until, in 1893, it reaches from ocean to ocean, and from gulf to gulf.

Their franchise was meant to be as exclusive as if they had had from the government letters-patent in the old royal fashion of close monopolies in East Indian trade, or salt, or tobacco at home, giving them by name the sole right to use the roads, and forbidding all others, under pain of business death, from setting their foot on the highway. But with this difference: the exclusive franchise in the latter case would exist by law; but in this case it was created in defiance of law, exists in contempt of the law, and in its living the law dies daily.

The refiners and producers who were pleading in this way with the railroads for a chance to live after May 1, never doubted but that, as they were told, and as their arrangements with the Pennsylvania road guaranteed, they were having and were to have at worst until that date, equal and impartial rates and facilities. Under this safe-conduct they parleyed for the future. But the Pennsylvania Railroad was at that moment negotiating with the oil combination to collect from the independents, under the guise of freight, 20 to 22½ cents a barrel on all they sent to market, and pay it over to the combination. The payments were made to one of the rings within the oil ring, called the American Transfer Company. "It is the same instrumentality under a different name," said the counsel of the New York Chamber of Commerce before the New York Legislature. The official of the Pennsylvania road who issued the order to take this money out of the treasury pleaded in excuse that proof had been given him that other roads were doing the same thing.[1] Receipted bills were brought to him, showing that the New York Central and the Erie had been "for many months" paying these men who called themselves American Transfer Company for having "protected" their oil business, sums ranging from 20 cents to 35 cents a barrel on all the oil those roads transported.[2] So deeply was the watch-dog of the Pennsylvania road's treasury affected by the proof that his company was doing less than the other roads, that he instructed the comptroller to give these men three months' back pay, which was done. Twenty cents a barrel was sent them out of all the oil freights collected by the Pennsylvania for the three months preceding, and thereafter the tribute was paid them monthly. Then it was increased to $22\frac{1}{2}$ cents a barrel. The same amount per barrel was refunded to them out of their own freight. They received this on all oil shipped by them, and also on all shipped by their competitors.[3] They who received this tribute pretended to the railroad officials that they "protected" the roads from losing business. The railroad men pretended to believe it.

The way in which this revenue was given and got shows what a simple and easy thing modern business really is—not in any way the brain-racker political economists have persuaded themselves and us. The representative of the oil combination writes a bright, cheery letter; the representative of the Pennsylvania answers it, and there you are; $22\frac{1}{2}$ cents a barrel on millions of barrels flows out of the cash-box of the railroad into the cash-box of the combination. In one year, 1878, this tribute, at the rate of $22\frac{1}{2}$ cents on the 13,750,000 barrels of oil shipped by the three trunk-lines, must have amounted to $3,093,750. The American Transfer Company

---

[1] New York Assembly "Hepburn" Report, 1879, Exhibits, pp. 479–514.

[2] This was always denied by the New York Central. "I never heard of the American Transfer Company," Vanderbilt told the New York Legislature. "I don't know that we ever paid the American Transfer Company a dollar. If we did, I have no knowledge of it." New York Assembly "Hepburn" Report, 1879, p. 1577.

[3] Testimony, Commonwealth of Pennsylvania *vs.* Pennsylvania Railroad *et al.*, p. 702. Same, Exhibits Nos. 45–47, pp. 732–33.

had a little capital of $100,000, and its receipts from this re-
bate in this one year would amount to dividends of 3093 per
cent. annually; the capital of the oil combination which
owned this Transfer Company was at this time $3,500,000.

There are reasons to believe that some of the very railroad
men who turned the money of the railroads over to the
American Transfer Company were among its members. But
if all the profit went to the combination, and none of it was for
the railway officials through whom they got it, their revenue
from that source alone would have paid in 1878 a dividend
nearly equal to this capital of $3,500,000. In this device of
the American Transfer Company we again see reappear in 1878,
in high working vitality, the supposed corpse of the South
Improvement Company of 1872. The American Transfer
Company was ostensibly a pipe line, and the railroad officials
met the exposure of their "nothing peculiar" dealings with
it by asserting that the payment to it of 22½ cents a barrel
and more was for its service in collecting oil and delivering it
to them; but the Third Vice-President of the Pennsylvania
Railroad admits that his road paid the money on oil which the
American Transfer Company never handled.

"This 22½ cents (a barrel) paid the American Transfer Company is not restricted to oil that passed through their lines?"

"No, sir; it is paid on all oil received and transported
by us." [1]

The American Transfer Company was not even a pipe line.
By the Pennsylvania laws all incorporated pipe lines must report their operations and condition monthly to the State. But
the publisher of the petroleum trade reports, and organizer
of a bureau of information about petroleum, with offices in
Oil City, London, and New York, issuing daily reports, testified that the American Transfer Company was not known in
the oil regions at all as a pipe line. It published none of the
statements required by law. "They do not," he said, "make
any runs from the oil-wells." It had once been a pipe line,

---

[1] Commonwealth of Pennsylvania *vs.* Pennsylvania Railroad *et al.*, 1879, p. 691.

but "years ago it was merged in with other lines," and consolidated into the United Pipe Line, owned and operated by the combination.[1]

When this arrangement was exposed to public view by the New York legislative investigation, the "expert" who appeared to explain it away in behalf of the railroads and their beneficiaries, paraded a false map of the pipe-line system, drawn and colored to make it seem that the American Transfer Company was a very important pipe-line.[2]   This was the same "expert" who, as we saw, defended the pipe-line holocaust of 1874 by asserting that "all were to be taken in alike."

There are three kinds of liars, an eminent judge of New York is fond of saying—liars, damned liars, and experts.

When the assistant secretary of the oil combination was asked about this "transfer" company, he replied, "I don't know anything about the organization."[3]   He had described himself to the committee as "a clamorer for dividends"; but he declared he knew nothing about an organization which was "transferring" him dividends at the rate of $3,093,750 a year on $100,000 of capital.   Almost at the very moment of this denial, receipts were being produced in court in Pennsylvania which had been given by the cashier of himself and his associates to the railroads for this money.[4]

Even if the independents succeeded in saving their oil from wasting on the ground, and got it into pipe lines, and had it refined, and were lucky enough to be given cars to carry it to the seaboard, they found that in leaving the oil regions they had not left behind the "no." Up to the very edge of the sea were the nets spread for them.

Part of the bargain of 1872 had been that the brothers of the South Improvement Company should provide the terminal facilities at the seaboard.[5]   Railroad companies are usu-

---

[1] Testimony, New York Assembly "Hepburn" Report, 1879, pp. 3666–69.
[2] Same, p. 3959.   [3] Same, p. 2664.
[4] Testimony, Commonwealth of Pennsylvania *vs.* Pennsylvania Railroad *et al.*, 1879, pp. 656–57.   [5] Art. 1, sec. 4.

ally supposed to have their own yards, storehouses, wharves, and the like, and, as a matter of fact, the railroads had these. The agreement of 1872 that the South Improvement Company should furnish the terminal facilities meant — it was discovered by the New York Legislature in 1879 — that such terminals as the road already had should be turned over to that concern, and that thereafter nobody should be allowed to build or use terminals except as it permitted.

The New York Legislature found, in 1879, that the oil combination thus owned and controlled the oil terminal facilities of the four trunk-lines at New York, Philadelphia, and Baltimore.

"They can use the power here given, and have used it to crush out opposition." [1]

"Of course, there is in the Erie contract a statement that every shipper of oil over the road shall be treated with 'fairness' by the Standard Oil Company, and our attention was drawn to that," the counsel of the Chamber of Commerce said. . . . "In the first place, they have the exclusive shipment of oil, and therefore nobody could ship oil, and there was no oil handled for anybody else; but if the Erie Company should send some for somebody else, why, the sloop could not get to the dock, and the machinery at the dock would not and could not work by any possibility so as to get that oil out of that dock and into a ship (except at the end of a lawsuit)." [2]

Evidently the "cancellation" of 1872 had not cancelled anything of substance. Indeed, the "no" of 1878 was wider than the embargo of 1872, for the fourth great trunk-line, the Baltimore and Ohio, was not one of the signatories then; but by 1878 it had, like all the others, closed its port to the people— farming it out as the old regime farmed out the right to tax provinces.

He used to meet the president of the oil combination "frequently in the Erie office," a friend and subordinate has

[1] New York Assembly "Hepburn" Report, 1879, pp. 40–44.

[2] Speech of Simon Sterne, counsel of the New York Chamber of Commerce, before New York Assembly "Hepburn" Committee, 1879, p. 3964.

recalled.[1]   Railroad offices are pleasant places to visit when such plums are to be gathered there as this of the sole right to the freedom of all ports and control of the commerce of three continents.

Down to this writing, when the little group of independents who remain masters of their own refineries along Oil Creek seek to send their oil in bulk abroad, or to transship it at any one of the principal ports for other points on the coast, the same power still says the same " no " as twenty years ago.[2]

[1] Testimony, same, p. 2772.   [2] See ch. xi.

CHAPTER IX

WHO PIPED AND WHO DANCED

THUS, by 1878, the independent producers and refiners found themselves caught in a battue like rabbits driven in for the sport of a Prince of Wales.

If the richest person then in America—that artificial but very real person the Pennsylvania Railroad—could not keep its pipe lines, nobody could. The war for the union, which ended with its surrender in 1877, closed the pipe-line industry to the people. The unanimous "no" of all the railroads which followed completed the corral.

Oil, when it got to market, found that those who had become the owners of the pipe lines were also the owners of most of the refineries, and so the only large buyers.[1] "Practically to-day there is but one buyer of crude oil for us. . . . We take our commodity to one buyer; we take the price he chooses to give us without redress, with no right of appeal."[2]

Then the sole carrier—the pipe-line company—refused to take the oil into its pipes—the oil as it came out of the wells —unless first sold to its other self, the oil combination. This was called "immediate shipment." Forced to waste or sell his oil, the producer, under this compulsion, had to take what he could get.[3] The Hon. Lewis Emery, Jr., a member of the State Senate of Pennsylvania, gave the authorities of the State an account of the "immediate shipment" evolution

[1] New York Assembly "Hepburn" Report, 1879, p. 44.

[2] Testimony, Commonwealth of Pennsylvania *vs.* Pennsylvania Railroad *et al.*, 1879, pp. 302, 314.

[3] Testimony, same, Pipe Line Appendix, pp. 36–37; Investigation, Pennsylvania Secretary of Internal Affairs, 1878, pp. 19, 29.

of American market liberty. "We go down," he said, "to the office and stand in a line, sometimes half a day—people in a line reaching out into the street—sixty and seventy of us. When our turn comes we go in and ask them to buy, and they graciously will take it. I am an owner in six different companies, and we all suffer the same."

To educate the producer to sell "always below the market," the Pipe Line let his oil spill itself on the ground for a few days. "We lost a considerable amount of oil, probably several thousand barrels," another producer said.

"Will you state at what price as compared with the market price, whether above or below, you sold that oil?"

"It was always below."

Asked why he sold it below the market, he said :

"Because the line would not run it until it was sold." [1]

The hills of Pennsylvania began to growl and redden as in 1872.

The Secretary of Internal Affairs was hung in effigy. Mass meetings were held — some tumultuous, others quiet; processions of masked men marched the streets, and groaned and hooted in front of the newspaper offices and the business places of the combination. In the morning the streets and sidewalks were frequently found placarded with cabalistic signs and letters, and occasionally printed proclamations and warnings. Most of the leading newspapers of the region had been either absolutely purchased by the oil combination or paid to keep silence. Others occasionally broke forth in violent articles advising the use of force. [2]

In the McKean County field the people rose in rebellion. They got up a Phantom Party, in its provocation and spirit much like a phantom party which, contrary to law and order, boarded some ships in Boston harbor a century before. One thousand men, wrapped in white sheets, marched by night

---

[1] Testimony, Commonwealth of Pennsylvania, etc., 1879, Pipe Line Appendix, pp. 36–37; Investigation, Pennsylvania Secretary of Internal Affairs, 1878, pp. 19, 29, 32, 42.

[2] A History, etc. Trusts, Congress, 1888, pp. 690, 697, 705, 706.

from Tarport to Bradford, the headquarters in that province of the sole buyer. Not a word was spoken.

It was not enough to make the people sell under compulsion. A day came when the only buyer would not buy and the only piper would not pipe. This brought the Parker district to the verge of civil war. The citizens were in a state of terrible excitement; the pipe lines would not run oil unless it was sold; the only buyers—viz., the agents of the oil combination—would not buy oil, stating that they could not get cars; hundreds of wells were stopped to their great injury. Thousands more, whose owners were afraid to stop them for fear of damage by salt water, were pumping the oil on the ground. The leaders used all the influence they had to prevent an outbreak and destruction of railroad and pipe lines. The most important of them went over to the Alleghany Valley Railroad office and telegraphed to the president: "The refusal to run oil unless sold upon immediate shipment and of the railroad to furnish cars has created such a degree of excitement here that the most conservative part of the citizens will not be able to control the peace, and I fear that the scenes of last July will be repeated on an aggravated scale."[1]

Three of the highest officials of the road sought an immediate interview with this leader of the producers. He warned them, and the Pennsylvania road which controlled their oil business, that unless immediate relief were furnished there would be an outbreak in the oil regions, because, as he told them, "The idea of a scarcity of cars on daily shipments of less than 30,000 barrels a day was such an absurd, barefaced pretence, that he could not expect men of ordinary intelligence to accept any excuses for the absence of cars, as the preceding fall, when business required, the railroads could carry day after day from 50,000 to 60,000 barrels of oil."[2] The warning was heeded. Thousands of empty cars, which the combination and its railroad allies had said couldn't be

---

[1] Testimony of B. B. Campbell, Commonwealth of Pennsylvania *vs.* Pennsylvania Railroad *et al.*, pp. 298–99. [2] Same, p. 300.

had anywhere, suddenly appeared hastening to Parker, blocking up the tracks in all directions, deranging the passenger business of the road. "They looked like mosquitoes coming out of a swamp." The sole buyer began buying again, and for the whole week, after having declared themselves unable to buy or move any, the railroads moved 50,000 barrels a day.[1] Producers under such rule saw their prices decrease and their land pass out of their possession, as was inevitable.

Ten years later in the Ohio oil-field all the substantial features of the plan we saw culminate at Parker are to be found in full play. There, also, the oil combination, Congress was told, is the only purchaser, and it fixes the price to suit itself. The production of the Ohio fields was between 18,000 and 20,000 barrels a day, but it could easily produce between 30,000 and 32,000. Because the only buyer refused to take care of the oil, wells have been shut back. Wells, which if opened up would run 1000 or 2000 or even more, were shut in four days out of the week.[2]

This culmination of 1878 made the people act. The producers were being ground to powder by the fact that an enemy had possession of their local pipes, their tankage, and their railways. "I am the unfortunate owner," said one of them, "of interests in nearly one hundred pumping wells. I have produced over half a million barrels of oil."[3] Oil was running out of the ground at the rate of 15,000,000 barrels a year, but the New York refiners who were in command of plenty of capital, said:

"We don't dare build large refineries, for we don't know where we could get the oil."[4]

At last the people organized the Tidewater Pipe Line. This was the first successful attempt to realize the idea often broached of a pipe line to the seaboard. It was the last hope

---

[1] Testimony of B. B. Campbell, Commonwealth of Pennsylvania *vs.* Pennsylvania Railroad *et al.*, p. 300.

[2] Testimony, Trusts, Congress, 1888, pp. 78–79.

[3] Testimony, Commonwealth of Pennsylvania *vs.* Pennsylvania Railroad *et al.*, 1879, p. 295.   [4] Same, p. 212.

of the "outsiders"—the "independents." "Nothing short of
the ingenuity that is born of necessity and desperation" produced that pipe line. It was well contrived and well manned,
and had plenty of money. It was organized in 1878, with
a capital of $1,000,000, which increased in a few years to
$5,000,000. It built a pipe from the oil regions to Williams-
port—105 miles—on the Philadelphia and Reading Railroad,
whence the oil was carried in cars by that company and over
the Jersey Central to Philadelphia and New York.

Unlimited capital and strategy did all that could be done
against the Tidewater. At one place, to head it off, a strip of
land barring its progress was bought entirely across a valley.
It escaped by climbing the hills. At another point it had
to cross under a railroad. The railroad officers forbade. Rid-
ing around, almost in despair, its engineer saw a culvert where
there was no watercourse. It was for a right of passage which
a farmer, whose land was cut in two by the railroad, had reserved in perpetuity for driving his cattle in safety to pasture.
It did not take long to make a bargain with the farmer for
permission to lay the pipe there.

The pipe line was finished and ready to move oil about the
1st of June, 1879. On June 5th a meeting was held at Saratoga of representatives of the four trunk-line railroads and of
members of the oil trust. The meeting decided that the new
competitor should be fought to the death. The rate on oil,
which had been $1.15 a barrel, was reduced to 80, then to 30,
to 20, to 15 cents by the railroads, to make the business unprofitable enough to ruin this first attempt to pipe oil to the seaboard. Finally the roads carried a barrel, weighing 390 pounds,
400 miles for the combination for 10 cents or less.[1] The representative of the Tidewater offered to prove to Congress,
in 1880, if it would order an investigation — which it would
not—that "the announced and ostensible object of the conference at Saratoga was to destroy the credit of the Tidewater, and
to enable the oil combination to buy up the new pipe line, and

---

[1] New York Assembly "Hepburn" Report, 1879, p. 45.

that a time was fixed by the combination within which it promised to secure the control of the pipe line—provided the trunk-lines would make the rates for carrying oil so low that all concerned in transportation would lose money.[1] There can be no doubt," he continued, "that, taking the avowed and ostensible object of the Saratoga meeting as the true one, it constituted, on the part of the willing participants, a criminal conspiracy of the most dangerous character."

One of the chief officials of the Pennsylvania Railroad testified to the competition which his road had carried on with the Tidewater. " It certainly was fought," he said ; "the rates were considerably reduced."[2] Rates were put down to points so low that the railroad men would never tell what they were. I have no knowledge—I have no recollection—was all the president and general freight agent of the Pennsylvania Railroad could be got to say, when before the Interstate Commerce Commission.[3] "Not enough to pay for the wheel grease," said the general freight agent.[4] The oil trust also cut the prices of pipeage by its local lines from 20 cents to 5 cents a barrel, turning cheapness into the enemy of cheapness.

But the Tidewater was strong enough to withstand even so formidable an assault as this. As its business was small, its losses were small ; but the railroads, making this war on it for the benefit of others, suffered heavily. The trunk-lines, it has been calculated, wilfully threw away profits equal to $10,000,000 a year for the sake of inflicting a loss of $100,000 on the pipe lines.[5] Enough revenue was lost to pay dividends of $2\frac{1}{2}$ to 5 per cent. on the total capital of the roads.

One effect that followed this reduction in rates was a corresponding decline in the price of oil at New York, in which the cost of freight is a constant element. The Committee of

---

[1] Franklin B. Gowen, before House Committee of Commerce, Washington, Jan. 27, 1880.

[2] Testimony, Titusville and Oil City Independents' cases, before Interstate Commerce Commission, pp. 299–300.   [3] Same, pp. 521, 539.   [4] Same, p. 534.

[5] Franklin B. Gowen, before House Committee of Commerce, Washington, Jan. 27, 1880.

the New York Legislature found in the testimony it heard reason to believe that the members of the oil trust took advantage of their advance knowledge to sell at high prices, to those who did not know, all they would buy for future delivery.

The "Hepburn" report of the New York Legislature of 1879 gives special prominence to the computations that $1,500,000 were the profits of this speculative deal.[1]

The customers of the Tidewater, the independent refiners in Philadelphia, were charged by the Pennsylvania Railroad on oil that came through the Tidewater 15 cents a barrel for one mile of hauling. The utmost the law allowed them was half a cent a mile, and they were carrying oil 500 miles to New York for the same charge of 15 cents a barrel, and less. Under such pressure these independent refineries, which the Tidewater had been built to supply, sold out one after another. The Tidewater was then in the position of a great transporting company, that had spent a large amount of money to bring a great product to its Philadelphia terminus, and found that refining establishments which had been begging it to give them oil had become the cohorts of its opponent. To meet this the Tidewater built refineries of its own at Chester, and at Bayonne, New Jersey, on New York waters.

When asked for a rate to another point, the Pennsylvania gave one that was three and four times as much as they would charge the oil trust, but added, " we cannot make a rate on the empty cars returning." That is, as it was interpreted, " we will carry the oil, but we will not permit the empty cars to come over the roads to get the oil. They must be taken on a wheelbarrow, or by canal, or by balloon."[2] The war went on. Attempts were made to seduce the officials of the Tidewater. A stockholder, who had been too poor to pay for his stock, received a large sum from the oil combination and began a vexatious suit for a receivership.[3] A minority

[1] Report, p. 45.
[2] Franklin B. Gowen, before Pennsylvania House of Representatives Committee on Railroads, Feb. 13, 1883.   [3] See ch. xiii.

forced their way into the offices of the company, and took violent possession of it by a "farcical, fraudulent, and void" election, as the court decided in annulling it. Its financial credit was attacked in the money market and by injunctions against its bonds.

Affidavits were offered from members of the oil combination denying that they had had anything to do with these proceedings. In reference to these affidavits, the representative of the Tidewater reminded the court that that combination was a multifarious body. "One-half of them," he said, "do a thing, and the other half swear they know nothing about it. In pursuance of this Machiavelian policy, they have eight or ten gentlemen to conduct negotiations, and eight or ten to say they do not know anything about them."

Then, with no visible cause, the capacity of the pipe fell below the demands upon it. This insufficient capacity was pleaded in court as one of the reasons why the pipe should be taken out of the hands of its owners. One day the cause was discovered—a plug of wood. Some mysterious hand had been set to drive a square block of wood into the pipe so as to cut down its capacity to one-third. The representative of the Tidewater declared in court his belief that this plug had been placed by "people on the other side who have made affidavits in this case." A similar deed, but much worse, as it might have cost many lives, was done during the contest with Toledo, nine years later.[1]

The Tidewater was successful, but not successful enough. It owned 400 miles of pipe, including the 105 miles of the trunk-line, and had control of nearly 3,000,000 barrels of tankage. It did a great work for the people. "It was," the Philadelphia *Press* said, in 1883, "the child of war. It has been a barrier between the producers and the monopoly which would crush them if it dared." While these words of exultation were being penned, a surrender was under negotiation. The Tidewater's managers were nearly worn out. These tac-

---

[1] See ch. xxvi.

tics of corrupting their officers, slandering their credit, buying up their customers, stealing their elections, garroting them with lawsuits founded on falsehoods, shutting them off the railroads, and plugging up their pipe in the dark, were too much. They entered into a pool. The two companies in the summer of 1883 "recognized" each other, as the trunk lines do, and agreed to divide the business in proportions, which would net the Tidewater $500,000 a year. The announcement that this pool had been forced on the Tidewater fell like a death-blow on the people of the oil regions. "The Tidewater," the Philadelphia *Press* said, editorially, "will probably retain a nominal identity as a corporation, but its usefulness to the public and its claim to popular confidence and encouragement were extinguished the instant it consented to enter into alliance with the unscrupulous monopoly which resorts to that means of conciliating and bribing what it had failed to destroy." As was anticipated by the *Press*, the Tidewater retained its nominal identity, but that was all. Its surrender was admitted by its principal organizer, Mr. Franklin B. Gowen. The officials of the Pennsylvania Railroad have testified to it. "They made an arrangement of some kind, the conditions of which I never knew; one swallowed the other or both swallowed the other, or something, and settled up their difficulties,"[1] said the general freight agent. The president said: "The competition between these pipe lines ceased."[2]

The attorney of the Tidewater was asked if there were any negotiations which resulted in a compromise of the differences with the oil combination.

"If by differences," he replied, "you mean competition in trade, I answer the question, yes. That resulted in a written contract. . . . The purpose of the contract was to settle the rivalry in business between the two companies, each company to take

---

[1] Testimony of General Freight Agent of Pennsylvania Railroad (Logan, Emery, and Weaver *vs.* Pennsylvania Railroad), McKean County Court of Common Pleas, 1889.

[2] Testimony, Titusville and Oil City Independents' cases before the Interstate Commerce Commission, Deposition, pp. 531–34.

a percentage of transportation and gathering, and each to do with the oil as it saw fit." [1]

The treasurer of the Tidewater, who had been in its service since 1880, corroborated its attorney. A contract had been made between the two; the date of it was October 9, 1883. Copies of the contracts are in the author's possession.

The Interstate Commerce Commission in 1892 judicially found the same fact. It says: "About December, 1883, the pipe lines, with the view of getting better rates, adjusted their differences, and the competition between them ceased. The pipe-line business appears then to have passed into the control of the National Transit Company." [2] All but 6 per cent. of the National Transit Company is owned by the oil trust. It formed practically one-third the imposing bulk of the $70,-000,000 of the trust of 1882. [3] If anything can be made certain by human testimony this evidence proves that these pipe lines stopped competing in 1883. The witnesses are the men who negotiated the contract, and upon whose approval it depended. But when the president of the trust was asked under oath, in 1888, if there were any pipe lines to tide-water competing with it, he named, as "a competing company," "the Tidewater Pipe Line."

"The Tidewater Company? Does that compete with your company?"

"It does."

"It is in opposition to it?"

"It is in opposition to it." [4]

In the same spirit he denied, in 1883, that he had anything to do with the company which had represented the oil trust in this "swallowing or something" of the Tidewater. This, the National Transit Company, was the most important mem-

---

[1] Samuel Van Syckel *vs.* Acme Oil Company, Supreme Court of New York, Buffalo, May, 1888, before Judge Childs; Deposition of David McKelvey.

[2] Titusville and Oil City Independents' cases; Interstate Commerce Commission reports, vol. v., pp. 4, 5.

[3] Trusts, New York Senate, 1888, p. 572.

[4] Same, pp. 389–99.

ber of the trust. Under its cover, by means like those described, from New York to West Virginia and Ohio, almost all the pipes for gathering and distributing oil have been brought into one ownership. Millions yearly of the earnings of this company were pooled with all the others in the trust, and the president was receiving his share of them four times a year. He was the sole attorney[1] authorized to sign contracts for the trustees, who thus held all the combined companies in a common control. These trustees, of whom he was the chief, not only controlled but owned as their personal property more than half the stock of every company represented. But these facts were not then known to the public. It was not intended that they should be known, as the struggle to conceal them from the New York Legislature five years later— in 1888—showed.

"Have you any connection with the National Transit Company?" he was asked, after taking the oath.

"I have not."[2]

When the Tidewater passed under this alien control, Mr. Franklin B. Gowen severed all his connection with it. He did not hold himself for sale to any man who had money to pay fees. He stood at a height where the profession of law was immeasurably above prostitution in the temples of justice — the odious aspect in which the sacrifice of purity in the ancient temples of Aphrodite is reproduced in our courts. It would have been impossible for him to combine the functions of a great law reformer and procurer of judicial virtue for railroad corporation wreckers. He never forgot what some successful lawyers seem never to remember—that the lawyer is, as much as the judge, an officer of the court and of justice. While he lived he was proud to be recognized as the chief defender in the courts of the rights of those whom it was sought to crush in this industry, although he thus allied himself with the poor and heavy laden. He could have used

---

[1] Trusts, New York Senate, 1888, p. 658.

[2] Testimony, Corners, New York Senate, 1883, p. 925.

his anti-monopoly eloquence as an advertisement of his value to monopoly; but he would not sell his soul to fill his stomach. His heart revolted against the wicked cruelty with which he saw the strong misuse the weak, and his penetrating vision saw clearly the ruin to which overgrown power and conscienceless greed were hurrying the liberties of his country. In his speech before the Pennsylvania Legislature in 1883, advocating a law to prevent the use of railway power by railway officials to redistribute the property of the people among their favorites, he said, speaking of what had been done in the oil regions of Pennsylvania: "If such a state of facts as I now call your attention to had been permitted by any government in Europe or Asia for a six months, instead of the sixteen years it has existed in this Commonwealth, the crown and sceptre of its ruler would have been ground into the dust, and yet the good, honest, patient, long-suffering people have submitted to it in this Commonwealth until the time has come that if we hold our peace the very stones will cry out.

"I for one intend to submit to it no longer. You may say it is unwise for me to attack this wrong, but I have attacked it before and I will attack it again. If I could only throw off the other burdens that rest upon my shoulders, I would feel it to be my duty to preach resistance to this great wrong, as Peter the Hermit preached the crusade. I would go through this State from Lake Erie to the Delaware; I would go into every part of this Commonwealth and endeavor, by the plain recital of the facts, to raise up such a feeling and such a power as would make itself heard and felt, and by the fair, open, honest, and proper enforcement of the law, right the wrong, and teach the guilty authors of this infamous tyranny

> " ' That truth remembered long:
> When once their slumbering passions waked,
> The peaceful are the strong.' "

Mr. Gowen bravely fulfilled his pledge not to submit. His principal occupation became the championship in the courts and the Interstate Commerce Commission of those who were

oppressed by this crushing power. His incorruptible lance
was always in place, until the morning he was found dead in
his room in Washington.

The oil combination had, up to this time, sent all its oil
east by rail as it had no pipe line, and its faithful fools, the
railroads, therefore burned their fingers with joy to roast the
Tidewater for so good a customer. But while the railroad
officials were wasting their employers' property to destroy the
combination's new competitor, its astute managers, seeing how
good a thing pipe lines were, quietly built a system of their
own to the seaboard. The railroads had helped them get hold
of the pipe lines—had in repeated cases, as the Erie, the Atlantic and Great Western, the Pennsylvania, the Cleveland
and Marietta did, allowed them to lay their pipes on the
lands of the railroads—and were now to see the pipe lines
used to replace the railroads in the transportation of oil.
These oil men saw what the railroad men had not the wit to
see—or else lacked the virtue to live up to—that the pipe line
is an oil railway. It requires no cars and no locomotives; it
moves oil without risk of fire or loss; it is very much cheaper
than the ordinary railway, for this freight moves itself after
being lifted up by pumps. The pipe line was the sure competitor of the railway, fated to be either its servant or master,
as the railroad chose to use it or lose it. The railways senti-
mentally helped the trust to gather these rival transportation lines into its hands; then the trust, with the real genius
of conquest, threw the railroads to one side. A system of
trunk-line pipes was at once pushed vigorously to completion in all directions. While the members of the oil trust
were building these pipe lines to take away the oil business of
the railroads, the officials of the latter were giving them by rebates the money to do it with. At the expense of their own
employers, the owners of the railroads, these freight agents
and general managers presented to the monopoly, out of the
freight earnings of the oil business, the money with which to
build the pipe lines that would destroy that branch of the
business of the roads.

It was the Tidewater that proved the feasibility of trunk pipe lines. The trunk pipe lines the combination has built were in imitation. Extraordinary pains have been taken to sophisticate public opinion with regard to all these matters—for the ignorance of the public is the real capital of monopoly—and with great success. The history we have transcribed from the public records is refined by one of the combination into the following illuminant:

"About 1879 or 1880 it was discovered that railways were inadequate to the task of getting oil to the seaboard as rapidly as needed. Combined capital and energy were equal to the emergency. No need to detail how it was done. To-day there reaches," [1] etc., etc. It must have been on some such authority that this, from one of our leading religious journals, was founded: "Only by such union"—of the refiners—"could pipe lines have been laid from the oil wells to the tide-water, reducing to the smallest amount the cost of transportation." [2] An account of the pipe-line system in the New York *Sun*, of December 14, 1887, describing the operations of the great pumps that force the oil through the pipes, says: "Every time the piston of the engine passes forward and back a barrel of oil is sent seaward. A barrel of oil is forced on its way every seven seconds of every hour of the twenty-four. Every pulsation of the gigantic pumps that are throbbing ceaselessly day and night is known and numbered at headquarters in New York at the close of each day's business." This heart of a machine, beating at the headquarters in New York, and numbering its beats day and night, stands for thousands of hearts whose throbs of hope have been transmuted into this metallic substitute. This heart counts out a gold dollar for every drop of blood that used to run through the living breasts of the men who divined, projected, accomplished, and lost.

[1] *Combinations*, by S. C. T. Dodd, p. 28.
[2] New York *Independent*, March 17, 1893.

CHAPTER X

CHEAPENING TRANSPORTATION

THROUGH all the tangle of this piping and dancing one thread runs clear. The oil combination had up to this time been dependent on the railroads for transportation, but it emerged out of the fracas the principal transporter of oil, made so by the railroads. It now had two trunk pipe lines to the sea-coast—the one it had conquered and the one it had built—and the railroads had made it a present of both of them.

The Tidewater—the first seaboard pipe line—had been built only because the Pennsylvania and other trunk lines had said "no" to every entreaty and demand of the oil regions for a road to the sea. That line the railroads had conquered for the combination, as they conquered for it the pipe lines of the Pennsylvania Railroad in 1877. The second seaboard pipe line was built by the combination with the railroads' money to take away the railroads' business, and best—or worst—of all, while the railroads were hard at work driving the Tidewater into its net. Such is the business genius of our "railroad kings."

This campaign closed, the duty of the hour for the oil ring was to get rates advanced by rail as well as pipe.

"Then they"—the pipe lines—"were anxious to get good paying rates,"[1] so that they could make a good thing out of the business of their own pipe and of the Tidewater which they had guaranteed $500,000 a year. The advent of the

---

[1] Testimony, Titusville and Oil City Independents' cases, Nos. 153, 154, 163, Interstate Commerce Commission; Deposition of General Freight Agent Pennsylvania Railroad, pp. 531, 534.

independent Tidewater had brought rates down. The restoration of exclusive control by its capture put rates up. But it was not enough for the oil combination to advance their own rates. It must induce the railroads to do the same. The railroads had furnished the means for the acquisition of both pipes, and they must now be got to drive business away from themselves to these competing oil railways. This would seem to be a delicate matter to achieve, but there was no trouble about it.

"It is our pleasure to try to make oil cheap,"[1] the president of the oil trust told Congress, but it did not use its new facilities to take in hand at reduced cost the carriage of all oil, and give the industry the economic advantage of the pipe-line idea. Quite the contrary. It united with the railroads to increase the cost. Under this new blow the independent refiners and producers whom the Tidewater had been built to keep afloat grounded again. Then the railroads—the Pennsylvania especially—repented of what they had done to these their oldest customers, and sent ambassadors to them to renew the broken promises of 1872, that if they would rebuild they should forever have equal rates and fair treatment. One of the highest officials of the Pennsylvania was sent to them to say: We recognize our error in permitting your refineries to be abandoned and the traffic destroyed. We wish to build up and maintain independent refining in the oil regions. We will give you every encouragement. We will insure you equal rates, on which you can ship and live.[2]

These invitations and guarantees were repeated and pressed. They were renewed by the officials of the Erie also: "You need have no hesitation in building up your business," said the officials of the Erie; "you shall have living rates."[3]

The independents listened and believed. They rebuilt their works and prospered.[4] This meant the return of cheapness—cheapness of transportation over the railroads, to en-

[1] Testimony, Trusts, Congress, 1888, p. 389.
[2] Testimony, Titusville and Oil City Independents' cases, p. 27.
[3] Same, p. 28.   [4] Same, p. 27.

able the refiners they had invited back to life to compete in
the market—cheapness of light.   Thereupon, incredible as it
seems, the Pennsylvania and the other railroads were influenced to declare war again upon the men who had reinvested
their money and their life energy in response to these solicitations.   This new war began with a secret contract, in 1885,
for an advance in rates against the independent refiners, who,
in trustful reliance on the pledged faith of the railroads, had
developed their capacity to 2,000,000 barrels a year.[1]

This campaign has lasted from 1885 until the present writing, 1894.   In it the pipe lines, the oil combination, the
Pennsylvania Railroad, and all the other great carriers between the independents and their markets in New England,
Europe, and Asia, have been mobilized into a fighting corps
for the annihilation of the independents.   This case illustrates
nearly every phase of the story of our great monopoly: dearness instead of cheapness; willingness of the managers of
transportation to deny transportation to whole trades and
sections; administration of great properties like the Pennsylvania Railroad in direct opposition to the interests of
the owners—to their great loss—for the benefit of favorites of the officials; great wealth thereby procured by destruction, as if by physical force, of wealth of others, not at
all by creation of new wealth to be added to the general
store; impossibility of survival in modern business of men
who are merely honest, hard-working, competent, even though
they have skill, capital, and customers; subjection of the
majority of citizens and dollars to a small minority in numbers and riches; subservience of rulers of the people to a
faction; last and most disheartening, the impotence of the
special tribunal created to enforce the rights of the people on
their highways.

This secret contract of 1885 was thus described by the
counsel of the refiners before the Interstate Commerce Commission: "It is a contract," he said, "so vicious and illegal

---

[1] Testimony, Titusville and Oil City Independents' cases, p. 17.

that the Pennsylvania Railroad refuses to bring it into court for fear a disclosure of its terms might subject it to a criminal prosecution."

The courts have never been allowed to see it, but its provisions are known. Some of them were admitted before the Interstate Commerce Commission to be what was charged, and others were described on the trial by the counsel of the independents from personal knowledge. By this contract the railroad and the oil combination bound themselves to advance rates, and to keep them the same by pipe and rail. In return for this pledge by the railroad not to compete it was guaranteed one-quarter — 26 per cent. — of the oil business to the seaboard. The Pennsylvania Railroad made no attempt to deny that it had made this contract. It admitted that it had an arrangement "substantially the same as stated." [1]

The combination was the largest shipper of oil, and yet it wanted freight rates advanced. It had pipe lines which could easily take to the seaboard all the oil that went thither, and yet it gave up a large part of the business to the Pennsylvania Railroad. The Pennsylvania Railroad knew that the pipe line was a competitor for the carriage of oil, and yet allowed it to dictate an arrangement by which the railroad got only one-quarter of the business, and signed away its rights to win a larger share if it could.

The railroad had persuaded the independent refiners to settle along its line by solemnly promising them fair and living rates, and yet now put its corporate seal to an agreement to make those rates whatever their enemy wanted them to be. Such was its honor. As for its shrewdness, that had at last brought it to this humiliation in a business where it had once been chief, of confining itself to this insignificant quarter of a restricted traffic instead of a competitive share of a traffic enlarged by freedom to the widest correspondence to the wants of the people. The mastery of the railroad men by

---

[1] Answer of the Pennsylvania Railroad; Testimony, Titusville and Oil City Independents' cases, p. 365.

the oil people was thorough. The latter did not agree to give the railroad one-quarter of their business. Not at all. All the traffic that came of itself to the railroad, or which its freight solicitors drummed up, must be put to the credit of the guarantee. All that was promised the railroad was that its total should amount to one-quarter of the whole traffic. All the rest the oil combination kept for itself.

The contract went at once into vigorous operation. Freight rates to the seaboard, which had been 34 cents, and, as was proved before the Interstate Commerce Commission, were profitable, were advanced to 52 cents a barrel—an increase of one-half. The railroad and the pipe line made the raise in concert, as had been agreed, and when the rates were changed again it was to still higher figures. Why should the clique, which had its principal refineries at the seaboard—to which it had to transport large quantities of oil—scheme in this way to raise the rates of transportation? Because it paid this excessive rate on only a small part of its own shipments, and compelled its rivals to pay it on all of theirs. The independents had no pipe line of their own, but the combination sent its own oil east by its own pipe line, excepting only the quantity it needed to add to the shipments over the Pennsylvania to make good its guarantee to that railroad of one-quarter of the traffic.

The cost of the pipe-line service to its owners is very small. When the manager of the pipe lines was before the Interstate Commerce Commission the lawyers of the railroads, as zealous for the oil combination, though it was not a party in the case, as for their own clients, fought through eleven pages of argument against having him compelled to tell the cost of pumping oil through the pipe to the seaboard; and when the Commission finally said, "Go on," all the general manager of the pipe lines had to say was, "I do not believe that it is possible to know." [1]

Finally, he was cornered into an estimate that the cost

---

[1] Testimony, Titusville and Oil City Independents' cases, p. 256.

of pumping was 6 or 7 cents a barrel. His questioner, who had been the organizer and manager of a great pipe line—the Tidewater—knew that oil had been pumped through for 4 cents a barrel, but he could not get his witness, who, no doubt, had done it still cheaper, to admit anything of the kind.

The net effect of this pool with the railroad was that the oil combination succeeded in making its rivals pay 64 cents a barrel to reach the East and the seaboard, while it paid only 16[1]—except on the traffic guaranteed the Pennsylvania Railroad—a difference against competition of 48 cents a barrel, a difference not for cheapness. "It only costs the pipe line 7 cents," the independents explained to the Interstate Commerce Commission, "and the published rate is 52. They are willing to pay 52 or even 70 cents on some of their product if they can make the other people pay 52 upon the whole of theirs."

So much of the contract as we have referred to was admitted. Why was it, then, the counsel for the railroad fought against showing it, even to the point of pleading that it might incriminate his client?[2] It was asserted, as of his personal knowledge, by the counsel of the independents that this was because another part of the bargain gave the proof that the rates which had been made under the agreement to put them up and keep them up were extortionate; that by a bargain within the bargain the oil combination carried oil for the railroad for the 280 miles for which they ran practically side by side, and for this charged it only 8 cents a barrel. The public, shipping either by the railroad or by the pipe line, had to pay 52 cents a barrel for 500 miles; but by this arrangement between themselves the two carriers would do business at 8 cents a barrel for 280 miles, at which rate the charge to the public to the seaboard should have been not quite 15 cents instead of 52 cents.

The statement was also made that the oil combination, in-

---

[1] Titusville and Oil City Independents' cases, Petition and Complaint.

[2] Same, Testimony, p. 367.

stead of giving the railroads the business it has guaranteed them, makes its obligation good by turning over to them periodically a check for the profits they would have had on hauling that amount of traffic.   As the guarantee was made as a consideration for the maintenance of high freight rates, such a payment by it would amount, in cold fact, to paying those in charge of the highways a large bribe to deny the use of them to the people.

This declaration of the provisions of the bargain was made by the counsel for the refiners seeking relief from the Interstate Commerce Commission.   In his argument demanding the production of the document he said : " I have had it in my hand and read every word of it, and know exactly what it contains." [1]

The sharpest legal struggle of the case was made on the demand that this paper be produced.   The Commission decided that it was " wholly immaterial," although the chairman had previously said : " It seems to us that we cannot exclude this evidence."   It was a document establishing interstate rates, and these are required by law to be published, and the Commission had always before this been liberal in compelling the production of papers which related to the making of rates. [2] The Commission had shortly before been threatened in this case by the counsel for the Pennsylvania Railroad with extinction if it insisted upon evidence of the cost of piping oil which the oil combination refused to give.

" It is possible that the powers of this Commission may be tested," [3] bullied the counsel of the railroad.   The members of the Commission laughed ostentatiously, but, for whatever reason, they gave the powerful corporations on trial no cause thereafter to " test their powers," which have slept while justice tarried, and the victims of this " contract " were kept under its harrow for three long years more, where they still lie.

The tax levied upon the consumers of oil by this agree-

[1] Testimony, Titusville and Oil City Independents' cases, p. 372.
[2] Same, pp. 380, 382.   [3] Same, p. 256.

ment for high freights amounts to millions a year. This agreement is at this writing still in force. There is reason to believe that similar arrangements exist with the other trunk-lines. The result is the surprising fact that "oil rates are very much higher than they were twelve years ago, and when there was no pipe-line competition!"[1] This is true also in the field of local pipeage—the transportation of the oil from the wells to refineries and railroads. Under the caption of "cheapening transportation" the counsel of the oil trust said, before the New York Legislature in 1888: "In 1872 the pipe-line system was in its infancy. A number of local lines existed. Their service was inefficient and expensive. There was no uniform rate. The united refiners undertook to unite and systemize this business. They purchased and consolidated the various little companies into what was long known as the United Pipe Line System. The first effect of this combination was a reduction of price of all local transportation to a uniform rate of at first 30, and soon after 20 cents per barrel."[2]

"The united refiners" and "to unite and systemize" are smooth phrases, full of the unction of good-fellowship and political economy. When the "united refiners" took possession of the pipe lines which had been forced into bankruptcy or "co-operation," they did not reduce rates—they advanced them. "The uniform rate of 20 cents," for instance, is an advance of 300 per cent. on the rate of 5 cents made by the trust's pipe-line system during the war with the Tidewater, and over the similar rates made during the earlier pipe-line competition.[3] The nominal rate, Congress learned from one of the oil-country men, was 30 cents for that service, but by competition the actual rate was down to 5 or 10 cents. "They consolidated and placed it at 20 cents, and it has remained at 20 cents, I think, since

---

[1] National Oil Company, Limited, to Interstate Commerce Commission, March 30, 1893.

[2] *Combinations: Their Uses and Abuses*, by S. C. T. Dodd, p. 26.

[3] New York Assembly "Hepburn" Report, 1879, p. 3688.

the year 1876. . . . The whole process of transportation
has been cheapened. Pipe that cost 45 cents a foot has
in that time been got for 10 cents. The quality of the
pipe was improved, so that there is not the leakage or the
wastage. There are all those improvements and inventions
that have cheapened it. We pay the same now as we did fifteen years ago. We have reduced the cost of our wells at
least 50 per cent. They have reduced nothing." [1] From
other sources, once in a while, facts have come to light showing how much less than cheap the local charge of 20 cents
a barrel is. For instance, it was shown before Congress that
a line which, with its feeders, had fifty miles of pipe, and
cost $70,000, made a clear profit in its first six months of
$40,000, charging sometimes less than this rate of 20 cents
a barrel.[2]

It is impossible to compute how much the defeat of legislation to regulate charges, or to allow the construction of competing lines, has cost the people. The Burdick Bill alone, to
regulate prices of pipeage and storage in Pennsylvania, it
was calculated by conservative men, would have saved at least
$4,000,000 a year. The killing of it was in the interest of
keeping up the high prices of the pipe lines, which finally
rest in the price of oil.

When the combination got possession of the pipe line to
Buffalo, which others had built in spite of every obstacle it
could interpose, it raised the rates of pipeage to 25 cents
a barrel from 10 cents,[3] and as happened in Pennsylvania
in 1885, the railroads to Buffalo in 1882 raised their rates
simultaneously with the pipe line. Pittsburg had the same
experience. When its independent pipe line was "united
and systemized" by being torn up and converted into "old
iron," as the Vice-President of the Pennsylvania Railroad had
told its projectors it would be, the rates of transportation for
oil went up.[4] The same thing happened at Cleveland. At

---

[1] Testimony, Trusts, Congress, 1888, p. 71.

[2] Same, p. 426.   [3] Same, p. 425.

[4] *The Railways and the Republic*, by J. F. Hudson, p. 83.

the rate at which the Lake Shore road carries oil from Cleveland to Chicago — 357 miles for 38 cents a barrel — it should charge less than 15 cents for the 140 miles between Oil City and Cleveland; but as late as 1888 it charged 25 cents. Why? The effect of the railroad charge is that little oil comes by rail to Cleveland from the oil regions; it goes by the pipe line of those whom the Lake Shore has been "protecting" ever since the South Improvement contract of 1872. There have been 3,000,000 barrels of this business yearly. The railroad officials exercise their powers to drive traffic from the railroad to a competing line. Why? We can see why the combination, which, by the possession of this pipe line, is a competitor of the Lake Shore, should desire such an arrangement; but it exists by the act of the Lake Shore Railroad. Why? The theories of self-interest would lead one to expect that the stockholders of the road would find out why.[1]

The pipe lines are the largest single item in the property of the oil combination. Here its control has been the most complete; and here the reduction of price has been least. This is a telltale fact, soon told and soon understood.

[1] See pp. 69-70.

CHAPTER XI

GENIUS could take so unspeakable a thing as a shirt and sing it into an immortal song, but a barrel—and an oil-barrel, greasy and ill-smelling—even genius could do nothing with that. But the barrel plays a leading rôle in the drama of the great monopoly. Out of it have flown shapes of evil that have infected private fortunes, the prosperity of more than one industry, the fiduciary honor of great men, the faithfulness of the Government to its citizens. Perhaps a part of what genius could do for the shirt—force a hearing for the wronged — may be done for this homely vessel of the struggling independent by the kindly solicitude of the people to learn every secret spring of the ruin of their brothers.

The market — the barrel that went to market—the freight rate that stopped the barrel that went to market—the railway king who made the rate that stopped the barrel that went to market — the greater king who whispered behind to the railway king to make the rate that stopped the barrel that went to market—this is the house that Jack unbuilt.

Such is the superiority of a simple business organization, where "evolution" has not carried the details of the industry out of sight of the owner, and where the master and man, buyer and seller, are in touch, that the independent refiners could overcome the tax imposed on them by this pooling of the pipe line and the railroads, and not only survive but prosper moderately. During the three years—from 1885 to 1888— following the first attack upon them under the contract just described, they state, in their appeal to the Interstate Commerce Commission in 1888, they were "enabled by their advantages in the local markets to keep up, maintain, and even increase their business."[1] These "outsiders" shipped their oil largely in barrels because the trunk-lines had made it as nearly impossible as they could for them to ship in tank-cars. They, like all in the trade, could not live without access to the European market. Out of every hundred barrels of various kinds of products from the distillation of petroleum, forty are of an illuminating oil not good enough to be burned in this country. It must be sold in Europe or not sold at all; and a manufacturer who cannot get rid of 40 per cent. of his product must give up manufacturing. To destroy the barrel method of shipment would destroy those who could use no other; and to close their outlet to Europe would make it impossible for them to continue to manufacture for the home supply. The barrel was the only life-raft left to the sinking independent.

They who had planned the secret pool of 1885 between the pipe line and the railroads, and the further advance of rates by both in 1888, now called upon the railroads to deliver a final stroke against the independents.[2] The railroads, when directed in previous years to say "no" to applications for transportation, and "no" to those who wanted the right to put their own tank-cars on the road, had obeyed; they obeyed again.

A pretext for the suppression of the barrel was easily found. It was a poor one, but poor pretexts are better than none. When the future "trustees" of the "light of the world" were doing a small fraction of the business, they got the contract of 1872 from the railroads to "overcome" all their competitors, on the pretext of "increasing the trade."[3] When by this contract and those that followed it they had secured nine-tenths of the trade, they got the railroads to say "no" to the remaining one-tenth, on the pretext that they could not ship as much.[4] When the Interstate Commerce law declared

---

[1] Titusville and Oil City Independents' cases, Nos. 153, 154, 163. Petition and Complaint, p. 4.

[2] Interstate Commerce Commission, "In the Matter of Relative Tank and Barrel Rates on Oil," 1888. Letter of G. B. Roberts.   [3] See ch. v.   [4] See ch. viii.

9

it to be a crime for railroads to forbid persons the road because they could not ship as much as others, the combination had the railroads shut out its rivals, on the pretext that they did not use tank-cars,[1] although tank-cars "are worse than powder." When regular tank-cars were offered by its competitors for shipment—as to the Pacific coast—the combination introduced an inferior tank-car, of which it claimed, without warrant, as the courts afterwards held, that it owned the patent, and so obtained the sole right of way across the continent, on the pretext that other shippers did not use this poor car.[2]

The pretext now used against the refiners of Pennsylvania was the passing phrase, "He must pay freight on barrels," in a decision of the Interstate Commerce Commission concerning Southern traffic. This decision had no relevancy to the oil business of the North. Six months went by after it was given with no intimation from any one that it related in any way to the situation in Pennsylvania, and to be so applied it had to be turned inside out and upside down. In the Rice case the Commission had decided that freight rates must be reduced on barrel shipments. This was, in the sharp language of the decision, to put an end to "the most unjust and injurious discrimination against barrel shippers in favor of tank shippers," a discrimination which the Commission has elsewhere said "inured mostly to the benefit of one powerful combination."

In ordering this reduction it said: "Even then the shipper in barrels is at some disadvantage, for he must pay freight on barrels as well as on oil."

By "must pay" the Commission meant "was paying." It was, as it afterwards protested, "rather a statement of a prevailing practice than a ruling."[3] And the remark furthermore concerned the trade in the South and Southwest alone, where special circumstances existed not found at the North.

Six months after this decision the Pennsylvania and other

---

[1] See below, and ch. xvii.   [2] See ch. xxxiii.
[3] Rice, Robinson & Witherop case, Interstate Commerce Commission, 1890.

Northern roads made these words, "He must pay freight on the barrels," the occasion of an increase of rates, which stopped the refineries of the independents. They were carrying free the heavy tanks—"the most undesirable business we do," in the language of their freight agent. They had been carrying the barrels of the independents free for twenty years. Now, continuing to carry the tank-cars free, they levied a prohibitory transportation tax on the barrels. To cap it all, they declared, in announcing the new rule, that it had been forced upon them by the Interstate Commerce Commission. But the President of the Pennsylvania Railroad is found admitting that it was the oil combination that dictated the move—"the seaboard refiners insisted." "Upon your decision" (in the Rice case) "being promulgated," he wrote the Interstate Commerce Commission, "the seaboard refiners insisted that we were bound to charge for packages," barrels, not tanks, "as well as for the oil." [1]

The seaboard refiners were the members of the oil trust; the others at the seaboard had been wiped out years before by the help of the railroads. Though the Pennsylvania Railroad was not a party to the case before the Commission, though it had not been called upon to change its practice, which was what it ought to be, it did now change it from right to wrong. The Commission had ordered that discrimination between the barrel and the tank should cease. The Pennsylvania, which had not, strange to say, been practising that forbidden kind of discrimination, immediately resorted to it, and, stranger still, gave as its reason the order of the Commission against it. It must have been a keen eye that could find in a "qualified and incidental remark," as the Interstate Commerce Commission styles it, in such a decision, a command to charge for the weight of the barrels and increase freight rates; but such an eye there was—an eye that will never sleep as long as Naboth's vineyard belongs to Naboth.

---

[1] In the matter of Relative Tank and Barrel Rates on Oil. Letter of President Roberts, Interstate Commerce Commission reports, vol. ii., p. 365.

All the trunk-line railroads to the East took part in the new regulation—September 3, 1888—that freight must be paid thereafter on the weight of the barrels as well as on the oil itself, and at the same rate. This increased the cost of transportation to New York to 66 cents from 52 cents, and to other points proportionately. Freight rates on the oil of "the seaboard refiners" who shipped in tanks were left untouched. In the circulars announcing the change it was said to be done "in accordance with the directions of the Interstate Commerce Commission." [1] When the refiners whom this advance threatened with ruin wrote to expostulate, they got the same reply from all the railroad officials as from President Roberts of the Pennsylvania Railroad : "The advance in rates . . . . has been forced upon us by the Interstate Commerce Commission." [2]

The Commission immediately called the responsible official of the Pennsylvania Railroad, which was the leader in this move, "to a personal interview," "expressed their surprise," and suggested the withdrawal of the circular and of the increased rates. This was in August.[3] No attention was paid to this by the road. The Commission waited until October 10th, and then sent a formal communication to the President of the Pennsylvania Railroad, which was followed by correspondence and personal conferences with him. The Commission pointed out that the statement of the circular was "misleading," "not true," "decidedly objectionable"; that the Commission had made no decision with reference to the rates of the Pennsylvania Railroad or the other Eastern lines; that its decision, applicable solely to the roads of the South or Southwest, had been that rates on barrels must be reduced, and that it was not right to use this as an excuse for increasing the rates on barrels. Finally, the Commission said that if it had made any ruling applicable to the Pennsylvania Railroad it would have

[1] Interstate Commerce Commission reports, vol. ii., p. 365.
[2] Titusville and Oil City Independents' cases. Exhibits, pp. 6, 7, 10.
[3] Interstate Commerce Commission reports, vol. ii., p. 365.

been compelled to hold that its practice, of twenty years' standing, of carrying the barrels free, since it carried tanks free, was "just and proper," and that there was nothing to show that an advance in its rates was called for.[1]

The Interstate Commerce Commission was the body specially created by Congress to interpret the Interstate Commerce Law. The Pennsylvania Railroad was one of the common carriers under the orders of the Commission, and its managers were subjects of jurisdiction, not judges. But its method of running the Supreme Court of Pennsylvania, as if it were one of its limited trains, was now applied with equal confidence to the Interstate Commerce Commission. It insisted that it was itself, not the Commission, which was the judge of what the latter meant by its own decisions. The road continued the rates against which the Commission protested. The Commission demanded that the assertions that the new rule of charging for the barrels and the advance of rates was made "in accordance with the directions" of the Interstate Commerce Commission be withdrawn. The Pennsylvania road responded with another circular, in which it changed the form but repeated the substance. "The action referred to was taken for the purpose of conforming the practice of this company to the principles decided by the Interstate Commerce Commission." The Commission protested that it was not laying down any such "principles," but the corporation declared that that was what it "understood," and held to the advance made on that understanding.[2]

To the almost weeping expostulations of the Commission in interviews and letters, to show that it had said nothing which could justify the action of the roads, the officials made not the slightest concession. "I did not consider it in that way," said one of them.[3] "That was their (the Commission's) view of the case, but it was not shared by us," said the

---

[1] Interstate Commerce Commission reports, vol. ii., p. 365.
[2] Same.
[3] Testimony, Titusville and Oil City Independents' cases, p. 462.

President of the Pennsylvania Railroad. "It was considered best to continue the practice," he said.[1]

"Why did you not rescind the order?" he was asked before the Interstate Commerce Commission.

"We understood their ruling to be a ruling for the whole country," he incorrigibly replied.

The railway president studiously withheld any assurance that he would obey if the Commission issued a direct command, which it had not done, though it had the authority.

"We would then take the subject up," he said.

Change the order to comply with the ruling of the Interstate Commerce Commission the roads would not and did not.[2]

All the roads to the seaboard and New England had made the order in concert, and together they maintained it. It was one hand, evidently, that moved them all, and though that hand moved them, for the benefit of a carrier rival of theirs —the pipe line of the trust—against their own customers, against their own employers, against the authority of the United States Government, all these railroad presidents and freight agents obeyed it with the docility of domestic animals.

These officials were the loyal subjects of a higher power than that of the United States, higher even than that of their railway corporations. They serve the greatest sovereign of the modern world—the concentrated wealth, in whose court the presidents of railways and republics, kings, parliaments, and congresses are but lords in waiting.

Thanks to the superior enterprise of their greater need, the independents of Oil City and Titusville had been able to survive the blows that had preceded, but this was too much. They had weathered the surrender in 1883 of the Tidewater Pipe Line, which had promised them freedom forever. Even the "contract" which made the allied pipe lines and the railroads in 1885 one, to tax them half as much again for transportation, had not broken them down. In spite of it

[1] Testimony, Titusville and Oil City Independents' cases, pp. 542, 543.
[2] Same, p. 542.

they had been able " to maintain and increase their business." [1]
But now they closed their works. The new attack had been
shrewdly timed to spoil for them in that year—1888—the
season of greatest activity in the export to Europe and Asia.
They appealed to the Interstate Commerce Commission.
"The greater proportion of our refineries are idle." [2]   "I
have not a customer in the entire New England States. I
have not had since the advance of last September."

"How was it before the advance?"

"I had a number of customers." [3]

Labor, though, as always, the most silent, suffered the most.
Three hundred coopers were thrown out of work in Titusville
alone within a short time, and the loss of employment to the
workmen in the refineries was still more serious. This was
not because trade was bad. Exports were never greater than
in 1889. Government statistics reveal as in a mirror what
was being done.

The exports of refined petroleum increased 21 per cent. in
1889 over 1888. But Perth Amboy, from which the independents shipped for the most part, showed a decrease of over
$18\frac{1}{2}$ per cent. By the stroke of a freight agent's pen the
business of these men was being taken from them, to be given
to others. The general tide was rising, but their feet were
sinking in a quicksand.

The export business of Boston in oil was given to the "seaboard refiners" by the same stroke. Freights that had been
$100 were now $174 to Boston, and $188 to New York.
These rates were so high as to stop oil from going through.
"The Nova Scotia trade," it was testified, "goes to New
York, and from there by water, whereas they used to buy in
Boston. Boston brokers will ship oil from New York and
get it to Nova Scotia cheaper than if it went from Boston,
whereas when we had the export rate we could compete in
that market." [4]   Two months later most of what remained of

---

[1] Titusville and Oil City Independents' cases. Petition and Complaint.
[2] Testimony, Titusville and Oil City Independents' cases, pp. 44, 110, 393,
396.   [3] Same, p. 401.   [4] Same, p. 335.

the business of the independents in New England was added
to the gift of their foreign trade, which had already been
made to the "seaboard refiners." By an order of October 25,
1888, the railroads made it known to these "pestilences," as
the lawyers of the railroads called the independent refiners in
court,[1] that they would not be allowed to send any more
through shipments into New England. This was done, as in
Ohio in 1879,[2] without the notice required by law, though in
the meantime a Federal law had been passed requiring notice.[3]

This order was the finishing touch in the task of using the
freight tariff to prevent freight shipment. It shut the independents—the hunted shippers—out of over 150 towns in New
Hampshire, Vermont, Maine, Massachusetts, including Manchester, Burlington, Portland, Salem, in which they had built
up a good business, and it made it impossible to reach these
places except by paying high local rates — from station to
station — which were not required of their competitor, who
shipped on through rates. The railroads would take the oil
of the independents for shipment, but would not tell them
what the rates would be. In this, as in all the moves of this
game, we see the railroad managers of a score of different
roads, at points thousands of miles apart, taking the same step
at the same time, like a hundred electric clocks ticking all
over a great city to the tune of the clock at headquarters that
makes and breaks their circuit.

The independents were saved by a Canadian railroad from
the destruction which American railroads had planned for
them. The Grand Trunk gave them a rate by which they
could still do some business in the upper part of New England, though to do this they had to ship the oil into Canada
and back into the United States. The effect of this abolition
of through rates in "cheapening" oil was that the people of
Vermont, for instance, had to pay 2 cents a gallon more than
any other place in New England.[4]

---

[1] See p. 145.　　　　　　　　　　　　　　　　　[2] See ch. xv.

[3] Testimony, Titusville and Oil City Independents' cases, pp. 283–84.

[4] Same, p. 283.

While all access for others to New England was cut off, the " seaboard refiners," sending the oil in free tanks to the seaboard, transshipping it there into vessels by the facilities of "which they have a monopoly,"[1] easily made their own the business of their rivals in the 150 towns from which the latter were thus cut off. No one has been able to move all the railroads in this way, as one interlocking switch, to obey a law or accommodate the public. But it was done easily enough for this kind of work. Possession was got of the railway managers at the initial points, as was done so successfully in another case,[2] and all the other railway managers, as far as Boston, followed in their trail. Reproducing the tactics in Ohio in 1879, it was only against oil that this attack of the tariff was made. Other freight for export, of which there was a vast variety, continued to be carried to Boston at the same rate as before.[3]

All the freight agent of the initial road had to do with the oil on its way to Europe was to pass it along to the next line. Whether, after leaving his road, it went by the way of Boston or that of New York made no difference to his road, and was in no way his affair. But it made a great deal of difference to those who wanted all the business of Europe and America for themselves, and we consequently find him serving them, and dis-serving his employer (the railroad), by charging 21 cents a barrel if the oil was going to Boston after leaving his line, but only $15\frac{56}{100}$ cents if it was going to New York. When asked if he thought he was justified as a railroad man under the law in making the charges for what he did vary according to what was done by the business after it left his hands, he refused to answer.

"You will not answer?"

"Not at present."[4]

All the connecting and following roads are on record as having protested against the measures in which they followed

---

[1] Titusville and Oil City Independents' cases, Interstate Commerce Commission Reports, vol v., p. 415.   [2] See chs. xv., xvi., xvii.

[3] Testimony, Titusville and Oil City Independents' cases, pp. 268–336.

[4] Same, p. 476.

the lead of the initial lines.[1]　The freight agent of the West
Shore Railroad declared that the prohibition of through shipments to the towns of Massachusetts, Vermont, New Hampshire, and Maine "occurred simply through mistake;" but
the mistake, he acknowledged, had never been corrected.[2]
This "mistake" and that of September, which preceded it,
put an end to a large business, amounting in 1888 to 900,000
barrels.　The men, whom the railroads began to massacre after
having pledged them full protection, saved a fraction of their
trade in New England, as we have seen, only by taking refuge
with a foreign railroad.　The railroads against their will, as
they swore, lost business as well as honor, but the mistake
was not corrected.

It would tax the imagination of a Cervantes to dream out a
more fantastic tangle of sense and nonsense in quixotic combat than that which these highwaymen spun out of the principles of "scientific railroading."　All that highway control
could do to destroy the barrel shippers for the benefit of the
tank shippers was done; and yet the barrel method is the safer
and more profitable for the railroads.[3]　The cars that carry oil
in barrels can return loaded; the railroads have to haul the
tank-cars back empty and pay mileage on them.[4]　For a series
of years on the Pennsylvania Railroad the damage from carrying oil in barrels was less than half the damage from the
carrying of oil in tanks.[5]　The general freight agent of the
Pennsylvania Railroad Company tells the Interstate Commerce Commission that the carriage of oil in tank-cars "is the
most undesirable business we do."　He described a smash-up
at New Brunswick where there was a collision with a line of
tank-cars.　The oil got on fire; it ran two squares, got into a
sewer, overflowed the canal, which was then frozen over, and
followed the ice a square or two beyond.　Besides having to

[1] Testimony, Titusville and Oil City Independents' cases, pp. 163, 461, 537.
[2] Same, p. 267.　　　　　　　　　　　　　　[3] Same, p. 296.
[4] Same, Testimony of General Freight Manager of the Lehigh Valley Railroad,
pp. 161–62.
[5] Same, Testimony of General Freight Agent of the Pennsylvania Railroad, pp.
523, 537.

pay nearly five hundred thousand dollars damages for the destruction done, the railroad lost its bridge, which cost two or three hundred thousand dollars. It lost more money than it could make carrying oil for ten years. "I regard it," he said, "as worse than powder to carry; I would rather carry anything else than oil in tanks."[1] Barrel shipments being the best for the railroads, these princes of topsy-turvydom move heaven and earth to destroy them.[2]

There was no end to the "mistakes" made by the railroads for the "self-renunciation" of their business, though this was in favor of those whose pipe line made them rivals. They charged more for kerosene in barrels than for other articles of more value, contradicting their own rule of charging what the traffic will bear. They let the combination carry sixty-two gallons in every tank free on the theory of leakage in transportation. "The practice," said the Commission, "is so obvious and palpable a discrimination that no discussion of it is necessary;" and they ordered it discontinued.[3]

Though the railroads brought back the tanks free, for the return of the empty barrels they never forgot to charge. This charge was made so high that at one time it prohibited the return from all points.[4] "The monopoly uses a large number of barrels in New York City," the independents said to the Commission; "it is to its interest that empty second-hand barrels should not be returned to the inland refiner." When this was brought out the Pennsylvania and other railroads promised to make reparation, but had not done so years later when the case was still "hung up" in the Interstate Commerce Commission.

It was not lack of capital or of diligence that made the in-

[1] Testimony of General Freight Agent of the Pennsylvania Railroad in Nicolai and Brady *vs.* Pennsylvania Railroad *et al.*, before Interstate Commerce Commission, Jan. 23, 1888.

[2] The new rates prohibited the traffic. Testimony, Titusville and Oil City Independents' cases, pp. 97, 110, 139, 141, 146–48, 383–84, 393, 396, 397, 400, 401, 402.

[3] Decision in Rice, Robinson, and Witherop case, Interstate Commerce Commission Reports, vol. iv., p. 131.

[4] Testimony, Titusville and Oil City Independents' cases, p. 282.

dependents use barrels instead of tanks; tanks were useless to
them. All the oil terminal facilities of the railroads at the
seaboard had been surrendered to the combination for its exclusive use.[1] These were the only places where tank-cars
could be unloaded into steamers. "There are no facilities to
which we, as outside refiners, have access to load bulk oil into
vessels," and none where these refiners could send oil in tank-
cars to be barrelled for shipment abroad.[2] No matter how
many tank-cars and tank-vessels the independents might have
provided, they could not have got them together. Between
the two were the docks in the unrelenting grip which held
solely for its private use the shipping facilities of these public
carriers. Not even oil in barrels could the independents get
through these oil docks.

The Weehawken oil docks of the Erie road on New York
harbor are the best in the world. The Erie Railroad has
$920,760 invested in them, but only one shipper can use them
either for tanks or barrels.

The Western traffic manager of the Erie was asked:

"Would you take a shipment there over the Erie road of
independent oil consigned to the New York docks?"

"No, sir."[3]

The Pennsylvania Railroad refuses to haul tank-cars for
the independents to any other point at New York than the
terminals so controlled by the combination. It will not haul
them to other docks of its own. It will not let oil be shipped
over its line to the points at which it connects with other
roads for other harbors, though it will take shipments of
anything else than oil.[4] This amounts to a refusal to allow
the independents to use tank-cars or tank-steamers. Practically the same policy is pursued by all the main trunk-lines.
These independents could get rid of their export oil only
by selling to the combination. Through its other self—the
company which controls the terminals—it has kept an agent

[1] New York Assembly "Hepburn" Report, 1879, p. 44.
[2] Testimony, Titusville and Oil City Independents' cases, p. 36.
[3] Same, p. 270.   [4] Same, p. 221.

in the oil regions for years to buy for export this refined oil which its owners and makers could not export themselves. This is the "immediate shipment" of 1878 in another phase.[1]

"You have to sell to the Standard Oil Company in order to get your oil shipped in bulk from Communipaw?"

"Yes, sir."

"The independent cannot get his oil into a bulk vessel at Communipaw?"

"No, sir."[2]

To meet these disclosures the Pennsylvania presented two affidavits. One was from its general freight agent that its tank-cars were offered freely to all; but it did not deny, for it could not deny, any of these facts about terminals, which explained why the flies did not walk into its parlor. The other affidavit was from the secretary of the corporation controlling the terminals for the oil combination, and it similarly declared that its accommodations were furnished "upon exactly the same terms to all." How long it had been doing so, or how long it would continue to do so, it did not state, as the independents pointed out to the Commission. If this were the truth instead of being, as the independents hinted, "evidently a situation that has been recently arranged for the purposes of this application"—to the Interstate Commerce Commission for further delay—why had none of the independents, dying for want of export facilities, resorted to it? This was not explained, for it could not be. The independents explained the situation to the Interstate Commerce Commission: "The inland refiner who intrusts his oil to a storage company at the seaboard with a view to exporting, puts himself completely into the power of such concern. The exactions that may be unfairly imposed in individual cases for 'loss by leakage,' 'dumping and mixing for off-color or off-test,' 'cost of water white oil for mixing,' 'tares,' 'tares guarantee,' 'commissions on sales,' 'interest on

---

[1] See ch. viii.

[2] Testimony, Titusville and Oil City Independents' cases, Mr. Confer, June 17, 1891, p. 12.

goods until loaded and paid for,' 'incidental expenses,' and many other known matters of charge, may amount to a partial confiscation of the cargo."

The corporation which manages this monopoly of the terminals at Communipaw is a mysterious concern. Who own its stock, and what its relations with the railroad are, the Interstate Commerce Commission could not find out. Its president and treasurer were summoned to testify, but refused to attend. The manager of the oil combination's pipe lines stated that he knew of stock in the company that was owned by a member of the trust, though he afterwards qualified that he did not know it "positively." [1] The charge that this company was controlled by the monopoly was specifically made before the Interstate Commerce Commission and was not denied, and the Commission found that the oil combination "have a monopoly of those facilities to the exclusion of complainants." [2] It thus reported the same state of facts in 1892 as the New York Legislature in 1879.

The barrel was therefore the fountain of life for the independent. Without barrels he could not get his oil on board ship for export, and without exporting he could not live and refine for the home market. The oil combination ships in barrels also. According to the figures given in this case by one of its "assistant managers" its shipments by barrel are very large. This testimony was introduced to make it appear cruel to insinuate that the difference between barrels and tanks was made by the railroads to favor it, since it as well as the independents used barrels. The Commission openly expressed its dissatisfaction with this evidence, and dismissed the subject by the conclusive observation that the combination gains more by the low tank-car rates than it loses by the high barrel rates. [3] For the independent, however, the difference in rates was almost all loss, for he at that time shipped mostly in barrels. The high prices it made for oil and for freights at Titusville and Oil City did not hurt the combina-

[1] Testimony, Titusville and Oil City Independents' cases, pp. 237–38.
[2] Same, Report and Opinion of the Commission.   [3] Same.

tion. It had only to close its refineries there and transfer their business for the time to its establishments elsewhere. This it did, keeping some of them idle for years.[1]

Such was the story told to the Interstate Commerce Commission, in many hundred pages of testimony, by the refiners of Oil City and Titusville, who appealed to it for the justice "without expense, without delay, and without litigation" promised the people when the Interstate Commerce Commission was created.[2] The game, of which you have perhaps been able to get a dim idea from the printed page, the Commissioners saw played before them like chess with living figures. For years the principal subject of their official investigations had been the manœuvres of the oil ring. They had been compelled by the law and the facts to condemn its relation with the railroads in language of stinging severity, as every court has done before which it has been brought. Better than any other men in the country, except the men in the ring, the Commissioners knew what was being done. They comprehended perfectly who the "seaboard refiners" were whose demand that their competitors should be shut out of Europe and New England was better law with the Pennsylvania Railroad than the decisions of the Commission. They needed no enlightenment as to the purpose of the secret contract between the members of the oil trust and the Pennsylvania, nor any instruction that the "pool" between the pipe line and the railroad was as hostile to the public interest as any pool between common carriers.

The chairman of the Commission had openly hinted that the relations of the oil trust and the railroads were collusive, and that the spring from which they flowed was a secret contract.[3] It was shown to the Commission that at the same time the railroads advanced their rates the oil combination bid up the price of the raw material of the Titusville and Oil

[1] Testimony, Titusville and Oil City Independents' cases, pp. 127–28.

[2] Report of Senate Select Committee, Interstate Commerce, 49th Congress, 1st Session, 1886, p. 214.

[3] Testimony, Titusville and Oil City Independents' cases, p. 252.

City refineries. This is called "advancing the premium." [1]
The raise of the freight rate added 14 cents a barrel to the
cost of production, and the increased price of oil put on 12
cents more, either item large enough to embarrass competition.
The Interstate Commerce Commission in its decision recognized the practical simultaneity of the three movements to the
disadvantage of the independent refiners: (1) the bidding up
of the price of crude oil against them; (2) the new rule of
charging for the weight of the barrel; and (3) the abrogation
of the through rates to New England. These three things
occurred in a period of about two months. This, the Commission says, lends color to the charge that there was concert of
action between the combination and the railroad.

The Commissioners in their sittings had seen that the
counsel for the railroads did not pretend to bring forward any
evidence to prove that their attack on the barrel shippers was
just or proper. Although "the seaboard refiners," for whose
pecuniary profit these things had been done, were not on trial,
their witnesses, agents, and attorneys were in constant attendance, and kept close watch of the testimony and arguments.
The Commission had its attention called specifically to the
fact that the defence of the railroads on trial was being directed by the same "seaboard refiners" who had "insisted"
that the railroads should violate the law. The counsel for the
Erie road was frank enough to admit that it was they who
had prompted that carrier in its litigation before the Commission. When the Erie appeared before the Commission to
give "further testimony," its representative could not tell at
whose request its application therefor had been made, and
said he had known nothing about the matter until the day before. Three of the six witnesses then examined were from
the offices of the oil trust, whose members had refused to
come when summoned. The only subpœnas they obey are
those issued from their own headquarters.

The president of the oil combination's pipe lines—who is

[1] Testimony, Titusville and Oil City Independents' cases, pp. 20, 45, 75, 128–29,
175–77.

also the president of the steamship line in which its members are interested—and the vice-president of the pipe lines, and the president and the treasurer of the company which holds for the trust the monopoly of the terminal facilities, and the President of the New York, Lake Erie, and Western Railroad, and its vice-president, were all served with official notice to come and testify. But these gentlemen refused to appear. " It is for your honors," said the counsel for the refiners, suggestively, " to determine what obedience shall be paid to your subpœnas." [1] But the Commission did nothing.

The defendant corporations, and their lawyers, officers, and witnesses, made no pretence of treating the Interstate Commerce Commission with anything more than a physical respect. The representatives of the railroad companies practically told the Commission that its decisions were subordinate to theirs, and that they knew better than it what its rulings meant. Witnesses refused to answer questions they found awkward, and the lawyers gave the court to understand that if it did what they did not like they would snuff it out. The Commission heard one of the refiners who was a petitioner before it assailed with coarse vituperation, described in open court as a "pestilence," [2] because he had dared to write more than once to the railroads for the reduction of rates which would save him from destruction, and which the Commission had, not once, but half a dozen times, said the railroads ought to give to all.

The Commission had itself, outrunning the complainants, been the first to " pointedly disapprove " the attempt to destroy the barrel shippers, and to call upon the railroads to rescind their action. This protest it had made repeatedly—first with the subalterns, then with the chief of the Pennsylvania Railroad, in personal interviews, letters, and finally in an official pamphlet, which was an appeal to the public to judge between it and the corporation. It had reiterated its protest in a formal decision rendered September 5, 1890, after delib-

---

[1] Testimony, Titusville and Oil City Independents' cases, pp. 304–5.
[2] Same, p. 486.

10

erating seven months on the evidence and arguments. In this "they recalled the fact, now almost ancient history, that" the change was "pointedly disapproved by the Commission" when first made, and with lamentations noted that, though almost two years had passed, "the carriers have failed to comply with the suggestions there made. In charging for the weight of the barrels as well as the oil, the carriers that make use of both modes of transportation have disregarded the principles plainly and emphatically laid down by the Commission in the cases cited, and have paid no attention to the subsequent official memorandum explanatory of the decisions in those cases, but have persisted in maintaining a discrimination against barrel shippers. An order requiring the discontinuance of the discrimination has therefore become necessary." [1]

An order has therefore become necessary. The Commission then ordered one road concerned in this separate case to " cease and desist" within thirty days. Although several cases affecting a number of refiners and a number of roads had been heard and submitted together, as practically one in traffic, territory, circumstances, and the main question, it confined its decision to the case which involved only one road, and that a subordinate. There the Commission stopped; and there it stuck for more than two years, from September 5, 1890, to November 14, 1892, refraining from a decision in the case of the principal offender, the Pennsylvania Railroad.

The Pennsylvania Railroad is the representative carrier in the oil traffic. It controls all the oil business that passes over its lines, no matter how far away it originates. The initial road which led the attack on the barrel shippers is subsidiary to the Pennsylvania in the oil business, and the Pennsylvania controls its rates and regulations.[2] The Pennsylvania has been the head and front of the railroad attack on these men, and has been the open nullifier of the law and the Commission in this matter. It was the principal defendant on trial, and its case

---

[1] Interstate Commerce Commission Reports, vol. iv., p. 131.

[2] Testimony, Titusville and Oil City Independents' cases, pp. 188, 193, 446, 466, 467.

was identical with that of the others, except that it was the most flagrant; but no order would the Commission issue against it for two years. Wendell Phillips says: "There is no power in one State to resist such a giant as the Pennsylvania road. We have thirty-eight one-horse legislatures in this country; and we have a man like Tom Scott with three hundred and fifty millions in his hands, and if he walks through the States they have no power. Why, he need not move at all; if he smokes, as Grant does, a puff of the waste smoke out of his mouth upsets the legislatures." When the Commission had ordered a change of rates on barrels in the South, the Pennsylvania did the Commission the double disrespect of declaring that that order was binding upon itself against the protest of the Commission, and of using an order to reduce rates as an excuse for raising them. But now when the Commission, September 5, 1890, made a decision on the same point in a case arising in the territory and traffic in which the Pennsylvania was the chief carrier — a case, too, of a bunch of cases in which the Pennsylvania was a defendant — that road ignored it. The Commission, in the Rice, Robinson and Witherop case, in 1890, promulgated the very rule which the Pennsylvania Railroad established, which it had been following for twenty years, and which its officers before the Commission swore was the correct one, but the Pennsylvania refused now to accept and follow it. The road which was now ordered to go back to the correct practice, and which had perforce done so, was the initial road. The Pennsylvania had followed its initiative in adopting a "false" and "misleading" and "unwarranted" practice, but would not follow it in changing to the good.

The attitude in which the Pennsylvania road and the Commission were thus placed towards each other was this: Shall the Pennsylvania Railroad be allowed to make a charge which the Commission volunteered to rebuke it for making, and which it had decided, in the parallel case of another road in the same situation, was altogether unwarranted and must cease? They stood thus facing each other more than two years. There was apparently no excuse for delay the

Commission would not accept. At one time it granted post-
ponement on the plea of a lawyer that his father was sick.
More than the lawyer's father were sick; a whole community
of business men were sick; the entire country was sick, its
industry, law, politics, morals—all. The administration of
justice was sick. If the facts had been uncertain, or the law
undetermined, the course of justice would still have seemed
cruelly sluggish; but here was a matter in which the facts and
the law in question had been settled, and by the Commission
itself, over and over again. The only thing remaining was
that the Pennsylvania Railroad, as well as the road which was
its next neighbor, must obey the law. The railroad against
which the Interstate Commerce Commission decided in 1890
on this point joined the Pennsylvania at Irvineton and Corry.
The Commission put the law into force on one side of those
points, but for two years gave the Pennsylvania Railroad
and others "rehearings" and other means of delay, and did
not open its lips to say that the same law must reign on the
other. The conduct of this corporation meant that it intended to respect neither the Interstate Commerce Commission nor the Interstate Commerce law; that it recognized the
will of cliqued wealth as the supreme law; that the protesta-
tions of loyalty to the law and the Commission with which it
accompanied its defiance of both were not offered as a disguise of respect, but were chosen as a method which would
most embarrass the people's tribunal in upholding itself and
the rights of the citizens. All that was needed by those who
had contrived and were continuing the wrong was time—they
had everything else. Time they got, and plenty of it.

July 15, 1891, the refiners said to the Commission: "Two
and one-half years have elapsed since these complaints were
filed, and the end is not yet. We earnestly hoped that we
had succeeded in convincing this Commission that this re-
spondent was inflicting on complainants a great and unnecessary wrong, which merited the most speedy remedy and redress possible. If we have failed in this we are unable to
ascribe the failure to a lack of evidence or promptness in pre-

senting it. It was not thought possible that all this great length of time would be required to reach a conclusion in these matters, under all these circumstances, especially after the decision in the Rice, Robinson, and Witherop case (September 5, 1890). The enemies of the complainants could scarcely have found or wished for any more effectual way of injuring complainants than by a long delay of their cause. Further delay simply means further injury to complainants." The two years and a half have gone on to more than five years. A decision has been made, but the end is not yet. The delay prevented the injured men from going to any other tribunal with their complaint. They have succeeded in keeping alive, though barely alive, because the price of their raw material has declined a little, and given them a margin to cling to. This delay has denied them justice in the special tribunal they were invited to attend, and has also denied them the relief they could have got from other courts.

The Commission heard all this urged by eloquent counsel. It heard the men who were being crushed tell how their refineries were being closed, their customers lost, their business wrecked, their labor idle, while the trade itself was growing larger than ever. It saw the statistics which proved it. But no practical relief have the independents of Oil City and Titusville been able to get from it. They have lost the business, lost the hopes of five years, lost the growth they would have made, lost five years of life.

This delay of justice is awful, but it is not the end, for the decision, though it came at last in November, 1892, has brought no help. It required the roads to either carry the barrels free or furnish tank-cars to all shippers, and for the past ordered a refund of the freight charged on barrels to shippers who had been denied the use of tank-cars. More than five months after it was rendered the independents, in an appeal (April 20, 1893) to the Interstate Commerce Commission, called its attention to the fact that " none of the railroads in any one of the cases has as yet seen fit to obey any of its orders save such and to such extent as they found them advantageous to themselves, although the time for doing so has expired." More appalling still, it appeared, in an application made in March, 1893, by the Pennsylvania Railroad for a re-opening of the case, that these years of litigation were but preliminary to further litigation. The counsel of the railroad, in the spirit in which it had previously warned the Commission that its powers "may be tested," now informed it that the road, if the application for further delay were not granted, would "await proceedings in the Circuit Court for enforcement of what it believed to be an erroneous order." And in another passage it referred to the proceedings before the Commission as being simply proceedings "in advance of any final determination of the case on its merits." Four years and a half had been consumed when, as the independents pleaded to the Commission, "it might reasonably have been expected that as many months would have sufficed," and yet these are only preliminary to "the final determination of the case on its merits."

"The delay suffered has been despairing—killing," was the agonized cry of the independents in their plea to the Interstate Commerce Commission not to grant this new delay. "We pray that no more be permitted." But in November, 1893, more delay was permitted by granting another application of the Pennsylvania Railroad for "rehearing." This was limited to thirty days, but these have run into months, and "the end is not yet." Five years have now passed in this will-o'-the-wisp pursuit of justice "without delay."

And another "outsider," who has been a suppliant since March, 1889,[1] before the Interstate Commerce Commission for the same relief—the free carriage of barrels where tanks are carried free—is still a suppliant in vain. The Commission consumed three years in hearings and rehearings, only to report itself unable to decide this and other important points raised by him. It was "a most perplexing inquiry," "we are not prepared to hold," "we desire to be made acquainted with the present situation," and "the results ex-

---

[1] See chs. xvi. and xvii.

hibited by recent experience." "No such intimation is intended," said the Commission, as that it is right for the roads to charge for barrels when they carried tanks free—not at all. "We simply refrain" from stopping the wrong, and "reserve further opinion for fuller information and more satisfactory inquiry." Perhaps, however, by "voluntary action" [1] the railroads which had contrived this wrong would be good enough to stop it, though the Commission was not good enough to order them to do so! The Commission held that the rates were "unlawful; but, for want of sufficient data, we do not undertake to point out the particular modifications and reductions which would satisfy the demands of justice." [2] "We are not now prepared to determine," "we feel unable to prescribe," "is not now decided," "reopened for further evidence and argument," are the phrases with which the Commission glided away from the settlement of other vital points as to which its intervention had been invoked for more than three years. Even when it directed the railroads to reduce their charge it added "to what extent the Commission does not now determine, and the cases will be held open for such further," etc. And there his case hangs even unto this day, for since this "not-now-decided" decision the "outsider" has never renewed his appeals to the Interstate Commerce Commission concerning these cases or others,[3] but, hopeless of redress, has let them go by default.

The secret contract stands, but the barrel men survive, barely, despite monopoly, by changing to tank-cars, and getting a pipe-line and some terminals. They create seaboard facilities and persuade the Jersey Central to haul their tanks. To meet this road they lay the pipe now to be described, and, to escape railroads altogether, will build to New York, if not ruined meanwhile.

---

[1] Rice cases, Nos. 184, 185, 194. Interstate Commerce Commission Reports, vol. v., p. 193. [2] Same.

[3] George Rice *vs.* The St. Louis Southwestern Railway Co. *et al.*, and same *vs.* Baltimore and Ohio Southwestern Railway Co. *et al.* Interstate Commerce Commission Reports, vol. v., p. 660.

BETWEEN May and December, Sherman made his march from Lookout Mountain to the sea, cutting the Confederacy in two. For thirty years the people of Pennsylvania have been trying to break a free way to the ocean through the Alleghanies and the oil combination, and in vain. For ten years the hope of independent outlet to the sea from the oil-fields of Pennsylvania lay prostrate under the blow of the surrender of the Tidewater. Twice the people have tried again, only each time to be headed off. The first of these two rallies collapsed in the shut-down of 1887; the second was stopped at the cannon's mouth by an armed force at Hancock, New York, in the year of peace, 1892.

By 1887 the people of the oil regions had recovered from the shock of losing the independent Tidewater Pipe Line,[1] and began to make new plans for getting to the sea. By some means the committee to whom they had intrusted the management of the new enterprise was persuaded to go to New York to confer with the officers of the oil combination, who had measures of conciliation to propose that would make it unnecessary to build the new pipe lines. This committee, and finally the constituency it represented, were made to believe that the cause of the woes of the oil country was simply and only that there was too much oil—not that there were too many empty or half-filled lamps. They agreed to cut down their business one-half, and were lured away from the project of getting full prices on a full product. The outcome was

[1] See chap. ix.

the "shut-down" of 1887. The producers were persuaded it would bring back oil to a dollar a barrel — to stay there; but after a brief and unremunerative spurt in values, a reaction, lasting to the present, carried prices to a lower level than ever, and the producers found that the last state of those who let such spirits enter them is always worse than the first.

Several times before this the oil producers had tried to imitate the policy of scarcity, which the most brilliant business successes are teaching to be the royal road to wealth. It is stated by the report of the General Council of the Petroleum Producers' Union [1] that the producers had twice entered into arrangements with the oil combination to lessen the product and regulate the price of crude petroleum, and that in each case the arrangement had been violated by the latter when it seemed about to become profitable to the producer. Hence, when invited to confer for a third venture of this sort, the Council declined to do so. But in 1887 the invitation, extended for the fourth time, was a third time accepted. The producers succeeded in the restriction, but they did not better their condition. These men gave the world the spectacle of the producers flirting with the solitary and supreme buyer of their product, in the belief that he would help them to raise their price against himself.

The agreement which was made with the producers was shown before Congress.[2] The producers were bound for a year from November 1, 1887, "to produce at least 17,500 barrels of crude petroleum less per day," and to make it, if possible, "30,000 barrels less per day." In return for this the oil combination agreed to give the speculative profits on 6,000,000 barrels of oil — the profits on 5,000,000 for them, and on 1,000,000 for their laborers. This move of those who want petroleum cheap to make it dear is one of the equivocations of policy in which princes have always distinguished themselves. The need of the hour was to stop the building of the competing pipe line. That was accomplished by the

---

[1] Trusts, Congress, 1888, p. 695.   [2] Same, p. 69.

scheme of the shut-down, which amused the producers, and, as subsequent prices proved, did not hurt the buyer of their oil; quite the contrary.

Drills and pumps at once ceased their operations throughout the oil regions. Working-men were thrown out of employment, stores were closed, hundreds of families had to subsist on charity. One of the Broadway producers who made this bargain for the shut-down admitted to the committee of the New York Legislature that "the oil-producing interest was abnormally depressed," and "that there was great distress."[1] The agreement itself recites that the price of petroleum had been during the preceding year "largely below the cost at which it was produced." The people of the oil country went to work with desperation to enforce the policy of oil famine. Committees were formed among the well-drillers in each district, "whose duty," the formal papers of organization stated, "shall be to keep a lookout for and endeavor to prevent the drilling of wells." "We have no way of stopping those who want to drill wells," one of the officers of the organization said, "only by good, reasonable talk." The Well-drillers' Union appointed and paid one of their members to reason with people who insisted upon digging wells. It is not necessary to question the good faith of the assurance their officials gave Congress that his duties did not require the use of nitroglycerine. But, "unofficially," nitro-glycerine was freely used to enforce the shut-down. Men who failed to feel the influence of the "good talk," and went on putting up machinery, and drilling wells, would find their derricks blown into kindling-wood. Referring to one of these occurrences, a member of the Well-drillers' Union told Congress it was a case where no permission had been granted by the union to drill.

"Was the rig destroyed?" he was asked.

"The derrick was blowed up by some kind of compound."

The quantity of the "compound" was enough to shake windows six miles distant. The derrick and the machinery were "cheapened" into junk.

[1] Testimony, Trusts, New York Senate, 1888, p. 449.

" Did you ever know of a case of any man's derrick and apparatus being blown up in the oil region before the formation of this association?" one of the shut-downers was asked.

" I could not say that I do." [1]

The owner of the apparatus destroyed, it was stated by the press, had been repeatedly requested to join the shut-down, but had refused. There were several such occurrences, recalling the affairs at the Buffalo refinery in 1885.[2] When the people in Pennsylvania saw apostles of the gospel of making oil cheap enter into a bargain with them to make it scarce, it is not surprising that they should have become bewildered to the point of thinking that the noise of nitro-glycerine was " good talk," and should have sunk into the depression, monetary and moral, that alone could make such haggard faces rise among an honest laborious people.

We have seen how the refiners who pass under the control of the trust are compelled to make monthly reports. The same perfectness of discipline appears at once among the producers in this shut-down. Every one of them had to make monthly reports of how much oil he had taken out of the earth. If the mobilization of industry goes on at the rate of recent years, it will not be long—not later, perhaps, than the end of the nineteenth century—before all producers, and all makers, will be sending monthly reports to New York of grain, cattle, iron, wool, lumber, leather, and the manufactures of them to trustees, whose "pleasure it is to try to make them " —the men as well as the commodities—" cheap." The supervision by means of these monthly reports was so close that over-production, however minute, was immediately known. If the owner of a well over-produced only the one-hundredth of a barrel, he got a notice to go slower.[3]

To the producers engaged in it the result of the shut-down was that when their representatives at the end of it called on the oil combination in New York for the profits on the 5,000,000 barrels of oil set apart for them, as agreed, they

[1] Testimony, Trusts, Congress, 1888, pp. 7, 19, 27, 28.   [2] See ch. xviii.
[3] Testimony, Trusts, Congress, 1888, p. 64.

were given a check for a sum between $200,000 and $250,000.[1]
This was divided among those who had co-operated—nearly
one thousand—in proportion to their share in the good work
of making the supply of the light of the people so much
"less per day." The drama of industry has not many scenes
more striking than this of these men—the principal producers
of the oil country, which had yielded in the thirty years up to
this time more than 300,000,000 barrels of oil—going to the
great syndicate in New York to buy the privilege of restricting the production of their own wells, thankfully accepting
the scanty profits on a speculative deal in the oil exchange of
5,000,000 barrels, receiving with emotions of enthusiasm a
check for a couple of hundred thousand dollars for a year's
"co-operation" from the men who had made out of their product hundreds of millions.

The shut-down was a great disappointment in prices. The
average price of petroleum at the wells for October, the
month before the shut-down, was $70\frac{7}{8}$ cents a barrel. The
highest monthly price reached during the restriction was $93\frac{5}{8}$,
in March, 1888. The average for October, 1888, the last month
of the year originally agreed upon, was $90\frac{1}{2}$. By a subsequent
understanding the restriction was continued until July, 1889.
The price then was $95\frac{1}{4}$. At no time during the shut-down
was the coveted dollar mark maintained, and it was barely
touched in March, 1888, after which there was a sharp decline to
$71\frac{3}{8}$ in June, with savage losses to "the lambs." High prices did
not come until the accumulation of 6,000,000 barrels set aside
"for the use" of the producers had been sold out. After that
there were in the winter following—1889–90—a few months
in which the price rose, as to 1.12\frac{1}{2}$ in November, 1889, but
it sank the year following to $60\frac{3}{4}$ in December, 1890, and it
continued to go down until crude oil reached 50 cents in
October, 1892, the lowest point known since there was an oil
market.[2]

[1] New York *Tribune*, June 29, 1889.

[2] United States Department of the Interior. "Petroleum," by Joseph D.
Weeks, p. 300. Annual Oil Supplement to *Oil City Derrick*, 1893 and 1894.

The men with whom the producers made their bargain, shrewder than they, and versed in the dynamics of the markets, knew that the effect of setting apart 6,000,000 barrels of oil would be ultimately depressive to prices, not stimulating. Not knowing when or at what price this vast amount would be unloaded, buyers, both for use and for speculation, would be made timid, and prices would be held in check. The shutdown produced a great gambling mania. Untold millions were lost by men in the oil country, who gambled on the exchanges to make the profits of the expected advance. Local panics, bank failures, ruin in all its shapes, were the escort of shame and loss which marched with the shut-down. Curiously enough, it was those who speculated for the rise who were the losers. There was against them an element which knew better than they what prices were going to be, for it made them. It is this ability of insiders to bet on a certainty which has been the destruction of the oil exchanges. From Pittsburg to New York they are now practically all dead.

The amount of the reduction effected by the shut-down, independent of a natural decline which had set in some months before, has been estimated at 11,000,000 to 15,000,000 barrels. The production ran down from 25,798,000 barrels in 1886 to 21,478,883 in 1887, and 16,488,688 in 1888. In 1889 it was up to 21,487,435 again, and in 1890, 29,130,910.

The price of light advanced. When the negotiations were in progress the producers were told that if the flow of oil glutting the market could be stopped the price of refined could be advanced, and that for every eighth of a cent a gallon advance in it the producers could expect an advance of 4 cents a barrel on their crude oil. Refined advanced during the shut-down to a price to correspond to which the crude should have risen to 96 cents a barrel. Instead, its price fell to 78 cents. The committee went to New York "to protest." Their New York ally said there was no change in the markets of the world. That they could get the price for the refined, but they did not propose to hold up the price of the crude. "If we could not do that, they could not help it."

" He had refined to sell, and crude to buy ?"

" Yes, sir." [1]

This shut-down, the New York *Tribune* said, was " one of the most interesting economical experiments made in recent years." It was, as the New York *World* said, " one of the largest restrictive movements ever attempted in commerce." The president of the trust, when examined on February 27, 1888, by the New York Legislature, as to the agreement for the shut-down, declared positively that nothing of the kind had been done.

" There has been no such agreement ?" he was asked.

" Oh no, sir ! . . . Oil has run freely all the time."

" And no attempt to do that ?"

" No, sir." [2]

He afterwards recalled these denials, and excused himself on the ground that as he had been in Europe when the arrangement was made he had known of it only " incidentally." [3] A " shut-down " on facts is as necessary to the success of the schemes for scarcity as a shut-down in oil. There are too many facts, as well as too much oil.

" By advancing the price of the crude material you necessarily advance the price of the refined ?" another of the combination was asked.

" Yes, sir." [4]

The average price of refined at New York for export was 6.75 cents a gallon in 1887. This rose to 7.50 in 1888, the highest average price for any year between 1885 and 1893. [5] The effect of the restriction — " one of the most extensive ever attempted in commerce " — was thus to make oil and light and all its other products scarcer and dearer. The producers really got no good. After the shut-down had been in progress five months, their committee issued an address congratulating them on the " glorious results " achieved in the

[1] Testimony, Trusts, Congress, 1888, p. 68.

[2] Testimony, Trusts, New York Senate, 1888, p. 387.

[3] Same, p. 405.   [4] Same, p. 449.

[5] Annual Oil Supplement to *Oil City Derrick*, Jan. 2, 1893.

fidelity with which the pledge of restriction had been kept, but continued, " But prices are not yet remunerative." [1]

" We do not seem to have gotten it," one of the producers said to Congress, referring to the assistance they expected in an advance of the price to profitable figures. [2] No lasting gain came to any one unless to the monopoly, and it is possibly too soon to tell whether its gain will be " lasting."

Part of the speculation was that the profits of 2,000,000 barrels, contributed equally by the combination and the producers, were to be distributed among the working-men affected by the loss of employment. Men who had been earning $12 a day received a dollar a day from this fund, and lay idle. [3] A blistering picture of the condition of the region is to be seen in the testimony of one of the producers.

" The payments that you have made, or that your assembly has made, have been to individuals ?"

" Yes, sir."

" State what the character of the occupation of the individuals thus relieved was in relation to the shut-in."

" Pumpers and roustabout men who had families sick and impoverished. That was a source of relief to them, and we did not withhold it. It was in our community, and we thought we could well afford to allow them that."

" For what did you pay them ?"

" For charity's sake."

"Did you give them any occupation ?"

" We had it not to give ; we gave them money instead." [4]

This was the melancholy end of the great shut-down. But the people were not broken by their new failure. They did not lie long in the cul-de-sac into which they had been trapped. There is a magnificent reserve force of public spirit and love of liberty in the province of William Penn and the chosen State of Benjamin Franklin. The oil business has been a thirty years' war. The people have been whipped until one would suppose defeat had become part of their daily routine,

---

[1] Trusts, Congress, 1888, p. 52.   [2] Same, p. 67.
[3] Same, p. 29.   [4] Same, p. 65.

but there have always been enough good men who did not know they were beaten to begin fighting again early the next morning. It was so when the independents of Pennsylvania took the pool of the oil trust's pipe lines and the railroads before the Interstate Commerce Commission, only to reap the unexpected demonstration that the tribunal created by Congress to prevent and punish discrimination was but one more theatre for litigation and delay.[1] Leaving their cause on the floor of the Interstate Commerce Commission, these men went forth for the seventy and seventh time to build a pipe line of their own, on which they are now busy. Their numbers, resources, and hopes are less, but their will and courage are undiminished. To-day, in northwestern and western Pennsylvania this small, determined body of men are going forward with a new campaign in their gallant struggle for the control of their own business. Their efforts have been, a friendly observer says, not too warmly, as heroic and noble and self-sacrificing as the uprising of a nation for independence.

Of all this very little has been known outside the oil regions, for the reason that the newspapers there are mostly owned or controlled by the oil combination,[2] or fear its power. The last independent daily in northwestern Pennsylvania became neutral when the threat was made to place a rival in the field. With sympathy from but few of the home press, ridiculed by the "reptile" papers, and met at every turn by crushing opposition, and annoyances great and little from spies and condottieri, these men are, in 1894, working quietly and manfully to cut their way through to a free market and a right to live. Their new pipe line has been met with the same unrelenting, open, and covert warfare that made every previous march to the sea so weary. The railroads, the members of the oil combination, and every private interest these could influence have been united against them. As all through the history of the independent pipe lines, the officials of the railways have exhausted the possibilities of opposition. At

---

[1] See ch. xi.   [2] See ch. xxiii.

Wilkesbarre, where a great net-work of tracks had to be got
under, all the roads united to send seven lawyers into court
to fight for injunctions against the single-handed counsel for
the producers. They pleaded again the technicalities which
had been invoked afresh at every crossing, although always
brushed away by the judges, as they were here again. Though
they have allowed their right of way to be used without
charge for pipe lines which were to compete with them, the
railroads refused to allow the independents to make a crossing, even though they had the legal right to cross. Not content with the champerty of collusive injunctions, they have
resorted to physical force, and the pipe-layers of the independents have been confronted by hundreds of armed railroad
employés. When they have dug trenches, the railroad men
have filled them up as fast. Appeal to the courts has always
given the right of way to the independents, but the tactics
against them are renewed at every crossing because they cost
them heart and money, and they have not the same unlimited
supply of the latter as of the former. Their telegraph-poles
have been cut down, lawyers and land-agents have been sent
in advance of them to make leases of the farmers for a year
or two of the land it was known they would want. For a few
dollars earnest-money to bind the bargain, a great deal of land
can be tied up in such ways. In some cases conditional offers
would be made guaranteeing the owner five times as much as
the independents would give, whatever that might be. Further to cripple them, a bill was introduced into the Pennsylvania Legislature and strongly pushed, repealing the law giving pipe-line companies the right of eminent domain.

The Erie, which has let the combination lay its pipe lines
upon its right of way, and bore there for oil,[1] has been conspicuous in its efforts to prevent the new pipe line from getting through. The line at last reached Hancock, New York;
there it had to pass under the Erie Railroad bridge in the bed
of the river. The last Saturday night in November, 1892,

---

[1] Testimony, New York Assembly "Hepburn" Report, 1879, p. 3482.

11

the quiet of Hancock was disturbed by the arrival of one hundred armed men, railroad employés, by special train. They unlimbered a cannon, established a day and night patrol, built a beacon to be fired as an appeal for reinforcements, put up barracks, and left twenty men to go into winter quarters. Dynamite was part of their armament, and they were equipped with grappling-irons, cant-hooks, and other tools to pull the pipe up if laid. Cannon are a part of the regular equipment of the combination, as they are used to perforate tanks in which the oil takes fire. To let the "independents" know what they were to expect the cannon was fired at ten o'clock at night, with a report that shook the people and the windows for miles about. These opponents of competition were willing and ready to kill though their rights were dubious, and there could be no pretence that full satisfaction could not be got through the courts if any wrong was done.

For weeks Hancock remained in a state of armed occupation by a private military force. Referring to this demonstration with a private army at a moment of profound peace, the Buffalo *Express* said of those responsible for it: "They continue to fight with their old weapons—incendiarism and riot." No case has been come across in which the railroads made any opposition in the courts to the oil trust crossing under their tracks with its pipe line. More than once the railroads have allowed this rival carrier to lay its pipes side by side with their rails.

"Now, is your pipe line to New York laid upon the right of way of any railroad?"

"It touches at times the Erie road, and crosses the Erie road."

"Did you pay anything for that to them?"

"No, sir."

"Nothing?"

"Nothing." [1]

But never have the railroads failed to compel an indepen-

---

[1] Trusts, Congress, 1888, p. 330.

dent pipe line to fight through the courts for every crossing it needed. It has made no difference how often or emphatically the law has sustained the right of the people to make such crossings. The next attempt would be resisted on the same ground, and with the same desperate determination "to overcome competition" for the favorite. The local line laid by the independents in 1892 between Coraopolis and Titusville had to pass under the Erie, the Lake Shore, the Pan Handle, the Western New York, and the Pennsylvania railroads, and in every case had to encounter needless litigation to do so. It was victorious, for the roads did not dare go to trial, though the managers, one after the other, to help cripple competition, spent the money of the stockholders in what was perfectly well known to be a hopeless opposition. A correspondent of the Bradford *Record* wrote: "When the news reached Bradford that the Erie Railroad had sold her independence to the combination, that the latter might defeat honorable competition and continue to rob the people, that one hundred men and a cannon confronted the United States Pipe Line at Hancock, who could have censured the outraged producers of Bradford for blowing the great Kinzua viaduct out of the Kinzua valley? Who could blame the bankrupt producers of the oil country for destroying every dollar's worth of the combination's property wherever found? The people are getting desperate; they are ready, like the blind Samson, to pull down the pillars of the temple, even though they themselves fall crushed to death amid the ruins." These are wild, even wicked words, but is it not a portent that such words rise out of the heart of an honest community?

This opposition, with show of force and threats of violence, was successful. In February, 1893, after months of facing the cannon and the private army which the railroad maintained for the oil combination, it was publicly announced by the president of the new pipe line that the route by Hancock must be abandoned. Many thousands of dollars and time worth even more were lost. "Suppose," said a daily paper of Binghamton, "that a body of laboring men had unlimbered a cannon and stationed armed men to suppress competition, what denunciation of the outrage there would have been !"

A new way through Wilkesbarre was chosen after the retreat from Hancock, and by that route the independent producers and refiners, with hope long deferred, are now seeking to finish their march to the sea.

The producers are poor men, and their resources for this unequal contest come from the sale of oil, and day by day the price of oil was depressed until it sank to the neighborhood of half a dollar a barrel. There has been some recovery since, but still the lowest prices of many years are being made, and the producers are finding the burden of their escape very heavy. "It is the honest belief of all oil men," says one of them, "that the low price of oil for the year is due to efforts to make the producer so poor that he cannot carry through his pipe line." This is the enterprise of the independent refiners as well as producers. Against these refiners, therefore, the market for refined oil also is manipulated. Very fantastic have been the operations of the "unchanging" laws of supply and demand under this manipulation. The independents found that in the export market of New York, in the spring of 1894, petroleum, just as it came from the pipe line crude from the nether earth, was quoted at a higher price a barrel than the same oil after it had gone through all the processes of refining and was aboard ship ready for the lamps of Europe or Asia.[1]

To throw another obstacle in the way of the new line, the oil trust in 1893 began again the game of 1878, of refusing to relieve producers of their oil with its pipe lines. As in 1878, the oil was left to run to waste. Then, the object was to compel the producers to sell it "always below the market";[2] now, it was to force them to sign a contract not to patronize any other pipe lines. Producers who refused to sign this contract, in order to be free to join the new line when it

---

[1] Testimony of P. M. Shannon, J. W. Lee, T. B. Westgate, in the case of J. J. Carter *vs.* Producers and Refiners' Oil Co., Ld., Court of Common Pleas, Crawford County, Pa., May, 1894.　　　　[2] See ch. viii.

was finished, were refused an outlet, and they had to pump their oil on the ground while appealing to the courts to compel this common carrier to do its duty.[1] When they applied for a mandamus the combination receded from its position without waiting for a trial.

This has been a warfare on more than a new competitor; it is an attempt to suppress improvement and invention. A new idea in oil transportation, which promises a revolution in the industry, was hit upon by these independents. This was that pipe lines could be used to send refined oil long distances to market as well as crude. The announcement of their plans to do this was met with the ridicule of those who control the existing pipe lines to the seaboard and do not wish to see their old-fashioned methods of piping crude oil alone disturbed. But the independents went on with their idea. They have proved it practicable. Now, for the first time in the history of the oil industry, a pipe line transports oil ready for the lamp. Refined oil is piped from Titusville to Wilkesbarre with no loss of quality. Many hundred thousand barrels of it have been piped for nearly three hundred miles, and not a barrel has been rejected by the inspection, either at New York or its destination abroad. The success of the experiment proves that it can be piped to New York.

The independents press on. Occasionally one of them, says a local journal, unhinged by the loss of property, commits suicide or is taken to an insane asylum, and another goes down out of sight in bankruptcy, but the others close the ranks and go on, and now about 4000 men, in a strongly organized association, are marching side by side towards the sea—the blue and free.[2]

---

[1] Commonwealth of Pennsylvania, *ex rel.* Bolard and Dale *vs.* National Transit Co., Court of Common Pleas, Philadelphia County, Pa., December, 1893.

[2] See ch. xxxi.

CHAPTER XIII

PURCHASE OF PEACE

HUNTING about for tax-dodgers, it was discovered by the authorities of Pennsylvania some years ago that many foreign corporations were doing business within the limits of the Commonwealth and enjoying the protection of her laws, and at the same time not paying for it. Foremost among these delinquents stood the principal company in the oil combination with its mammoth capital, practically buying, refining and controlling nearly the entire oil production of the State, "and yet failing to pay one cent into the public treasury." So wrote the Auditor-General to his successor in 1882. The combination, beginning, like creation, with nothing, had grown, until in 1883 it was so rich that, according to the testimony of one of its members, it owned "between $40,000,000 and $50,000,000" in Pennsylvania alone.[1] But though doing business in Pennsylvania, and legally within the grasp of the taxing power, as decided by the courts, this company paid no taxes, and would not give the State the information called for by law as to its taxable property. It practised "voluntary taxation." "For eight years," Auditor-General Schell says, "it had been doing business in this Commonwealth, and had failed in all that time to file a single report." "It was not necessary for the department to call upon it to make reports." The law required these reports specifically and in details that could not be misunderstood, and that was notification enough. But year after year the Auditor-Generals, whose duty it was to collect due contribution from each taxpayer, made special

---

[1] Proceedings of Joint Committee Pennsylvania Legislature on Standard Oil Company and its Taxes, 1883, p. 527.

demands upon this one for reports in compliance with the law, but with no effect.

In 1878 William P. Schell became Auditor-General, and began, shortly after taking his oath, to see if he could find out what taxes were due from this concern, and how they could be collected. He sent official circulars to the company in 1878, 1879, 1880, but "there was no reply made at any time."¹ His predecessor had had the same experience. He then sent one of his force to Pittsburg, Philadelphia, and New York to investigate. Whenever he could get the names of persons familiar with the workings of the company he would visit them, to find himself usually "not much further ahead than when he started."² "It was impossible to get any information. Even the men we talked to deceived us. Men came to Harrisburg to give us information, and afterwards we found they were in the interests of the company."³ The department found itself, the Auditor-General wrote to his successor, "foiled at all points, not only by the refusal of the company to respond to the notices sent to its officers, but also by the great reticence of all persons in any manner connected with or employed by the company."

These efforts to find out the nature and character of the business of the company extended through two or three years. The first workable indication that the company was taxable in Pennsylvania came when the Governor of Ohio, in answer to inquiries, sent the Attorney-General a copy of the charter of the company. The Auditor-General wrote to the Governor and Auditor-General of New York and the Governor of Ohio for information. Letters were sent to the president and principal members of the company at Cleveland, Oil City, New York, and elsewhere. An answer was finally received from the company's attorney. He said that the company was not subject to taxation. The department

¹ Proceedings of Joint Committee Pennsylvania Legislature on Standard Oil Company and its Taxes, 1883. Testimony of Auditor-General Schell, p. 11 *et seq.*, pp. 394–95, and of Corporation Clerk, same, p. 58 *et seq.*

² Same, pp. 60, 61, 62.　　　　　　　　　　³ Same, pp. 374, 383.

replied the same day refusing to accept this view, and insisting on reports. Then the lawyer replied that the books and papers "were at Cleveland, and it would take some time to prepare reports." The Auditor-General offered to send his clerk to Cleveland "by first train," to prepare the reports for the company if assurance was given that he would be permitted to examine the books of the company when he got there.

No reply to this request was ever received. Then telegrams were sent, several days in succession, asking for reports, offering more time if the company would agree to report within any reasonable time, and finally warning the company that if it did not comply with the law and file its reports the Auditor-General would act under the authority given him by the law, and charge it with taxes estimated on such "reasonable data" as he could procure. All the department could get were evasive letters or telegrams from the counsel in New York, such as "letter explaining on the way." The letter came with the valuable information that "the officers are out of the city, and the company will answer on their return." Another "reply" was: "I have failed to get replies from the absent officers."[1] No reports forthcoming, the Auditor-General at last, on the best information he could get, backed by affidavits which were placed on file in the archives of his office, calculated the taxes due from 1872 to 1881, with penalties, at $3,145,541.64. This was totalled on an estimate, supported by affidavit, that the profits of the company had been two to three millions a year from 1872 to 1876, and ten to twelve millions a year from 1876 to 1880, figures which what is now known show to have been near the truth. After fixing upon this amount, and before charging it against the company, the latter was given still another chance, and another. Two telegrams were sent notifying that the estimated tax would be entered up if "the refusal to report" was persisted in. The last telegram said: "Still hoping that reports

[1] Proceedings of Joint Committee Pennsylvania Legislature on Standard Oil Company and its Taxes, 1883, pp. 68, 69, 70, 381.

will come from the company, so that we will have some data to act upon."

No word of reply came.

Then the Auditor-General formally entered the amount he had estimated on his books, as the law authorized him to do.[1] His investigations had consumed his entire term, and the filing of this estimate was almost his last official act. It is a fact of record that after all this, officers of the company, in seeking to have this estimate of taxes due set aside, stated in writing that "there was no neglect or refusal on the part of said company to furnish any report or information which could lawfully be required of it by any officer or under any law of the State of Pennsylvania."[2]

Suit was now brought by the Attorney-General of the State to recover this tax, as was his duty, and then the company began to stir itself. To assist him in procuring and interpreting evidence the Attorney-General, who knew nothing of the oil business, obtained the services of a man who knew more about it than any one else in Pennsylvania. This person was a practical oil man. He was one of the leaders of the producers and refiners' association, which in the exciting times of 1872, when law and order in Pennsylvania stood on the edge of a crater, compelled the railroads to abandon the South Improvement scheme, "in name," and to give in writing the pledge that "all arrangements for the transportation of oil after this date shall be upon the basis of perfect equality to all," though he could not find a way to make them keep the pledge. He was prominent six years later in the uprising of the people when they found that all these promises were being broken, and all their rights on the highways being violated. It was largely through his influence that the producers determined to proceed against the oil combination as a criminal conspiracy, and procured the in-

[1] Proceedings of Joint Committee Pennsylvania Legislature on Standard Oil Company and its Taxes, 1883, pp. 53, 70, 81–85.

[2] Appeal of Standard Oil Company to the Court of Common Pleas of Dauphin County, Pennsylvania, June 20, 1881.

dictment of its principals in Clarion County, Pennsylvania, on charges of crime.[1] "When," as was said before the Pennsylvania Legislative Committee of 1883, "the doors of the penitentiary were gaping wide to receive them; when a true bill had been found before the Grand Jury; when, if they ever were in jeopardy before to-day, they were in jeopardy."

He was chairman of the Committee on Transportation of the Oil Producers' Association, and was one of the "legal committee" of five who represented the producers in having the "anti-discrimination suits" brought and pushed against the Pennsylvania Railroad by the State in 1879. By these suits the discriminations and favoritisms, which, though known, it had till then been impossible to prove, were forced into the light as facts, and the evidence was furnished without which the indictments just referred to could not have been found. When the accused, frightened at last, succeeded in getting the aroused producers to agree not to push the criminal trial, in consideration of a solemn pledge that all secrecy and favoritism in transportation should be given up, he withdrew from the negotiations and would not sign the compromise. He had assisted the Congressional Committees of Commerce at Washington in 1872 and 1876 in their ill-starred investigations, and had been active in the effort to get another investigation begun in 1880. He had also been one of the principal witnesses before the New York Legislative investigation of 1879. For eighteen years he had been on this quest. With him the Attorney-General now arranged to get the evidence on which the State could support its claim for taxes.

The members of the great corporation saw that they must act. In out-going Auditor-General Schell they had met the first officer of the people who was as determined to make them pay as they were not to pay. The policy of silence and nullification was abandoned. One of the members of the trust came in person to the State capital to see the Attorney-

---

[1] Trusts, Congress, 1888, p. 707.

General. He made an unexpected overture. He volunteered to furnish the State with a full disclosure of the facts it needed to prove its claim.

"I confess," said the Deputy Attorney-General, "that I little knew in what direction to cross-examine him."[1] He therefore sent for the expert who had been employed by the Attorney-General. The "trustee" protested against his presence; but the Deputy Attorney-General said that he had been employed by the State, and it would be necessary that he should take part. The representative of the trust, moved, as he afterwards testified, by the patriotic consideration that "the regular cumbersome way of taking oral testimony . . . would result in great labor and expense to the State, and would be an obstruction and labor to us that could be avoided," made a suggestion that the State go to the trial of the case upon a statement of facts of their business which he and his associates would make. This offer to become a volunteer witness was agreed to, and the delinquent corporation and the State went into court with an "agreement as to facts." The Attorney-General reserved for the State the right to add to these facts, but did not at any time during the proceedings do so.

His expert shrewdly foresaw that another defeat for the people was to be the result of this policy. "I objected very strenuously," he says. "It was my pet scheme to examine them orally in court or by commission, and I gave it up very reluctantly. I told the Attorney-General I could not believe those gentlemen were in earnest, that I knew I could ask a string of questions of any one of them which if answered would have given the case away to the State."[2] But the Attorney-General, the same who as counsel for the people, in 1879, against the members of the same corporation, led his clients to defeat, overruled him. The old campaigner saw the mistake of 1880 about to be repeated, and an agreement with the offenders substituted for trial and for the defeat of them he

[1] Proceedings of the Joint Committee of the Pennsylvania Legislature, etc., pp. 143, 196, 476.   [2] Same, pp. 316–17.

believed would follow. He determined to prevent the consummation of this second catastrophe. He sent his counsel to New York to the headquarters of the oil combination with a notice that he would not adhere to the bargain made by the Attorney-General at Harrisburg with reference to " the agreement of facts." " I propose to attack," was the message he sent.[1] He was to have received compensation from the State. He believed that this gave him an interest in the matter sufficient to gain a footing in the courts for action by himself independently of the Attorney-General. In pursuance of this idea, when the case came up for trial, he appeared with his private counsel ready to take part in the proceedings if permitted.

The notice of attack was received " with surprise," but was met with a characteristic move. " I raised the question with him "—the counsel—" as to what possible motive " his client " had in the matter," the " trustee " testifies, " and as to whether it would not be better for him to desist from it; whether it would not be possible for us, if he was needing business, to find some position in which he could legitimately earn a living." [2] The lawyer replied that he had no right to treat on any such basis, and withdrew from all connection with the case. But this was the opening of a negotiation which through another lawyer " resulted," as the expert of the State afterwards confessed, " in peace between us." He had given notice that he meant to attack, and the " negotiation " which followed " was whether anybody would give me as much as there was in my contract with the State if I would not attack." [3]

Meanwhile the Attorney-General marched gayly to another defeat of his client—the people—going into court with no other ammunition than the facts furnished by the men he was suing. He did not put his expert, nor the Auditor-General, nor his assistant, nor the men on whose information and affidavits the estimate had been made of taxes due, nor any one else on the stand. He was " perfectly satisfied," he says,

---

[1] Proceedings of the Joint Committee of the Pennsylvania Legislature, etc., pp. 229, 478.　　　[2] Same, pp. 478–79.　　　[3] Same, pp. 228-29.

"that these facts were true," and that the company were "in good faith doing exactly what they undertook to do—namely, to furnish me with all the information that was necessary to establish the Commonwealth case." [1]

His method was as singular with the argument as with the testimony. He insisted, in opposition to the opinion of Auditor-General Schell, that such a corporation must pay taxes on all its capital stock, whether it represented property in the State or out of it. The court decided against him. It held that it was taxable "only on so much of its capital stock as was represented by the business and property of the company within the State." As to what the amount of this property and business within the State was the court took the facts furnished by the delinquent itself, as they were the only ones presented to it by the Attorney-General. The amount originally charged for taxes by Auditor-General Schell, who had forced the fighting, was $3,145,541.64. The Attorney-General, on his mistaken theory of the law and on the facts volunteered by those he was suing, had "split the difference" and sued for only $796,642.20. The court cut this down to $33,270.59, and on appeal this was still further reduced to $22,660.10. [2]

This decision was not final or conclusive as to either the State or the company, both of whom afterwards sued out writs of error. The expert, who had been pushed to one side, at once determined to take what steps he could to reopen the case and mend the fortunes of the State. The moment the decision was announced he telegraphed the Attorney-General again for another conference, and was told to come to Philadelphia. He told the Attorney-General that he thought "the hope of the State to get the largest amount of money was to get a rehearing and let us have an oral examination." But the "satisfied" Attorney-General refused to do anything but carry the same argument and the same agreement of facts up to the Supreme Court. He refused to move for a new

[1] Proceedings of the Joint Committee of the Pennsylvania Legislature, etc., pp. 163, 185. [2] Same, p. 631.

trial, and not only told his expert so, but told the "trustee" so. The trustee, by one of those coincidences which prove how much better it is to be born lucky than rich, happened to have come at the same time to stay in the same hotel with the Attorney-General.

It was in vain that the expert pointed out omissions of property and facts which he thought "had not been clearly shown in the agreement as to facts," and afterwards other matters he had discovered. After the defeat of the State he prepared an affidavit containing additional facts. He employed an attorney in the preparation of this affidavit and a petition to the court to have the case reopened. His purpose was "to get another chance at this trial."

"To get another trial?"

"Anything."

"Another hearing?"

"Anything." Anything to prevent the miscarriage of this last attempt to "round up" the men he had been trying for nearly twenty years to bring to justice. The Attorney-General would not present this petition. After this, still before the final decision, he saw the Attorney-General again to renew his pressure for a change of policy. Three times he saw the Attorney-General to lay his additional facts before him, and urge that a different method of conducting the case be tried.[1] Some of the new points he raised the Attorney-General referred and deferred to the company he was pursuing, and "we showed him how they were fully included in the statement rendered by us to the State, and he (the Attorney-General) expressed his entire satisfaction with every point raised." Others of the new points the Attorney-General declared to be "immaterial."[2] The Attorney-General showed no wish to bring proof into the case of any facts except those furnished by the people being sued. Although the decision of the lower court had been a warning that the theory on which the State had gone into court was bad, and that the

---

[1] Proceedings of the Joint Committee of the Pennsylvania Legislature, etc., pp. 267–70, 762–63.   [2] Same, pp. 310, 789.

amount of taxes to be recovered depended on the amount of tangible property in the State, he refused to use the right he acknowledged he had—to call other witnesses, to put the men who had made the agreed statement of facts upon the stand, and cross-examine them.

From the Attorney-General, who knew little of either the facts, as he confessed, or the law as the court declared it, who accepted their statements as gospel, and who asked them whether new facts offered him should be admitted into his side of the case against them, the company had nothing to fear. But this old opponent of theirs, whom the Attorney-General had employed, was at large, and was a dangerous man. He knew the facts; he had the right theory of the law; he was tremendously in earnest. The case had only got as far as the first decision of the lower court. There were still opportunities for all kinds of legal proceedings. By virtue of this contract he claimed such an interest in the proceedings as to give him a right to ask the courts to interfere. He might get a new trial and carry out his "pet scheme of oral examination." He might rouse the people as he had roused them before. He might interfere through the Legislature. He might raise a storm which could not be quieted until in this suit, or some other, his pet plan might be carried out, of getting these silent gentlemen into a witness-box. He considered himself to be in the service of the State. "I was under a contract with the State," [1] he says. And we find the Attorney-General in close consultation with him in Philadelphia down to the very last day.

The company sees that something must be done, and does it. Its "trustee" calls upon the expert at his hotel. [2] He renews the suggestion he had made in New York when word had been sent by the expert that he would not be bound by the agreement of facts, and "proposed to attack." He finds his man cast down, utterly discouraged by the decision of the lower court and the attitude of the Attorney-General. Time

---

[1] Proceedings of the Joint Committee of the Pennsylvania Legislature, etc., pp. 640–43, 830. [2] Same, p. 231.

and again he had seen the people denied justice, and their
enemies escape even so much as the necessity of appearing
in court.   He had seen, in every one of the proceedings
against them, from 1872 to 1880, committees of Congress,
State governors, judges of the Supreme courts, State legislatures, attorney-generals, railroad officials, every trustee of the
people, wilt, like green leaves in a fire, before this flashing
wealth.   His resolution gave way.   He was to have received,
under his agreement with the Attorney-General, in salary and
commissions, $23,000, or less, according to the amount re-
covered.   That he saw fading out of sight in consequence of
the, to him, inexplicable course of the Attorney - General.
Every one else who had tried to stand up for the people
against this power had gone down ; why should he be quixotic
and poor ?

"We want peace," the "trustee" said, and the, till then,
faithful friend of the people sold him all he had of that commodity for $15,400, to be paid in instalments, and a salary of
$5000 for a year.

"I proposed to reopen it"—the case—"and I did not."

"Why did you not?"

"Simply because I was assured I should have just as much
money out of the transaction as my original contract would
have paid me."

This confession made on the stand, under the strain of
cross-examination in a civil suit in which he was a witness,
startled the country with its first hint of the real cause of the
failure of the great tax case, and led to an investigation by
the Legislature of Pennsylvania.[1]

The first payment was $7500.   This was paid, not in a
check, as is the usual method between business men in legitimate transactions, but in bank - notes — $500's or $1000's.[2]
That this method of payment was inconvenient and unusual
was shown by the statement of the recipient, that he went to
the Chemical Bank and got a bank certificate for his $7500 of

---

[1] Proceedings of the Joint Committee of the Pennsylvania Legislature, etc., pp.
229–30, 284–95.   [2] Same, p. 498.

bank - notes. "Of course I did not carry that amount of money around with me." [1] Bank-notes and bank drafts, not the company's checks, were used in the succeeding payments also.

"In sending him money to Titusville, where you had a bank account, why did you not send him a check on your own bank or draft?"

"Well, there was nobody at Titusville who had any knowledge of the matter. It was not necessary to acquaint them with it," said the "trustee." [2]

This representative of the company was diligent in business, as he understood business, and was always forehanded. He made the first moves and kept the lead. He went all the way to Harrisburg to meet the Attorney-General. He got control of the case by making the overture to volunteer testimony. He called first on the lawyer sent to New York with notice of "attack," called first on the State's expert in Philadelphia and New York, made the first suggestion for "peace," and got it "cheap." [3] But after he had bought "peace" the next interview is at the company's office. The other man must walk now. When put on the stand, the purchaser, of course, denied that this "purchase of peace" had anything to do with the case against his company, or with the suppression of the only expert in the employ of the State in that suit.

"With reference to the tax case," he said, "the payment of this money had no bearing whatever."

"Then why did you pay him the money?"

"Well, I have already said, two or three times, that I paid him the money for the purpose of having him desist from further malicious attacks upon our company."

The man of whom he had bought "peace" was not then engaged in any proceedings against "our company," except the tax case. He had been engaged in nothing for two years, since the proceedings of the Producers' Association in 1880. There were no other movements in prospect. The only war,

[1] Proceedings of the Joint Committee of the Pennsylvania Legislature, etc., p. 343.　　　　　[2] Same, p. 500.　　　　　[3] Same, pp. 339–41.

12

actual or contemplated, was this tax war. Pressed through several pages of cross-examination, and challenged to name a single instance of war by this man upon them, at the time of the purchase of "peace," or since 1880, which would account for their willingness to pay him so large a sum, he was finally forced to say: "I cannot do it." [1]

The Attorney-General, who had thought it unnecessary to collect more testimony by putting the defendants on the stand under oath, testified, of course, that there had been no suppression of testimony. The seller of peace himself, when he was afterwards brought to book before the Legislature, attempted to stand to a similar denial that he had in any way been unfaithful to his trust as the expert of the State and representative of the people. But he broke down. He was asked if his agreement with the company had any relation to this case.

"Unquestionably. To all cases—this case and all others."

"You were to do nothing further for the Commonwealth in this or any other case?"

"Precisely."

"If the Supreme Court had subsequently reversed the case, and it had gone back for a new trial, and had been tried before a jury, so that the company's officers could have been subpœnaed and compelled to testify, would you then, after receiving this money, have been at liberty to assist in getting that testimony together for the Commonwealth, and aiding the Commonwealth?"

"I should say not."

"You were free to do it prior to your arrangement?"

"Certainly."

"By whom was it"—the negotiation—"begun?" he was asked.

"By the representative of the company," he replied, naming him. [2]

When this bargain was arranged and the first payment

---

[1] Proceedings of the Joint Committee of the Pennsylvania Legislature, etc., pp. 502-6. [2] Same, pp. 297, 310, 315, 327.

made only an opinion had been filed. No judgment had been entered. There was still time to make any one of many moves. Reargument and new trial both were possible.

These men seduced this representative of the people only to cast him aside, as seducers always do. They did not pay him "cash down" when they bought his "peace," but in instalments, and part of his pay was in the shape of $5000 for a year's service for which he was to do no work. This kept the whip-hand of him until the tax matter was finally settled and irrevocably past reopening. When that had been done they cast him off with scorching contumely. The secretary of the trust waved him into obloquy as a black-mailer.

When the trustee who negotiated the "peace" was before the committee of the Pennsylvania Legislature in 1883 which investigated this miscarriage of justice in the tax cases, he was asked if the man of whom he had bought "peace" had used the positions he had held in the producers' and other associations to further his own ends. He answered: "I think he would prostitute anything to further his own mercenary ends."[1]

The committee of the Legislature appointed to investigate this "purchase of peace" furnishes in its report the facts we have recited, which were uncontradicted, but declares that the transactions they disclose "did not prejudice the rights of the Commonwealth," and that nobody had done anything wrong. An effort was made after the failure of the tax case to get the Attorney-General of the State to issue a warrant against the purchaser of peace, upon which he could have been held to trial in a criminal court for bribery and corrupt solicitation of a public officer. An affidavit charging the crime in the usual form was presented to the Attorney-General. There was by this time a new Attorney-General, but he ditched this move with the same skill for the management of his adversaries' case that his predecessor had exhibited in the tax suit. He de-

---

[1] Proceedings of the Joint Committee of the Pennsylvania Legislature, etc., pp. 467, 521.

manded that affidavit be made by some one who could testify
to the bribery of his personal knowledge before the committing magistrate.   As the facts were known only to the two
principals, and neither of them could be expected to come
forward to make affidavit and application for his own com-
mitment, the Attorney-General demanded the impossible.[1]
The fact of bribery was publicly known by the confession
under oath of one of these principals, and the Attorney-General had been presented with the affidavit of a citizen, prepared in due and regular form, upon which he could have
proceeded to issue a warrant, as is done in the case of less
powerful offenders.   Failing with the Attorney-General to
have this transaction taken into the courts, the effort was
renewed with the committee the Legislature had appointed to
investigate.   It was asked to do as committees had done
before—to send the case to a criminal court and let it be
tried.   The distinguished lawyer acting for the people before
the committee offered to appear as a volunteer Attorney-
General in the prosecution of the trustee.   " There is not an
honest jury," he said, " in the State of Pennsylvania which
upon the testimony would not send him to the penitentiary
for the crime of bribery."[2]   The committee refused to send
the matter to the courts.

Upon the only occasion when the " Trustees" seemed in real
danger of being brought in person and on specific charges to
trial, criminally, the Supreme Court of Pennsylvania saved
them.   In the Clarion County cases it took the unprecedented
step of interfering with the criminal jurisdiction of the lower
courts.   It was in reference to this that Mr. Gowen said
before the Committee of Commerce of Congress in 1880: " I
was a member of the Constitutional Convention of Pennsylvania, and I know that if that convention did anything
effectively it was when it declared that the Supreme Court
should not have original jurisdiction in criminal cases, and yet
I have seen three judges of the Supreme Court lay their

[1] Proceedings of the Joint Committee of the Pennsylvania Legislature, etc., p
661.   [2] Same, F. B. Gowen, p. 650.

hands upon an indictment in a county court and hang it up."
The effect of this interposition of the Supreme Court is
summed up as follows in the history of the contest between
the Producers' Union and their powerful antagonists: " This
practically terminated the last legal proceeding conducted by
the general council of the producers of petroleum." " It was
the greatest violation of law," said Mr. Gowen before the
Pennsylvania Legislative Committee, "ever committed in the
Commonwealth."[1]

That some such action might have been expected could be
inferred from the remark in *Leading Cases Simplified*, by
John D. Lawson, warning the student of the law of carriers
"not to pay much heed to the decisions of the Supreme Court
of Pennsylvania—at least, during the past ten or fifteen years.
The Pennsylvania Railroad appears to run that tribunal with
the same success that it does its own trains."[2]

Some time after these events the purchaser of this peace
gave some money to a hospital for cancers, and, in recognition
of his philanthropy, was made its president. This hospital
was for cancers of the body—not for moral cancers of the
kind propagated for money by men who corrupt the Commonwealth. It would have been full expiation in the good old
times of the priest and the baron Ruskin describes to donate
to the cure of an evil a fraction of the profits of the culture
of it. The newspapers in May, 1891, chronicled the opening
of another pavilion of this hospital, and the delivery of "an
interesting address" by the new president. One of the journals remarks that "this interest, combined with his well-
known liberality in Church and humane matters generally,
suggests a thought concerning the peculiar development on
this line of many of our very rich men." But what the
"thought" was the journalist did not go on to state.

[1] Proceedings of the Joint Committee of the Pennsylvania Legislature, etc., p.
713.

[2] Hudson's *Railways and Republic*, p. 465.

CHAPTER XIV

"I WANT TO MAKE OIL"

AT this writing there is an old man named Samuel Van Syckel, over eighty years of age, partly paralyzed, but still vigorous, living in an obscure back street of Buffalo, very poor, though his fertile brain has helped to make millionaires of many others. Van Syckel's life has been one of ups and downs, possible only in the case of an adventurous mind seeking the golden-fleece in a new industry and in a new country. Of all the brave and ingenious men who have experimented, invented, and pioneered to realize for mankind all the surpassing possibilities of the coming oil age, he is one of the most notable. He had already made and lost one or two fortunes when we find him, about 1860, with a little still in Jersey City, making roof-tar.

He was born in Hunterdon County, New Jersey, the son of a farmer, and worked on the farm until he was of age, when he went into business. The panic of 1857 caught him with sails wing-a-wing, conducting all at once, and prosperously, grist-mills, linseed-oil mills, grain distilleries—these he had to take for a debt—several stores, cooper-shops, and two or three farms.

He failed because he had gone security for others, but he paid 100 cents on the dollar, and went to New York City. There he became a member of the Corn Exchange, and opened a commission-house for the sale of produce. His country friends had such confidence in his honesty and judgment that within six months he had done a business of $400,-000. But he discovered that of the 1500 members of the Exchange all but one had failed, and many of them several times. He saw that he was in a position where, through the inability of some other dealer to fulfil his contract, he might be swamped any day, and lose all he had himself and all the thousands intrusted to him by his friends. He had old-fashioned notions about losing friends' money, to himself or to any one else. He left the produce business. He went to making roof-tar in Jersey City, and in 1860 built one of the first refineries for making kerosene out of petroleum. When "Colonel" Drake, in 1859, found out that oil could be got by drilling, Van Syckel was one of those the new source of supply found wait-ing for it. He began refining in a small way, and, with an ardor which he has carried into everything he has done, he plunged into the study of new ways of refining the oil which then started to flow with embarrassing riches out of thousands of wells. The study of oil-refining became his passion, as, fortunately for us less gifted folk, the study of the effects of heat on clay, of sulphur on the gum of the caoutchouc-tree, of steam on the lid of the teakettle, were in their time passions with Palissy, Goodyear, and Watts. In the work of his life, forcing its secrets out of this difficult liquid, he has been very successful. Earthly reward the old inventor has none, but, sitting in his story-and-a-half cottage, what he mourns most is that he has been and is denied the opportunity of work. Tortured by restless and inventive energy, which age and dis-appointment and betrayal have not sufficed to· snuff out, his continuous word is: "I want to make oil."

When petroleum from the new wells began to come to New York, dozens of little stills were built all over the Jersey flats, many of them by Jews and Greeks. "Stills kept burn-ing up all around," he says to his visitor. "Almost every day there was an explosion somewhere from the gases. I told my wife to give me my oldest clothes and send me my meals. I was going to find out all about this business. There was a pile of roofing-gravel under a shed by my stills. I went there and slept and ate, day and night, and watched the stills and the pipes, the gases, the oils, and all. All the sleep and rest I had for months was there. It was while watching these work that my greatest idea came to me, of making oil by a continuous process, so that I could feed in petroleum at one end and have kerosene running out at the other in an unceasing stream, day after day, without stopping the whole establishment, as the oil-refineries still do, every day or two, to cool off and clean up. By the old process, still in use, when the charge in the still of perhaps 1000 barrels had been refined, we had to draw the fires and wait perhaps ten hours—the best part of a day—for the still to cool off, so that the men could go in with iron chisels to chop it all loose and clean it out. This would take four or five men from four to six hours. The still would be idle for a day and a half, and then the same process would have to be gone through with again with every charge. All over the flats the Jews and Greeks kept burning up. The Common Council of Jersey City said we must stop refining. The rest joined a great combination to fight the Common Council, but I made up my mind to go where the oil was produced. I went to Titusville in 1865. I had all the money I could want. Some rich men told me to draw on them up to $100,000 for anything there was 'snacks in' for them."

This was about the time the founders of the oil combination began in Cleveland, with "no money."

"What makes I found in Titusville!" continued Van Syckel. "I went all up and down the creek. They were glad to get 65 gallons of kerosene out of 100 gallons of petroleum, while I could get 80. I think the head of the oil combination had a little still cocked up in the woods there —a one-horse, pig-pen kind of a place at the bend of the creek, a cobbled-up sort of a mud-hole, with a water-trough to bring the oil to the still. He was not there himself; he stayed in Cleveland. I didn't ever think anything about him then. I was 'way above him. I first saw him some years after, about 1872, in a refiner's office. He was talking up some scheme he had for a combination of refineries. He said he didn't want to have the market overstocked. He was just a common-looking kind of a man among the rest of us there. I saw, when I reached Titusville, that the most money was to be made in shipping oil. I made a dollar a barrel, and in six months I was $100,000 in pocket. The land speculation I wouldn't touch. It was wild. It scared me to see men sitting around on logs, and trading off little pieces of land for hundreds of thousands of dollars. I was the first man to lay a pipe line to carry oil up and down the hills of Pennsylvania."

"The first successful pipe line," says the United States Census Report of 1885, "was put down by Samuel Van Syckel, of Titusville, in 1865, and extended from Pithole to Miller's Farm, a distance of four miles." [1]

"When I first came to the oil country all the oil had to be teamed from the wells to the railways, over roads with no bottom in wet weather. Sometimes a line of teams a mile long would be stuck in the mud. Often the teamsters would dump their load, worth $5 a barrel, and abandon it. Mules would get so discouraged that they would lie down and die in the roadway before they could be helped. The teamsters knew their power. They charged accordingly. They charged for looking at the oil to see how many barrels their teams could draw. They charged extra for every mud-hole they struck, and if the wagon-wheels went to the hubs they doubled their bills. I paid $2 to $4 a barrel for teaming, and was shipping 4000 barrels a week. The teamsters were making more money than the well-owners, and didn't care whether they hauled oil or not. All this set me to thinking. I hit on the pipe-line idea, and announced that I would carry the oil by pipe from the wells to the railroad. That was too much for the people of the oil regions. Everybody laughed me down. Even my particular friends, with whom I used to take my meals at the hotel, jeered and gibed me so that I took to coming and going through the back door and through the kitchen, and ate by myself. 'Do you expect to put a girdle around the earth?' was the favorite sarcasm. I knew it

[1] "Petroleum and Its Products," by S. F. Peckham, Special Agent, U. S. Census, 1885, p. 93.

would cost a great deal—$100,000 perhaps; but I had the money. I built it—two two-inch lines, side by side—between June and November in 1865, and turned the oil in. The pipe was a perfect success from the first barrel of oil that was pumped in. It flowed, just as I expected, up hill and down dale. The line was four miles long—from the Miller Farm to Pithole—with two or three branches.

"Then the teamsters threatened to kill any one who worked on the pipe line or who used it. They would drive astraddle of it, dig down to it, put logging chains around it and pull it out of the ground, and leave the oil, worth $4 to $5 a barrel, running to waste out of the holes. I sent to New York for some carbines, hired 25 men to patrol the line, and put a stop to that. I put up the line as security for some debts owed by my partner, under an agreement that when its profits had paid the debt it was to be returned to me. The debt was wiped out in a few months, but I never got the line back. . . . I had no money left to sue for it. This was the end of my pipe line. It has grown into a system thousands of miles long, second in importance only to the railroad, and out of it many, many millions of profit have been made, but not a cent has it yielded me. Then I went to refining oil, and, with a partner, built one of the first big refineries in the oil regions. There has been no oil refined in this country since 1870 without the help of my improvements. Some I patented, some I did not. The refiners at Titusville were hard put to it for pure water. I drove pipes through the river into the second gravel under the river, and got the finest cold water there could be. This anticipated the 'driven wells' several years. I put steam into the stills" (this had been done before both by European and American refiners). "I found out how to burn the uncondensable gases. I showed one of my neighbors how to do this, and he saved $20 a day after that in his coal bills, but I got nothing for it. Each new thing I proposed, up would go everybody's hands and eyes, and oh, what a rumbling there would be! I never made money so fast as in this refinery. We did not use the continuous process. I had not patented it, and I had partners whom it would not have been right for me to experiment with. Our profits were over a dollar on every barrel. We sold our product as fast as we could make it. We made $125,000 in fifteen months, although we paid as high as $8 a barrel for crude. I worked like a slave to make good the loss of $100,000 in my pipe line. I worked and watched day and night, and knew I was beating them all making oil. My partners were church elders, who could never find words enough to express their indignation about the way my pipe line had been taken away from me, and so virtuous that they never smoked a cigar nor drank a drop. I got into no end of lawsuits with them, and I lost my property again. I sold a part interest in my patent to some one who was afterwards taken into this oil combination, and it now claims that they own all my patents. They have frightened off or bought off every one who has tried to use any of my inventions."

The rest of the old man's story was told by him under oath in a suit he brought against members of the combination.[1] "The idea of continuous distillation, as it was suggested to me at Jersey City, was always in my brain ever since. I made an attempt to construct such works in 1876 under Mr. Cary. I run out of money. I had been robbed out of my pipe line that cost me $100,000, and my oil-refinery in which I had more than $100,000. Mr. Cary said he was going to build a little refinery. He said he had $10,000 that we might use in making oil in a continuous way. We got our lease and broke ground in 1876. We had not got very far—we got the pipe on the ground and some brick and one old-fashioned still —when" the representative of the oil combination, one of its principal members, "came on to the ground . . . the 15th of December, 1876. He asked me if I would not take a salary and not build these works in opposition to them. I told him 'No.' Then he wanted I should take a life salary, one that would support me for life comfortably. I told him I did not

---

[1] Samuel Van Syckel *vs.* Acme Oil Company. Tried in the Supreme Court at Buffalo, N. Y., May 14, 1888.

want his salary; I wanted to build this refinery and make oil in a new continuous way. He then wanted me to let him build it. He said, 'We will build it for you.' I objected to this. He then said that I could make no money if I did refine oil. He also said if I did I could not ship it. He said he would say to me confidentially that they had made such arrangements with the railroads in reference to freight—in reference to getting cars—he knew I could make no money if I did make oil."

Almost on the same day—May 14, 1888—on which Van Syckel was giving the jury this undisputed account, sustained by the judge and jury, of how the combination used "arrangements with the railroads" against its rivals, another pioneer, even more distinguished, was relating his almost identical experience before the committee of Congress investigating trusts, May 3, 1888. This was Joshua Merrill, "to whom," said S. Dana Hayes, State Chemist of Massachusetts, "more than to any one else, belongs the honor of bringing this manufacture to its present advanced state."[1] Merrill's inventions and successful labors are described in the United States Census Report on Petroleum, 1885. He was at work guessing the riddles of petroleum as long ago as 1854.[2]

From 1866 to 1888 he and his partners ran a refinery at Boston.

"What has become of it?"

"We have recently dismantled it."[3]

For several years their business had been unprofitable. There were two causes, he explained. One was that they made a better quality of oil than the average, at a cost which they could not recoup from the prices established in the market by poorer oils. The other cause was the extraordinary charges made against his firm by the railways in Boston which brought their crude.

---

[1] *The Early and Later History of Petroleum*, by J. G. Henry, 1873, p. 186.

[2] "Petroleum and Its Products," by S. F. Peckham, Special Agent, U. S. Census, 1885, p. 9.

[3] Trusts, Congress, 1888, Testimony of Joshua Merrill, p. 566.

His firm had their own tank-cars, in which their crude oil came from Pennsylvania. From Olean to Boston his freight cost him the last few years 50 cents a barrel. From the depot in Boston, to get it over two miles of track to his refinery, cost him $10 a car, or about $1.25 a barrel. This was at the rate of about 42½ cents a ton a mile. The average freight rate for the United States is about half a cent a ton a mile. His rate was an advance of 8400 per cent. on the average. He appealed to the Railroad Commission of Massachusetts.

"We wrote to the commissioners that we thought the charge was very high, and they ought to interfere to have it reduced. But it was not done.

"We made repeated efforts, personal solicitations, to the railroad officers, and to the railroad commissioners also, but it was the established rate."[1]

Two roads participated in this charge of $10 for hauling a car two miles. One of these was the New York and New England road, whose haul was a mile and a half, and its charge $6.

"Who was president of the New York and New England road?"

The dismantled witness's experience had made him timid.

"I do not know."

"Do you not know," he was asked, "that one of the oil trustees is president?"

"Yes, sir."[2]

The same railroad is the principal New England link in the lines of circumvallation which the combination in coal, hard and soft, American and Nova Scotian, is drawing about the homes and industries of the country. His company sold their tank-cars to the oil combination, as "we no longer had any use for them."[3]

"I was thirty-two years in the oil business," the veteran said, mournfully, as he left the stand. "It was the business of my life."[4]

To return to Van Syckel. After his warning to the inventor

[1] Trusts, Congress, 1888, Testimony of Joshua Merrill, pp. 567–69.
[2] Same, p. 568.   [3] Same, p. 568.   [4] Same, p. 570.

that he could get no cars and make no money, even if his new idea proved a success, the representative of the combination invited Van Syckel to put himself in its hands.

"He said they would furnish the money to test the invention and pay me all it was worth. I felt a little startled at the rebates, and I knew it before, but I did not know it was so bad as he had figured it out. I then asked him who of his company would agree to furnish me money to test the patent and to pay all it was worth. He asked me who I wanted to agree with. I then asked him if a man" (naming him) "that I had had more or less dealings with" (one of the trustees) "would agree to what he had said. He said he had no doubt he would. He said, 'We will go and see him, and go at his expense.' He said he would take the works off my hands at cost, and would satisfy my partner to stop building them if I would go to New York, and I think it was the next day when we went to New York."

They went to the office of the member of the combination whom Van Syckel had said he would confide in. "He seemed to be very glad to see me, and very sorry to learn I had been so unfortunate in the oil regions. He then asked me what these patent works would cost in a small way to prove that oil could be successfully made under continuous distillation. I told him it could be done for about $10,000. He said they would give it, . . . and if it proved a success they would give me $100,000. He said it was worth more. He would give me $125 a month to support my family during the time I was building and testing it. I said, 'Let us put what we have agreed upon in writing.' He begged off for a time. He said it could be done at Titusville just as well. He saw I was not quite satisfied being cut off in that way, so he took my hand and said he would give me his word and honor what they had agreed upon there should be put in writing at Titusville Monday morning. I did not want to press him any harder. I told him I would take the $125 a month until the thing was tested. If it proved a failure the whole thing should come back where it started from, and if it proved a success he was to pay me $100,000" (for the patents and the business). "He said we all understood it, then. I went home." Van Syckel called upon the Titusville member of the trust. "He begged off from me the same as the other did in New York; said they were pressed with business. He said they would fix it this afternoon, or words to that effect." Instead of building for him, as it had agreed, the combination, the moment he placed himself in its hands, destroyed the building he had already begun.

"What did they do with the works when they bought them?"

"They took the brick that was on the cars and hauled them to other places, I suppose, and I don't know where they threw the still. They kept that leased property during the five years for a junk-yard. I went the next day to see him, and pressed him about it the best I could. I could not accomplish anything; he appeared to be busy, or kept out of the way. I kept chasing to his office. I tried to catch him and talk over what I should depend on, where we were going to build; but he kept out of the way. He said he had not seen their folks. In July, 1879, more than three years after our contract in New York, he said they had had a meeting of all their wise-heads, and they had called in chemists, and they all unanimously agreed that oil could not be made by a continuous process, and gave that as a reason for not furnishing the money to build these works. I said, in reply, 'I am not responsible for the knowledge that the "oil combination" has for refining oil; neither would I exchange mine for all they have got combined. You said you would furnish me the money and build these works, and do as you had agreed to do.' I walked out. That was about the last I had to say to him on that subject."

"Did you after that build, or undertake to build, an oil refinery to test your continuous process?"

"Yes, sir; in connection with a German. He was going to build a small refinery. He said he would build it my way, if I would let him use it in the new way. He constructed it on that principle; but he was slow—he was a very slow man to deal with. We ran . . . twenty days without stopping" (to clean out the stills).

"And it actually ran that length of time?"

"Yes, sir."

"What became of these works?"

"Hauled off to the junk-yard"—by one of the companies in the combination. It "bought them out after we just got them under way, and then tore them down and hauled them off."

"You then brought them up to Buffalo, and tried to put them into the Solar Works?"

"Yes, sir."

"What became of those?"

"They eventually went the same way."

In court the combination claimed that Van Syckel's was an inferior process, but it had not left it to die the natural death of the inferior process.

"And how about the expense of the two ways?" he was asked.

"The same help that would make 1000 barrels the old way, to take three or four days, I would make in the new process in one day; the old way takes about a ton of coal more and gets less oil, and the oil is not near so good."

No contradiction was offered by the defendants of any of these statements. Uncontradicted evidence showed that the new process was cheaper and produced better oil than the old processes. Stillmen from the Herman and Solar refineries, in which Van Syckel tried his new process after the combination refused to build for him, testified to the practical success of his method. "We must have run these continuous works for two months while I was there" (at the Solar).[1]

"We kept Van Syckel's process running right along continuously for sixteen days" (at the Herman refinery).[2]

"We did not have to clean out the patent stills, while by the old process they would have to be cleaned out about every day or thirty-six hours."[3]

[1] Supreme Court of New York: Samuel Van Syckel *vs.* Acme Oil Company. Tried at Buffalo, New York, May 14, 1888.

[2] Testimony, same.

[3] Testimony, same.

A number of residents of Titusville, dealers in oil and consumers, testified to the superiority of the illuminant Van
Syckel produced. It burned much better than that made by
the monopoly, several said. "The burning qualities was
extraordinarily good." "It gave better satisfaction to my
customers." "It did not gum the lamp-wicks, and did not
smell." [1]

This was done in spite of rusty and choked-up pipes, defective stills and apparatus.

One of the owners of the Solar, who was a practical refiner
and the overseer of the works, testified that he had seen Van
Syckel's continuous process run successfully both in Titusville
and Buffalo:

"The result was much beyond my expectation."

"How long did you run the works?"

"I think about two weeks."

"What was the cause of it stopping?"

"The president of the company, also the treasurer, had been
to New York two or three times; after the second or third
visit he came back seemingly disgusted with the business;
afraid of losing his money if he continued any longer, and
quit."

"Was there a mortgage upon your property?"

"Yes, sir." It had been foreclosed, he said, in conclusion,
by one of the leading members of the oil combination. [2]

The only thing Van Syckel can do to carry out his part
of the contract he does. He develops his invention. He is
successful in his application to the United States patent-office.
He made his contract with the combination in 1876, and got
four patents thereafter in 1877, 1878, and 1879.

"Well," it was said in court, "they are a large concern;
they would make money out of this; I should think they
would want it if it is such a good thing." "Why, my dear
man, they have got a monopoly of the business, anyway,"
Van Syckel replied. "They don't care what kind of oil they

---

[1] Supreme Court of New York: Samuel Van Syckel *vs.* Acme Oil Company.
Tried at Buffalo, New York, May 14, 1888.   [2] Testimony, same.

13

sell; but they have got a plant that has cost them millions of dollars that they have got to change, and all that sort of thing, if they take my patent. That is the situation."

He lived on the $125 a month while he was testing and proving the invention. In July, 1880, when four years of his life had been thus wasted, the allowance was changed, without notice or his consent, to $75 a month. The next month he was refused even that sum "unless I signed a receipt in full of all demands, and I walked out without it."

His pipe line has become a part of the net-work of pipe lines of which the oil combination boasts. His refinery of 1869, one of the largest built in western Pennsylvania up to that time, passed into its hands. Three times in succession, after it refuses to build for him as it agreed, he arranges to put his idea of continuous distillation into use, and in each case the refinery in which he sets up his pipes and stills is bought up by it and destroyed. He is kept dangling for years by its policy of delay. Then his independent efforts are broken up; capitalists are made afraid of him. He can get no means for building new works. "Ever since I went into their hands," he said in court, "I have been just as I am now. I could not make oil; could not build a refinery; could not get anybody help me to do it; and here I have stood these last twelve years, and I want to be out. That is just where they want to keep me, so I cannot make any oil. It is the whole profit of the whole of it. They hold me to my contract, and they break theirs."

When twelve years had gone by, and he found that they would neither build for him as agreed nor let any one else build for him, Van Syckel turned to the law and sued them for damages. On the trial all the facts as we have stated were admitted—the abandonment of the enterprise in consequence of the threats that he would not be allowed to ship and market his oil; the interviews in New York; the contract; the sale; Van Syckel's later efforts to make oil in other refineries; his success in producing better and cheaper oil; its popularity; the purchase and destruction of the works using the new method. Not a word of evidence was adduced in disproof. The judge and the jury found all these questions in Van Syckel's favor.

The defence was twofold. It was admitted that the two representatives Van Syckel had dealt with had made the contract as he described it. The members of the combination did not deny that. But, they argued, it was not legally binding. "We simply concede," said these great men to the Court, "that they made a contract, but leaving it to the corporation itself to decide upon it. . . . There cannot be the slightest claim that the company was bound by a contract of that character." On this point they were defeated in the trial. Their second defence was that there were no damages. "The trouble is," they said, "that there are no damages sustained, no damages whatever sustained." They took the ground that his possessing a creative mind was the cause of Van Syckel's ruin, not their betrayal of him. "Mr. Van Syckel," they argued to the Court, sympathetically, "is an instance of what it means to get out a patent, and deal in patents—in nine cases out of ten. He was an inventive man. He has got out a good many patents. No question they were meritorious patents. And what is the result? Poverty, a broken heart, an enfeebled intellect, and a struggle now for the means of subsistence by this lawsuit. So that, if your honor please, there is nothing here from which we can determine what the original value of this patent was." The jury and the judge decided against them, and held there was a contract, legal and binding. That brought them face to face with the question of damages, and here the ruling of the judge saved them, as the decision of another judge saved other members of the combination in the criminal case in the same city, about the same time.[1] The judge ordered the jury to find the damages at six cents, and the jury—in the evolution of freedom juries appear to have become merely clerks of the Court —did so. "This direction of a verdict," said the Court to

[1] See ch. xxi.

Van Syckel, "decides every other question of the case in your favor."

Six cents damages for breach of such a contract, and in Buffalo $250 fine for conspiracy to blow up a rival refinery! Here are figures with which to begin a judicial price-list of the cost of immunity for crimes and wrongs.

Lawyer Moot, Van Syckel's counsel, deferentially asked the Court to suggest where was the defect in the proof of damages. It would be "the wildest speculation and guesswork," the Court said, for the jury to attempt to compute the damages.

"Then the Court is unable to suggest any particular defect in the proof?"

The Court evaded the point of the counsel, and repeated in general terms that there was no testimony upon which a jury could assess damages.

Those whom he was suing did not disprove that, by threats of making it impossible for him to get transportation, they had driven Van Syckel to abandon his own business, and make a contract with them by which they were to pay him $100,-000 for his new process, if successful. The Court held the contract binding. They had not furnished the money and works to test the inventions as they had agreed to do; but he had nevertheless gone on and completed the invention, so that patents were granted for it by the government. He had tested the invention in other works, they failing him, and had proved it a success; they had thereupon purchased and destroyed these works; he was beggared, and nobody else under these circumstances could be induced to venture money on his invention. Upon these facts, judicially ascertained, the judge refused to let the jury compute the damages, and ordered them to find the damages "nominal," as another judge sentenced their associates in Buffalo to "nominal" punishment.

"There are many things known to the law," said Parnell to the president of the Special Commission trying the Irish members of Parliament, "which are strange to a non-legal mind."

This pioneer, inventor, and true Captain of Industry, real

creator of wealth, has ever since had his neck bent to the pressure of hands too heavy for him. While all over the earth homes are brighter, knowledge is more easily got, and civilization forwarded, because of what his head has thought and his hands have done, he has retired to what is, in fact, a life of penal exile. He has been cut off from the darlings of his brain. Like the political prisoners of Siberia, he can eat and sleep and dress, but he cannot go into the world. His mind is at work there, in every factory and pipe line and lamp; but he must sit, unknown and unrewarded, in his pine cottage on unpaved Maurice Street, ploughed up in the prairies on the outskirts of Buffalo. Dearer than money to him, as to all such creative minds, would be the privilege of feeding the appealing activities of his brain with work. But he is banished from work. He has been set down outside the frontier of industry, and commanded never to return. No one dares buy or sell of him, nor adventure labor or money with him. He is an outcast. This is his greatest grief. The day I visited him he came into the sitting-room from the patch of garden behind the house. "I keep busy," he said, "to keep my mind off—anything to keep busy, if it is only pulling weeds." He is glad to see visitors. "I have been knocked out," he said, "so that nobody now comes to see me." His clear gray-blue eyes, tall, strong frame, firm mouth, large features and limbs, eager face, fit the facts of his career. He is one of the type of country-bred, hard-working American manhood of the last generation. There are no visionary lines in his face, as in his life there have been no impracticabilities, except his too great trustfulness. Gambling oil exchanges, wild oil-land speculations, inside "deals" with railroad freight agents, have never caught him. He has been a money-maker— not a money-taker. To-day, at eighty, the only thing he asks is that he may have the chance to work out his ideas. He talks patiently and courteously, with perfect intelligence and memory, but every once in a while breaks in with an outburst of what is evidently an unceasing refrain within—"I want to make oil."

The diminutive room we are in is stark in its simplicity and poverty. A paragraph in the morning paper on the table tells of "a massive oaken case, similar to a bookcase," which one of the chief reapers where Van Syckel has sowed is having put into his stable in New York. "It has doors of polished oak, with brass hinges, and heavy plate-glass. The inside will be lined with purple plush, and, when completed, the bits which shine in the mouths of his trotters and coach-horses will be arranged inside of this magnificent case in rows, ready for use, as well as an appropriate ornament for the stable."

It is better to be one of the king's horses than one of the king's men. But no words of envy pass his lips. He does not seem to repress them. He simply appears never to feel them. It chanced that as I left him, standing on the uppermost of the three wooden steps of his cottage, bleakness all about, "plain living" within, plain enough to satisfy the hardest climber for "high thinking," it chanced that his last words to me were—"I want to make oil," with an appeal to seek for him the opportunity so long denied. These words, plain and homely as they must seem to those who feed their appetite for the sublime and heroic with the highly varnished sayings of the battle-field and illustrious death-beds, will never cease to ring in my ears with a tone of greatness.[1]

[1] Samuel Van Syckel died in Buffalo, March 3, 1894, aged 83.

CHAPTER XV

Some day, perhaps, when more of our story-readers have learned that there are things in the world quite as important as the frets, follies, and loves of boys and girls half-grown, more of our story-tellers will hold their magic mirror up to the full-pulsed life with which mankind throbs through the laboring years that stretch along after the short fever of mating is over. George Rice, coming from the Green Mountains of Vermont, entered the oil business twenty-nine years ago, when he and it were young. He was one of the first comers. Beginning as a producer in the Pithole region, in the days of its evanescent glory, in 1865, he prospered. Escaping the ruin which overtook those who stayed too long in that too quick sand, he was one of the first to develop the new field at Macksburg, Ohio, and to see the advantages of Marietta, on the Ohio River, as a point for refining. Crude oil could easily be brought from Ohio and Pennsylvania by barge down the Ohio River. The field he entered was unoccupied. He drove no one out, but built a new industry in a new place. In 1876 he had risen to the dignity of manufacturer, and had a refinery of a capacity of 500 barrels a week, and later of 2000 barrels. Owning wells, he produced, himself, a part of the crude which he refined. His position gave him access to all the markets by river and rail. Everything promised him fortune. His family took hold with him in the work of bread-winning. "The executive part of the business is done altogether by my family," he says. "One daughter keeps the books, another daughter does nine-tenths of the correspondence, and my son-in-law is the general manager."[1] One of

[1] Trusts, Congress, 1888, p. 573.

the daughters was a witness in one of her father's cases before
the Interstate Commerce Commission. "She discussed with
counsel," said the New York *World,* "the knotty points involving tank-car rates, mileage, rebates, and the long and short
haul as familiarly as any general freight agent present."

Several other refiners, seeing the advantages of Marietta,
had settled there. They who elected themselves to be trustees
of the light of the world, thus having the advantages of the
place pointed out to them by practical men, determined that
Marietta must be theirs. They bought up some of the refiners.
Then they stopped buying. Their representative there, afterwards a member of the trust, "told me distinctly that he had
bought certain refineries in Marietta, but that he would not
buy any more. . . . He had another way," he said, "of getting
rid of them."[1] Of these "other ways" the independents were
now to have a full exposition. In January, 1879, freight rates
on oil were suddenly and without previous notice raised by
the railroads leading out of Marietta, and by their connections.
Some of the rates were doubled. The increase was only on
oil. It was—in Ohio—only on oil shipped from Marietta; it
was exacted only from the few refiners who had not been
bought, because there were "other ways of getting rid of
them."[2]

This freight-tariff attack on the independent refiners was
arranged by their powerful rival and the railroad managers at
a secret conference, as the latter admitted.

"Did you have any consultation or invite consultation with
other manufacturers of oil at Marietta?"

"No, sir."[3]

When the representatives of the combination in this market
were taxed by a dealer with getting the benefit of this manipulation of freight, "they laughed." All the railroads took
part in the surprise. Curiously enough, the minds of the
managers of a dozen roads acted simultaneously and identi-

---

[1] Railroad Freights, Ohio House of Representatives, 1879, p. 28.

[2] Testimony, same, pp. 5, 41, 42, 124, 141, 162, 166, 170.

[3] Testimony, same, p. 129.

cally, over thousands of miles of country—some, as they admitted, with suggestion, and some, as they testified, without suggestion—upon so precise a detail of their business as the rates on oil at one little point. "I did it at my own instance," said the freight agent of the Baltimore and Ohio. Freight officials of railways as far apart east, west, and south, and in interest, as the Baltimore and Ohio, and the Pennsylvania, and the Lake Shore, which had no direct connection with Marietta, and reached it only over other lines, stopped their "wars" to play their part in the move by raising the rate on oil only, and, most remarkable of all, to a figure at which neither they, nor the railroad connecting them with Marietta, nor (and this was the game they were gunning for) the independent refiners could do any business. From other points than Marietta, as Cleveland, Parkersburg, Pittsburg, and Wheeling, where the combination had refineries, but the Marietta independents had none, the railroads left the former rates unchanged.[1]

Rice was "got rid of" at Columbus just as effectually as if Ruskin's "Money-bag Baron," successor of "the Crag Baron," stood across the road with a blunderbuss. His successful rival had but to let its Marietta refineries lie idle, and transfer to its refineries at Wheeling its Marietta business—and Rice's too. By the pooling of the earnings and of the control of all its refineries—the essential features of the combination—its business could be transferred from one point to another without loss. One locality or another could be subjected to ruinous conditions for the extermination of competitors, and the combination, no matter how large its works there, would prosper without check. It gets the same profit as before, but the competitor by its side is ruined. All its refineries along a given railroad can be closed by high rates made to "overcome competition," but profits do not cease. Their business is done elsewhere by its other refineries, and all the profits go into a pool for the common benefit.

From Rice's point of view, Marietta was the storm-centre;

---

[1] Railroad Freights, Ohio House of Representatives, 1879, pp. 12, 34, 172.

but the evidence before the Ohio Legislative Investigation of 1879, before the Legislative Committee of New York of 1879, before Master in Chancery Sweitzer in Pennsylvania, and in the suit against the Lake Shore Railroad, showed that the low barometer there was part of a disturbance covering a wide area. The demonstration against the independent refiners of Marietta was only part of a wider web-spinning, in which those at all points—New York, Boston, Philadelphia, Pittsburg, Oil City, Titusville, Buffalo, Rochester,[1] and Cleveland—were to be forced to "come in" as dependents, or sell out, as most of them did.

That rates were not raised from points controlled by the combination is only part of the truth. At such places rates were lowered. This, like the increase of rates, was done at a secret conference with the oil combination and at its instance.[2] Where it had refineries the rates were to be low; the high rates were for points where it had competitors to be got rid of without the expense of buying them up. The independents knew nothing of the increase of freights prepared for them by the railroad managers and their great competitor until after, some time after, it had gone into effect.

The railroad company gave notice to their rivals what the rates were to be, but withheld that information from them.[3] That was not all. Before the new rates were given all the old rates were cancelled. "For a few days," said an independent, "we could not obtain any rates at all. We had orders from our customers, but could not obtain any rates of freight."

As to many places, the withholding of rates continued. "There's many places we can't obtain any rates to. They just say we sha'n't ship to these other places at any price."[4]

When the Ohio Legislature undertook to investigate, it found that the railroad men professed a higher allegiance to their corporations than to the State. They refused to answer

---

[1] See ch. xviii.

[2] Railroad Freights, Ohio House of Representatives, 1879, p. 129.

[3] Trusts, Congress, 1888, p. 579.

[4] Railroad Freights, Ohio House of Representatives, 1879, pp. 33, 40-42.

the questions of the committee, or evaded them. "I am working under orders from the general freight agent," said one of them, "and I don't feel authorized to answer that." The arguments of the committee that the orders of an employer could not supersede the duty of a citizen to his government, or the obligations of his oath as a witness, were wasted. "I will tell you just how I feel," said the witness to these representatives of an inferior power. "I am connected with the railroad company, and get my instructions from the general agent, and I am very careful about telling anybody else anything." The Legislature accepted the rank of "anybody else" to which it was assigned, and did not compel the witness to answer.

To a question about the increase in freight: "I object," said another railroad officer, "to going into details about my own private business." [1]

One peculiar thing about the action of the railroads was that it was an injury to themselves. The Baltimore and Ohio, for instance, by raising its rate, cut off its oil business with Marietta entirely. "What advantage is it, then?" the freight agent of the road over which the Baltimore and Ohio reached Marietta was asked.

"There is no advantage. . . . We had revenue before this increase in rates, and none since."

"What would be the inducement for her (the Baltimore and Ohio) to do it, then?"

"That is a matter I am not competent to answer." [2]

The railroad men testified positively that the increase affected all alike at Marietta. It was supposed even by those who thought they saw to the bottom of the manœuvre that the combination would close its Marietta works temporarily, in order to seem to be equally affected with all the rest. It could do this with no loss whatever, since, as explained, no raise in rates had been made from Wheeling, Parkersburg, Pittsburg, Cleveland, where it was practically alone, and it

[1] Railroad Freights, Ohio House of Representatives, 1879, pp. 49, 51, 56.

[2] Same, pp. 159, 163.

could reach all its customers from those places as well as from Marietta.   But the combination kept on filling orders from its refineries at Marietta at the old freight rates, while by its side the men it was hunting down sat idle because the discriminating rates of freight made it impossible for them to use the highways.   It was so careless of appearances that oil ordered of its works at Parkersburg would be sent from the Marietta branch,[1] and at the old rate of 40 cents, while the other refineries could not ship because the rate to them was 65 cents; the increase at Marietta was not enforced against it, but only against the three independents—just as planned in the South Improvement scheme.

The move was far-reaching—as far as Chicago, the rate to which was made $1.20 a barrel, instead of 90 cents a barrel.

"Then they cut you off from the Western trade as well as this State?"

"Yes, sir; almost entirely. . . . I was selling in Chicago, and it cut trade entirely off."[2]

"Before the rates were changed did you run to your full capacity?"

"Yes, sir; about that."[3]

At one stroke the independents lost the business which it had cost them years of work to get.   As the testimony of witness after witness showed, the merchants who had been their customers in Chicago, Columbus, and other places, now had to send their orders to those for whose benefit the railroad men had raised the rates.   This sweeping change was not due to any change in their desire to sell, or of their old customers to buy.   They could still make oil which was still wanted.   But they were the victims of a competitor who had learned the secret of a more royal road to business supremacy than making a better thing, or selling it at a better price.   Their better way was not to excel but to exclude.   When their "secretary" was called before the Ohio Legislature, after this freight ambuscade had transferred the bulk of the business of the inde-

---

[1] Railroad Freights, Ohio House of Representatives, 1879, p. 169.
[2] Same, pp. 249–50.   [3] Same, p. 250.

pendent refineries at Marietta to him and his associates, he declared that the sole cause of their success was the "large mechanical contrivances" of the combination, its "economy," and its production of the "very best oil." "With an aggregation of capital, and a business experience, and a hold upon the channels of trade such as we have, it is idle to say that the small manufacturer can compete with us; and although that is an offensive term, 'squeezing out,' yet it has never been done by the conjunction of any railroads with us."[1]

The small manufacturer did compete and flourish until these railroad men literally switched him out of the market. He competed and got his share of the business, until the men who wanted monopoly, finding that they had no monopoly of quality or price or business ability, resorted to the "large mechanical contrivance" of inducing the managers of the railroads to derail the independent, throwing him off the track by piling impassable freight tariffs in his way. The successful men secured their supremacy by preventing their competitors from entering the market at all. Instead of winning by "better" and "cheaper," they won by preventing any competitor from coming forward to test the questions of "better" and "cheaper." Their method of demonstrating superiority has been to prevent comparisons.

All the independent refiners at Marietta, except Rice, died. "Most of those we received from have gone out of the business," a Cincinnati dealer told the Legislature. Some had fled; some had sold out.[2] Rice set himself to do two things: the first, to drag into the light of day and the public view the secrets of these "better methods"; and the second, to get new business in the place of what he had lost. He succeeded in both. It was in January that he had notice served upon him that he could no longer go to market. In two months he had the Ohio Legislature at work investigating this extraordinary administration of the highways. This was a great public service. It did not yield the fruit of immediate reform, but it

[1] Railroad Freights, Ohio House of Representatives, 1879, p. 260.
[2] Same, p. 116.

did work which is the indispensable preliminary. It roused the people who were still asleep on these new issues, and were dreaming pleasant dreams that in George III. they had escaped from all tyrants forever, and that in the emancipation of the blacks they had freed all slaves forever.

Rice knew that the Legislature were planting trees for posterity, and did not wait for help from them. He set about looking up markets where the public were free to choose and buy. He could not go West or East or North. He went South. The little family kept the refinery at Marietta running, and the father travelled about establishing new agencies in the South, and studying freight tariffs, railroad routes, and terminal facilities for loading and unloading and storing. In 1880, through all the storm and stress of these days, he was able to double the capacity of his refinery. Again he succeeded in building up a livelihood, and again his success was treated as trespass and invasion. His bitter experience in Ohio in 1879 proved to be but an apprenticeship for a still sterner struggle. Rice was getting most of his crude oil from Pennsylvania, through a little pipe line which brought it to the Alleghany. The pipe line was taken up by the oil trust.[1]

This compelled him to turn to the Macksburg, Ohio, field for most of his petroleum. He had one tank-car, and he ran this back and forth faster than ever. Then came the next blow. The railroad over which he ran his tank-car doubled his freight to 35 cents a barrel, from 17½. That was not all. The same railroad brought oil to the combination's Marietta refineries at 10 cents a barrel, while they charged him 35. That was not all. The railroad paid over to the combination 25 cents out of every 35 cents he paid for freight. If he had done all the oil business at Marietta, and his rival had put out all its fires and let its works stand empty, it would still have made 25 cents a barrel on the whole output. Rice found a just judge when he took this thing into court. "Abhorrent," "danger-

---

[1] Trusts, Congress, 1888, p. 574.

ous," "gross," "illegal and inexcusable abuse by a public trust," "an unparalleled wrong," are the terms in which Judge Baxter gave voice to his indignation as he ordered the removal of the receiver of the railroad who had made this arrangement with the combination, to enable it, as the judge said, "to crush Rice and his business."[1]

In an interview, filling four columns of the New York *World* of March 29, 1890, the head of the trust which would receive this rebate is reported to have made this attempt to reverse the facts of this and similar occurrences: "The railroad company proposed to our agent," he said. But the judge who heard all the evidence and rendered the decision, which has never been reversed or impaired, declared that it "compelled" the railroad to make the arrangement, "under a threat of building a pipe line for the conveyance of its oils and withdrawing its patronage." This arrangement was negotiated by the same agent of the oil combination who engineered the similar "transfer" scheme by which the trunk-line railroads gave it, in 1878, 20 to 35 cents a barrel out of the freights paid by its competitors in Pennsylvania, as already told.[2]

"I reluctantly acquiesced," the receiver said, writing in confidence to his lawyer, anxious lest so acquiescing he had made himself legally liable. The interview describes the arrangement as an innocent thing: "A joint agreement for the transportation of oil." It was an agreement to prevent the transportation of oil by anybody else. Judge Baxter shows that it was a joint agreement, procured by threats, for the transportation of "$25 per day, clear money," from Rice's pockets into the pockets of the members of the trust for no service rendered, and without his knowledge or consent, and with the transparent purpose of transporting his business to their own refineries. Judge Baxter called it "discrimination so wanton and oppressive it could hardly have been accepted by an honest man, and a judge who would tolerate such a

[1] Trusts, Congress, 1888, pp. 577–78.
[2] See ch. viii.

wrong or retain a receiver capable of perpetrating it, ought to
be impeached and degraded from his position." [1]

This matter was also passed upon by the Select Committee
of the United States Senate on Interstate Commerce. "No
comment," the committee say, "is needed upon this most im-
pudent and outrageous proposition"—by the oil company to
the railroad. [2]

"Are you going to deny that story?" a great American
statesman of the latter-day type was asked by one of his
friends.

"Not I," was the reply. "The story's false. When you
find me taking the trouble to deny a thing, you can bet it's
true!"

This "agreement for the transportation of oil" had its calculated effect. It put a stop to the transportation of oil from
the Ohio field by Rice over the railroad, just as the destruction by the same hands of the pipe line to the Alleghany had
cut him off from access to the Pennsylvania oil-fields. He
then built his own pipe line to the Ohio field. To lay this
pipe it was necessary to cross the pipe line of his great rival.
Rice had the pluck to do this without asking for a consent
which would never have been given. His intrepidity carried
its point, for, as he foresaw, they dared not cut his pipe for
fear of reprisals.

In turning to the South, after his expulsion from the Ohio
and Western markets, the Marietta independent did but get
out of one hornet's nest to sit down in another. His opponent was selling its oil there through a representative who,
as he afterwards told Congress, "was very fortunate in competing." He thought it was "cheaper in the long-run to
make the price cheap and be done with it, than to fritter away
the time with a competitor in a little competition. I put the

---

[1] Trusts, Congress, 1888, p. 578. Hardy and another *vs.* Cleveland and Marietta Railroad *et al.*, Circuit Court, Ohio, E. D., 1887. *Federal Reporter*, vol. xxxi.,
pp. 689–93.

[2] 49th Congress, 1st Session, Report of the Senate Select Committee on Interstate Commerce, p. 199.

price down to the bone." [1]   Rice, in the South, ran into the embrace of this gentleman who had the "exclusive control" of that territory, and whose method of calling the attention of trespassers to his right was to cut them "to the bone."   The people and the dealers everywhere in the South were glad to see Rice.   He found a deep discontent among consumers and merchants alike.   They perhaps felt more clearly than they knew that business feudalism was not better, but worse, because newer, than military feudalism.   This representative of the combination assured Congress that "99.9 of all the first-class merchants of the South were in close sympathetical co-operation with us in our whole history"—that is, out of every hundred "first-class merchants" only one-tenth of one merchant was not with them.   This is a picturesque percentage.

Rice's welcome among the people would not verify his opponent's estimate that his vassalage included all but one-tenth of one dealer in every hundred.   From all parts came word of the anxiety of the merchants to escape from the power that held them fast.   From Texas: "Most of our people are anxious to get clear."   From Arkansas: "The merchants here would like to buy from some other."   From Tennessee: "Can we make any permanent arrangement with you by which we can baffle such monopoly?"   From Kentucky: "I dislike to submit to the unreasonable and arbitrary commands."   From Mississippi: "It has gouged the people to such an extent that we wish to break it down and introduce some other oils."   From Georgia, from different dealers: "They have the oil-dealers in this State so completely cooped in that they cannot move."   "We are afraid." [2]   As Rice went about the South selling oil the agents of the cutter "to the bone" would follow, and by threats, like those revealed in the correspondence described below, would coerce the dealers to repudiate their purchases.   Telegrams would pour into the discouraged office at Marietta: "Don't ship oil ordered from your agent."   "We hereby countermand orders given your agent yesterday."   One

[1] Trusts, Congress, 1888, pp. 534, 535.
[2] Same, pp. 730–38.

14

telegram would often be signed by all the dealers in a town, though competitors, sometimes nearly a dozen of them, showing that they were united by some outside influence they had to obey.[1]

Where the dealers were found too independent to accept dictation, belligerent and tactical cuts in price were proclaimed, not to make oil cheap, but to prevent its becoming permanently cheaper through free competition and an open market. Rice submitted to Congress letters covering pages of the Trust Report,[2] showing how he had been tracked through Tennessee, Missouri, Nebraska, Georgia, Kansas, Kentucky, Iowa, Mississippi, Louisiana, Texas, Arkansas, Alabama. The railroads had been got to side-track and delay his cars, and the dealers terrorized into refusing to buy his oils, although they were cheaper. If the merchants in any place persisted in buying his oil they were undersold until they surrendered. When Rice was driven out prices were put back. So close was the watch kept of the battle by the generals of " co-operation" that when one of his agents got out of oil for a day or two, prices would be run up to bleed the public during the temporary opportunity. "On the strength of my not having any oil to-day," wrote one of Rice's dealers, "I am told they have popped up the price 3½ cents."[3]

The railroad officials did their best to make it true that "the poor ye have with you always." By mistake some oil meant for the combination was delivered to Rice's agent, and he discovered that it was paying only 88 cents a barrel, while he was charged $1.68, a difference of 80 cents a barrel for a distance of sixty-eight miles.

"Could you stand such competition as that?"

"No, sir. Before that I went up there and sold to every man in the place nearly. They were glad to see me in opposition. . . . I lost them, except one man who was so preju diced that he would not buy from them."

" Your business had been on the increase up to that time?"

[1] Trusts, Congress, 1888, p. 743.
[2] Same, p. 729.   [3] Same, p. 732.

"Increasing rapidly. . . . I haul it in wagons now forty miles south of Manito."

"The rates against you on that railroad are so high that you can for a distance of forty miles transport your oil by wagon and meet the competition better than you can by using their own road?"

"Infinitely better." [1]

---

[1] Trusts, Congress, 1888, pp. 416-20.

CHAPTER XVI

A SPY at one end of an institution proves that there is a tyrant at the other. Modern liberty has put an end to the use of spies in its government only to see it reappear in its business.

Rice throughout the South was put under a surveillance which could hardly have been done better by Vidocq. One of the employés of the oil clique, having disclosed before the Interstate Commerce Commission that he knew to a barrel just how much Rice had shipped down the river to Memphis, was asked where he got the information. He got it from the agents who "attend to our business."

" What have they to do with looking after Mr. Rice's business? . . . How do your agents tell the number of barrels he shipped in April, May, and June ?"

"See it arrive at the depot."

"How often do your agents go to the depot to make the examination ?"

"They visit the depot once a day, not only for that purpose, but to look after the shipment of our own oil."

" Do they keep a record of Mr. Rice's shipments ?"

"They send us word whenever they find that Mr. Rice has shipped a car-load of oil."

" What do their statements show with respect to Mr. Rice's shipments besides that ?"

"They show the number of barrels received at any point shipped by Mr. Rice, or by anybody else."

"How often are these statements sent to the company ?"

"Sent in monthly, I think."

"It is from a similar monthly report that you get the statement that in July, August, and September, Mr. Rice shipped 602 barrels of oil to Nashville, is it?"

"Yes, sir."

"Have you similar agents at all points of destination?"

"Yes, sir."[1]

This has a familiar look. It is the espionage of the South Improvement Company contract, in operation sixteen years after it was "buried." When the representative of the oil combination appears in public with tabulated statements exhibiting to a barrel the business done by its competitors for any month of any year, at any place, he tells us too plainly to be mistaken that the "partly-born," completely "buried" iniquity, sired by the "sympathetical co-operation" of the trustees and their railroad associates of easy virtue, is alive and kicking—kicking a breach in the very foundations of the republic.

A letter has found the light which was sent by the Louisville man who was so "fortunate in competing," immediately after he heard that one of "his" Nashville customers had received a shipment from the Marietta independent. It was addressed to the general freight agent of the Louisville and Nashville Railroad. It complained that this shipment, of which the writer knew the exact date, quantity, destination, and charges, "slipped through on the usual fifth-class rate." "Please turn another screw," the model merchant concluded. What it meant "to turn another screw" became quickly manifest. Not daring to give the true explanation, none of the people implicated have ever been able to make a plausible explanation of the meaning of this letter. The railroad man to whom it was sent interpreted it when examined by Congress as meaning that he should equalize rates. But Congress asked him:

"Is the commercial phrase for equalizing rates among railroad people 'turn another screw'?"

[1] Testimony, Rice cases, Interstate Commerce Commission, Nos. 51–60, 1887, pp. 442–43.

He had to reply, helplessly, " I do not think it is."

The sender before the same committee interpreted it as a request "to tighten up the machinery of their loose office." [1] Rice found out what the letter meant. "My rates were raised on that road over 50 per cent. in five days."

"Was it necessary to turn on more than one screw in that direction to put a stop to your business?"

"One was sufficient." [2]

The rates to the combination remained unchanged. For five years—to 1886—they did not vary a mill. After the screw had been turned on, he who suggested it wrote to the offending merchants at Nashville, that if they persisted in bringing in this outside oil he would not only cut down the price of oil, but would enter into competition on all other articles sold in their grocery. He italicized this sentence: "*And certainly this competition will not be limited to coal-oil or any one article, and will not be limited to any one year.*" [3] "Your co-operation or your life," says he.

"Have you not frequently, as a shipper of oil, taken part in the competition with grocers and others in other business than oil, in order to force them to buy oil?"

"Almost invariably I did that always." [4]

"The expense and influence necessary for sustaining the market in this manner are altogether expended by us, and not by the representatives of outside oil," he further wrote. "Influence," as a fact of supply and demand, an element of price-making, is not mentioned in any political economy. And yet the "influence" by which certain men have got the highways shut to other shippers has made a mark as plain as the mountains of the moon on our civilization. "If we allow any one to operate in this manner," he continued, "in any one of our localities, it simply starts off others. And whatever trouble or expense it has given us in the past to prevent it we have found it to be, and still believe it to be, the only policy to pursue." [5]

[1] Trusts, Congress, 1888, pp. 524–30.   [2] Same, p. 620.
[3] Same, pp. 534–36.   [4] Same, p. 533.   [5] Same, p. 536.

They "are threatening," his Nashville agent, after the screw was turned, wrote Rice, "to ruin us in our business." [1]

The head of the Louisville "bone-cutters," when a witness before Congress during the trust investigation, stigmatized the action of his Nashville victims as "black-mail." They were "black-mailers" because they had sold a competitor's oil, and refused to continue to sell his own unless it was made as cheap or cheaper. Competition, when he practised it on others, was "sympathetical co-operation." Tried on him, it was "black-mail." "That man wanted us to pay him more than we paid the other jobbers"—*i. e.*, he wanted them to meet the prices of competitors "because he thought we had the market sustained, and he could black-mail us into it. I bluffed him in language, and language is cheap." [2] The "language" that could produce an advance of freights of 50 per cent. in five days against a competitor was certainly "cheap" for the man whose rates remained unchanged, and who thereby absorbed his neighbor's vineyard. The inevitable result followed at last. Rice fought out the fight at Nashville seven years, from 1880 to 1887; then, defeated, he had to shut up his agency there. That was "evacuation day" at Nashville. It was among his oldest agencies, he told Congress, "and it was shut out entirely last year on account of the discriminations. I cannot get in there." [3]

State inspection of oil and municipal ordinances about storage have been other "screws" that have been turned to get rid of competition. City councils passed ordinances forbidding oil in barrels to be stored, while allowing oil in tanks, which is very much more dangerous, as the records of oil fires and explosions show conclusively. His New Orleans agent wrote Rice concerning the manœuvres of his pursuer: "He has been down here for some time, and has by his engineering, and in consequence of the city ordinances, cut me out of storage. As matters now stand, I would not be able to handle a single barrel of oil." [4] In Georgia the law was made

[1] Trusts, Congress, 1888, p. 729.
[2] Same, p. 534.
[3] Same, p. 730.
[4] Same, p. 733.

so that the charge to the oil combination shipping in tank-cars was only half what it was to others who shipped in barrels. The State inspector's charge for oil in tanks was made 25 cents a barrel; for oil in barrels it was 50 cents a barrel. But as if that was not advantage enough, the inspector inspected the tanks at about two-thirds of their actual capacity. If an independent refiner sent 100 barrels of oil into the State, he would have to pay $50 for inspection, while the oil combination sending in the same would pay but 25 cents a barrel, and that on only 66⅔ barrels, or $16 in all. This difference is a large commercial profit of itself, and would alone enable the one who received it to sell without loss at a price that would cripple all others. In this State the chief inspector had the power to appoint inspectors for the towns. He would name them only for the larger places, where the combination had storage tanks. This prevented independent refiners from shipping directly to the smaller markets in barrels, as they could not be inspected there, and if not inspected could not be sold.[1] All these manœuvres of inspection helped to force the people to buy of only one dealer, to take what he supplied, and pay what he demanded. Why should an official appointed by the people, paid by them to protect them, thus use all his powers against them? Why?

" State whether you had not in your employ the State inspector of oil and gave him a salary," the Louisville representative of the combination was asked by Congress.

" Yes, sir." [2]

Throughout the country the people of the States have been influenced to pass inspection laws to protect themselves, as they supposed, from bad oil, with its danger of explosion. But these inspection laws prove generally to be special legislation in disguise, operating directly to deprive the people of the benefit of that competition which would be a self-acting inspection. They are useful only as an additional illustration of the extent to which government is being used as an active

---

[1] Trusts, Congress, 1888, p. 735.　　　　[2] Same, p. 535.

partner by great business interests. Meanwhile any effort of the people to use their own forces through governments to better their condition, as by the ownership of municipal gas-works, street-railways, or national railroads and telegraphs, is sung to sleep with the lullaby about government best, government least.

This second campaign had been a formidable affair—a worse was to follow; but it did not overcome the independent of Marietta. With all these odds against him, he made his way. Expelled from one place and another, like Memphis and Nashville, he found markets elsewhere. This was because the Southern people gave him market support along with their moral support. Co-operation of father and son and daughter made oil cheaper than the "sympathetical co-operation" opposing them, with its high salaries, idle refineries, and deadheads. Rice had to pay no dividends on "trust" stock capitalized for fifteen times the value of the property. He did not, like every one of the trustees, demand for himself an income of millions a year from the consumer. He found margin enough for survival, and even something more than survival, between the cost of production and the market price. "In 1886 we were increasing our business very largely. Our rates were low enough so that we could compete in the general Southern market."[1]

Upon this thrice-won prosperity fell now blow after blow from the same hand which had struck so heavily twice before. From 1886 to the present moment Rice and his family have been kept busier defending their right to live in business than in doing the business itself. Their old enemy has come at them for the third time, with every means of destruction that could be devised, from highway exclusion to attacks upon private character, given currency by all the powerful means at his command. The game of 1886 was that of 1879, but with many improvements gained from experience and progress of desire. His rates were doubled, sometimes almost tripled; in some cases as much as 333 per cent. Rates to his adver-

[1] Trusts, Congress, 1888, p. 578.

sary were not raised at all. The raise was secret. Suspecting something wrong, he called on the railroad officer July 13th, and asked what rates were going to be. The latter replied that he "had not the list made out." But the next day he sent it in full to the combination. Rice could not get them until August 23d, six weeks later, and then not all of them. As in 1879 the new tariff was arranged at a conference with the favored shippers.[1]

This was the first gun of a concerted attack. Rice was soon under fire from all parts of the field. One road after another raised his rates until it seemed as if the entire Southern market would be closed to him. While this was in progress the new Interstate Commerce Law passed by Congress—in part through the efforts of Rice—to prevent just such misuse of the highways, went into effect. But this did not halt the railway managers. A month after it was passed the Senate Committee on Interstate Commerce was shown that discrimination was still going on, as it is still. At points as far apart as Louisville, New Orleans, Atlanta, St. Louis, and San Francisco switches were spiked against Rice, and the main lines barricaded of all the highways between the Ohio River, the Atlantic and Pacific oceans, and the Gulf of Mexico. In the face of the Interstate Commerce Act the roads raised his freights to points in Georgia, Alabama, Tennessee, Kentucky, Louisiana, and Mississippi in no case less than 29, and in some cases as high as 150, 168, and 212 per cent. more than was charged the oil combination. Where the latter would pay $100 freight, he, shipping the same amount to the same place, would sometimes pay $310—if he got it taken at all.[2]

The general freight agent of one of the roads, when before the Interstate Commerce Commission, denied this. When confronted with written proof of it he could only say, "It is simply an error."[3]

Rice shows that in some cases these discriminations made him pay four times as much freight, gallon for gallon, as the

[1] Trusts, Congress, 1888, pp. 579–80. [2] Same, p. 584.
[3] Testimony, Rice cases, Interstate Commerce Commission, Nos. 51–60, p. 147.

monopoly. The differences against him were so great that even the self-contained Interstate Commerce Commission has to call them "a vast discrepancy."[1] The power that pursued him manœuvred against him, as if it were one track, all the railroads from Pennsylvania to Florida, from Ohio to Lake Superior and the Pacific coast. "Through its representative the oil combination was called before the Interstate Commerce Commission to explain its relation to this 'vast discrepancy.'"

"Your company pays full rates?"

"Pays the rates that I understand are the rates for everybody."

"Pays what are known as open rates?"

"Open rates; yes, sir."[2]

That the increase of rates in 1886, like that of 1879, was made by the railroads against Rice, under the direction of his trade enemy, is confirmed by the unwilling testimony of the latter's representative before Congress. "I know I have been asked just informally by railroad men once or twice as to what answer they should make. They said, Here is a man —Rice, for instance—writing us that you are getting a lower rate." He was asked if he knew any reason, legal or moral, why the Louisville and Nashville Railroad should select his firm as the sole people in the United States. "No, sir," the witness replied; but then added, recovering himself, "I think they did because we were at the front."[3] The railroads bring the people they prefer " to the front," and then, because they are "at the front," make them the "sole people."

Rice did not sleep under this new assault. He went to the Attorney-General of Ohio, and had those of the railroads which were Ohio corporations brought to judgment before the Supreme Court of Ohio, which revoked their action, and could, if it chose, have forfeited their charters. The Supreme Court found that these railroads had charged "discriminating

<hr>

[1] Trusts, Congress, 1888, pp. 682–83.
[2] Testimony, Rice cases, Interstate Commerce Commission, 1887, Nos. 51–60, p. 57.   [3] Trusts, Congress, 1888, pp. 529–32.

rates," "strikingly excessive," which "tended to foster a monopoly," "actually excluded these competitors," "giving to the favored shippers absolute control."[1] Rice went to Cincinnati, to Louisville, to St. Louis, and Baltimore to see the officials of the railroads. He found that the roads to the South and West, which took his oil from the road which carried it out of Marietta, were willing to go back to the old rates if the connecting road would do so. But the general freight agent of that company would give him no satisfaction. He wrote, October 3d, to the president of the road over which he had done all his business for years. He got no answer. He wrote again October 11th, no answer; October 20th, no answer; November 14th, no answer. Rice had been paying this road nearly $10,000 a year for freight, sending all his oil over it. The road had used its rate-making power to hand over four-fifths of his business to another, but he has never been able to get so much as a formal acknowledgment of the receipt of his letters to the head of the road, asking that his petitions for restoration of his rights on the highway be considered. A part only of the letters and telegrams which he sent during these years—to get rates, to have his cars moved, to rectify unequal charges, to receive the same facilities and treatment others got—fill pages of close print in the Trust Report of the Congressional Committee of Manufactures of 1888.

"Your time is a good deal occupied with correspondence, is it not?"

"I should say so. If the rates had been more regular, I would not have had so much correspondence. It takes about all my time to look after rates."[2]

Driven off his direct road to market, Rice set to hunting other ways. The Baltimore and Ohio, he found, was, though very roundabout, the only avenue left by which he could get his oils into Southern markets. He began to negotiate with

---

[1] Supreme Court of Ohio: the State, *ex rel.*, *vs.* The Cincinnati, New Orleans and Texas Pacific Railway Company. The State, *ex rel.*, *vs.* The Cincinnati, Washington and Baltimore Railway Company, 47 Ohio State Reports, p. 130.

[2] Testimony, Rice cases, Nos. 51–60, p. 384.

it immediately, but it was not until several months later—the middle of November—that he succeeded in closing arrangements. To get to Chattanooga, Tennessee, over this route his oil had to travel 1186 miles as against 582 miles by the roads which had been closed to him, and yet the rate was lower over the more than double distance. Again, he could send a barrel of oil 1213 miles by the Baltimore and Ohio to Birmingham, Alabama, for $1.22, while the roads he had been using put his rate up to $2.26, although their line to Birmingham was only 685 miles.

All the arrangements had been concluded to the mutual satisfaction of Rice and the Baltimore and Ohio Railroad. After this thorough discussion of four months, in which every point had been examined, Rice sends forward his first shipment December 1st. He is not a little elated to have blazed his way out of the trackless swamp in which he had been left by the other roads. His satisfaction is short enough. In about a fortnight—on December 15th—the then general freight agent of the Baltimore and Ohio telegraphed him that he could not be allowed to ship any more. "We will have to withdraw rates on oil to Southern points, as the various lines in interest"—the connections to which the Baltimore and Ohio delivered the oil for points beyond its own line, and which shared in the rates—"will not carry them out."

This was stunning. It nullified the labor of months which had been spent in opening a way out of this blockade. It put the cup of ruin again to the lips of the family at Marietta, innocent of all offence but that of trying to make a living out of the industry of their choice, and asking no favors, only the right to travel the public highway on equal terms, and to stand in the open markets. The excuse given was heavy-laden with inaccuracy. Rice immediately found out by wire that the Piedmont Air Line, one of the most important of the connections, had not refused to carry at the agreed rate. Its traffic manager telegraphed the Baltimore and Ohio people to reconsider their action, and continue taking Rice's oil. When asked first by Rice, and afterwards by Congress, to name the lines which refused, as he alleged, to carry out the rates he had agreed upon, the general freight agent of the Baltimore and Ohio could not give one. He escaped from Congress by promising to send its committee, "within a day or two," all the correspondence with these other companies. Once out of the committee-room, he never sent a scrap of paper to redeem his promise, and the whole matter was lost sight of by the committee.[1]

Rice, badly shattered, still sought and managed to find a few long-way-around routes. He presented to Congress in 1888 a table showing how he still managed to get to some of his markets. To Birmingham, Alabama—the direct route of 685 miles, as well as the Baltimore and Ohio, being closed to him—he shipped over seven different railroads forward and backward 1155 miles. The rates of all these roads added together made only $2.10 a barrel instead of $2.66, to which the shorter line had raised its price, for the purpose, as this comparison shows, not of getting revenue, but of cutting it off. To get into Nashville he had to go around 805 miles over five different lines instead of 502 miles, as usual, and still had a rate of $1.28 instead of $1.60.

From 1880, the moment he turned to the Southern field, after the destruction of his business in the West, everything that railroad men's ingenuity could do was done to prevent him from becoming a successful manufacturer who might increase the amount to be shipped, open new markets, and steady the trade by making it move by many minds of different views and reasons instead of by one. In order barely to live he was kept writing, telegraphing, travelling, protesting, begging, litigating, worrying, and agitating by press, prosecutions, private and public, and by State and national investigation. The ingenuity of the railroad officials in chasing him down was wonderful. Nothing was too small if it would hurt. Sometimes the railroad made through rates so high that it was cheaper for him to ship his oil along by short

---

[1] Trusts, Congress, 1888, pp. 397, 398, 615–17.

stages, paying the local rates from place to place until it reached its destination. In this way he got a car from Cincinnati to Knoxville at the rate of 32 cents altogether, when, if it had been shipped at once all the way on the through rate, it would have cost 40 cents a hundred. The railroads have spent hundreds of thousands of dollars, used up armies of gifted counsel, and spoiled tons of white paper with ink to argue out their right to charge more for short hauls than long hauls; but when some traffic manager wants to crush one of his employer's customers, no short-haul long-haul consistency stands in his way.[1] It was not enough to fix his rates at double what others paid. All kinds of mistakes were made about his shipments. Again and again these mistakes were repeated; nor were they, the Interstate Commerce Commission shows, corrected when pointed out.[2] One of the stock excuses made by railroad managers for giving preferential rates to their favorites is that they are the "largest shippers," and, consequently, "entitled to a wholesale rate." But when Rice was the largest shipper, as he was at New Orleans, they forgot to give him the benefit of this "principle." When Rice wrote, asking if a lower rate was not being made, the railroad agent replied: "Let me repeat that the rates furnished you are just as low as furnished anybody else." "This lacks accuracy," is the comment of the Interstate Commerce Commission.

Wishing to know if the Louisville and Nashville would unite with other roads in making through rates to him, Rice asked the question of its freight agent. He replied: "I do not see that it is any of your business." "It was undoubtedly his business," the Interstate Commerce Commission says, sharply; "and his inquiry on the subject was not wanting either in civility or propriety." When Rice asked the same road for rates, the officials refused to give them to him, and persisted in their refusal.[3] Like Vanderbilt before the New

---

[1] Trusts, Congress, 1888, p. 622.

[2] Same, pp. 586, 676. Testimony, Rice cases, Interstate Commerce Commission, Nos. 51–60, 1887, pp. 391–92.   [3] Same, pp. 676–77.

York Legislative Committee, they seemed to think excuses to shippers were a substitute for transportation, and evidently thought they had done more than their duty in answering Rice's letters. But as the Commission dryly observes, their answers to Rice's letters did not relieve him of the injurious consequences. In attempting to explain these things to the Interstate Commerce Commission, the agent of the railroad said :

"If I have not made myself clear, I—"

"You have not," one of the Commission interrupted.[1]

The refusal to give Rice these rates was an "illegal refusal," the Commission decided ; "the obligation to give the rates . . . was plain and unquestionable." This general freight agent was summoned by Congress to tell whether or not lower rates had been made to the oil combination than to their competitors. He refused to produce the books and papers called for by the subpœna. He had been ordered by the vice-president of the road, he said, to refuse. He declined to answer the questions of the committee. Recalled, he finally admitted the truth : "We gave them lower rates in some instances."[2]

Rice took to the water whenever he could, as hunted animals do. The Ohio, Mississippi, Tennessee, Missouri were public highways that had not been made private property, with general agents or presidents to say "No" when asked permission to travel over them. He began to ship by river. The chairman of the Committee of Commerce rose in his seat in Congress to present favorably a bill to make it illegal to ship oil of less than 150 degrees fire-test on the passenger boats of inland waters. The reason ostentatiously given was public safety. But, as was at once pointed out in the press, the public safety required no such law. The test proposed was far above the requirement of safety. No State in its inspection laws stipulated for so high a test. Most of the States were satisfied with oil of 110 degrees fire-test ; a few, like Ohio, went as high as 120 degrees. All but a very small

---

[1] Rice cases, Nos. 51–60, 1887, p. 119.　　　[2] Trusts, Congress, 1880, p. 520.

proportion of the oil sent to Europe was only 110 degrees fire-test. The steamboat men did not want the law, and were all against it. There was no demand from the travelling public for such legislation. General Warner, member of Congress, said, in opposing the bill: "Petroleum which will stand a fire-test of 110 degrees is safer than baled cotton or baled hay, and as safe as whiskey or turpentine to be carried on steamers. What is the object, then? There can be but one, and I may as well assert it here, although I make no imputation whatever upon the Committee of Commerce, or any member of it. It will put the whole carrying trade of refined petroleum into the hands of the railroads and under the control of . . . a monopoly which has the whole carrying trade in the oil business on railroads, and they will make it as impossible for refiners to exist along the lakes and the Ohio River as it is impossible for them now to exist on any of the railroads of the country." Why the trust, though it was the greatest shipper, should seek to close up channels of cheapness like the waterways was plain enough. They were highways where privilege was impossible. With its competitors shut off the railroads by privilege, and off the rivers by law, it would be competition proof.

The United States authorities, too, moved against Rice, responsive to the same "pull" that made jumping-jacks for monopoly out of committees of commerce and railway kings. When the Mississippi River steamer *U. P. Schenck* arrived at Vicksburg with 56 barrels of independent oil, the United States marshal came on board to serve a process summoning the officers and owners to answer to the charge of an alleged violation of law. Several steamboats were similarly "libelled."

"We were threatened a great many times," the representative of the steamboat company told Congress.[1] The steamboat men were put to great expense and without proper cause. When the cases came to trial they were completely cleared in every instance. But the prosecution had done its work

---

[1] Trusts, Congress, 1880, pp. 410–11.

of harassing competition. The success of the campaign of 1879 in Ohio was now repeated over a wider field. The attack of 1886, "in a period of five months," Rice said before Congress, "shut up fourteen of my agencies out of twenty-four, and reduced the towns we had been selling in from seventy-three to thirty-four."[1] This was a loss in one year of 79 per cent., or about four-fifths of his business.

[1] Trusts, Congress, 1888, p. 599.

CHAPTER XVII

IN THE INTEREST OF ALL

THE difference in freights against Rice was so great, as the Interstate Commerce Commission found, after taking hundreds of pages of testimony, that he had to pay $600 to $1200, "or more," on the same quantity his opponent got through for $500. These discriminations were made, as the commissioners say, "on no principle. . . . Neither greater risks, greater expense, competition by water transportation, nor any other fact or circumstance brought forward in defence, nor all combined, can account for these differences."[1]

The railroads had, of course, to give some reason, and they put forward the plea that it was much more expensive and dangerous to carry Rice's shipments, which were in barrels, than those of the combination, which were in tank-cars.[2] This excuse for charging him rates at which he could not ship at all did not stand examination by the Interstate Commerce Commission.

But he did not wait for that. When he found the railroads were so fond of tank-cars, he set about getting them. He wrote the general freight agent and the president of the road that he would build tank-cars, and asked what his rate would be then; but he got no answer. He wrote other roads, but got no answer. He asked the general manager of the Queen City and Crescent Route the same question. After a correspondence of five months with him and other officials, in which he was shuttlecocked from one to another and back again, he had not only not succeeded in getting any tank-car

---

[1] Trusts, Congress, 1888, pp. 688–89.   [2] See ch. xi.

rates, but at the end of that protracted exchange of letters the general manager wrote : " I was not aware that you had asked for rates on oil in tank-cars." [1]   Rice wrote the Louisville and Nashville : " I will build immediately twenty tank-cars if you will guarantee me . . . as low a net rate as accorded any other shipper."   Commenting on his failure to get answers, the commissioners say : " Complainant did not succeed in obtaining rates.   The denial of his right was plain, and stands unexcused. . . . What reason there may have been for it "—the refusal of rates—" we do not know, but find that they were not just or legal reasons." [2]

How history is made !   One of the reasons given by the solicitor of the oil trust [3] for its success is its use of the tank-car, with the obvious inference that its would-be competitors had no such enterprise.   And Peckham, in his valuable and usually correct " Census Report on Petroleum," in 1885, says that the railroads require shippers to use tank-cars ! [4]

Determined to keep in the field and to have tank-cars, if tank-cars were so popular with the railroad officials, Rice went to the leading manufacturers to have some built.   He found they were glad to get his contract.   After making arrangements at considerable trouble and expense to build him the cars, they telegraphed him that they had to give it up. Bankers, who had promised to advance them money on the security of the cars, backed out " on account of some supposed controversy which they claim you have had with the Standard Oil Company and various railroads in the West.   They feared you could not use these cars to advantage if the railroads should be hostile to your interests." [5]

Through the all-pervading system of espionage, to which cities [6] as well as individuals were subject, his plans had been discovered and thwarted.   The espionage over shipments provided for by the South Improvement scheme has now

[1] Trusts, Congress, 1888, p. 607.   [2] Same, p. 678.

[3] *Combinations*, by S. C. T. Dodd, p. 29.

[4] " Petroleum and Its Products," by S. F. Peckham, U. S. Census, 1885, p. 92.

[5] Trusts, Congress, 1888, p. 614.   [6] See ch. xxiv.

extended to business between manufacturer and manufacturer. Why should it stop at unsealing private correspondence in the post-office in the European style, and making its contents known to those who need the information for the protection of their rights to the control of the markets?

Rice, who was nothing if not indomitable, finally got ten cars from the Harrisburg works. But this supply was entirely inadequate, and he had to continue doing the bulk of his business in barrels. What a devil's tattoo the railroad men beat on these barrels of his! They made him pay full tariff rates on every pound weight of the oil and of the barrel, but they hauled free the iron tanks, which were the barrels of his rivals, and also gave them free the use of the flat-cars on which the tanks were carried.[1] Hauling the tanks free, on trucks furnished free, was not enough. The railroads hauled free of all charge a large part, often more than half, of the oil put into the tanks. In the exact phrase of the Interstate Commerce Commission, they made out their bills for freight to the oil combination "regardless of quantity." This is called "blind-billing."

Of the 3000 tank-cars of the combination only two carried as little as 20,000 pounds; according to the official figures there were hundreds carrying more than 30,000 pounds, and the weight ran up to 44,250 pounds, but they were shipped at 20,000 pounds.[2] A statement put in evidence showed that shipments in tank-cars actually weighing 1,637,190 pounds had been given to the roads by the combination as weighing only 1,192,655 pounds. Cars whose loads weighed 44,250, 43,700, 43,500, 36,550 pounds were shipped as having on board only 20,000 pounds. At this rate more than one-quarter of the transportation was stolen.

The stockholders of the road were paying an expensive

---

[1] Testimony, Rice cases, Interstate Commerce Commission, Nos. 51–60, 1887, p. 144.

[2] Trusts, Congress, 1888, pp. 587, 675, 680. Rice cases, Nos. 51–60, 1887, pp. 487–88. For similar preferences to the palace cattle-car companies, see report on "Meat Products," United States Senate, 1890, p. 18.

staff of inspectors to detect attempts of shippers to put more in their cars than they paid for, but these shippers paid for three car-loads and shipped from four to six regularly, and were never called to account. This "blind-billing," the Commission said, was "specially oppressive." It was done by the roads in violation of their own rule. It had been mutually agreed among them, and given out to the public, "that tank-cars shall be taken at actual weight." [1]

When Rice was trying to get the roads to allow him to use tank-cars, he asked how the charge on them was calculated. Of those that answered none answered right. None of them gave him the slightest intimation that there was any such practice as "blind-billing." On the contrary, they assured him he would have to pay for every pound he shipped. The Missouri Pacific replied with a "statement not warranted by the facts," as the Commission softly put it. They said they charged for the "actual weight," while, as the Commission shows, they made shipments "regardless of quantity." Rice asked the Newport News and Mississippi Valley Railroad for tank-car rates. "A tank-car is supposed to weigh (carry) 20,000 pounds; if it weighs more, then we will charge for it." At the same time the agent wrote Rice this, he was hauling cars containing 35,000 pounds "with no additional charge." "If this statement was made in good faith," the Commission says, "it is difficult to account for it, and it is not accounted for." "Had he (Rice) provided himself with cars for tank shipment, and been charged as he was told he would be, the discrimination against him would have put success in the traffic out of the question."

When they wanted to turn some new screw in freight rates against Rice, the railroad officials would whip themselves around the stump by printing a new tariff sheet on a type-writer, and tacking it, perhaps, as one of the Interstate Commerce Commission said, on some back door in their offices. This they called "publishing" their rates, as required by the

---

[1] Rice cases, Nos. 51–60, 1887, p. 477.

Interstate Commerce law. To Rice, asking for tank-car rates, they would send this printed sheet, showing that if he shipped by tank-car he must pay for every pound, and they held him off with this printed, official, and apparently authentic tariff, though shipping 44,000 for 20,000 pounds for the trust. This was done after the Interstate Commerce Act went into force.[1]

One of these roads assured Rice that its rates had been fixed "by the special authority of the National Railway Commissioners." The fact was, as the Commission declares: "The Commission never investigated coal-oil rates, or gave special authority for their renewal; it never sanctioned any difference in the rates as between tank-car and barrel shipments, and had never, up to the date of this letter, had its attention called to them in any way."[2]

The representative of the combination was called as a witness before the Interstate Commerce Commission. "We pay for exactly what is put in the tanks,"[3] he testified. "In fact, this was never done," says the Commission.[4] Even the railroad officials, who could go any length in "blind-billing"'for him, could not "go it blind" on the witness-stand to the extent of supporting such a statement. "Our price per tank-car was not based on any capacity or weight; they have been made simply per tank-car."[5]

"What, generally, is the object of false billing?"

"I suppose to beat the railroad company."[6]

In defence of the discrimination against the barrel shippers, a great deal has been made of danger from fire, damage to cars from leakage, and trouble of handling in the case of barrel shipments, but the best expert opinion which the Interstate Commerce Commission could get went against all these plausible pretences.[7] The manager of the tank line on the Pennsylvania roads showed that the risks were least when the transportation was in barrels. Another reason given for the lower rates on tanks was that they returned loaded with

---

[1] Trusts, Congress, 1888, pp. 675, 679–87.   [2] Same, p. 682.
[3] Rice cases, Nos. 51–60, 1887, p. 47.   [4] Trusts, Congress, 1888, p. 675.
[5] Rice cases, Nos. 51–60, 1887, pp. 108–9.   [6] Same, p. 120.   [7] See ch. xi.

turpentine and cotton-seed oil from the South; but, as the
Interstate Commerce Commission shows, this traffic was taken
at rates so astonishingly low that it was of little profit;[1] and
the commissioner of the Southern Railway and Steamship
Association informed the Commission that the return freight
business in cotton alone, brought back by the box-cars, to say
nothing of other freight, was worth more than these back-
loads of turpentine in the tank-cars.[2] It was, consequently,
the box-car in which barrel shipments were made, and not
the tanks, on which the railroad men should have given a
better rate, according to their own reasoning. Turpentine
and cotton-seed oil are worth three or four times more than
kerosene, and it costs no more, no less, to haul one than the
other; but the railroads would carry the cotton-seed oil and
turpentine for one-third or one-fourth the rate they charged
for kerosene. The Commission could not understand why
the rates given by the roads on these back-loads of turpentine
and cotton-seed oil were so low. "This charge, for some
reason not satisfactorily explained to the Commission, is made
astonishingly low when compared with the charge made upon
petroleum, although the cotton-seed oil is much the more valuable article."[3]

The newspapers of the South have contained many items
of news indicating that the men who have made the oil
markets theirs have similarly appropriated the best of the
turpentine trade, but nothing is known through adjudicated
testimony. The trustees of oil have always denied that there
was any connection between them and the Cotton-seed Oil
Trust, although the latter shipped its product in the oil trust's
cars. The reasons, therefore, for the "extraordinarily low"
rates made on the turpentine and cotton-seed oil shipped
North in its tank-cars must remain, until further develop-
ments, where the Commission leaves it—"not satisfactorily
explained." The railroads said they made the rates low for
tanks because of the enticing prospects of these back-loads,

---

[1] Trusts, Congress, 1888, p. 674.   [2] Rice cases, Nos. 51-60, 1887, p. 480.
[3] Trusts, Congress, 1888, p. 674.

in which there was no profit to speak of ; but they extended
these special rates to points from which there was no such
back-loading.[1] Rice saw how the cost of sending his oil
South could be reduced by bringing back-loads of turpentine
at these "astonishingly low" rates. He found there was still
turpentine in the South he could buy; but the railroads
would not so much as answer his application for rates.

"They absolutely refused."

"Was this refusal since the Interstate Commerce decision
in your case?"

"Yes, sir ; since that decision."[2]

It might have been thought this would have been enough—
hauling the tank itself free; furnishing the flat-cars free for
many tanks; carrying free a quarter to a half, "or more."
But there was more than this. The railroads paid the combination for putting its tank-cars on their lines. For every mile
these cars were hauled, loaded or empty, the roads paid it
a mileage varying from $\frac{3}{4}$ to $1\frac{1}{2}$ cents. This mileage was of
itself a handsome revenue, enough to pay a profit of 6 per
cent. on its investment in the cars. But when Rice asked
what the railroads would charge him for hauling back his
empty tank-cars, he was not told that he would be paid for
their use, as others were. He was told that he would be
charged "generally a cent and a half a mile," or, "we make
the usual mileage charge on return of empty tanks." "This
last statement," the Interstate Commerce Commissioners say,
"was not warranted by the facts."[3] The vessel which contains
the oil of the combination "receives a hire coming and going,"
Mr. Rice's lawyer said before the Committee of Congress on
Commerce; "that which contains Rice's oil pays a tax." When
Rice tried to sell his oil on the Pacific coast he found that if
he shipped in tank-cars he would have to pay $95 to bring
the empty car back, which others got back free.

The representative of the oil combination was questioned
about all this by the Interstate Commerce Commission.

[1] Trusts, Congress, 1888, pp. 531–33.   [2] Same, pp. 646–47.
[3] Same, pp. 668–85.

"Are you allowed mileage on tank-cars?"

"No, sir."

"Neither way?"

"Neither way." [1]

But the railroad officials again could not "blind-bill" him as far as this. Asked what mileage they paid him, they replied:

"Three-quarters of a cent a mile." [2]

When the freight agents who did these queer things at the expense of their employers—*i.e.*, their proper employers, the stockholders—were put on the stand before the Interstate Commerce Commission to explain, they cut a sorry figure. "It was an oversight," "a mistake," said one. Another could only ring confused changes on "I think it is an error. . . . I cannot tell why that is so. . . . It is simply an error. . . . I cannot tell." [3] There were never any errors, suppositions, oversights for Rice. [4] Referring to this, the Commission says, caustically:

"The remarkable thing about the matter is that so many of these defendants should make the same mistake—a mistake, too, that it was antecedently so improbable any of them would make. The Louisville and Nashville, the Cincinnati, New Orleans and Texas Pacific, the Newport News and Mississippi Valley, and the Illinois Central companies are all found giving out the same erroneous information, and no one of them can tell how or why it happened to be done, much less how so many could contemporaneously, in dealing with the same subject, fall into so strange an error. It is to be noted, too, that it is not a subordinate agent or servant who makes the mistake in any instance, but it is the man at the head of the traffic department, and whose knowledge on the subject any inquirer would have a right to assume must be accurate. In no case is the error excused." [5]

The cases in which Rice prosecuted the railroads before

---

[1] Rice cases, Nos. 51–60, p. 65. [2] Same, p. 131.

[3] Same, pp. 128–29, 143–47, 239.

[4] Same, p. 109. Trusts, Congress, 1888, pp. 675–76.

[5] Trusts, Congress, 1888, p. 688.

the Interstate Commerce Commission are among the most important that have been tried by the Commission. The charges made by Rice were conclusively proved, except as to some minor roads and circumstances. The Commission declared the rates that were charged him to be illegal and unjust, and a discrimination that must be stopped. It ordered the roads to discontinue using their power as common carriers to carry Rice's property into the possession of a rival. " The conclusion is irresistible that the rate sheets were not considerately made with a view to relative justice." [1]

The facts of these discriminations — " unjust," " illegal," and " abhorrent "—are on the records as judicially and finally determined. But one of the combination said before the Pennsylvania Legislature, at Harrisburg, as reported in the Harrisburg *Patriot*, February 19, 1891:

" I say to you all, in good faith, that since the passage of the Interstate Commerce law, and the introduction of that system, we have never taken a rebate. I mean we have taken no advantage over what any other shipper can get. I make the statement broadly, and I challenge the statement to the very utmost, and will pay the expenses of any litigation undertaken to try it."

When it was found that this practice of charging the preferred shipper for only 20,000 pounds when it shipped 25,000, 30,000, 40,000, or 44,000, was going to be investigated by the Interstate Commerce Commission, there were intellects ready to meet the emergency. A pot of paint and a paint-brush furnished the shield of righteousness. Each car being known by its number, and only by its number, all the old numbers of the 3000 tank-cars of the oil trust were painted out, and new numbers painted on. Whether its mighty men left their luxurious palaces in New York, and stole about in person after dark, each with paint-pot and brush, or whether they asked employés to do such work, the evidence does not state. The device was simple, but it did. Rice was suing for his rights to use the highways before the Interstate Commerce Commission, and before the Supreme Court of Ohio, through

---

[1] Trusts, Congress, 1888, p. 689.

the Attorney-General of the State, who had found the matter of sufficient importance to use his official power to institute suits in *quo-warranto* against two railroads.   It was necessary that evidence should be forthcoming in these suits to prove what his rate was in comparison with the others. The only way this could be done was by comparing the actual size of the cars with the size given in the freight bills, or manifests. The cars are known in the bills only by their numbers, and without its number no car could be identified. The report of Congress reprints the following from the testimony of the representative of the trust before the Interstate Commerce Commission :

" Has there recently been any general change in the numbering of the cars ?"

" Yes, sir; there has been quite a general renumbering, repainting, and overhauling."

" When did that change take place ?"

" I think it was commenced some time in July ; it may have been later."

The result of that renumbering made it practically impossible to identify any car as connected with any shipment made before that time. The cars were there, looking as fresh and innocent as good men who have donned robes of spotless white earned by the payment of generous pew-rent. The cars showed even to the unassisted eye, as the Interstate Commerce Commission said, how much larger they were than was pretended. There were still the accounts of the railroads, showing that these cars had been " blind-billed " as containing only 20,000 pounds, but the cars mentioned in the manifesto could no longer be identified with the cars on the tracks. The sin of " blind-billing " was washed out in paint. Rice went to the Interstate Commerce Commission with his complaint in this case in July. Immediately the repainting and renumbering took place. " It was commenced some time in July ; it may have been later." [1]

---

[1] Trusts, Congress, 1888, pp. 598–99. Testimony, Rice cases, Nos. 51–60, 1887, p. 28.

In such cases time is money, and more. "Seest thou a man diligent in business, he shall stand before kings. He shall not stand before mean men."

The members of this combination have many thousand tank-cars engaged in carrying their oil, and some of them have another kind of tank-car travelling about the country. Under the head of the "Gospel Car" the *Daily Statesman*, of Portland, Oregon, printed the following article, Sunday, December 13, 1891: "THE GOSPEL CAR.—The mission car 'Evangel' arrived yesterday, and was side-tracked on the penitentiary switch. A song service attracted many people during the morning. There will be services at 10.30 this morning, and in the afternoon, at 3 o'clock, a Sunday-school will be organized. This will be the first Sunday-school ever organized from the gospel car, which has been on the road since last spring. The 'Evangel' is sixty feet in length, ten feet wide, and seats nearly one hundred people. It is the generous gift of "—several New York millionaires, the most important of them belonging to the oil trust—". . . to the American Baptist Publication Society. The reverend gentleman who was in charge of the 'Evangel,'" the *Statesman* continued, "will visit the smaller towns along the railway, and conduct evangelistic meetings in the car." One of these cars was in Chicago early in 1893, and was admiringly described by the Chicago press. Though corporations have no souls they are ready to help save the souls of others, for the railroads give these cars free hauling, and the messages and the packages of its occupants are franked by the telegraph and express companies. The contents of this tank-car are distributed by its donors to the people without money and without price. It is conceivable that by making it so "cheap" and by multiplying the "Evangel" into an evangelical tank line of thousands of cars, the donors might drive the churches, which have no tank-cars, out of the business, as they have done the tankless refiners, and ultimately add to their monoply of the Light of the World that of the Light of the other World.

The effect of all this on the family co-operation at Marietta does not need to be described. Its head told Congress that if he had had no difficulty in getting the same freight as others he could have run his refinery to its full capacity, and could have increased his works largely.

"Are not your expenses less than theirs?"

"Yes, sir. . . . I am running very moderately now. . . . One-third to one-half generally." [1]

"I am virtually ruined," he says still later in a statement of his condition in a circular to the public, urging them to petition Congress to make the imperfect Interstate Commerce law operative. He is virtually ruined, though he has won his cases before the Interstate Commerce Commission, and that Federal tribunal has ordered the roads to give him his rights on the highways; but it has been a barren victory. His circular is entitled "My Experience Very Briefly Told." Its opening sentences give us in a phrase the secret of the significance of Rice's story, and dignify his appeal to the public. They show how thoroughly adversity had driven home into this plain man's mind a great civic truth which his fellow-citizens have not yet learned, probably because they have not yet had adversity enough. His solitary and fruitless, although successful, struggle taught him that the citizens of industry can no more maintain their rights acting singly than the citizens of government. He had learned that "competition," "supply and demand," "eternal laws of trade," were catch-words as impotent in the markets to give individuals their rights, if unassociated, as the incantations of royalty and loyalty, and law and order, to save people from their king until they made themselves a People. Persons fail; only a People can get and keep freedom. This Rice had begun to learn from his failure to enforce single-handed rights which all the courts declared were his, but which no court could secure. In his card to the people, he said: "I am fighting for my rights and for my existence (which happens to be in the interest of all) single-handed and alone, at my own expense and time lost. . . .

[1] Trusts, Congress, 1888, p. 622.

I am here . . . to do what I can to get the Interstate Commerce Act amended at this present session of the Fiftieth Congress, to cure existing evils, and all I ask is that you will take hold and assist me by your signature and approval to the enclosed petition. You are subject to the same influences, and now is your time, my fellow-countrymen, to come forward and assist a little to stop this nefarious work."

"In the interest of all." This is exactly the relation which the struggle of this common citizen bears to the general welfare. The investigation by the Ohio Legislature in 1879;[1] the removal by the United States Court of the railroad receiver who agreed to pay the oil trust $25 out of every $35 freight collected from Rice;[2] the refund ordered by the Supreme Court of Ohio from a pipe-line company which had charged Rice 15 cents extra on every barrel he shipped to pay it to his competitors;[3] the successful prosecution, by the Attorney-General of Ohio before the Supreme Court, of the railroads discriminating against Rice;[4] the cases before the Interstate Commerce Commission from its beginning till now, involving hundreds of railroads, and decided, so far as it did decide, on almost every point in Rice's favor;[5] the disruption, as far as forms go, of the oil trust in Ohio by the Supreme Court of the State ousting corporations from the right to become members of such combinations and to pool their earnings therein;[6] the investigation of the oil trust by Congress in 1888 and 1889, devoted in large part to the various aspects of Rice's experience—these are some only of the public functions which had to be invoked in the ineffectual attempt to protect this one man on the high-road and in his livelihood, and they show how little his was merely a "private affair."

[1] See p. 205.   [2] See p. 206.

[3] Brundred, *et al. vs.* Rice, decided November 1, 1892, 49 Ohio State Reports.

[4] See p. 219.

[5] For the decisions in these Rice cases see Interstate Commerce Commission Report, vol. i., p. 503; same, p. 722; vol. ii., p. 389; vol. iii., p. 186; vol. iv., p. 228; vol. v., p. 193, and same, p. 660.

[6] The State of Ohio *ex rel.* David K. Watson, Attorney-General, *vs.* The Standard Oil Company, *N. E. Reporter*, vol. xxx., p. 279; 49 Ohio State Reports, p. 317.

When the amendment of the Interstate Commerce law was before Congress in 1889, eminent counsel were employed by Rice to explain the defects of the law to the committees, and petitions to Congress through his instrumentality were circulated all over the country, and numerously signed. Though a poor man, who could ill afford it, he gave time and money and attention, frequently spending weeks at Washington, discussing the subject with members, and presenting petitions. The act was amended in partial accordance with these petitions and recommendations.

To obtain the elementary right of a stockholder, never withheld in the course of ordinary business — to vote and receive dividends on stock in the oil trust which the trustees had sold and he had bought in the open market—Rice had to sue through all the New York courts from 1888 to 1892. The Court of Appeals decided that there had been no lawful reason for the denial of his rights, and ordered that they be accorded him. This was another barren victory. The trust had meanwhile ostensibly been dissolved; but the dissolution has every appearance of being like that of its progenitor, the South Improvement Company, a dissolution "in name" only; not in reality. In place of the old trust certificates listed on the New York Stock Exchange, new certificates have been issued which were selling in the spring of 1894 at about the same quotation as the former ones.

In this case the trust asked the New York courts to deny Rice his rights because he had in other matters, and as to other parties, appealed to other courts. His other suits had been against the railroads, not against the oil combination. He acted on the defensive, and went into court only to save himself from commercial strangulation. In all of them that went to trial he was successful, with but one or two exceptions. He was so successful that even the judges who heard his case and decided in his favor were moved to outbursts of unaffected indignation on the bench. The only result aimed at or procured was that the courts decreed that these common carriers must in the future give this citizen his legal rights on the railways; not that he must have the same rates as his opponent, but only that the difference in their favor shall not be "excessive," "illegal," "unjust."

Because of this attempt to secure the fair use of the highways side by side with it, the trust pleaded in the Supreme Court of New York that his appeal to courts as a shipper was a reason why the courts should withhold his rights as a stockholder.

In making this plea the trustees described themselves as having been for years persecuted by the independent of Marietta, and moistened the dry pages of their legal pleadings with appeals for the sympathy of the courts and the public. He has "diligently and persistently sought to become acquainted with" our "methods of business and private affairs;" "he has used efforts to injure" our "business"; "he is attempting to harass, injure, and annoy" us; "he has ever since . . . 1876, when he first engaged in business, . . . maintained a hostile attitude, and been engaged in hostile transactions and proceedings against" us, . . . "for the purpose of injuring" us and our "business"; he "has been uninterruptedly prosecuting . . . a series of litigations . . . in the courts, as well as before the Interstate Commerce Commission, and before an investigating committee of Congress . . . for the purpose of harassing and annoying" us.[1] And when in 1891 Rice was appealing to the Attorney-General of New York to bring suit in the name of the State against the oil combination in New York, like that which had been successfully brought in Ohio, he was publicly stigmatized in court as a "black-mailer" because he had once named a price at which he was willing to sell his refinery and quit. So the citizens of Nashville were called black-mailers for competing, and the citizens of Buffalo for bringing a criminal conspiracy to justice.

---

[1] Rice *vs.* Standard Oil Trust. New York Court of Appeals — Case on Appeal, 1888.

16

It is this dancing attendance upon State legislatures, courts, attorney-generals, Congress, the Interstate Commerce Commission, as shown in this recital, which the modern American business man must add to Thrift, Industry, and Sobriety as a condition of survival.

CHAPTER XVIII

ORDINARY SUPPLY AND DEMAND

"Do I understand you that they have not sought in any way to make the operations of refineries outside the trust so unprofitable that parties would either come into the trust or have to abandon the business—has anything of that sort been done?"

"They have not; no, sir, they have not," was the triple negative of the president.

"They" (the trustees) "have lived on good terms with what I may call their competitors?"

"They have; and have to-day very pleasant relations with those gentlemen."

"So far as you know," he was asked, "the product of the crude oil and the manufacture and sale of the refined oil has been absolutely left to the ordinary rules of supply and demand, has it not?"

"It has." [1]

In the winter of 1873 a young farmer living among the blue hills of Wyoming, in western New York, where he had been born and bred, was asked by a stranger from Rochester to help him in a search for oil lands. The old-fashioned quiet of the little community was agitated by the hope that the milk and honey of their valleys might be replaced by a more precious flow. The stranger and his son were prosperous oil refiners, but a little cloud, about the size of a "trustee's" hand, had crept into their sunshine. As they set about drilling a well on some "likely-looking" land

---

[1] Testimony, Trusts, New York, 1888, pp. 385–87.

they had leased, the stranger told the farmer why he was so
anxious to strike oil for his own exclusive use. The reader is
better prepared to understand his explanation than the then
inexperienced agriculturist to whom he gave his confidence.
It had begun to be difficult for him to get a full and regular
supply of the crude petroleum for his works. There were
restrictions, he said, about the shipments.[1] What that meant
the young farmer was to learn for himself.

There was no oil in Wyoming, and the refiner went back
to Rochester, and, as so many others have done, sold the control of his works, the Vacuum, to the "successful men"
of the combination, and stepped silently into the minority
place. His Wyoming friend, Charles B. Matthews, had continued in his service, and when the Vacuum was sold he and
two other of its employés made up their minds to go into
the business of refining in Buffalo on their own account.
They were under no obligations or contract to remain, and
did not suppose themselves to have been sold along with the
concern. They were capable men, and showed great business
sense in their arrangements. Buffalo, by its connections by
rail and the lake with the market, and its nearness to the oil
supply, was a much better situation than Rochester or Cleveland. An independent refining company — the Atlas — was
then constructing an independent pipe line from the oil regions to Buffalo. "This made Buffalo the best point for establishing refining industries in the country, with its canal
and lake transportation for the products of the factory, and
with a pipe line, in the hands of independents, from the crude
oil wells to the city," said the Buffalo *Express*. Matthews
had by this time had several years' experience in the business.
Of the two with him, Albert was a laborer, who had worked
his way up in the Vacuum refinery until he could run the
stills, and had learned how to make oil. He and his thrifty

---

[1] People of the State of New York *vs.* Everest *et al.* Court of Oyer and Terminer, Erie County, February, 1886, court stenographer's report. This item is
omitted in the transcript of evidence furnished by the oil trust to the Committee
of Congress investigating trusts in 1888. See Trusts, Congress, 1888, p. 801.

wife had saved a few thousand dollars. He was ambitious. He had learned at school and in the army and at Fourth-of-July celebrations that America is a free country for all, and that there are no classes here, and that any workman may go to the top. Farmer Matthews had fed his boyhood with stories of country boys who had gone to the city and matured into business magnates. He and Albert pooled their visions and their savings, borrowed some money, and went to work. As for competition, though they knew it was close, they were not afraid but that they could hold their own in a fair fight, and of anything but a fair fight they never dreamed.

"How are you going to get your crude oil?" Albert and Matthews were asked when they went to tell their employer what they were going to do.

"From the Atlas pipe line."

"You will wake up some day and find that there is no Atlas Oil Company.

"We have ways," he continued, "of making money you know nothing about," using, singularly enough, the phraseology employed by a greater man in the interview with another would-be competitor.[1]

"As gentlemen," he went on to say, "I respect you, but as to the Buffalo Lubricating Oil Company I shall do all in my power to injure or destroy it."[2]

Afterwards Albert alone was sent for. "Don't you think it would be better for you to leave these men, and have $20,000 deposited to your wife's credit than go with these parties?"

"I went out with them in good faith, and I propose to stay."

"It will be only a matter of a few days with the Buffalo institution at the furthest. We will crush them out, and you will lose what little you have got."

Albert was shown an elaborate statement of the cost of making oil and its selling price, proving that there was no money in oil.[3] The record of dividends was produced in

[1] See p. 52. [2] Testimony, Trusts, Congress, 1888, pp. 814, 882, 883.
[3] Same, p. 815.

court afterwards. It showed that just before this—January 18, 1881—a dividend of 50 per cent. had been paid in one month.[1] Dividends of $300,000 had been paid in 1881 on the capital of $100,000. "No wonder they did not want competition," said the New York *World*.

These negotiations had been with the son. Albert not yielding to this pressure, and pushing ahead with the construction of the rival stills, the father, who was in California, came back. At his request Albert again interrupted the work on the new refinery, which he alone of the partners could direct, and came from Buffalo to Rochester for an interview.

"You have made a grand mistake," said his old employer, "by going out with those fellows. . . . The company will not last long. . . . The result will be, if you stay with them, you will lose all you have got in it. . . . We are going to commence suits against them. We will not only sue them, but serve an injunction on them and stop their work. The result of it is that when these suits commence, if you are in it, you will be responsible, and you have got a little money, and you will lose it all. . . . If you come back and work with us everything will be all right, and we will make everything satisfactory to you."

"If I leave them it will leave them in bad shape," Albert urged.

"That is just exactly what I want to do,"[2] his former employer replied.

Albert began to weaken. "I had," he afterwards told in court, . . . "about $6000 altogether, or a little more. They had reason to know that I had some property there."[3] This was all he had to show for the work of a lifetime, and it began to look as if it were fading away under these reiterated threats and warnings, which went on from March to June. Albert gave way. He went to his lawyer, Mr. Truesdale, of Rochester. "We have come," said his former em-

---

[1] Court Stenographer's Report, p. 1135.
[2] Testimony, Trusts, Congress, 1888, p. 816.   [3] Same, p. 816.

ployer, who accompanied him, "to see what disposition can be made of Al's property."

"They are going to bust the company up," said Albert to his lawyer, when asked why he was going back to the Vacuum Company. "I am an indorser on one of its notes, and if I do not come back with the Vacuum, what property and money I have will be taken away from me."

The lawyer was pressed to tell how Albert could get out of his arrangement with his company. They could not get along without him, and were not likely to discharge him.

"If they won't release him or buy him out, the only other way," said the lawyer, "is to leave them, and take the consequences. If he has entered into a contract and violated it, I presume there will be a liability for damages as well as for the debts."

"I think there is other ways for Albert to get out of it," said the representative of the Vacuum method in commerce and morals.

"I see no way except to back out or sell out; no other honorable way," persisted the lawyer.

"Suppose he should arrange the machinery so it would bust up or smash up, what would the consequences be?"

"If negligently, carelessly, not purposely done, he would be only civilly liable for damages caused by his negligence; but if it was wilfully done, there would be a further criminal liability for malicious injury to the property of the company."

"You wouldn't want me, would you," said the poor man to his late employer and friend, "to do anything to lay myself liable?"

"You have been police justice," said the Vacuum man to the lawyer, "and have had some experience in criminal law. I would like to have you look up the law carefully on that point, and we will see you again."[1] Or, in effect: "See about how much crime we can commit," District Attorney Quinby paraphrased it afterwards to the jury.

[1] Testimony, Trusts, Congress, 1888, pp. 817, 872–74.

In a day or so the two managers of the Vacuum—father and son—came back again with Albert.

"Have you looked up that matter, Mr. Truesdale?" asked they.

"Yes, I have looked it up."

"What do you think about it?"

"My impression has not changed. Such a course would involve him in a criminal liability if he did it on purpose. Everybody who advised or counselled him in such a course would be equally liable with him. The consequences, if you follow that course, would be that you would get into State's prison. If he is an honest man he won't think of taking any such action as that. I advise him to keep out of any such thing."

"Such things will have to be found out before they can be punished," was the Vacuum reply. "They will have to find him before they can do anything to him. We will take care of him." "Having in mind," said District Attorney Quinby to the jury, "what happened afterwards—that they should spirit him away."

"The suggestion is altogether wrong," persisted the lawyer. "The action would certainly be very hazardous as well as wrong."

On leaving, the elder of the two, evidently persisting in his plan, said to the lawyer, "If you want to communicate with Albert, you can do so through C. M."[1]—his son.

These men were too careless to note that the lawyer they were talking to was not their lawyer, but Albert's. When they were brought to trial for the crime that followed, and Albert, repentant, told the truth, the lawyer was free to testify against them. "I am entirely willing," said Albert in court, "that Mr. George Truesdale shall state what took place. I withdraw any legal objections I might have."

The accident which has let us see how the employés of a trust coolly debated with lawyers the policy of blowing up a

---

[1] Testimony, Trusts, Congress, 1888, pp. 818, 873.

competitor's works, is one of the few glimpses the American public will ever get into the relations of great legal lights and law-reformers with the mighty capitalists who wreck railroads and execute wholesale corruption of courts, legislatures, and trustees, and evade and transgress the laws with the sure march of those who know that indictments and bail-bonds and verdicts of "guilty" and the penitentiary are only for men not rich enough to plan crime "by advice of counsel." When such men went marauding through the treasury of a great railroad and the courts of an Empire State, we saw the greatest of law-reformers, with a host of legal luminaries, picketing and scouting for them. Every sound in nature is phonographed somewhere, as its waves strike, and Judgment Day will be rich with the revelations from these invisible rolls of the confidential conversations between "trustees" and counsel, who are not honorable lawyers as George Truesdale was, prostituting their functions as "officers of courts" into those of officers of crime.

All these trips from Buffalo to Rochester for these interviews made bad breaks in the construction of the works of the new company at Buffalo. The partners, who were wholly dependent upon Albert's knowledge and experience for the building of the refinery, and running it when built, were mystified and alarmed. Time and again he ran away without a word to them, and all work would stop until he came back. When he was on hand his task did not prosper as if his heart were still in it. When one of the three stills of the refinery had been set up ready for use, and before any oil was run, Albert went up to Rochester again. At this rendezvous the sinister suggestion of "doing something" was repeated. "You go back to Buffalo and construct the pipes and stills so that they cannot make good oil, and then if you would give them a little scare ... they not knowing anything about the business ... you know how to do it." Swearing he would not consent, but already succumbing to this temptation, as he had given way to the threat of ruin, he replied as before: "I don't propose to do anything to make myself criminally liable."[1]   At their suggestion he took a man they sent all through the new works, showing him how the stills had been constructed, how the oil was to be made, and all the details of the refinery.[2]

The day came at last—long expected, delayed by these un-accountable absences—when the members of the new company were to have the happiness of seeing their enterprise set going.   The one still that was ready was filled with crude oil.   The morning of the start Albert weighted down the safety-valve with heavy iron, and packed it with plaster of Paris.   "Fire this still," he said to his fireman, "as heavy as you possibly can."   The fireman did as he was ordered. During the forenoon Albert came to him.   "Damn it!" he said, "you ain't firing this still half.   Fire this still!   I want you to fire this still!   You ain't got no fire under it!"   He took the shovel himself and threw some coal in, although there was, as the fireman expressed it, "an inordinary fire." The fire-box grew cherry red.[3]

Albert knew well enough what the next chapter in the history of his associates was likely to be.   He had carried a dark-lantern into the still-room one day when he was superin-tendent of the Vacuum.   "I was badly burned by the explo-sion," he testified before the coroner's jury investigating the explosion in Rochester, in 1887.   There were four explosions in the Vacuum works while he was there.   In the second, four men were burned.   As one of them ran to get water, with his clothes burning, he set fire to the gas coming out of the sewer.   Flames flashed all about him.   "There's hell all around!" he exclaimed.   The third explosion came from an overheated condensing-pipe, and destroyed one of the build-ings.   The fourth burned up three tanks.   Remembering all this, he now took himself off to the grounds of the Atlas Company, out of harm's reach.   The brickwork about the still cracked apart with the heat.

But the "smash-up or something" had not been thoroughly

[1] Trusts, Congress, 1888, p. 820.   [2] See p. 64.
[3] Trusts, Congress, 1888, p. 854.

arranged. Despite the heavy weight and the packing of plaster, the safety-valve lifted itself under the unusual pressure, and was a safety-valve yet. It was blown open, and a large mass of vapor rose and spread. This was the real accident: that the safety-valve broke loose instead of keeping the gases in to explode, as had been planned. The spreading vapor was not steam, as that had not been admitted to the still, but the gas of distilling petroleum, as inflammable as gunpowder. There was danger still, as great almost as that of explosion. A spark of fire, and it would have wrapped all within its reach in flames. The boiler fires were but twenty feet distant; not far from them the distilled oil was being gathered in the "tail-house"; near the tail-house stood the tanks of crude oil, hundreds of barrels of the fuel that conflagration loves — the kind of fuel the cooks use who, beginning with kerosene for kindling, make the whole house into a stove, and cook themselves and the family with the breakfast.

The kindly wind of a June day carried the cloud of gas away from the fire until it passed out of sight. The unsuspecting, inexperienced men, whose lives and property had been at the mercy of explosion, knew nothing of their peril until years afterwards. The worst they knew then was that the "batch" of 200 barrels of petroleum was spoiled, and that Albert, the only practical man among them, was gone, leaving them crippled for a year. They waited for him, but he did not come. They looked for him, but could not find him. Matthews went to the depot night after night, sometimes at midnight, or later, to watch the trains, but Albert never came.

" What would be the consequences?" Albert was asked afterwards in court, when he was telling about " the pretty heavy fires " he had made under the still—" what would be the consequences in case too hot fires were applied, and the gas should blow off the pipes and become ignited ?"

" The consequences would be that, if ignited, there would be a fire." [1]

[1] Trusts, Congress, 1888, p. 826.

An Associated Press despatch from Louisville, Kentucky, June 30, 1890, describing an explosion in an oil refinery there, and the "five acres of fire" that followed, reproduces for us the picture which it had been planned to paint at Buffalo as part of the panorama of "the ordinary rules of supply and demand." A tank-car had been opened to run some oil out. As the workmen lifted the cap from the manhead of the tank a cloud of gas poured forth. It had been generated simply by the heat of the summer sun, without the aid of an "inordinary" hot fire. The men jumped and ran. Before they had taken a dozen steps the vapor, spreading over the ground and moving with the wind, had reached one of the sheds near by in which there was a fire. There was a flash. The men were bathed in a lake of fire. They ran with the flames streaming from them. At the infirmary their bodies were found to be charred in spots, literally roasted alive, and the flesh dropped off as their clothing was removed. Three men died and several were injured.

Several years after the Buffalo explosion, when those convicted for their part in it were fighting for stay of proceedings, new trial, anything to escape sentence, and were trying by every means in their power to impress upon the public the altogether innocent character of the little incident at the works of their rival, something happened at their own works—the Vacuum in Rochester—which gave the people an appalling sense of the terrors of the new school of supply and demand. Naphtha is one of the by-products of petroleum distillation, and is used by the gas companies in the manufacture of the greased air they furnish under the name of gas. The Vacuum Company were selling their naphtha to the Rochester Gas Company. It was delivered to the gas company through a pipe line. On the afternoon of December 21, 1887, there was an explosion on Platt Street, Rochester, tearing away the pavement, shattering the basement of a building, and filling the air with missiles. In a few seconds another explosion occurred a short distance away, making a hole in the street several feet in diameter, from which came large volumes of smoke and flame. A third and fourth "bust-up" rapidly followed, and then a fifth, in the Clinton Flouring Mill, tearing away a considerable portion of the building, blowing off the roof and upper stories of the Jefferson Mill adjoining, and shattering the Washington Mill. The Jefferson and Clinton and Washington mills were burned to the ground. People were killed by flying débris, burned to death, smashed by falling walls, crippled by jumping from the upper stories of factories and mills on fire. "There is probably no chemical product," says Professor Joy, of Columbia College, "which has occasioned the loss of so many lives and the destruction of so much property as naphtha. . . . From its highly explosive and inflammable nature it has proved little better in the hands of ignorant people than so much gunpowder."

"The counsel for the defence," said District Attorney Quinby, in summing up the case before the jury, "laughed at the idea of Matthews and his associates coming to Buffalo with a little money to compete. I congratulate him that instead of defending for conspiracy he is not here to-day pleading for the defendants' lives. If a person had been killed, and it had been under the advice and instruction of his clients, he would have been differently situated from what he is to-day. How well you men may be thankful that the gases from this still did not flow down and, becoming ignited, explode and kill the fireman! You ought to get down on your knees and thank your God that Providence prevented any such terrible thing as that for you."

After the "bust-up" had been planned, and before it was done, one of the Vacuum managers went to New York, where the "trustees" for whom he was managing the company were. After the "bust-up" Albert heard by telegram from New York, as had been arranged, and went to meet his old employer. "What do you say to going down to Boston?" he was asked on his arrival. Later a man came in and was introduced by the name of one of the three trustees who purchased and directed the Vacuum. On leaving, this "trustee" said: "I will see you again if you do not go to Boston." He thus showed that he knew of the plan that Albert should be taken away, and that they should go to Boston. The manager of the Vacuum now gave the world a genuine illustration of the harmony of labor and capital. He couldn't let Albert out of his sight. They went to Boston on the Fall River boat. The representative of a hundred millions took the laborer into his own state-room, and at Boston carried him into the splendors of Young's Hotel, where he registered, naming himself "and friend," and they shared one bedroom. They went to church together, and to Nantasket Beach, his friend introducing Albert to those whom they met under an assumed name. "You don't want to be known here," he said, "and I will introduce you by the name of Milner."

"That is the name I was known by while I was there."

"Albert has nothing to fear," said District Attorney Quinby on his trial. "He had never been in Boston before in his life. He had no acquaintance there. There was no reason why he should be registered 'and friend' at the hotel. There was no reason, so far as he was concerned, that he should be introduced under a fictitious name, except that his employer had been schooled in the wonderful university known as" the oil combination. In Boston, on a Monday, on the Common, within sight of the equestrian statue of the Father of his Country, his former employer made a contract with Albert to pay him $1500 a year for doing nothing except staying away from Buffalo.

"You won't have much to do, and you can stay here in Boston, and keep away from those fellows, and we will protect you."

"Who's going to make up if those fellows come on and sue me for damages? Who will make up this loss that I have been going to by sacrificing my property?"

"Leave that to me; I will fix that all right. You do just as I tell you, and you will come out all right. . . . Go wherever you like, stop where you like, and we will pay all your expenses while you are here." [1]

[1] Trusts, Congress, 1888, pp. 821–22.

Albert loafed about Boston several weeks, sometimes helping to roll a barrel of oil in the Vacuum's store. When he wanted money he asked for it and got it. He had once been a hard drinker. Destruction was as carelessly invited upon the soul of a poor brother as upon the lives and property of competitors. He hung around Boston and Rochester nearly a year. Then his old employer, who was in California, sent for him to come there to help in a fruit cannery, his salary continuing as before. From the moment he deserted his partners, as Judge Edward Hatch, the counsel for Matthews, stated in the civil suit for damages in this conspiracy, Albert "never earned enough to cover the end of your knife-blade with salt at your dinner. But they pay him, in salary and bonus, over $4000. Why? To get him away, and to stifle lawful, legitimate, and honest competition ; to stifle that which brings into every poor man's home an article of necessity at a cheaper rate." He stayed in California a few months, and, finally, sickened of the disgraceful part he was playing, turned at bay, and gave notice that he was going to leave. "This is kind of sudden," the agent of his employers replied, but said he would write to the principal director in New York and advise that he release him. "You will give me time, won't you ? You know it takes a couple of weeks or longer to do business from here to New York." Albert waited, and in time the word came from New York. "I have heard from these parties, and they are willing to release you." [1]

Albert, who had put himself into the extraordinary position in which he was on the repeated pledges of the tempters that they would make it "all right" with him, and protect him from loss and harm, found that he had put his "trust in princes." When he came to settle he expected that those for whom he had sacrificed his honor, his property, and his career would make him some compensation. In answer to the question how much they ought to make up to him, he named $5000 or $10,000, which was certainly little enough, in view

[1] Trusts, Congress, 1888, pp. 824–25.

of the fact that the business he had sacrificed to them was one in which, as the Vacuum's career showed, $100 shares came to be worth $2666 each. But the representative of the trust declared he could not think of such a thing, and in full of all obligations gave him nothing but the balance due of the wages agreed on. Then he asked Albert to hold himself still further at their service. As they parted, he said: "Now we have settled up; now we are good friends. . . . If anything ever comes up in this matter I would like to have you stand by us. . . . We will see that you are paid all right, and give you $25 a day while we need your services." Albert replied that he did not feel under any obligations to the oil combination. "I do not know as my interest lays that way. I do not think I shall do anything to benefit them; they have injured me all that they can; they have switched me all around, all over the country; they have got me out of employ, not given me anything to do, which I sought to have them do. I do not think they have used me right, and I have sacrificed considerable money by this transaction, and you have always promised that it would be made good, and you have not done so." [1]

[1] Trusts, Congress, 1888, pp. 825–26.

CHAPTER XIX

MATTHEWS knew nothing and suspected nothing about the worst part of the plot against him until Albert's lawyer, Mr. Truesdale, nearly four years later, was called upon to testify in the suit Matthews brought for damages against the Vacuum people. This suit was to recover from them for having enticed Albert away, and having persecuted Matthews with false and malicious suits; but Truesdale's evidence at once revealed that there had been a deeper damnation still in the conspiracy against him. Mr. Matthews, one day on the street in Buffalo, ran across Albert, who had just come back from California.

"No man ever used another meaner than I have you," said the now repentant man to him, volunteering all the information he had, and agreeing to testify if called on. This revelation made the farmer-refiner a reformer. This was the public's business. If such things could be plotted and done with impunity by one man against another, there was an end forthwith of every liberty the republic boasted. Especially menacing was such a conspiracy when concerted by the rich fanatic of business against the poorer citizen to prevent the latter from disputing the claim that a great market was a private preserve, and that the right to trade in it is a privilege which "belongs to us." [1] Matthews could have used his discovery as an irresistible weapon to force his enemy to his knees, but he laid his evidence before the district attorney. This official presented it to the grand-jury, which found that

[1] See ch. xxxi.

17

the facts warranted indictments. When the first indictment was quashed on technical grounds a second grand-jury, sifting the facts, agreed with the first that the accused should be held to answer in the criminal courts. This was six years after the crime. The five persons indicted were the two former owners of the Vacuum, now the resident managers of it for the combination, and the three members of the oil trust, as the combination then called itself, who had bought the Vacuum for it, and had been elected by the trustees directors to manage it for them, and had so managed it even to the most picayune details. The case caught the ears of the world, not because crime was charged against men who had dazzled even the gold-filmed eyes of their epoch by the meteor-like flash of their flight from poverty into a larger share of "property"— the property of others—than any other group of millionaires had assimilated in an equal period; not for that, but because the charges of crime against these quickest-richest men were to be brought to trial. Members of the combination had been often accused; they had been indicted. This was the first time, as District Attorney Quinby said in his speech to the jury, that they had found a citizen honest enough and brave enough to stand up against them—the only one. "There is no man," he said, "so respected to-day in Buffalo as he for the method he has used to bring these men to justice." He succeeded in doing alone what the united producers of the oil regions failed to do, although their resources were infinitely greater. The people of the entire oil country failed utterly to do so much as get the members of the oil combination, when indicted for conspiracy in 1879, to come into court to be tried. All its principal men were indicted—the president, the vice-president, the secretary, the cashier, and others. They could not even be got to give bail. One of them had said when the indictments were found, that the case would never be tried, and it never has been. The Governor would not move to have those of the accused who were non-residents extradited, as he would have done, does daily, in the case of poor men, and the courts so tangled up the questions of procedure that the people withdrew, and left the indictments, as they remain to this day, on file in the Clarion County court, swinging like the body of some martyr on a road-side gibbet in the pagan days, polluting the air and mocking justice.[1]

That the trust was thoroughly alarmed, and saw the necessity of rallying all its resources to save itself, was apparent from the formidable display with which it appeared in the court-room. Present with the five defendants, as if also on trial—a solid phalanx—were its president, the vice-president, the manager of its pipe-line system, the principal representatives of the trust in Buffalo, and many others. Their regular attorney of New York was present with two of the leading lawyers of Buffalo. Besides these there was a distinguished man from Rochester, reputed the ablest lawyer in western New York, whose voice is often heard in the Supreme Court at Washington. He had two important members of the Rochester bar as assistants, one of them in the summing up unmercifully scored by the District Attorney for fixing witnesses; and, not least, a well-known United States District Attorney, who made the convention speeches by which a distinguished citizen of Buffalo was nominated, successively and successfully, for Sheriff, Mayor, Governor, and President. The defendants come here, said the people's attorney, with the best legal talent the country affords, the best the profession can furnish; for the trust—"they are practically the defendants in this action—with its great wealth, has the choice of legal talent." Other eminent lawyers were also consulted, but were not present. Never was a weak defence made the most of with more skill than these gentlemen exhibited upon the trial. . . . But great as was the ability of the defence, Mr. George T. Quinby, the District Attorney, and his assistant, William L. Marcy, proved a match for them. Every political and moneyed influence that could be brought to bear was used to mislead the District Attorney, but all to no purpose. The jury could see that the complainant, Charles B.

[1] History, etc., Petroleum Producers' Unions. Trusts, Congress, 1888, pp. 690–716.

Matthews, did not get the indictment to sell out, otherwise he would have sold it out and not have insisted upon a trial.   The fact that the case was on trial, at a cost of many thousands of dollars to the defendants, was conclusive upon that point. An emissary, trying to get Matthews to call off the District Attorney and to hush up this criminal prosecution, said the oil trust could "give him anything, even to being governor of a Western territory." [1]   "You will have a chance," Matthews told the District Attorney, "to line the street from your house to the City Hall with gold bricks."   But this public prosecutor had no price.   He grasped the full scope of this extraordinary case, which involved not only a crime against persons and against the people, but against that true commerce of reciprocal and equal service on which alone the new civilization of humanity can rest.

The room in the Buffalo court-house, where the case was being heard, was bright with the sunshine of a May day, putting out the shadows of indictments and verdicts lurking in corners and pigeon-holes.   Although it was a criminal case, the on-looker saw, strange as it seemed, that whatever strain there was in the situation appeared to be felt least by the accused, and most by the public and the jury.   The nearer the eyes of the on-looker travelled towards the prisoners, the lighter and brighter was the scene.   Close to the accused sat a bench full of notables, evidently friends lending moral support.   That the bench was occupied by men of importance was evident.   They were supported by platoons of eminent counsel and detectives.   Only the judge betrayed no consciousness of the presence of the herd of millionaires.   The whisperings and pointings and namings by one spectator to another showed that the people's curiosity was greatly excited by the sight of the richest men in the country, if not in the world, with attendant millionaire esquires in or about the dock of a criminal court.   On this particular day the notables and their suite had come in specially good-humor.   Nods of kindly

---

[1] Testimony, Trusts, Congress, 1888, p. 942.

recognition went about and smiles rippled everywhere as, settled into their seats, they listened to the recital by the witnesses. It had been as good as a play to hear the working-man, Albert, tell on the stand how he had been bribed and threatened with ruin until he yielded to the suggestion that he should "bust up" the works of his friends, partners, and employers, and run away. There had been nothing funny to Albert in those threats: "We will ruin you," "We will crush you," "You will lose what little you have got left." [1]

"Then the compensation you got was $300 and the pleasure of selling out your friends?" Albert was asked by one of the great lawyers.[2] Albert did not smile, but "they seemed to enjoy hugely," reported the press, "the idea that men could be bought so cheap." The eminent counsel of the prisoners took the cue from their clients, and treated the proceedings as a farce. When the State's Attorney was questioning his witnesses, they objected to his questions with laughs and sneers until he became indignant, and asked, with considerable emphasis, to have the joke explained to him—a need the jury also felt, as their verdict showed. When the Boston agent of the trust told that his instructions from headquarters were that if there was to be any selling at a loss to let the new competitor have the loss,[3] they all laughed again.

So all the morning there had been fine sport in the court-room, and the good-humor had risen higher with every fresh incident in the entertainment until Albert's wife took her place in the witness-box. She, too, raised a laugh, but it was not she who laughed. Serious enough she was when taking her place on the witness-stand. She had to face these gentlemen, before whose hundreds of millions her husband's little venture had withered, but, as she herself afterwards said: "I wasn't afraid of them, but I was nervous. But as soon as I got talking I didn't care anything for them, although they all sat there in front, in a row, looking straight at me."

The wife's story to the jury showed how such an adventure

---

[1] Trusts, Congress, 1888, pp. 814–15.   [2] Same, p. 834.   [3] Same, p. 847.

appeared when looked at and experienced from the woman's stand-point—the home-maker's and the home-keeper's—which the smiling row before her were as little able to grasp as the participants in a pigeon-shooting match to look upon that vision of flames, demons, and death-dealing thunder from the point of view of the hapless birds. A bright-faced, brown-eyed, pleasant-looking woman, as she took the stand she looked what she was—an artisan's honest wife. " My husband," she said, "had been employed in the Vacuum oil works at Roches-ter thirteen or fourteen years, and we had accumulated some property—mortgages and money and real estate. We moved to Buffalo, April 5, 1881, where he was superintending the building of the Buffalo works." [1] After Albert had yielded to the threats and the temptation, and had fixed the stills and the fires for an explosion, he fled without a word to his wife or his associates, hid, under an assumed name, in Boston, and then travelled over the continent for a year—from Buffalo to Boston, to Rochester, to San Francisco.

" When you left Buffalo did you leave any word with Matthews where you were going ?"

" No, sir."

" Or your wife ?"

" No, sir."

While the wife was in Buffalo wondering what had become of her husband, he was in New York with his venerable ex-employer, getting lessons like the following in the secrets of building up a great commercial enterprise:

" The best thing you can do, Albert," said the latter, " is to go and write a telegram, and tell your wife to go back to Rochester."

" You'd better write it; I am a poor writer," said Albert.

" No," he said; " I do not want to appear in this case at all. Write it so," he continued, " that she can move on the Fourth of July, and they can't attach her things." [2]

The first word she got from her husband was this telegram

---

[1] Trusts, Congress, 1888, p. 842.

[2] Testimony, Trusts, Congress, 1888, p. 821.

to move between two days, and back to Rochester the dutiful woman packed herself and her things.

"It was two or three weeks before I heard from him direct or knew just where he was," she said.

"I asked Charles"—one of the two managers—"how Al was, and he said Al was all right."

"Would he tell you where he was?" the State's Attorney asked.

"No, sir; when I wrote to my husband I left the direction blank, and gave the letter to Charley. I got an answer through Charley." [1]

For three weeks they would not let her know where her husband was. "Think of that," said the District Attorney. "She had to go and take her poor little letter to her husband, thinking, perhaps, if he was away from her tender care he might get to drinking, because he does drink some; but when with his wife they lived year in and year out without his tasting a drop; . . . afraid that he might get to drinking, and that she could not watch over him. . . . It was a cruel thing to do."

"C. told me to go to the real-estate agents," Albert's wife continued, "and try to sell our property and get it into money. He made out a list of real-estate agents from the city directory. I guess that is all he did about assisting me in the sale of the property."

"I asked C. if my husband could not come home from Boston. I was sick. He said 'Yes.' Al came home and stayed a week or two. Then he went back to Boston. C. told me they did not want the Buffalo company to know where Al was." [2]

Albert was a man infirm under temptation. The employer knew, by fourteen years' acquaintance, the weakness this man had acquired in his service in the army. He gave him idleness, money, temptation, and an assumed name to go to the devil with, if that agent of the trust was to be found in Boston.

"You want to take good care of Al," said the good old man

---

[1] Testimony, Trusts, Congress, 1888, pp. 842–43.   [2] Same, pp. 843–44.

to his clerk in Boston, "and not let him get homesick. If he wants any money, let him have it." Albert travelled the broad way made smooth for him.

"Of course I never went around with him," said the clerk, in a deposition ; "a porter that I had was the party that went around with him in the evening. I would hear what was going on, and I could judge about the size of Al's head when he came around in the morning."

With all Albert's faults he kept one dignity to the end which makes him tower above his seducers—the dignity of the laborer. A life's discipline in daily toil had made his whole fibre too honest to enjoy idleness, even at the rate of $1500 a year. He was free to come and go amid the gaudy joys of a great city, as irresponsible under the assumed name given him as if he wore the ring of Gyges. He had money for the asking, and boon companions. But the habit of a lifetime of honest, hard manual work was too deeply ingrained into the very substance of his nature for him to become a cheap American Faust, revelling in a pinchbeck paradise. This simple son of poverty had all his life handled only real things, and had at every point had the mind's native wantonness and riot checked by the hard surface which had calloused his hands, and the outer air which had cooled him as he worked. His were dreams of honest rest earned by honest work, and of family joys. The self-indulgence that was revealed by the "size of his head in the morning" was an animal exuberance that, as the result showed, did but stain the "rose-mesh of his flesh," and went no deeper. Albert could not stand the idleness of his Boston life. He went back to Rochester.

"I want something to do."

"What brings you here?" said his employer. "Go back."

After hanging around the office in Boston a few weeks longer, the workman's nature reasserted itself again. He went back again to Rochester. "I want something to do." "We have not got anything for you to do just now," he was told. "You are all right."[1]

[1] Trusts, Congress, 1888, p. 823.

Months of idleness were interrupted only by odd jobs, like superintending the digging of a ditch or the sinking of a salt-well. Time and again, though he was drawing his pay of $125 a month, he went, as he told the story in court, to repeat the plea for "something to do." Finally, the elder of the managers, who was in California, sent for him. He was to be made "an independent man," the new promise ran, but really, as the sequel showed, was, if possible, to be kept out of the way of too inquisitive juries and prosecuting attorneys. The wife, treated as a mere pawn in the game, protested vehemently. "I went down to the Vacuum Oil Company's office, and asked C. to give Al something else to do. I didn't want him to go to California. He said that there was not anything that he knew that he could do."

"I don't want Al to go. I won't go. Give him something else to do."

"I have nothing else." [1]

She had to yield, and her husband left her to go to California. His employer persuaded Albert to buy a piece of land in California. "He seemed to be very anxious to locate me there." [2] Albert sent to his wife for the money, but the shrewd little woman sent only half. "I thought I would let him pay it out of his pay." With the same good sense the wife had not sold all the property when sent out alone among the real-estate men. "I did not sell the real estate," she said; "I thought there was too much expense." [3] She was not with her husband when the rupture came in California. The first news the anxious wife had of a change in her husband's affairs was when "Charley" came to her, as she was sitting one summer evening on the porch of a neighbor's house, and told her "Al" had quit them. "I do not know what to make of it," he continued; "I think he must be crazy or something." [4]

It was not until his return that she learned the details of the painful experience he had been through. When it was

[1] Trusts, Congress, 1888, p. 844.   [2] Same, p. 825.
[3] Same, p. 845.   [4] Same, p. 844.

heard that Albert, upon his return from California, had made restitution as far as he was able, by telling what he knew to the authorities, to aid them in bringing the principals in the crime to justice, there was consternation in the trust. One of its detectives had been captain of the company Albert was in during the Civil War. The captain now presented himself before Albert as he went to his work in Corry, Pennsylvania, where he had gone after his return from California, and became sociable rapidly. He had great plans for Albert, and came to the house to discuss them confidentially. Albert and his wife had been simple folks to start with, but they had learned a thing or two by this time. The captain's desire for confidential talk with his old comrade was so intense that it would have been rude in Albert's wife to thwart it. She packed off her daughter on an errand, and announced that she had a call up the street, and would leave them to themselves; but she did not add, as she might have done, that during her absence she would be represented by the Chief of Police, whose appetite for confidential communications was as keen as the captain's, but whose retiring disposition kept him in the dark seclusion of an adjoining room, with his ear to the crack of the door.

"Wouldn't Albert like to go to Russia?" the captain asked his dear friend the private, whose existence he had never personally recognized when they were so close together during the Civil War. "If the Court will allow me to show by this witness," said the prosecuting attorney, "that the captain came there as a detective for the oil trust, and made a proposition, after the indictments were found, to Albert to flee the country, and go with him to Russia." One of the army of trust lawyers was instantly on his feet with "I object." The judge sustained him, and the testimony was shut out.

Albert's wife kept close to his side, and held him steady. No, Albert did not care to go to Russia. Advertisements of an alum-mine in Corry then began to appear in newspapers where Albert's attention could be called to them. By a lucky chance the captain happened to know the capitalists whose boundless powers of enterprise could find full outlet only by developing the hitherto unsuspected resources of Corry for supplying the nations of the earth with alum. By a joyful coincidence, these capitalists wanted for superintendent of their bottomless alum-mines just such a man as the captain knew his dear Albert to be. Would Albert like to go to Italy to learn the true science of alum manufacture, and to show the effete monarchies how an American could disembowel the earth of its alum? Salary, $5000 and expenses. No, Albert had no unslaked ambition to go to Italy as superintendent of mines of alum, or green cheese, or any other lunar commodity.

At least, Albert would take a drink? That poor Albert would do; and when he failed to come home at night his wife went up and down the streets seeking him. "A persistent effort had been made" by the trust, Mr. Matthews testified, "to get Albert out of the country. I was afraid they would get him away, as he might not be used in this case. Men had been sent there to get him drunk, and had debauched him."[1] Money was potent enough to persuade lawyers to make it a part of their professional duty to help in this. One of the trust's lawyers sat with Albert and its detective in the stall of a cheap saloon, and plied him with liquor to get from him some letters of Matthews' they wanted. "There they sat," said the keeper of the saloon; ". . . they got what they called for, probably. . . . I couldn't tell how many drinks they got into Albert on that occasion; I think they drank there."[2]

While this courtship was in progress with Albert in Pennsylvania, wires were being pulled to get him indicted in New York. The grand-jury of Rochester was asked to indict him for receiving stolen property in a watch trade he had made seven years before. This would have ruined him as a witness in the forthcoming criminal case against the members of the oil trust, but the grand-jury decided that there was no evi-

[1] Court Stenographer's Report, p. 2049. The last statement is omitted in the transcript furnished by the trust for the Congress Trust Report of 1888.

[2] Testimony, Trusts, Congress, 1888, p. 911.

dence on which to indict.   When Adam Cleber, a stolid-look-
ing German laborer, who worked in the same place with
Albert in Corry, took the stand for the State at the close, an
eager excitement filled the court-room.   The State's Attorney
was known to have his darkest sensation still in reserve.
What it was he would not, of course, disclose in advance, but
those hardly less familiar than he with the evidence hinted
that the fertile genius of the captain, having exhausted itself in
the ideas of the trips to Russia and Italy, had fallen back upon
the genius of his superiors, and had arranged to have Albert
go a-hunting, and get a "bust-up" as much as possible like
the one he had been induced to attempt upon his employers
and partners.

"Did the captain tell you what he wanted you to do to
Albert?" Cleber was asked.

"Yes—"   That was as far as Cleber got.

"I object!" screamed one of the lawyers.

"I propose to show that the captain made a request of this
witness in regard to what he should do to Albert, and what
he should come and swear to about Albert, there being no
truth in the matter he wanted Cleber to swear to," the State's
Attorney urged to the Court.   The judge took the matter
home for consideration over-night, and announced in the
morning that he would not admit the evidence.   It was acknowledged by one of the lawyers for the members of the
trust on trial that he had employed the captain to get evidence for them; but the judge, instead of admitting Cleber's
testimony, and leaving the question of its value to be settled
by the jury, excluded it.

In his closing speech District Attorney Quinby said:
"Why, in Heaven's name, my friends, didn't you place the
captain on this witness-stand?   He would have been a feast
for you and a feast for me.   His ways have been curious and
sinuous, his methods have been peculiar and corrupting, and
they did not dare to put him on the stand because if they
did he would have left it to go to prison.   That is the reason.
They know it."

The brave and steadfast woman told her part of this story on the witness-stand. Her home had been broken up again and again. As she herself said afterwards: "I had to live with my carpets packed, and moved around like a gypsy." Her husband had been tempted to commit a crime which compelled him to lead the life of a fugitive. He had been spirited away and secreted; she had not been allowed to know where he was, and could communicate with him only through a third person; they had moved around, in her expressive phrase, until they had moved into two rooms; the savings of fifteen years' hard work were all gone, and the independent business, in which her husband had just got his footing, swept away. He and she faced the world with no other assets than their child and the palms of their hard-working hands.

"Well, it's taken all we had," she says; "we've lost it all, but I'd rather it would be so than to have the money they have, and go about hiding and sneaking. I'd like money, but not so well as that. When I said to 'Charley,' 'I shall have to sell all my furniture'—'Oh, that's nothing.' And when I told him it had cost us $100 to pay the expenses of selling real estate—'That isn't much.' It wasn't much to them, but it was to us, who had made every dollar by hard work. Well, we'll have to do without the money, and just live along by honest work. We can live that way. We have had all this trouble and lost our money, and haven't made money enough to buy a calico dress."

All the good that had come of this loss of savings and home and honor had gone to those at the bar of justice and their associates sitting in the tickled row before her. On the cross-examination, which was to crush the witness and her damaging testimony, the distinguished counsel, not content with all the suffering and loss already inflicted on this wife, tried to humiliate her still further, but the woman's wit of truth was too much for the lawyer's wit of wile.

"Don't you recollect," the lawyer asked, "that you went to the house of the manager of the Vacuum, and that you saw him in the parlor, and that you asked him to take your husband back?

"I never asked him to take my husband back."

"Then you did not ask him at the time and place I spoke of?"

"I never asked him anywhere to take him back."

"Don't you recollect upon that occasion being considerably affected, and asking him to take your husband back, and his speaking of the way in which he had left the company, which he characterized as shameful, and that you cried—shed tears?"

"I never asked him to take him back. I recollect going there. I recollect I felt bad, because I was talked to so much about it. I had reason to feel bad. I am trying to tell the truth as near as I can."

"Then what was the occasion of your bad feeling?"

"It was because I thought we were going to lose everything, and would not have nothing left. That is what I felt bad for—was shedding tears for, if I did. I don't know as I did." [1]

Then came the laugh. From millionaire to lesser millionaire went the enlarging laugh. The mighty cortege of the retained ex-judges, famous constitutional and criminal lawyers, detectives, camp-followers laughed. It was the laugh of hundreds of millions, and it clinked and tinkled and rang. As if every mouth were a bagful of gold, and as if every bag had burst, the golden notes of mirth filled the air, and struck the ceiling, and rolled over the floor, rebounded and fell and rose in mellow chimes of sound, and the golden rain dripped everywhere. Millions on millions, tens of millions, hundreds of millions of the coin of the republic, and in every coin a cackle.

"Yes, they all laughed at me," the little woman told her friends; "it looked like such a great joke to them. Perhaps I did not tell it very well, but I told the truth."

In closing the case the State's Attorney said to the jury:

[1] Court Stenographer's Report, pp. 454–55.

"A sorrow was placed on that woman's heart that can never be removed. One of the pathetic things in this case was that when this woman was on the stand, telling her little story, how they were afraid they might lose the few thousand dollars they had saved, the $6000 or $7000 they had been struggling for for fifteen years, these New York gentlemen with their millions laughed in her face at the idea of her being sorry to lose the pittance of $6000 or $7000. It was the only time in the case, really, I felt that these gentlemen were outraging common decency."[1]

Some time after the trial was over, and sentence passed and satisfied, these men sent for Albert to come to Rochester. He went with witnesses. There in the office of a leading lawyer he was tempted with desperate propositions to do something or say something that would break the force with which these disclosures must act on public opinion. "They need not think," he replied, "that they can get me to make a false oath to let them out of a hole. I would not do it for all the combined wealth of the trust. When my wife was on the stand they laughed her in the face when she told about losing all we had. Do you suppose any man with a particle of American blood could have any love for them? I think as much of my wife and daughter as any of them of theirs, and I will do nothing to disgrace them." This hard-working and hard-living laborer and his wife had, by thirteen or fourteen years of toil and stinting, saved $6000. The laughers had in the same time saved about $300,000,000, and somebody else had done all the work. The poor man and his wife had been afraid that the $300,000,000 would devour the $6000. It said it would, and it had. Shall not they laugh who win?

[1] Court Stenographer's Report, p. 2164.

CHAPTER XX

THE District Attorney put the president of the light of the world on the stand. His evidence showed that the purchase of the three-quarter's interest in the Vacuum Company, sold because "there were restrictions in the shipments," was made by the three New York men on trial. "They are shareholders in the trust," he said. When they bought the stock they transferred it to the oil trust. He had known of the contemplated purchase. Having thus proved that the three indicted directors from New York on trial were members of the oil trust, and were managing the Vacuum for it, the District Attorney proceeded, in pursuance of a logical plan of inquiry, to bring before the jury what the trust was, and its relations to the companies it covered.

"What is it . . . if you know?" the District Attorney asked. The president, through his counsel, objected to the question.

"What is the object of this?" the judge asked the District Attorney.

The trust, the District Attorney explained, owns a majority of the stock of this Vacuum Company and others, and controls the manufacture in this country of substantially all the lubricating and illuminating oils. These defendants belonging to the trust, and "one of these being chairman of a committee of the trust, it was the desire and motive of the three to do away with competition, to destroy and ruin the competitive works in Buffalo."

The Court asked the president of the trust if it was a manufacturing company.

"It is not, your honor."

The Court ruled out the question "What is it?" although in doing so he used language apparently contradicting his ruling, saying, in effect, that it was "quite immaterial what the objects or purposes of the oil trust are, unless these defendants are in some way interested so as to create a motive to do what it is claimed they did do." Again, when the District Attorney sought to ascertain in what other corporations engaged in the manufacture of oil in 1879, 1880, and 1881 the trustees on trial owned stock, it was objected to and the objection sustained, although the Court but a few moments before had said, "I will allow you to show everything these defendants have done upon the question of motive, . . . to show what their business is, the companies they have stock in, whether it is an oil company or some other company—that is, any company engaged in the manufacture of oil that would come in competition with the Buffalo company. . . ."

The judge, declaring that he would admit such evidence, refused to admit it. What the District Attorney would have been able to uncover as to the responsibility of the "trustees" for what was done by the subordinate companies, the reader, freer than the jury in this case, can find out for himself.

The nine trustees, of whom three were on trial, owned as their individual property more than half of this as of every establishment in the trust. They decided who were to be elected directors and officers of each company. They exercised full control over these officers when elected. They declared the dividends. The profits of all these shares are put into one purse, and distributed in quarterly dividends among the trustees in proportion to their interest in the trust —the purse-holder.[1] In the case of the Vacuum Company, accordingly, we find that the minutes of stockholders' meetings record the presence of members of the oil trust, in person and by proxy, representing a majority of the stock, electing the officers and directors, and declaring the dividends. How

---

[1] Testimony, Rice cases, before Interstate Commerce Commission, 1887, Nos. 51–60, p. 367. Testimony, Trusts, New York Senate, 1888, pp. 571, 577, 578, 579, 658. Testimony, Trusts, Congress, 1888, p. 295.

18

thorough and minute is the supervision over the vassal companies an employé, who had been in the service of the combination for several years in a confidential way, and "had access to every book and paper and their cipher arrangement," has told.[1] They "control every movement of every branch of their business." The subordinate companies "make a report every day of all their business. . . . They have blanks there on which they make a report of all their shipments, where shipped, and who shipped to, and all their purchases; and they report every month the exact percentage they have made out of their crude oil, of all the different products they get out of it. They report everything in detail."

This was in 1879. Ten years later, in 1888, the testimony of the president shows that the system is the same. "They know the cost at every refinery. They get such reports once in thirty days; each report shows just what it has cost for everything. . . . Made out on regular blanks."[2]

But when put on the stand in this case, in Buffalo, he had professed himself altogether ignorant of any such reports.[3] Asked if the Vacuum Company had made them, he replied:

"I can't recall any such reports."

Asked if it was obligatory upon the Vacuum Oil Company to make reports, he said:

"I can't state."

But the manager's testimony in the same case shows that the system of reports which his superior "could not recall" was in regular operation.

"There are reports of sales of the Vacuum Oil Company made to certain parties in New York."[4]

The three trustees who bought the control of the Vacuum stock did not keep it for themselves. They transferred it to the trust, and received for it shares in the trust. They were

[1] Testimony, Alleged Discriminations in Railroad Freights, Ohio House of Representatives, 1879, pp. 36–39.

[2] Testimony, Trusts, New York Senate, 1888, p. 410.

[3] Court Stenographer's Report.

[4] Testimony, Trusts, Congress, 1888, p. 871.

not stockholders in the Vacuum, but stockholders in the trust. It was the trust which was the real stockholder in the Vacuum. The profits on this Vacuum stock, therefore, went into the common fund in which the trust accumulated the profits of all its controlling ownerships in companies all over the country — all over the world. Every trustee shared in the profits of every company so controlled, whether in the United States or Europe or Asia. The president of the trust, now on the witness-stand, was a large participator in the profits of the Vacuum, because he was a large owner in the trust which possessed three-quarters of it. Similarly as to the three trustees indicted and on trial, and every other trustee.[1] The case was interwoven, notwithstanding the exclusion of this by the judge, with evidence that the three members of the trust on trial were the managers of the company for the trust, and were consulted habitually about the current details by the salaried agents.

"After this purchase was made did you continue to represent the purchasers in the management of the affairs of the Vacuum Oil Company?" one of the three was asked.

"I did."

After the purchase of the Vacuum by the trust, Mr. Matthews, before he left to go into business on his own account, had to go to its office in New York half a dozen times, to see the New York directors when he wanted instructions. His testimony on this point covers thirty pages of the official testimony, and shows repeated interviews between him and the members of the trust about every kind of detail of the business of the Vacuum. When Matthews asked the manager of the Vacuum to give him more pay, the latter had told him to speak to one of the trustees — one of the three now on trial. "It will be as he says about it." Again, as to another matter, he said to Matthews: "I cannot tell you. There is no use for me to pretend that we run our business, for we do not."[2]

This evidence must be sought in the original records of the

---

[1] Trusts, New York Senate, 1888, pp. 456, 571.
[2] Court Stenographer's Report, p. 892.

case at Buffalo, as it is left out in the transcript furnished by the trust to the committee of Congress, which represents the case against the two local managers only. The Rochester manager, after the explosion, and at the time of sending for Albert to come to New York, telegraphed to his son: "Our views with regard to Albert confirmed." By whom? as Matthews' lawyer asked. The manager saw one of the three accused trustees in New York after he returned from the trip to Boston to hide Albert. "I told him that I had hired him," he testified.

The trustee denied this, as the president denied the monthly reports. But he has himself furnished the evidence that his employé told the truth. In their answer in court to the allegations of the suit against them for damages, he and the other two trustees concerned in the Vacuum direction testified that they advised the Rochester managers " to endeavor to retain the said" Albert, . . . "and after" he "had left the employment of the Vacuum Oil Company . . . they further advised that he should be re-employed if it could be done by reasonable increase of his wages. They were afterwards informed that he had been re-employed." This shows they knew about the negotiations before, during, and after. They knew the man was to have more wages, though the increase was only $300 a year, and their income was millions yearly. When he had been gotten away they were informed of that too. The District Attorney knew all about this answer in the civil case, but under the statutes of New York it could not be used in a criminal prosecution against those who had made it. He put the trustee on the stand, and did his best to get him to tell the same story, but in vain.

The body-guard of lawyers surrounding the great men who made the court-room a veritable curiosity-shop for the people of Buffalo, did a deal of acting throughout the trial to impress on the jury that the whole proceeding was a farce. They laughed and yawned and pooh-poohed, and sneered at the District Attorney's questions and points, and went through all kinds of dumb-shows of indignation and ennui that their clients should be so needlessly called on to waste priceless time. But this could not prevent their faces from lengthening as the story was told by witness after witness, as more than one observant reporter saw and noted. When the evidence was all in, and District Attorney Quinby had closed his case, the situation was desperate. There was no doubt about that. The great men of the trust on trial had been proved to be the actual directors of the Vacuum at every turn of its daily affairs. Before any evidence was introduced for the defence, one of the distinguished lawyers arose and moved the discharge of the three members of the trust, who were a majority of the Board of Directors of the Vacuum Company, and managed it for the trust. The prosecution were not taken unawares by the motion. The District Attorney's able assistant, William L. Marcy, had gathered all the precedents and equipped himself to resist the discharge. He and the District Attorney fought hard to have the principals in the company go to the jury with their agents, but in vain. Mr. Marcy pointed out that, as shown in the case of The People *vs.* Mather, "to charge partners as conspirators it is not necessary even to show that they were the original conspirators. It is sufficient if at a subsequent time they become party to it by accepting the benefits derived from the conspiracy. The case lays that down in exact terms."

The Judge: "Must there not be an adoption?"

Mr. Marcy: "That is an adoption—accepting the benefits."

The Judge: "They may accept the benefits without knowing."

Mr. Marcy: "Then the jury may infer that knowledge from all the circumstances. The jury are the tribunal to determine whether or not the parties had the knowledge." Mr. Marcy pointed out that there was everything to lead the jury to infer that these men were parties to the plan. "Where did the meetings of the Board of Directors take place? At Rochester, where the works are? No; at New York, where these men carried on their other business. The Rochester representatives dance in attendance wherever these New York parties desire them to go." He pointed out to the judge that the trustee whom Albert met in New York after the explosion knew of the plan to take him to Boston. He showed that the same trustee, when remonstrated with by Matthews for bringing patent suits without foundation, said that he intended to carry them on, and if he was beaten in one court, he would carry them to a higher court. Just in the same way the Rochester representative of the trust had said: "I will bring lawsuits against you. I will get an injunction against you." "When the Rochester manager," said Mr. Marcy, "hired Albert, he did not pretend to be able to make a bargain until he had been to New York and consulted about it. He was in New York before he telegraphed to him to come to New York. This significant fact points home the conspiracy upon the gentlemen who reside in New York."

But the judge, and not the jury, rendered the verdict as to the three members of the trust on trial. He failed to remember or observe the law that leaves it to the jury to render the verdict. He announced that he had decided to grant the motion for their discharge. There was silence in the court-room for a moment. Then: "Gentlemen of the jury, hearken to your verdict as advised by the Court," came in sonorous tones from the clerk; "you find the defendants"—naming the three members of the oil trust at the bar—"not guilty of the crime, as charged in the indictment, so say you all."

The jury looked scared at being addressed so peremptorily, but said nothing.

"The New York men looked happy," said one of the observers, "but their Rochester associates and codefendants did not smile." Upon the discharge of the trustees, one of the Buffalo dailies said that whether there was any conspiracy at all is an undecided question, but it should be remembered that the oil trust and the Vacuum Oil Company "have been honorably acquitted of the charge of having anything to do with the matter. As the case now stands, it is simply The People against" —the two Rochester managers.

Poor men! It was for this that they succumbed to the

attacks of the oil trustees upon their business, sold them for $200,000 three-quarters of a concern which produced $300,-000 in dividends in one year for the lucky conquerors, became vassals instead of masters in their own refinery. It was for $10,000 a year, divided into $6500 for one and $3500 for the other, that they undertook to fetch and carry for their suzerains, even to the gates of the penitentiary; and when discovery and conviction came, to bear in silence upon their own shoulders the guilt and shame from which others got only "more."

The trial of the two remaining defendants proceeded. Neither of them took the stand. In a deposition the elder said it was Albert who had spoken about misplacing the pipes; but when asked what he said in reply to a suggestion, which no one better than he knew the significance of, he replied: "I made no reply to it, but I thought it would be a very scandalous proceeding." [1] Albert had told how, in conversation in California, his employer had described his plans with regard to Matthews.

"We would have just got them fellows in a boat, right in the middle of the stream, and we would have tipped them two over, and drowned them, and you would have been all right." [2] "If I ever made such a remark," this defendant deposed, "it was in a playful humor. I am in the habit of making playful remarks."

Witness after witness had to confess, under cross-examination, that his testimony had been written and rewritten by himself or the lawyer for the defence, and carefully conned before coming on the stand. The District Attorney asked one of these tutored witnesses why he had read over the written preparation of his testimony in the rotunda of the court-house just before going on the stand.

"I read it over," he replied, lucidly, "for the simple reason of reading it over."

"Just to practise in reading?"

[1] Testimony, Trusts, Congress, 1888, p. 869.　　　[2] Same, p. 825.

"Well, perhaps we might call it practice in reading." [1]

"This preparation of the testimony," said the District Attorney to the jury, "which I stigmatize as infamous, this going to a witness and writing him down, and having him fix it, and write it over again, and keeping it in his mind, and reading it over, and so going on the stand, is not the way to try a lawsuit, in my mind. I write nothing down. I coach no witnesses. I want a witness to tell me his story. I put him on the stand and he tells me his story; but no writing down, no reading over. It is not right, and it is very liable to be very wrong."

Several witnesses were introduced to prove that Matthews had offered to settle the criminal prosecution. He could not have done so had he wished to. The criminal case was in the hands of the State. Of the witnesses who made this charge against Matthews, one was a stockholder in the trust, another had been a stockholder in one of its pipe lines, and both had to admit on cross-examination that the occasion of his alleged agreeing to settle the case had been that they had gone to him for their friends, unsolicited by him and unexpected, to find out at what price he would sell his works to the combination. "I was anxious to settle the criminal prosecution," said one of these ambassadors.

"Anxious for whom?" asked the ever-ready District Attorney.

"I should say—nobody," replied the witness, in confusion.

"Mr. Matthews told him," said Mr. Hiram Benedict, one of the best-known citizens of Lockport, who was present, "that if they bought the capital stock of the company they could do what they chose with the civil suits, but with the criminal suit he had nothing to do; the people had that in charge." [2]

The lawyers tried to make a jest of the whole proceeding, and affected to look upon the incidents of this rivalry with their powerful client as something too trivial to be noticed. "Is it a trivial matter," asked District Attorney Quinby, "that

---

[1] Testimony, Trusts, Congress, 1888, p. 902.   [2] Same, pp. 905–41.

it shall be decided, once for all, in a court of justice, that in an alleged republic you and I shall not start a business which is a rival to some one else? That is the issue here, and yet the lawyers for the accused tell us it is trivial. It is the most important question that was ever left to a jury of twelve men in this or any country in this age of monopoly." The jury thought so too. The meaning of the policy of suppressing competition was skilfully described by Judge Edward Hatch, Mr. Matthews' counsel in the civil suit for damages, and here again the jury, representing the people, thought so too. "When a man or a corporation is in a position to control the market as to a given article, then everybody is within their power, and it rests with their conscience to determine what shall be the price. Every time you farmers at home, or your wives or daughters, take your oil-can, turn it up, fill your lamp, and then sit down to read by it, you can understand what is meant by this proposition to crush these men out. . . . It was a matter that not only these three men were interested in, but every person that lived in the community. Competition would run along to a point where you could get the oils that you use in your families, to grease your wagons, and to burn in your houses, or for any other purpose, at a price that should give the manufacturer a fair profit, and at the lowest possible price. On the other hand, if you leave that open to these parties to regulate as they saw fit, having a monopoly of the market, then you rest upon the conscience of a corporation and put your faith in a soulless individual."

It is one of the few bright lines in this picture that whenever the people got a chance to make themselves heard, their utterance was always right and true. The four juries which passed upon the facts understood them, and had the moral standard by which to judge them aright.

One of the trust's employés was put on the stand to break the effect of the evidence that the competition of the new works had put down the price of oil. "In the early part of 1881 — the winter of 1881 " — he said, " common oil was $5\frac{1}{2}$ cents a gallon "—this to prove that the reduction had preceded the appearance of the new refinery. He was confronted by the District Attorney with one of his own bills of oil sold in February, 1881. " That would seem to be a sale of 120 degrees oil at 12 cents a gallon," he confessed, and added, awkwardly, " I was asked as to the winter of 1881. That is not the winter of 1881 as I understand. I meant to speak from July, 1881, and so on." [1]

The great lawyers held up to the ridicule of the jury the idea that the gases of distilling petroleum were dangerous. Matthews stated on the stand that he had seen this gas burn up derricks, property, and several men. The lawyers could not let anything so absurd go unchallenged.

" Did it explode ?" he was asked smartly.

" Yes, sir."

" And how did the ' explosion ' burn up the men and property ?" with a knowing look to the jury.

" The gases crept quietly to the boilers, unobserved," said the witness, " and all at once the whole atmosphere was ablaze."

The witnesses who tried to prove that no harm could have resulted from the tampering with the still broke down. One of them was the inspector of oils at the combination's refinery at Cleveland. He, too, had once been an independent refiner, but had passed under the yoke. He declared with every possible variation of phrase that there could not have been an explosion at the Buffalo works; but the District Attorney got out of him piecemeal admissions that the " escaping petroleum gases would be inflammable"; that " in a damp day you would expect them to settle close to the still"; that then, if they came in contact with fire, " you would have a large flash, and consume those vapors; if a person was in the vicinity he would burn."

" I ask you if it would be a safe thing to fill a still with 175 barrels of petroleum, put under it an extremely hot fire, so that the front portion of the still is a cherry red, and a weighted safety-valve is blown off—would you consider that a safe thing to do ?"

[1] Testimony, Trusts, Congress, 1888, p. 939.

"I would not."

Still another of these witnesses ended, like Balaam, by saying just the opposite of what had been wanted of him. He testified that the escape of gases from the stills, and even their ignition, was a matter of no consequence — "it may occur at any time"—until he was cross-examined. It turned out then that his own works had been burned three times by the gases from distillation taking fire. "These gases," he had to admit, "took fire and burned the receiving-house. A man got burned up with it."

"Are you willing," the District Attorney asked, sarcastically, "to go down to the Buffalo works and have them run some vapor, on a quiet day, on the ground, and let you stand in the middle of it and touch it off?"

"I am not anxious to do that."[1]

Every one looked to see Matthews crushed by the cross-examination, in accordance with the widely advertised promises of the counsel on the other side.

"As he stood up to take the oath," said the New York *World*, "and confronted the men with whom he had been at sword's-point for six years, men of unlimited wealth and almost unlimited influence, and controlling the most gigantic monopoly of any age or any country, Charles B. Matthews looked, as a good observer said, what he proved himself to be, a fighter, who will never know when he is whipped. Hard knocks and a struggle of years against an all-powerful enemy have whitened his hair, and set firm, hard lines about his face. His eyes are deep-set under a protruding forehead and black, bushy lashes, and are dark, firm, and searching. His jet-black beard is luxuriant but coarse, his whole head and face bespeak the dogged persistence in following a foe that is characteristic of the man. He is tall, well built, and with those whom he knows to be friends he is kindly and almost jovial in his manner." He told his story, and the jury believed it. One of the most damaging portions of his testimony was that

---

[1] Testimony, Trusts, Congress, 1888, pp. 932–33, 937.

given to connect the New York members of the trust with the conspiracy by showing that they had the actual, practical, continuous management of the Vacuum in matters small as well as large. Matthews, when in their employ, was kept running to New York continually to see one or the other of them about some detail of the business. Seeking to break down the force of this testimony, the big gun of the legal battery opened on him.

"But you did not see the name" of the oil combination "up over the office that you went into (in New York)?"

"I do not think I ever saw the name over the office that I went into. I think that name is not often in view over where they do business."

"What makes you think so?"

"My experience and observation."

"What experience and observation have you had?"

"Do you want I should tell it all?"

"No, you need not tell it all. We will let that go now." Matthews had been in their employ. He knew about the staff of lobbyists they keep to go from capital to capital as needed.

For lack of evidence the jury was offered abuse of Matthews, spoken by the brilliant attorney on a shout which enabled the populace outside the court-house to hear his speech, and, as the verdict proved, deafened the jury to his eloquence. The jury preferred the view given by the District Attorney. "When I look upon the troubled face of Matthews," said District Attorney Quinby in his closing of the case, "I know what is coming upon his head. When I know the struggle he has gone through, the integrity that is in his heart, I would say to him, 'Well done, good and faithful servant, you have withstood the powerful arm of this insatiable corporation. You stand to-day honored from one end of this land to the other.' ... I am proud that in the county of Erie has been born a gentleman who has had the bravery and fortitude he has shown."

CHAPTER XXI

CRIME CHEAPER THAN COMPETITION

THE jury was composed of nine farmers, one tailor, one store-keeper, and one railroad foreman. "So intelligent a jury," said the Buffalo *Express*, "is proof perfect that the verdict it returns is the only one warranted by the law and evidence." The jury found all the defendants guilty whom the court allowed them to try. The verdict, "Guilty as charged in the indictment," was given May 18, 1887. Every possibility of appeal and reversal was resorted to. The judge granted a stay, and this left the defendants unsentenced. A motion for a new trial postponed the day of fate until December 24, 1887.

When the judge decided against the new trial an appeal was taken, and was carried through every court except the highest. Legal procedure in New York makes the courts a hunting preserve for those who can afford the luxuries of litigation. The law was changed by the Field code so that demurrers and counter-appeals, proceedings and ancillary proceedings, on technical points can be carried, one after another, from court to court, while the real point at issue has to wait untried below for the results of this interminable contest. By grace of this power to carry preliminary and technical questions from court to court, at the pleasure of quibbling and appealing lawyers and procrastinating judges, from courts of Oyer and Terminer to the Supreme Court at General Term, to the Court of Appeals, rich corporations and individuals are able to tire out altogether all ordinary opponents. It was only by help of very able and highly paid lawyers, officers of the courts and of justice, that the law of New York was " reformed," so that the technical parts of a case could be to such an extent disengaged from the main body, and sent forward and backward, up and down, through the whole series of appeals, consuming endless time and money, while poor men seeking justice kick their heels in the lowest courts.

As the time for pronouncing sentence came on, petitions for mercy were circulated in Buffalo and Rochester. The members of the jury which had found the accused guilty were labored with separately to sign a recantation. Only six succumbed and signed a statement that the prisoners were found guilty, not because they had conspired to blow up their rival's refinery, but because they had enticed away Albert. This recantation was in the face of the judge's charge, which had made the plot to blow up the Buffalo works the chief and the important inquiry in this case, and the verdict had been given under the influence of this view of the case. Six of the jury saw the impropriety of making this statement after they had disbanded and passed from under the legal and moral restraints they felt when sitting under their oath of office, and refused to sign it.

When the paper from the complaisant six jurors was handed in, the District Attorney said in court: "These jurors received money for making these affidavits. If required to do so I will prove the statement." He was not called upon to do so. "These affidavits," he said afterwards, "were procured for the purpose of influencing the Court to administer the lighter punishment, since they tended to show that the verdict was directed against the lighter offence. One of the jurors told me he had been offered money to sign one of these affidavits, and he knew of one juror who had received $10 for signing one."

When the last possibility in the way of proceedings for a stay or for a new trial had been exhausted, except argument of an appeal in the Court of Appeals, which was known to be useless, sentence was pronounced. The penalty provided in the statutes was imprisonment for one year in the penitentiary, or a fine of $250, or both. The lawyers pleaded that the elder of the convicted men was old, that the younger had just returned from a wedding tour in Europe, that some of the wealthiest and most prominent citizens of Rochester had petitioned for mercy, and that six of the jury had done like-wise. Each was sentenced to pay a fine of $250. Notice of appeal was given by the convicted, and a year was consumed on both sides in preparations to fight the case to a bitter finish. But the appeal was abandoned. A new trial and new sentence might have ended worse. The fine was paid, and these employés of the trust, upon whose record as reputable and inoffensive citizens for all the years of their business career no shadow had fallen till they entered its employ, took thereby the place assigned them by the jury—that of convicts guilty of crime.

Crime, it seems, may in this country be cheaper than competition. They who received the larger part of the benefit of the enticement of Albert, of the harassing litigation, of the damage done by the explosion, and of the bankruptcy which was finally produced by these means, went free of all punishment; and the employés found their crime but little less than a pastime. After his conviction, and before his sentence, one of the two married. His wedding was attended by many of the great men of the trust—magnates in the New York world of affairs and its affiliated interests. It glittered with gold and silver and precious stones which they sent to signify to the world that they stood sponsor for him.

The case of some humble boycotters was then fresh in the public mind. Certain working-men, on strike, handed around printed circulars in the streets of New York, requesting people not to buy beer sold by their employer. In a few weeks from the time they dropped those circulars in the streets they were in the penitentiary at Sing Sing. It was shown on their trial that they were entirely ignorant of the fact that they were violating any of the laws of the State in what they did. It was shown on the trial of the oil men that they did know that the course they had in view was criminal, and were warned by a lawyer it might land them in prison. "It was very fortunate," said the New York *World*, "that they were not poor men convicted of stealing a ham."

One of the reasons given by the judge for his leniency was that prominent citizens of Buffalo and Rochester had begged for mercy. "With the very highest respect for the judge," said the Buffalo *Express*, "as the *Express* has often demonstrated, we must say that this is a mighty queer excuse. Three-fourths of those citizens are in one way or another identified in interest with the oil trust, as the judge could readily have ascertained, and their names on that petition were entitled to no more moral weight in the consideration of this case than the names of the two guilty men should have had if they had seen fit to sign it."

The sentence raised a whirlwind of indignation. "As ridiculous as anything that could be imagined," said the Philadelphia *Ledger*. "It is high time," said the New York *World*, "that the lines were drawn between competition and conspiracy, between business and brigandage." Referring to the golden harvest of $300,000 dividends in one year on a capital of $100,000, representing an original investment of only $13,500, the *World* said : "The monopoly of this sort of business is a very seductive thing. It is calculated to make men of more boldness than morals blow up factories, or do almost anything else to control the field." "It can afford to blow up a rival refinery every day in the year at that price," said the Erie *Dispatch*. "There have been conspiracies," said the Oil City *Blizzard* (Pa.), "to injure the business of opposition concerns right here in Oil City, and the conspirators have never been punished." "It is — a light sentence," was the comment of the Buffalo *Commercial*. "Poor criminals," the Buffalo *Express* declared, "may well wonder why rich ones are let off so easily. It is equivalent to deciding that wealth may securely indulge in that inexpensive sort of amusement as a mere pastime. Who's afraid?" it asked. "What conspirator 'in restraint' of trade is afraid of a $250 fine?" "Certain it is that no wealthy criminals convicted of such a crime ever before received from a court such a mockery of justice," was the verdict of the Springfield (Mass.) *Republican*.

The facts of this case have not been carelessly examined or decided. Two grand-juries in succession passed upon the evidence and found it good enough for indictments. Two petit juries heard the evidence, both for and against, in the civil and criminal suits, and found it good enough—one jury for $20,000 damages, another for a verdict of criminally guilty. Seventy picked citizens have unanimously concurred in the decision "Guilty." And this scarlet letter the monopoly will always have to carry.

"So surely as Matthews lives, and so long as he lives," District Attorney Quinby said in the criminal prosecution, " he will never again make another dollar upon a barrel of oil he may manufacture. The word has gone forth, right in this court-room, that this man shall be crushed, and he can never again run his works successfully. That is going to be one of the results of this case." The fulfilment of this prediction came swiftly. This sentence of ruin upon Matthews was executed before sentence was even pronounced upon the conspirators against him. He had been left crippled by the flight and corruption of his partner, the only practical oil man in the enterprise. When he tried to obtain some one to take his place, he could not get word of any one not connected with the oil combination. He did not dare to advertise, and knew no one in Buffalo he could venture to speak to. He had made contracts before opening the works, and was unable to fill them. The pipes had been laid wrong; it took him a year trying one way and another, and making a great many mistakes, to set them right. His third partner was frightened back into the employ of the oil combination by threatening litigation.

Then came the suits to destroy, punctually as threatened.[1] "If one court does not sustain the patents, we will carry them up until you get enough of it," one of the trustees said to Matthews. One of the Rochester managers, in speaking of these

---

[1] Testimony, Trusts, Congress, 1888, p. 816.

19

suits, said: "I don't know as we will gain anything really, but we will embarrass them by bringing these suits, and, if it is necessary, we will bring them once a month; yes, we will bring them once a week." One, two, three, four, five suits came with injunctions. "Null and void" was the verdict of court after court on the worthless patents and pretended trade-marks on which he was sued.

Matthews had to keep pushing his pursuers to trial. What they wanted was not decisions but delays, to ruin him by the waste of time and money.[1] "It cost me one-third of my time, and $25,000 or more to defend these suits." These suits were used to scare away his customers. "I was instructed," said the Boston representative of the combination, "to tell the customers that the Buffalo company were using their patents."[2] The sole legal victory the combination won was the recovery of six cents damages on a technical point.

Matthews, on his side, took to the courts. He sued his persecutors as individuals and corporations. He pursued them civilly and criminally. He was successful in defending himself against their suits. All his suits were successful as far as he was able to carry them. One suit for damages produced a $20,000 verdict; another was for $250,000, on the still stronger evidence procured in the criminal trial. It took Matthews two years—from 1883 to 1885—to get his first case for damages for conspiracy to trial. All that time was consumed by his opponents in quibbles about procedure, technical objections, and motions for delay, appealing them from court to court. The judge, in taking from the jury afterwards the three trustees who had been brought to trial for conspiracy, declared that he could see no reason to believe that these suits had been brought without probable cause. But the jury before which the suit for damages was tried saw plenty of such reasons, and gave Matthews' company a verdict of $20,000 damages. The views of the judge and jury might have varied in the same way on the question of the guilt of the three members of the trust.

---

[1] See chs. xxii. to xxvi.   [2] Testimony, Trusts, Congress, 1888, p. 847.

Matthews woke up one morning to discover, as he had been told he would, that there was no Atlas Company to get his oil from. Corporations may have no souls, but they can love each other. The Erie Railroad killed the pipe line of the Atlas Company for the oil combination.[1] The courts had been kept busy granting injunctions against it on the motion of the Erie. These were invariably dissolved by the courts, but an application for a new one would always follow. At one time the lawyers had fifteen injunctions all ready in their hands to be sued out, one after the other, as fast as needed. The pipe line was finally destroyed by force. Where it crossed under the Erie road in the bed of a stream grappling-irons were fastened to it, and with an immense hawser a locomotive guarded by two freight cars full of men pulled it to pieces. The Atlas line and refinery became the ".property" of their enemy. Matthews' supply of crude oil was not cut off immediately. He was tapered off. One of the superintendents of the Atlas testified in the suit for damages Matthews brought against the Atlas after it passed into the hands of the combination, that by the order of the manager of the refinery he mixed refuse oil with the crude which they sold to the Buffalo Lubricating Oil Company. Finally the supply was shut off altogether.

Matthews turned to the railroads connecting Buffalo with the oil country. They all put up their rates. At the increased rates they would not bring him enough to keep him going; they would not give him cars enough, and told him they would not let him put his own cars on the road. Even the lake steamers raised their rates against him. The farmer-refiner was taking his lesson in the course which had driven his first employer to dig oil-wells because "there were restrictions in the shipments." Cut off from a supply by either pipe or rail at Buffalo, Matthews made an alliance with the Keystone Refinery in the oil regions. War was now made upon the Keystone. It was finally ruined.

[1] Testimony, Trusts, Congress, 1888, p. 424.

Packs of lawyers were set upon Matthews, and they finally brought him down. An attorney appeared before a judge and made a motion that the property of Matthews' company be taken out of Matthews' hands and be placed in the charge of a receiver, as officer of the court, to secure a debt due a Buffalo bank. This done, the lawyer appeared before the judge who afterwards decided that $250 fine was punishment enough for criminal conspiracy, with an offer from the monopoly to pay $17,300 for the discontinuance of the suits for damages which Matthews had instituted, and $63,700 for all the other assets. The other creditors and all the stockholders opposed the motion, but the judge granted it. There were two suits. One had produced a verdict of $20,000, and the other one for $250,000 was brought on the new and much stronger evidence secured in the criminal trial. As to the value of the property, Matthews had brought his enterprise to the point where it was worth $20,000 a year. It was capable of producing many times that amount of profit. Had not Albert been enticed away, the new works would have yielded a profit of over $100,000 the first year. They had a capacity of 70 to 80 barrels a day of lubricating oil, and the profit was $5 to $6 a barrel at the time Matthews and Albert went into the business.[1] The judge, overruling a majority of the creditors, ordered the receiver to accept the offer. He gave as his reason for selling these damage suits that a criminal prosecution had already taken place for the same offences, and a person could not be punished twice for the same offence. As they had not yet been punished, this meant, if it meant anything, that the suits were to be sold out for this inconsiderable sum, and the guilty men were to get their punishment in the sentence he was to pass upon them in the criminal court.

Three months later, before the same judge, these convicted agents stood up to receive their criminal sentence. The judge gave them the lightest sentence in his power, " nominal punishment." He did so, he was reported by the Buffalo press

---

[1] Testimony, Trusts, Congress, 1888, p. 849.

to have said, because "it has come to the attention of the court that civil suits have been brought to recover damages sustained by reason of the same overt acts. Large punitive damages are demanded in those actions. It is fundamental that a person cannot be punished twice for the same offence."

The judge released them from the suits for damages because they were to be punished criminally. Then he released them from any but nominal punishment, because there had been suits for damages. One would infer that the civil suits for damages were in full career in the courts, to end possibly in hundreds of thousands of dollars' damages against the convicted. No one would infer what was the truth—and who should have remembered it so well as the judge, for it was he who had done it?—that the civil suits had been ordered sold. The judge had ordered his officer—the receiver—who had the luckless Matthews' affairs in his grip, not to try the cases, but to sell them. The suits had been ordered sold in February preceding, and they were as dead as—justice. But as all the technical formalities and slow proceedings needed to consummate the sale had not been completed when sentence was passed in May, the damages they might produce were made a reason for inflicting none but nominal punishment. The order of sale made it impossible that they should ever be tried.

Of the money paid into court, nearly half—$30,000—went to the lawyers, and, cruelest stroke of all, the attorney who had made the successful motion before the judge to take Matthews' property away, and to order the forced sale, got $5000. Matthews got nothing. Even his right to sue his destroyers had been sold to them on their own motion and at their own price.

The crime was plotted in March, 1881. The participants were indicted in 1886. It took until May 15, 1887, to secure conviction. While sentence was still unpronounced Matthews' property was put into the hands of a receiver of the court, January 16, 1888; the property was sold by order of the court, February 17, 1888; sentence was pronounced May 8, 1888; the formalities of the sale were consummated July

11, 1888; and the sentence, coming last of all—the fine of $250—was executed May 1, 1889.

Matthews had tried to make money in oil, and had failed; but his competition had forced those in control of the markets to increase the price to the producer, and he made light cheaper to the community. In Buffalo his enterprise had caused the price to drop to 6 cents from 12 and 18 cents, in Boston[1] to 8 cents from 20. Oil has never since been as high in Boston or Buffalo as before he challenged the monopoly. And he forced the struggle into the view of the public, and succeeded in putting on record in the archives of courts and legislatures and Congress a picture of the realities of modern commerce certain to exercise a profound influence in ripening the reform thought with which our air is charged into reform action.

Nothing is so dramatic as fact, when you can find the fact. The treatment his church gave the brother, who had been the victim, as judicially declared, of a criminal conspiracy, is described in the following letter from Matthews:

"BUFFALO, January 19, 1888.

"MY DEAR FRIEND,—As your father was a clergyman, and as you feel an interest in church affairs, I think you will wish to know of my recent experiences. My church here is not a rich one, but we pay as much for church music as we do as salary to our pastor. Probably the wealthiest man in our church is an agent of the oil trust. He receives a salary of $18,000 per year, and keeps their retail store here, and has been a witness for them in important suits. He does not belong to our church, but is a trustee and treasurer of the Church, and is very kind to our pastor, whom he took last summer on quite an extended vacation trip in New England. But you know the class of men that usually become trustees in our city churches these days.

"My pastor surprised me a few days ago by making a visit at my office, and telling me that as my term of office as member of the session expired soon, it might be best for me not to be a candidate for re-election, in view of what the newspapers had said about me, and the opposition there was. He said, however, that he personally felt friendly to me, and regarded me highly. He seemed to be embarrassed, but I quickly relieved the situation by saying that I had told my family some months before that I should not again hold a church office. I told the doctor he well knew I

[1] Testimony, Trusts, Congress, 1888, p. 847.

did not desire office in or out of the Church. True, the newspapers, under the influence of the oil trust, had ridiculed me as 'farmer Matthews from the country.' But why should my pastor mock me with such shallow pretences for reasons for church opposition to me? I had engaged in the oil business without the consent of the oil monopoly, and my pastor then and there told me my friends thought me foolhardy in doing so. I could hardly suppress my feelings on hearing this said by the man who baptized my children and ministers at the church altar. What could all this mean? I had only fought for my rights as an American citizen, as a manufacturer and shipper of oil. I had been sustained in every detail by the courts. I had convicted in our courts prominent men of conspiracy, little thinking that the subtle power of these men could come to dominate the Church itself. My feelings were intense, and words came thick and fast—all too tame to express my feelings. I told the doctor how I had struggled on from boyhood, and at middle age had accumulated a few thousand dollars, and in all these years had never sued a man or been sued, and that my struggle with the oil monopoly was for rights that no one worthy to be called a man dare to surrender. I told the doctor how I had been hounded, and my business beset by spies—that my friends had often told me I was in danger of assassination if I continued the fight in the courts. He, having done his errand, seemed uneasy, and anxious to go. I told him I had seen the rising and corrupting power of this trust in their control of our aldermen and courts, in state and national legislation. I could witness all this with comparative composure; but it made every drop of my blood hot to see them erect their altars for Mammon worship in the Church of the living God. I had seen the hard-won earnings of a lifetime swept away, and had hoped that at least one word of sympathy might come from the Church. If I had been robbed by old-fashioned highwaymen and the Church received none of the loot, church sympathy would have been hearty and abundant. But no; Sabbath after Sabbath our reverend doctor rises in the pulpit, and, at the regular time, says: 'Let us worship God in the gift of money.' Religion, divine worship, and money all seem to have a like meaning as they are alternately mentioned in our pulpit. My ancestors far back were church people, but this worshipping money, or worshipping God with money, is all new to me. It was not the acceptable worship required by Christ and taught by his disciples. After the conversation I had with my pastor that day I trudged home, but could not sleep that night. My heart was too full of sorrow as well as anger. I hope you will forgive me for writing you so long a letter. I have written much more than I intended to, but did not see where to stop. There are many things I wish you could see but not experience in the life of a business man nowadays. I want you to write often, as every word from a true friend is prized highly in these dark days for me."

The action of the judge in this and another celebrated case was made an issue in the elections in New York in 1889. In

June, 1882, the railroads in New York City, rather than pay
the freight-handlers the 20 cents an hour they asked for,
instead of 17 cents, brought the business of the city to a
stop.   They refused to employ their old men at that price,
and did not supply their places.   Trucks by thousands, heavy
with merchandise, stood before the railroad freight-houses
for days, waiting in vain to be unloaded.   The trade of the
metropolis was paralyzed, and the railroad officials sat serene-
ly in their offices, letting the jam pile up until the freight-
handlers were starved into accepting the wages they were
offered, and commercial distress had made the business community desperate enough to tolerate that injustice, or any
other iniquity, provided the "Goddess of Getting-on" were
allowed to get on again.   It was so clear that the price asked
by the men was fair, and that the refusal of the railroads to
set them at work and keep the channels of trade open was
due to a purpose to manufacture such widespread loss and
trouble that the public should be goaded into forgetfulness of
the rights of the men, that public opinion forced the Attorney-General of the State to act.   Re-enforced by able counsel,
he applied for a peremptory writ of mandamus to compel the
roads to resume operations.   This motion came before this
Buffalo judge, then sitting by assignment in New York.   He
kept the people waiting ten days, and then quashed and dismissed the petition.   The decision of the Supreme Court,
composed of judges of both parties, reversing his action, was
unanimous, but the mischief he had done was by that time
—January 17, 1883—long past mending.

When he was nominated to be judge again, after his inde-
cision and decision had swelled the dividends of the great
railways of New York, the presiding officer of the convention
which was to choose him to be their candidate was, by a coincidence, also the president of one of the great railway corporations which had been involved in the judicial proceeding
of 1882.   The judge's record was made one of the issues in
the State election which followed the defeat of justice in
Buffalo.   He was nominated by the Republicans in 1889 for

Judge of the Court of Appeals, the highest court in the State of New York, and the nomination was asserted by the New York *Times*, in a leading editorial, to have been procured by the oil trust. Its "influence was active," said the *Times*, "in securing the nomination of" this judge. "... An attorney who has labored in its interests at Albany during the last two sessions of the Legislature was conspicuous among the men who did the work." The New York *Times*, the Buffalo *Courier*, the New York *Star*, the New York *World*, and other leading journals of the State retold the story of the trial, and declared that the judge's action in taking the case of the members of the trust from the jury, and the sentence he gave the convicted agents, made it clear that he was unfit to be a judge. The oil combination, the *World* said, editorially, "have had agents busy this year trying to secure his elevation to the highest court in the State. ... We say confidently that the history of the case establishes his conspicuous unfitness for a place on the bench of the Court of Appeals. He should be defeated, and with him the oppressive monopoly which is actively seeking his election."

He was defeated with the rest of the ticket. District Attorney Quinby was re-elected several terms in succession. After their victory the people went to sleep, but not the sower of tares. At the election of 1890 the nomination of this judge to a seat on the bench was secured from both parties. For fourteen years, therefore—from 1890—a seat of the Supreme Court, one of the most important tribunals of justice in New York State, will be occupied by this judge, before whom must come many questions affecting oil transportation, electric lighting, natural gas and illuminating, street railways, banking, and other interests of the oil trust.

Monopoly cannot be content with controlling its own business. It is the creature of the same law which has always driven the tyrant to control everything — government, art, literature, even private conversation. Any freedom, though seemingly the most remote from any possible bearing upon the tyrant, may—will grow from a little leak of liberty into a mighty flood, sweeping his palaces and dungeons away. The czar knows that if he lets his people have so much freedom as free talk in their sitting-rooms their talk will gather into a tornado. In all ages wealth, like all power, has found that it must rule all or nothing. Its destiny is rule or ruin, and rule is but a slower ruin. Hence we find it in America creeping higher every year up into the seats of control. Its lobbyists force the nomination of judges who will construe the laws as Power desires, and of senators who will get passed such laws as it wants for its judges to construe.

The press, too, must be controlled by Power. During the criminal trial at Buffalo one of the oil combination's detectives was put on the stand. He was compelled to produce his written instructions from the counsel of the trust.[1] These had been given him at the office of the oil trust in New York. He forwarded his reports to its office in New York, and received his pay from the same place.[2] He sent his subordinates to get employment in Matthews' works, and through them obtained information from the inside. The monopoly paid one of these detectives $2.50 a day for spying, while he could earn only $1.50 a day for working.

"I see here further," said the District Attorney, "'Why the *Express* published the last complaint'"—in Matthews' suit for $250,000 damages. "Did he ask you to find out about that?"

"He did."

"That is, he wanted you to find out what arrangements were made with the Buffalo *Express* to have the complaint published?"

"Yes; the whole complaint. It covered the whole of the newspaper."

"And do you know 'how many copies were taken by Matthews?' Did he tell you to find that out, too?"

"Yes, sir."[3]

---

[1] Testimony, Trusts, Congress, 1888, pp. 429, 894.　　　　[2] Same, p. 894.

[3] Testimony, Stenographic Report, p. 895. This passage also is omitted in the transcript furnished the committee of Congress by the counsel of the trust.

CHAPTER XXII

ANOTHER TALE OF TWO CITIES

THE South is the most American part of America. Close observers note as its especial characteristic the preservation of the original Anglo-Saxon types, which gave this country its first and deepest impress.

The South is not yet so steeped as the North in the commercialism to which it is all of life to buy and sell, and its population, less affected by trade and immigration, remains more nearly American, as the fathers were American, than the parts of the country flooded by the full force of the modern tide. Only in the South is there record all through this history of a man "too prejudiced to buy" from those who claimed the sole right to sell.

The merchants of Columbus, Mississippi, were buying their oil of the southern branch of the combination when they were offered a supply at cheaper prices by an independent refiner. They asked the combination to meet this competition of the market. This was refused. There were eleven firms there which sold oil in connection with other things. The combination "coolly informed us," wrote one of the firms to a journal of the trade, "that we were in their power, and could not buy oil from any one else, and that we should either pay such prices as they demanded or not sell oil. We immediately formed an association among ourselves and ordered from other parties. On receipt of our first car they immediately put the retail price below the cost per car lots, and for some time tried to whip us in that way, as we still declined to handle their oil. They then wrote offering to rebate to several of the larger firms if they would withdraw and leave the smaller ones to fight the battle alone. This proposition we declined, and they again tried the low-price dodge, their agent telling us that they would spend $10,000 to crush us out. This game they have now been trying for three years, and in that time we have not handled one gallon of their oil." As these devices, irresistible in more commercial civilizations, did not fool the brotherhood of Columbus, a special agent was sent to Columbus to carry on the war.

"You can tell the Columbus merchants if this does not succeed we will have it out on other lines," the agent was instructed, in the strain of the letter to the merchant of Nashville.[1] "The battle has not fairly opened yet; sharpen up your sword, we mean war to the knife." And again: "We want Columbus squelched," was the word sent the agent from the headquarters at Louisville.

He was ordered to start a grocery store in Columbus, to compete in their entire business with the "black-mailers." While the fight was on, and it was still hoped to conquer Columbus, the following was kept prominently before the people in the daily papers:

"We desire to state that we did not establish an agency in Columbus to force the wholesale grocers to handle our oil."

But seven years later the general in command of this department told Congress it was his practice to fight in that way. "Almost invariably I did that always."[2]

"To threaten the people elsewhere with Columbus," the agent at Columbus was told, "will make them scat, as it were, and take our oil at any price." But the people of Columbus did not "scat." The new store had a complete stock of groceries. Prices on everything, including oil, were put "down to the bone." But one essential feature of the enterprise all the ingenuity and power of the invader could not furnish—customers. Goods were advertised at cost; alluring signs were hung out with daily variations; but the people would not buy. A few citizens who bought at the beginning,

---

[1] See p. 214.   [2] Testimony, Trusts, Congress, 1888, p. 533; see also p. 734.

without understanding the plan of campaign, came out in the newspapers with cards of apology, and pledges that they would not repeat the mistake. Local bankers refused to honor the drafts of the enemy, threw out its accounts, and gave notice that they would advance no money to persons who bought at its store. The public opinion of Columbus so bitterly resented the attack upon the livelihood of its merchants, because they had dared to buy where they thought best, and so clearly saw that the subjugation of the merchants would be but the preliminary of a conquest of themselves, that any one seen within the doors of the odious store fell into instant and deep disgrace. " Their store is regarded as a pest-house," wrote one of the leading business men, "and few respectable people ever darken their doors, their trade being confined mostly to negroes. Their oil trade has dwindled down to almost nothing, and we are selling now to merchants in other towns who heretofore bought exclusively from them."

At the first sign of aggression the merchants had given up competition, which they saw meant only mutual ruin, and had tied themselves together in an association. Now as the struggle widened the people did the same, and found a greater benefit and pleasure in co-operation than in keeping up the delusion of the "higgling of the market" where there was no market. The *Index*, of Columbus, printed an agreement signed by hundreds " of those who will sustain our home merchants in the struggle they are making. . . . It will receive many more signatures among our citizens. . . . The people have only to understand to properly decide in this matter between right and wrong."

" You ask if the feeling is bitter against them in our ' community,' " one of the merchants wrote. " I can only liken it to the spirit which prevailed when the people of Boston emptied King George's taxed tea into Boston Harbor."

Attempt was made to intimidate the press. Advertisements were discontinued because the papers supported the cause of the people. "If the agent," said the *Index*, of Columbus, "thought the cash that might be obtained for such advertisements could purchase the silence of this journal when it should speak, or its support in a wrong cause, he reckoned without his host." "The pledge" was signed by practically every man in the place. The country people about Columbus, when they came to town to sell produce and buy supplies, took back with them blanks of the agreement not to buy the obnoxious oil, and circulated them among their neighbors for signature. Agents were sent among these country people to win back their trade, but they could not be moved. The competition was made "war to the knife," and the knife "to the bone." It was a singular sight—this concentration of millions to "kill" these little men in this remote country town in far-off Mississippi. Nothing was too small to do. When one of the Columbus "rebels" bought oats for his trade, a competitive stock of the same kind of oats was hurried into Columbus, and these instructions sent with it: "Put your sign out. Rust-proof oats to arrive at 98 cents to $1 a bushel. This will kill him. The same signs should be posted about meats, sugar, coffee, etc."

The plan of action of the Merchants' Association was simple: they declined to handle the enemy's oil at any price. "Then to have a stock of our own always on hand, ready to sell whenever we could at a profit, and hold in reserve whenever they put prices below cost; and in this way we have made it a losing business to them for over three years, and will continue to do so as long as they remain in our town. . . . When our association buys a car of oil, each member pays for and takes charge of an equal share, but the oil remains the property of the association; and should any member sell out before the others, he has the right to buy from them at cost, and the next car is not ordered until all are nearly sold out."

It is "our pleasure to make oil cheap"; but a written proposition was made to the merchants that if they would repent and return, the price would be 20 cents a gallon, with a rebate to the loyal dealers. As this oil could be, and was being, laid down in Columbus at 12 cents a gallon, the proposition amounted to a request that the merchants join in imposing a tax on the people of 8 cents a gallon, which must be added to the retail price, and go to swell the profits of the "sympathet-ical co-operation." "Can any one," said the *Index*, "after knowing these facts, doubt that in a pecuniary point our mer-chants could have done better by surrendering the principle and joining the ring? But, at the same time, could any reason-ing man (even viewing it in the light of policy alone) advise such a course?—one which, if adopted, would only open the door for other monopolies to enter and demand high prices on meat, flour, and the other necessaries of life, until our city becomes the highest market in the land. Let all good citizens, then, unite in a steady effort to resist the yoke which this monopoly is now trying to force upon us, and let us teach them and all others that our people are too loyal to each other and too in-telligent to allow themselves to be made the instruments of their own destruction.

"Remember, that should our merchants be forced to yield, the day of low prices will be a short one, and then these stran-gers, having accomplished their purpose and forced their yoke upon you and us, will return to their homes, and while rioting in the taxes wrung from you, with your own assistance, will laugh at you for allowing yourselves to be so easily duped, and, emboldened by their success in forcing upon you high-priced oil, will soon return to demand high prices on sugar, coffee, and every other article of trade."

The nose for news of the American press scented out the novelty of a whole community acting as one man in successful resistance to those who had till then found nowhere any cohe-sive brotherliness to make a stand against them. The newspa-pers of the country took the matter up. It was absolutely the first time any method had been found that could prevail against the tactics of divide and conquer, which had been elsewhere irresistible. Public attention was fascinated by the revelation that a brotherhood to ravage the people turned impotent when the people were roused to meet it with their brotherhood of the commonwealth. There was in the spectacle a moral illu-mination—the light that never fails. Instead of becoming, as had been planned, a warning to all the people of the dire destruction to be visited upon any who dared to disobey, the encounter between the one-man power of united Columbus and the one-man power of hundreds of millions of dollars became every day more brilliantly a sign in the sky, showing all the people how the invasion of their industrial liberties could be changed into a ruin more complete than the retreat from Moscow. Scores of such assaults on the people had been won before. "What was being done at Columbus," said one of the papers, "is but what they have done before at Aberdeen, and at hundreds of other places North and South."

But as despoilers always have to fear, one defeat may undo a lifetime of conquest. The success of the people of Columbus was teaching the people of the whole country, and of all markets, that their real enemy was not the oil trust, but the lack of trust in each other. The people were learning there was a magic in association more potent than the trick of combinations. The *Index* proposed to the people of the South to join the citizens of Columbus, and make the fight general. "There is this about it : if there was concentrated action among the smaller cities and towns throughout even this section of the State, we would have no fear of the result. The oil trust may be too strong for a single small locality, but if a combination of a certain number of localities handling oil were effected, they would soon be forced to retire. Such a combination can be and should be brought about at once."

The struggle at Columbus lasted three years. It had seemed unequal enough—a few thousands of dollars against hundreds of millions. But three years of this commercial warfare failed to break the spirit or resources of the brave—and wise because brave—people. The community never broke rank. They laughed when they were tempted with cheap coffee, flour, sugar, to join in the attempt to bankrupt their home merchants. They could see that the gift of forced cheapness, used to destroy natural cheapness, was a Trojan horse bearing within itself the deadliest form of dearness. Defeated, the oil lords gave up the contest, closed their store in Columbus, and left the people of that place free.

"England," says Emerson, "reaches to the Alleghanies; America begins in Ohio." In the Western Reserve of Ohio, hive of abolitionists and Union soldiers, was the same spirit of America which, at Columbus, Mississippi, had defended its market rights as outposts of all other rights. It was only a few years ago discovered that the flames of the "burning springs" of the Caspian Sea, China, and America, whose torches kindled the lamp of history, were beacon-fires uncomprehended by a procession of civilizations, and waiting to light man to the knowledge that the earth beneath him was a city of domes, huge receivers storing up the products of vaster gas-retorts below. Man found that he need not wait for this spirit to come to him out of the "caverns measureless to man." He could go to it, as in oil, and, tapping the great tanks, could lead their flighty contents to homes and mills, to emerge there as light and warmth and power.

Experience in oil had made ready skill and capital to use the new treasure. In a very few years thousands of miles of pipe were laid, and millions of capital invested in the natural-gas business, mainly in Ohio and Pennsylvania. The gas was found in the same general localities as oil, and the methods of procuring and distributing it were similar, and the similarity easily extended to the methods of administering this bounty of nature as "property." Toledo began to be supplied in 1887 with the new fuel through pipe lines by two companies. They obtained their franchises as competitors, but were soon found to be one in ownership, prices, and all details of management. The discovery that the two companies at Toledo were really one, and that one the evil one of the oil trust, aroused the apprehensions of the people, and these were increased by a number of circumstances.

The Toledo companies got from the city as a free gift a franchise worth hundreds of thousands of dollars, on condition that they would supply Toledo before a certain date. But in the midst of the work of laying pipes they suspended operations, and declared that they would do nothing more unless the City Council fixed, at rates dictated by them, the prices the peo-

20

ple were to pay.   These rates were enough to pay not only a
fair dividend, but to return in a few years every dollar of
capital invested in lands, pipes, etc.   Later they demanded
another increase which, according to the sworn statement by
their superintendent of the amount of gas supplied daily,
would have amounted to $351,362.50 a year.   They made the
charges regardless of the ordinance, and used delay in furnishing gas as a means to make people willing to pay these illegal rates.   Consumers seeking to renew their contracts were
informed that the price would be doubled.   The companies
had assured the people that they should get their heat at half
the price of coal; but when the bills were footed up, the gas
in many cases cost more than coal.   The companies refused
to supply fuel to an oil refinery which had been built in Toledo in opposition to the trust refineries.   The companies discriminated against some customers, and in favor of others.
The power to say which manufacturer should have cheaper
fuel than his competitor was a power to enact prosperity or
ruin.[1]   It was a power to force themselves into control of any
business they desired to enter.

Those who controlled these gas companies appeared in the
Circuit Court of the city in a proceeding which alone contained warning enough to put any self-governing community
on guard.   The Court was asked to deny the right of farmers
in Wood County to give a way over their lands to the Toledo,
Findlay, and Springfield Railway, being built to give the independent oil-refiners and producers of the Ohio oil-field a
route to market.   The farmers in question had made leases to
an oil corporation of the trust, giving only the specific right
to bore for and pipe and store oil and gas.   The farmers supposed that they had parted only with what they had signed
away in the leases.   They supposed they still owned their
farms.   When the new railroad sought the privilege of a right
of way the farmers granted it.   Suit was at once brought for
an injunction to prevent this use of the land.   According to

---

[1] See ch. xxv.

the logic of the claim in these cases a farmer who has made such a lease could not build a road across his own farm without permission. "Most certainly not," was the reply made by one of the lawyers to the judge who asked if the farmer could do so.

By occurrences like these an increasing number of influential citizens were convinced that the gas companies would hold a power over the comfort and daily life of the people not wise to surrender entire to any corporation. An agitation was begun for the supply of gas to the people by themselves acting through the municipality. Six thousand citizens sent a petition, in the session of 1887–88, to the Legislature to pass the necessary enabling act. There was a discussion of the project for two years. Public opinion grew more favorable every day. The citizens chartered a special train to carry a delegation to Columbus the day the pipe-line law came before the Senate. The Legislature in 1889 passed the law. It authorized the people of Toledo to issue bonds to the extent of $750,000 to buy gas land and build pipe lines. This legislation was, of course, bitterly opposed by the existing gas companies, and they demanded of the Legislature that before the law became operative it should be ratified by a three-fifths vote of the people. The friends of this scheme of municipal self-help and independence accepted the challenge. In the ensuing campaign the opposition to the people was officered by the president of one of the natural-gas companies, twice Governor of Ohio, afterwards United States Secretary of the Treasury. The natural-gas trustees of the City of Toledo in an official communication said : "There is reason to believe the money of the natural-gas companies was freely spent to defeat it."

The act was ratified April, 1889, by a vote of 7002 for to 4199 against—" a vote," say the trustees, " in which the heavy taxpayers were largely acting with the majority." [1] Organized labor took an enthusiastic part in the work of this election. The Central Labor Union held a special meeting which

[1] Report of Citizens' Committee on City of Toledo and Its Natural Gas Bonds, p. 5.

filled the largest public hall.   Men paraded the streets with
banners favoring the policy of independence.   The Knights
of Labor held meetings to discuss the project, and the Central
Council, representing all the assemblies in the city, passed
unanimously resolutions appealing to all members of the order and all working-men to support no candidate who would
not pledge himself to the city pipe line.   At a meeting of the
glassworkers it was resolved to be "the duty of every working-man to vote 'Yes' for the pipe line next Monday."   "Many
of us glassworkers," said the resolutions adopted, "have been
employed in factories in the Ohio Valley, receiving their natural-gas fuel from a gigantic corporation similar to that which
now supplies Toledo.   We have seen our employers unfairly
dealt with, and arbitrarily treated in the matter of making
rates.   Some of them were forced to go into the courts, to
prevent the extortion of the piratical company who were bent
on assessing each citizen and industry at the highest rate possible, irrespective of its effect on the industries or the wages
of the employés.   Many manufacturers were compelled to
move their plants to the cheap gas-fields of Ohio and Indiana.
The employés were compelled to break up their homes and
emigrate, in order to follow their trade for a livelihood."   The
question came before the people again the next spring, when
both the Republican and Democratic parties by acclamation
renominated a natural-gas trustee, whose term was expiring,
to succeed himself.   At the election the vote was 8958 for,
and only 58 against—a practically unanimous indorsement of
the project by the people.

Toledo now began to make history.   "It is entirely safe to
say," a well-known citizen declared in the Toledo *Blade*, "that
in the history of this country no other people have been called
to the experience which Toledo has been undergoing for the
past year.   Communities often are agitated and divided on
questions of local policy; but no second case will be found in
which a people, after settling such questions among themselves according to recognized rules, were confronted with
warfare, bitter and persistent, such as this city is now called

to meet, and at the hands of a combination wholly of non-residents, without the slightest proper voice in their domestic concerns." In every direct encounter with the "commons" the "lords" had been defeated—in the two years' debate which preceded the first appeal to the Legislature; in the Legislature, where the bill passed the House almost unanimously, and the Senate more than two to one; in the appeal to the voters; before the governor, who had been approached to cripple the enterprise of the municipality by naming unfriendly trustees. The gas companies had tried at each city election, after the Legislature acted in 1889, to seat in the City Council a majority in their interest; but the people, making the city pipe line the issue of the election, gave an overwhelming preponderance of their votes to the men pledged to see it through.

"Strong and subtle opposition"[1] was then brought to bear on the Common Council to prevent it from passing the necessary ordinances; but, in spite of it, both branches of the Council voted them unanimously. A clearer case of the will of the people and of law and order there could not be. A free and intelligent community, in a matter of vital concern to its industrial freedom and business prosperity, after thorough discussion, in which all sides had been freely heard, had by constitutional proceedings decided by an overwhelming majority upon a policy altogether within its legal, moral, and contract rights. The ablest lawyers, writers, and financiers that money could hire had had it under the microscope to find some breach for attack, but had not been able to find a flaw. All was constitutional, legal, proper, and expedient. A glance at the contestants brings out in clear outlines some conditions of our modern development which have come upon us almost unawares. The City of Toledo was a vigorous community of 90,000 people; its opponent was a little group of men; but they controlled in one aggregation not less than $160,000,000, besides large affairs outside of this. The assessed valuations of the property of the people on which Toledo could levy

---

[1] City of Toledo and Its Natural Gas Bonds, p. 5.

taxation was, in 1889, but $33,200,000. The total income of the municipality was $961,101; that of a single member of the little group opposing them had been acknowledged to be $9,000,000 a year, and was believed by the best informed to be several times as much. This individual income was greater than the product of all the manufactories of the city, and three times greater than the combined wages of the workmen in these establishments. There were several members of the natural-gas syndicate who collected and disbursed every year more than the community. Toledo had about the same population as Kansas in 1856. The slave power of the South that assailed the liberties of the 90,000 in Kansas numbered millions, but the new power in the North, which in a short generation had grown so strong that it did not fear to attack the 90,000 freemen of Toledo, counted only nine names. The people could act only after public deliberation, and through the slow stages of municipal and State procedure. Their antagonist met in secret council, and devised plans executed by a single hand, armed with the aggregated power of hundreds of millions of dollars, and liable, if found illegal or criminal, to only "nominal" punishment, or only 6 cents damages.[1]

At Columbus the struggle was with something very simple but extraordinarily difficult to overcome, as simple things often are—an obstinate, immovable, thoroughly angry public opinion, acting only through private voluntary means, its set will to exchange the fruits of its labor with whom and on what terms it pleased. There was absolutely no leverage to be got to bear upon the people of Columbus except by changing their feelings. Compulsion was out of the question. But at Toledo compulsion was possible. There the people had acted not through unofficial combination as at Columbus, but through the official machinery of the town and State. If the law could be turned against them by able counsel or compliant judges; if any smallest fault, however technical, could be found in the legislation of the State or the city or the

---

[1] Chs. xiv. and xxi.

practical administration of the official machinery provided for the natural-gas business of the city—if this could be done, the people of Toledo could be compelled, however little their will had changed, to see their enterprise of independence balked; this compulsion could be carried to the use of force if they resisted, and the militia of the State and the regular army could be brought into the conflict.

Such is the prize of power which tempts—more than tempts, drives as by fate—our overgrown wealth to fortify itself by control of judges, governors, presidents, commanders-in-chief —all the agents of the supreme authority and force.

Columbus was so local that its people were sufficient unto themselves. All they had to do was to keep on saying, We will not buy. But Toledo was a citizen of the great world of affairs and finance. It was part of London, New York, Chicago. Much of it was owned as an investment elsewhere. Sensitive nerves connected it with all the markets, especially the greatest of all—the money-market. It sold and bought and borrowed and lent far beyond its own border. What Wall Street gossips said about the people of Columbus would not make a dollar's difference to the whole town in a year, but a whisper started through the offices of the great capitalists in New York and abroad would flash back by wire to Toledo, and go like a quick poison through its industries and credit, private and public.

"Private enterprise" could not afford to let the people of Toledo go forward with their public enterprise. Many millions had been invested in getting control of a business representing $200,000,000. Many towns and cities, as Fostoria, Sandusky, Fremont, Clyde, Bellevue, Norwalk, Perrysburgh, Tiffin, and Detroit, were being supplied with gas at a handsome profit. If Toledo should set a successful example of self-supply, it would find imitators on every side. The essence of "private enterprise" was that the people should get their gas from Captains of Industry, and pay them for their captaincy two or three times the real cost as profit, just as monarchical countries pay kings for kindly supplying the people with the government which really comes from the people. The essence of municipal supply was that the people should supply themselves at cost without profit, and without Captains of Industry, except as the people provided them. Toledo, in fine, proposed to keep step with the modern expansion of self-government, which finds that it can apply principles and methods of democracy to industry. It proposed to add another to many demonstrations already made, noticeably in this very department of gas supply to municipalities, of the truth that the ability to carry on the business of supplying the various wants of mankind is not a sort of divine right vouchsafed from on high to a few specially inspired and gifted priests of commerce, by whose intermediation alone can the mysteries of trade be operated; but, like the ability to govern and be governed, is one of the faculties common to mankind, capable of being administered of, by, and for the people, and not needing to be differentiated as the prerogative of one set of men. The Toledo experiment was another step forward in the world-wide movement for the abolition of millionaires—a movement upon which the millionaires look with unconcealed apprehension for the welfare of their fellow-beings.

Mankind views with equanimity the expulsion of the profit-hunter from the businesses of carrying letters, minting coins, administering justice, maintaining highways, collecting taxes, in which millionaireism has been universally put an end to. It views with hopes of larger results the newer manifestations of the same tendency which in England have abolished millionaireism in telegraphs and parcel express; in Germany and France, Australia, and India have gone a long way towards the abolition of the millionaire in railroads; and in various cities and towns in Europe, America, and Australia have put up local signs, "No millionaires allowed here," by the municipalization of trade in water, gas, electricity, street-railways, baths, laundries, libraries, etc. The trust of millionaires was therefore fighting for a principle, and what will good men not sacrifice to principle!

CHAPTER XXIII

Towns, like men, stamp themselves with marked traits.
Toledo had an individuality which showed itself from the
start. Its leading men clubbed together and borrowed money
as early as 1832 to build one of the first railroads constructed
west of the Alleghanies—the Erie and Kalamazoo, to connect
Toledo and Adrian. When, in 1845, the steamboats on the
lakes formed a combination, and discriminated against Toledo,
the city through its council refused to submit, and appropriated $10,000 to get an independent boat to Buffalo. The city
appropriated its credit and revenues to other important and
costly enterprises, including four railroads, to keep it clear of
the cruel mercies of private ownership of the highways. In
1889 it expended $200,000 to secure direct railway connec-
tions with the Pennsylvania and the Baltimore and Ohio railways for competition in rates with the Lake Shore Railroad.

As it had been authorized to do so by the State, the City
Council of Toledo, April 29, 1889, ordered gas bonds to the
amount of $75,000 sold, that work on the city pipe line
might begin. Before proceeding with the enterprise confided
to them, the natural-gas trustees gave the private companies
an opportunity to save themselves from the competition of
the city. They asked them in writing if they would agree
to furnish gas cheaply for a term of years, or if they would
sell their entire plant to the city? They did this, as they expressed it, as "an honorable effort . . . to obtain cheaper gas
without unnecessary expenditure, and without injury to established rights." After a delay of nearly a month a reply
was received, refusing to enter into negotiations either for a

reduction of charges or for the sale of the private plants to the city. The trustees then asked for a personal interview, but this was refused. Then when the city began preparations to sell its bonds, a cannonade was opened on it in the courts, the money-market, the gas-fields, the city government, the press, among the citizens, and everywhere. Injunctions were applied for in three courts, unsuccessfully in all instances. No injunction was ever granted in these or any other of the many suits brought for the purpose of enjoining the sale of the bonds. Courts will usually grant temporary injunctions awaiting a hearing on the merits when complainants will enter into ample bonds and indemnify defendants. But the parties instigating this litigation would not put up the necessary bonds. They thus could smirch the bonds without incurring any personal liability in so doing.

An expensive array of lawyers was sent before the United States courts to prevent the issue of the bonds on the ground that they were illegal, and the law under which they were issued unconstitutional. The principle involved had been frequently discussed and always upheld both by the Supreme Court of Ohio and the Supreme Court of the United States.[1]

"Does not your argument appear to be in conflict with the views of the Supreme Court of Ohio and the Supreme Court of the United States?" the judge asked. The counsel for the gas companies responded in substance : " If so, then so much the worse for the views of those courts."

As it was through the suffrage that the people of Toledo were able to do this, the attack was widened from an attack on the enterprise to one upon the sovereignty of the citizens which made it possible. "Everybody votes in Ohio—in fact, too many people," said the lawyer who applied for an injunction against Toledo. If he had his way, he declared, there would be fewer voters, and he stigmatized the arguments of Toledo as those of John Most, the communist.

"Unquestionably," decided Judge Jackson, "the Legisla-

---

[1] State, *ex rel.*, *vs.* City of Toledo, 48th Ohio State Reports, p. 112.

ture may authorize a city to furnish light, or facilities for transportation, or water to its citizens, with or without cost, as the Legislature or city may determine. . . . Since the decision in Sharpless *vs.* Philadelphia it is no longer an open question whether municipalities may engage in enterprises such as the one contemplated by the act in question in this case. The act of January 22, 1889, authorizing the city of Toledo to issue bonds for natural-gas purposes, is clearly within the general scope of legislative power, is for a public use and purpose, and is not in contravention of any of the provisions of the constitution. The court being of the opinion that the legislation is valid, it follows, of course, that the injunction applied for must be refused." [1] When the news of Judge Jackson's decision was telegraphed to Toledo nothing less than the booming of cannon could express the joy of the citizens. They sent this message to the just judge : "One hundred guns were fired to-night by the citizens of Toledo in honor of your righteous decision to-day." Judge Jackson again upheld the bonds at Toledo, January 14, 1890, when he again dismissed the case against the city "for want of equity, at cost of complainants."

The favorable decision by Judge Jackson, although an appeal was taken, made it possible for the city to sell the $75,000 bonds which had been issued by order of the Council. The bonds brought par, interest, and over $2000 premium. With the money thus procured the city's Board of Natural Gas Trustees began operations. Their opponents had spread far and loud among the voters before the election—among those who would be likely to buy the bonds, everywhere it would hurt—the assertion that all the territory that was good had been bought up by them, and the city's trustees would not be able to get any. One of the companies had no less than 140,000 acres of gas lands in its possession or under contract, at a cost in rentals and royalties of $100,000 a year.[2] But the city trustees, even with the small sum at their com-

---

[1] *Federal Court Reporter*, vol. xxxix., pp. 651–54.

[2] Report of the Northwestern Ohio Natural Gas Company, January 7, 1889.

mand, were able to secure at the very beginning wells with a capacity more than four times as great as the private companies had had when the latter began the investment of a million or more to lay their pipe lines to Toledo.[1]   Together with this supply the city trustees got 650 acres about 35 miles from Toledo of as choice gas territory as there was in Ohio, almost all of it undrilled, and they had offers amounting to 5000 acres more within piping distance from the city.   The city's trustees made their purchases with success, and received the laudations of their constituents for having got lands and wells at better prices than the private companies.

August 26, 1889, after a decision in the United States courts that there was no ground on which to object to the issue of the bonds, the City Council voted the issue of the remaining $675,000.

Defeated in the public debate which preceded the decision of Toledo to supply itself; defeated at the State Capitol; defeated at the polls of Toledo time and again—every time; defeated in the Common Council; defeated in the gas-fields; defeated in the courts of their own choosing, the opponents of the city, thorough as only the very good or the very bad can be, refused to submit.   When the two corporations, in 1886, were seeking the franchise indispensable for doing business in Toledo, they said to the Board of Aldermen: "We ask no exclusive privilege. . . . We cannot have too many gas companies."   They also said: "If the city desires to furnish its own gas, there is nothing in this ordinance to hinder it.   We are ready and willing at any time to enter into competition with the city or any other company."   They said, on the same occasion, in answer to apprehensions which had been expressed about the danger of putting the fuel supply of the city into the hands of a monopoly: "You can go before the Legislature and obtain the right to issue bonds for furnishing yourselves with gas."   It was by these assurances the companies induced the Common Council to grant

---

[1] Toledo and Its Natural Gas Bonds, pp. 36–37.

them gratuitously the very valuable franchises they were seeking.

The right of the people to compete was not left to these assurances. It was specifically and formally asserted in the ordinance of July 5, 1887, fixing rates. This was the ordinance to procure which the gas company suspended its operations in mid-course, and declared it would not continue unless the prices which it wanted were made. The ordinance was, in fact, prepared by the company. It said: "Provided that nothing herein contained shall be construed as granting to existing companies any exclusive rights or privileges, or prevent any other company from furnishing natural gas to the citizens of said city." But the same learned counsel who, in behalf of the companies, had assured the city that "there was nothing in this ordinance to hinder it," went before the United States Court and pleaded that ordinance as good reason for the intervention of the Federal Government to prevent the city from going on with its enterprise.

The only morning paper—an able advocate of the city pipe line — suddenly changed owners and opinions. Among its new directors were two of the lawyers of the trust opposing the city, a director in one of its companies, and, besides them, the manager, a contract editor from Pennsylvania. His sole conspicuity there had been won in turning against the people of the oil regions a paper which had been their stanchest defender. This Toledo daily, in its espousal of the cause of the city, had been firing hot shot like this against the oil combination: "It wants a monopoly of the natural-gas business. This is what it is driving at." Under its new management it roared like a sucking dove, thus: "It is fashionable with demagogues and men who are not capable of appreciating the worth of brains in business to howl against it"—the oil combination—"as a grasping, grinding monopoly." Just after the people had decided in favor of the pipe line, and only a few days before it changed owners, it had said: "All manner of influences were brought to bear to defeat this proposition.... All the plausible falsehoods that could

be invented, and all the money that could be used, were indus-
triously employed, but the people saw the situation in its true
light, and the majority voted right." It now made the defeat
of the city's pipe line the chief aim of its endeavors. In this
work "no rule or principle recognized in decent journalism
was respected."

In all the history of Toledo no interest on its bonds had
ever been defaulted or delayed; no principal ever unpaid at
maturity. The city was prosperous, its growth steady; its
debt growing less year by year in proportion to its population and wealth. Its bonds ranked among the choicest investments, and commanded a premium in the money-market.[1]
But the credit and fair fame of the city were now over-
whelmed with wholesale vituperation by this paper, and others
elsewhere under similar control. Articles were carefully prepared for this purpose by skilled writers. These were then
copied from one newspaper to another. By some arrangement insertion was obtained for them in financial journals in
New York and in London, and in other foreign capitals. The
Toledo organ declared that Toledo was an unsafe place for
the investment of capital in any form. Its public affairs
were said to be run by a set of "demagogues and speculators,"
whose administration was "piratical mob rule." The city
pipe line was a "monstrous job," and the men who favored it
were "a gang of throttlers and ravenous wolves." They were
"blatant demagogues, who made great pretence of advancing
the city's interest, but whose real aim is to enrich themselves
at public expense." The bonds, which had been issued in due
form by special authority of the Legislature, ratified by a vote
of more than three-fifths of the citizens, and declared to be
valid by the United States Court, were described as "chro-
mos," "worthless rags," "bad medicine," "disfigured securities," "like rotten eggs, highly odorous goods," "but few persons at most can be found ignorant enough to buy them."

The Mayor, City Auditor, Board of Natural Gas Trustees,

---

[1] City of Toledo and Its Natural Gas Bonds, p. 3.

united with a citizens' committee of the Board of Trade in a plan to promote the sale of the bonds direct to the people of Toledo through a financial institution of the highest standing. This action the paper described as "a scheme for gulling simples," "a blind pool," "an unpatented financial deadfall"; compared it with "gambling, pool-playing, and lottery selling." These grave charges were widely circulated throughout the country. Bankers and capitalists in other cities who received them had no means of knowing that they were not what they pretended to be—the honest if uncouth utterances of an independent press chastising the follies of its own constituency. Newspapers which supported the city's project were assailed as ruthlessly as the community and citizens. The *Blade* was constantly referred to as "The Bladder." Another journal was given a nickname too vulgar to be printed here. One of the most prominent journals of Ohio was punished by the following paragraph, which is a fair sample of the literary style of monopoly : "That aged, acidulous addlepate, the monkey-eyed, monkey-browed monogram of sarcasm, and spider-shanked, pigeon-witted public scold, Majah Bilgewater Bickham, and his backbiting, black-mailing, patent-medicine directory, the *Journal*."

An old journalist and honorable citizen who wrote over his initials, " C. W.," a series of able and dignified letters in the *Blade*, which had a great influence in the formation of public opinion in favor of the pipe line, was assailed with " brutal falsifier," "hoary old reprobate," " senile old liar." Caricatures were published depicting the buyers of the bonds as "simple greens." When the County Court of Lucas County, following the United States Court, sustained the bonds on their merits, and did so on every point in question, because, as the judge stated, "the equities of the case are with the defendants," the organ falsely stated that judgment for the city was given "because the merits of the case are involved in a higher court." When a capitalist of New York, who had been an investor in the bonds of Toledo and a taxpayer there for twenty-five years—one of the streets of the city was named for him — bought $10,000 of the city pipe-line bonds, the paper attacked him by name in an article headed "Bunco Game," charging him with being a party to a bunco game in connection with "public till-tappers" for "roping Toledo citizens into buying doubtful securities." When the Sinking Fund Commissioners of Toledo very properly invested some of the city's money in the gas bonds, they were held up by name as "public till - tappers," "menials" of a "hungry horde" of "boodle politicians," accomplices of "plunderers of the public treasury," unable to withstand "the brutal threats and snaky entreaties of the corrupt gas ring." For one of the associate editors the position of Deputy State Inspector of Oil was obtained—an appointment which cost the Governor who made it many votes in the next election, and did much to defeat him. Such an appointment might give a versatile employé the chance to do double duty : as editor to brand as bad good men who could not be bought, and as inspector to brand as good bad oil for sale.[1]

One of the means taken to defeat the pipe line was the publication of very discouraging accounts of the "failure" at Indianapolis, where the citizens had refused to give a natural-gas company belonging to the oil trust the franchise it demanded, and, forming an anti-monopoly trust, had undertaken to supply themselves. Some "influence" prevented the Common Council of Toledo from sending a committee to Indianapolis to investigate. A public-spirited citizen, prominent and successful in business, came forward, and at his own expense secured a full and accurate account of the experience of Indianapolis for the city. This proved that the people were getting their fuel gas at less than one-half what Toledo was paying. The contest against giving the Indianapolis franchise to a corporation of the trust had been a sharp one. Its success was due to the middle classes and the working-men, who stood together for freedom, incorruptible by all the powerful influences employed. "We will burn soft coal all

---

[1] See ch. xxix.

our lives," one of their leaders told the Toledo committee, "rather than put ourselves in the power of such men."

In Indiana the Legislature meets only once in two years, and when this issue arose had adjourned, and would not meet again for a year. The people, not being able to get authority for a municipal gas pipe line, went to work by voluntary co-operation. Every voting precinct in the city was organized and canvassed for the capital needed. The shares were $25 each, and they were bought up so rapidly that the entire amount—$550,000—was subscribed in sixteen days by 4700 persons, without a cent of cost to the city. When subscriptions to the amount of $550,000 had been raised, $600,000 more was borrowed on certificates of indebtedness.

Gas lands were bought and 200 miles of pipe lines laid, all at a cost of about $1,200,000. The income in one year, during a part of which the system was still under construction, was $349,347. In the first year of complete operations the Indianapolis people's trust paid off $90,000 of the principal. The income for the year ending October 31, 1892, was $483,258.21, and the bonded debt has been paid. The stock, since January 1, 1893, has been paying dividends at the rate of 8 per cent. a year.

A prominent citizen of Indianapolis, one of the State judges, told the Toledo papers, in an interview: "The private companies had their gas laid to the city and along the streets several months in advance of the Citizens' Trust, but it did them little good. Everybody said: 'I will wait for the Consumers' Trust.' 'Yes, but we will furnish you gas just as cheap,' said the Indianapolis company; 'why not take it of us?' To this the citizens replied: 'To take gas of you means cheap gas to-day, but high gas to-morrow.' And wait for the gas they all did." The charge to manufacturers was $2\frac{1}{2}$ cents a thousand feet, as against 8 cents, at that time charged at Toledo. There were 12,000 private consumers. Cooking-stoves in Indianapolis were about $12 a year, against $19.50 in Toledo. One of the representatives of the private company declared at a public meeting at Indianapolis that its charges were made

21

such as to give a full return of all the invested capital in three years, as that was the probable life of the supply. A year after the inauguration of the Indianapolis movement a committee of the citizens at Dayton, who had risen against the extortionate prices charged them, investigated the condition of affairs at Indianapolis. They reported that Indianapolis had paid $200,000 on its bonded debt, and was getting ready to pay as much more. The Consumers' Trust supplied between 10,000 and 11,000 consumers, and spent $1,000,000 less than the Dayton private company spent to supply 3000 fewer consumers. The annual charge at Dayton was $54.80 ; at Indianapolis only $26.80—less than half.

When facts like these were brought out, to the demolition of the fictions circulated in Toledo, the answer was characteristic. The "organ" could not deny the statements, but it fell upon the citizen through whose generosity the information had been got for the people, and assailed his private character in articles which, one of the daily papers declared, editorially, "would almost, if not quite, justify him in shooting their author on sight."

This newspaper charged the city natural-gas trustees with being "rotten to the core," and with every variation of phrase possible to its exuberant rhetoric sounded the changes upon their official career as a "big steal," "fostered by deception, falsehood, and skull-duggery." It sought to intimidate the Legislature and the courts when they failed to enact or construe laws against the people. It said : "Law-makers, judges, and others may feel the force of this element when the proper time comes and political preferment is sought."

It was money in pocket that facts like those of the experience of Indianapolis, Detroit, and other places should not be made known. Even ideas must not be allowed to reach the public mind. Professor Henry C. Adams, the well-known political economist, lectured in Toledo during this contest, in a University Extension Course, on "Public Commissions Considered as the Conservative Solution of the Monopoly Problem." The "organ" gave a synopsis of the lecturer's views, which is printed herewith in parallel columns, with a synopsis of what Mr. Adams really said, as revised by himself:

WHAT THE ORGAN OF MONOPOLY REPORTED.	WHAT THE LECTURER REALLY SAID.
The lecturer made reference to Toledo as an unfavorable place to discuss the matter of municipal control of quasi-public business and competition of municipalities with private corporations. But he deprecated anything in that line. He did not mention particular instances, but broadly condemned the policy pursued by this city in matters of this kind, and his remarks had a visible effect on his audience. He considered municipal control of business enterprises the worst form of monopoly, as they began by having the unfair advantage of the law-making power, and the tendency to corruption was greater than when individual enterprises were asking privileges. The audience was much pleased with the lecturer.	Professor Adams thought the solution of the monopoly problem must be found either in public control or in public ownership. He advocated public control, and held that the State and Federal railroad commissions should have a fair trial, that their hands should be strengthened by further and adequate legislation. He entertained the hope that this control and regulation would ultimately protect the interests of the public in a satisfactory manner. He was willing to admit, however, if this effort to secure the needed public control by the aid of commissions and legislation should fail, then public ownership was the only remaining solution. He held that in local monopolies it may still be wise to try the experiment of public control by aid of commissions. He said, however, that if anything should be owned and controlled by and for the people it would be street-railroads, gas and water works. He admonished his audience not to be misled by the argument that municipal ownership would be dangerous because of undue political influence, for the local monopolies under private ownership were already in politics, and in a most dangerous manner. He observed facetiously that he hesitated to discuss the question of municipal control or ownership before a Toledo audience.

From the control of the markets to the control of the minds of a people—this is the line of march.

So direct, persistent, and bold were the charges of corruptions rung day after day by this journal against all the officials concerned in the city gas enterprise that some people began to believe there must be truth in them.   But when the community at last turned upon its maligners, and the grand-jury brought indictments against the active manager of the paper and his chief assistant for criminal libel upon the city's natural-gas trustees, the whole structure of their falsehood went down at a breath.   They had no defence whatever. They made no attempt to justify their libels or even explain them.   Their only defence was a series of motions to get the indicted editor cleared as not being responsible for what had appeared in the paper.   Counsel labored over the contention that the accused was none of the things which the language of the law holds for libel. He was neither the "proprietor," "publisher," "editor," "printer," "author," nor a person "who uttered, gave, sold, or lent" a copy of the newspaper, but only the "manager."   The employés gave testimony which would have been ludicrous but for the contempt it showed for court and community.   The journalist who was the "managing editor" of the paper under the indicted chief editor was asked :

"Who was the head of the paper when you entered upon your duties as managing editor ?"

"I do not know."

"Who hired you as managing editor ?"

"I really can't say that I was hired at all."

"Who employed you to come to Toledo ?"   The witness had been an employé in Pennsylvania of the editor on trial, and had followed the latter to Toledo to take the place of managing editor.   "Nobody employed me."

The son of the indicted editor had also followed his father to Toledo, and was employed on his paper.   Asked for what purpose he came, he said : "I had no purpose in coming."

The gentleman who had charge of the counting-room was asked who fixed his salary.

"I regulate my own."

The advertising manager declared :

" I have no knowledge who is my superior."

The accused had to let the case go to the jury without a spark of proof of the accusations which had filled the paper every day for months. He had no evidence to offer either that the charges were true, or that he believed them to be true. He stood self-confessed as having for years printed daily gross libels on citizens, officials, and community, as part of the tactics of a few outside men to prevent a free city from doing with its own means in its own affairs that which an overwhelming public opinion, and the legislative, executive, and judicial authorities, and its present antagonists themselves, had all sustained its right to do. The agent of this wrong was found guilty, and sentenced to imprisonment in the county jail, with heavy costs and fine ; like the unhappy agents at Buffalo—" made cheap " for others.[1] But sentence was suspended pending hearing of the motion for a new trial. This did not come up for a year. The court could find no error in the proceedings of the trial court, and could not sustain any of the objections made. But it found a point which even the lawyers had not hit on, and strained this far enough to grant the new trial. Then the convicted editor went before another judge—not the one who had tried him—pleaded guilty, and was fined, and so saved from jail.

One of the last scenes in this Waterloo was the abandonment of the newspaper with which the corruption and intimidation of public opinion had been attempted. Failure was confessed by the sale of the paper, and it was bought by a journalist who had been especially prominent in the defence of the city, and against whom on that account a bitter warfare had been waged by the daily which now passed into his possession. The *Sunday Journal* of Toledo, in commenting on the surrender, declared that the course of the organ had been one of the strongest factors of the success of the people. " In every possible way it slandered and outraged the city, where of necessity it looked for support. There could be but one result. Scores who had opposed the pipe line became its most ardent advocates purely in the general defence."

[1] See ch. xx.

CHAPTER XXIV

HIGH FINANCE

WHEN Judge Jackson refused to enjoin the city from issuing its bonds an appeal was taken. The court and the lawyers of the city were promised that it would be carried up without delay. Months passed, and no use was made of the privilege of filing new pleadings and taking new testimony— that is, no use but to make the suits the basis for libels on Toledo and its bonds.

Time ran on until the day was at hand for opening bids for the bonds. That was to be Wednesday. Then the counsel for the opposition notified the city that on Monday they would begin the taking of depositions. This was not then or afterwards done, but on the strength of the notification news despatches were sent over the country that the proceedings against the legality of the Toledo bonds were being " pressed." In consequence of this and other manœuvres, when Wednesday came there were no bids. A hasty rally of some public-spirited capitalists at home, learning of the emergency, made up a subscription of $300,000. The names of the citizens who made this patriotic subscription were printed in the daily paper under the heading of "The Honor Roll."

Only by extraordinary manœuvres could the market for such securities offered by such a community have been thus killed in a time of great general and local prosperity, and extraordinary they were. What they were was formally and authoritatively ascertained by an investigation made by a committee appointed at a mass - meeting [1] of the citizens of

[1] October 19, 1889.

Toledo called by the mayor, the Hon. J. K. Hamilton. The call ran:

"For the first time in the history of Toledo, its general bonds, secured by the faith and property of the city, and bearing a fair rate of interest, have been offered, and only such of them sold as were taken at home by popular subscription. It is deemed desirable that under such circumstances the citizens of Toledo should meet together and determine what further steps should be taken to carry out the will of the people as expressed by 62 per cent. of the voters of the city.

"It is believed that with proper effort a large additional popular subscription may be obtained, and thus notice given to the world that notwithstanding all opposition the citizens of Toledo have confidence in and will maintain the credit of this fair city, and that a great enterprise undertaken by its people will not be defeated by the machinations of private opposing interests, no matter how powerful and unscrupulous."

The meeting appointed a committee of three—David Robinson, Jr., Frank J. Scott, and Albert E. Macomber—"to prepare and circulate throughout the financial circles of the country a pamphlet which shall set forth the case of the city of Toledo in its struggle against those who by anonymous circulars and other dishonorable ways have attempted to prevent the sale of the Toledo natural-gas bonds." This committee put the facts before the public in a very able pamphlet, "The City of Toledo and Its Natural Gas Bonds." In an official statement asked for by this committee the city natural-gas trustees say: "Skilled writers were employed to furnish articles for Eastern financial journals, to cast discredit on the bonds on the very grounds that had been set aside by Judge Jackson's decision. Not content with this open warfare, anonymous circulars were sent to leading investment agencies in the United States, warning them to beware of these bonds, as they were under the cloud of doubtful constitutionality and an impending lawsuit. When the day arrived for bidding for the bonds no bids were made. Agents of investors were present, who came to bid, but by some unknown and powerful influence they were induced not to put in their bids. The writers are not aware that any similar mode of striking at the credit of a whole community was ever before resorted to in this country. It is an insult and a wrong not only to this city, against which it is aimed, but to people of independence everywhere in the United States who have a common interest in the maintenance of the rights of all." [1]

Press despatches impugning the validity of the bonds and misrepresenting the facts were sent all over the country. The anonymous circulars referred to were mailed to all the leading banks, investment agencies, capitalists, and newspapers. The New York *Mail and Express* said: "It would be decidedly interesting to know who is responsible for the . . . methods by which it was thought to prevent the city from undertaking the enterprise. A number of volunteer attorneys and correspondents deluged bankers and newspapers with letters warning them against the bonds which the city proposes to issue, on the ground that it had no right to issue them. The *Mail and Express* received several communications of this kind."

"Not only the financial centres of this country," say the city's natural-gas trustees in their official report for 1890, "but those of Europe were invaded with these circulars." [2] The circular was headed "Caveat Emptor." It contained twenty-four questions, and every one of the answers, except those which referred to matters of record and routine, like the date, amount, name, etc., of the bonds, was incorrect. What hurt the people of Toledo most, as it was most base and baseless, was its attack on their hitherto unquestioned credit and financial honor. Asking the question, "How does the credit of the city stand?" the circular answered: "Refunding has been going on ever since 1883. The bonded debt was greater at the beginning of 1889 than of 1888; bonds bearing interest at 8 per cent. will become due in three or four years. The mayor, in his last annual message, admits the inability of the city to pay much of these except the refunding." "Willing to wound, and yet afraid to strike," the authors of this attempt to pull down an entire city managed, by the inter-

---

[1] City of Toledo and Its Natural Gas Bonds, pp. 6–7.
[2] Annual Report of the Natural Gas Trustees, 1890, p. 9.

weaving of such phrases as "ever since 1883," "bonded debt greater," "inability of the city to pay," to create by insinuation the feeling of financial distrust for which their greatest industry and ingenuity had been able to find not a particle of foundation. No modern municipality is asked or expected or desired "to pay much except the refunding." Capitalists would greatly prefer that even the refunding should not be carried on, but that the debt should run along at the original high rates of interest, which they regretfully see dwindling away. The circular failed to state that the city was borrowing money at 4 per cent. to pay off debts bearing 8 per cent. The insinuations of the circular could have been used of "the credit" of the United States, New York, Paris, London, Chicago, with the same appropriateness—with this exception, that Toledo's municipal financial credit was relatively to its resources on a sounder and more conservative basis than these much more highly financed cities. The circular did not state that the proportions of debt to population had been decreasing for many years past.[1]

"Toledo has not two years' supply of gas," the circular said, "in all the territory acquired." The State Geologist, in his annual report for 1890, said that Toledo would have no gas to supply its pipe lines or citizens in 1891. In 1892 the city pipe line supplied gas to the value of $168,954.46. Three years have passed, Toledo wells still flow, and new ones are being found continually. "Whatever may have been his object," say the city gas trustees, "in volunteering such a statement, we know that so far in 1891 it is untrue, and that such positive declarations, based upon hypothetical conditions, are utterly unworthy of scientific pretensions."[2] The State Geologist also took part in his annual report in the debate between municipal control and private enterprise, siding altogether with the latter.

The quantity of gas land owned by the city was put by the circular at 300 to 500 acres. The city had 650 acres. The

[1] City of Toledo and Its Natural Gas Bonds, p. 3.
[2] Toledo Natural Gas Trustees' Report, 1890, p. 7.

circular declared the life of an ordinary well to be one to three years. There is no such limit. Referring to the quantity of gas land the city had, the circular asked and answered:

" Cannot other territory be acquired ?

" Not in Northwestern Ohio, and not nearer than the gas fields of Indiana."

This was untrue, for the gas trustees had already been offered, as stated, several thousands of acres of the best gas lands in addition to those they had bought. But the authors of the circular did their best to make it true. The city's natural-gas trustees say in their report for 1890: " As soon as the trustees were prepared to negotiate for gas wells and gas territory, the field swarmed with emissaries and agents of the Northwestern Ohio Natural Gas Company to compete with the trustees. In order to prove what had been previously stated, ' that Toledo could procure no gas territory,' no means were left untried ; agents of that company even fraudulently represented themselves to the owners of gas property that they were connected with the gas trustees and working in their interest, and in some instances introducing themselves as the president of this board. Prices went up 1000 per cent. in some instances rather than let it fall into the hands of the trustees. A conspicuous officer of that company, as an excuse for paying an enormous sum of money for a gas well, is reported as saying, ' We did not want the gas well, but we had to buy it in order to keep Toledo from getting hold of it.' " [1]

Referring to the private companies, " Are the people of the city already supplied with natural gas for public and private use ?" the circular asked. " They are," it answered, and goes on : " Why does the city want to go into the natural-gas business, then ?" " To boom the lands of real-estate speculators." This is a charge affecting the Legislature and Executive and State courts of Ohio, the courts of the United States, the people of Toledo, and all the members of their

---

[1] Annual Report of the Natural Gas Trustees, 1890, p. 8.

city government. Burke confessed that he did not know how to draw up an indictment against a whole people. That art has been acquired since his day.

"Are these bonds of unquestionable validity?" this catechism of libel upon a community queries.

"By no means. Prominent taxpayers have suits pending attacking the constitutionality of the act under which they are issued."

"Have these cases," the last question ran, "ever been tried on their merits?"

"They have not."

They had been tried so far that the United States and State courts had refused on every ground urged to interfere with their issue and sale, declaring the legislation authorizing them to be valid. They had never been tried any further in the United States courts for a very good—or bad—reason. The "prominent taxpayers," after their defeat before Judge Jackson, took every possible means to prevent the case from reaching a final adjudication. The invariable rule of the United States Supreme Court has been to treat as final and conclusive the decisions of State courts as to such domestic issues. During the hundred years of its existence not a case can be found in which that court has overruled the fixed and received construction given to a State law by the courts of that State.[1] The only hope for the suit of the "prominent taxpayers" was, therefore, that the Supreme Court of the United States would for their special profit reverse the practice to which it had consistently adhered since the establishment of the government. What they really thought of their prospect of success in that effort they confessed when their case, no longer delayable, was upon the point of being reached.

They who had been so "anxious to get to the case as soon as possible" refrained from printing the record, a condition precedent to putting the case on the docket of the United States Supreme Court. The city wanted the decision, and in order

[1] "Constitutional History as Seen in the Development of American Law." Lecture by D. H. Chamberlain. G. P. Putnam's Sons, New York.

that the case might not be dismissed for this failure to print
the record, and a decision upon the merits be thus prevented,
the city's gas trustees advanced the money—$1100—to the
court printer for printing the record. Pushed thus against
their will to trial, when the day came on which they must
rise to state their case the opponents of Toledo folded their
tents and stole silently away. On the motion of their attorney the case was dismissed, against the protest of the city.
They paid all the costs, including the money advanced by the
city for printing the record. To their defeat all along the
line they did not want to add a formal decision against them
from the Supreme Court, which was inevitable. And they
ran away to fight another day.

Another purpose of these suits was confessed only a few
weeks after this circular was issued. The existence of the
suits was used to try to frighten the city's natural-gas trustees into accepting a "compromise." The compromise was
that they should abandon the enterprise, sell out pipes and
lands for a fraction of their worth, get their gas from the
private company at higher rates, and put the city in its power
for all time to come. "It will be three or four years before
your case is through the Supreme Court," its representative
told the natural-gas trustees, in urging them to accept. "You
can't sell your bonds," he continued; "you have no money."
The "compromise" was refused, but the city's pipe line had
been delayed so long that the profits of the company for
another twelvemonth were secure.

The demonstration against the bonds in the United States
Circuit Court had been followed by similar suits in the State
courts. Here again the city was successful. It was upheld
on every controverted ground—in the enabling act, in the vote
of the people, in the appointment of the trustees by the governor, and in the issue of the city bonds. Appeal was taken
here, as in the United States courts, and, as there, for delay,
not for decision. To checkmate further use of this lawsuit to
smother the law and cripple the city, the friends of the pipe
line began a suit against the authorities to force an immedi-

ate decision from the Ohio Supreme Court as to the legality of the bonds. It was certainly, as was said in the press, "a curious state of things when the defendant is compelled to bring suit against himself because the plaintiff refuses to allow trial in his own case."

These litigations, the circulars, the press, were only part of the campaign. One of the committees of the Common Council was brought under control, and induced to throw technical difficulties in the way of the sale of the bonds, which caused months of delay.[1] Effort was made to get the Governor to appoint natural-gas trustees hostile to the city, but failed. It was attempted, also without success, to get the Legislature to prevent the sale of the bonds at private sale. During all this controversy the city was most fortunate in receiving the needful authority from the State Legislature. This was due mainly to a faithful and able representative of Toledo in that body, the Hon. C. P. Griffin. He was offered every promise of political preferment and other allurements to betray his constituents, but he always remained faithful. Without his support the efforts of the city would have failed. His services amid great temptations deserve the grateful remembrance of the public.

Some of the devices of "private enterprise" were childish enough. "A Business Men's Protest" was published, which proved under the microscope to have been largely signed by men whose names could not be found in the directory. A similarly formidable-looking remonstrance against the pipe-line bill was sent to the Legislature. It had 1426 names; of these 464 could not be found in the directory, and over 300 of the 962 remaining names signed the petition for the city's bill. Many of them avowed that when they had signed the "Remonstrance" it had a heading in favor of the pipe line, which must have been changed afterwards. As part of the tactics of misinformation, a report was published—in January, 1890—claiming to give the business of both the private com-

[1] Report of the Toledo Natural Gas Trustees, 1890, pp. 8–9.

panies; but the members of the Council Committee on Gas, when afterwards examining the books for the gas company, found that it gave the receipts of only one company. A paper was prepared by a citizens' meeting for circulation among the manufacturers to ascertain how much they would contribute towards the city pipe line; but when reported back to the meeting it had become, in some mysterious way, a paper asking the manufacturers how much they would advance to quite a different scheme, the effect of which would be to sell out the city pipe line or convert it into a manufacturers' line.

These were the infantile methods of men who could not see the ludicrousness of the position they put themselves in by such efforts to keep a business which they were constantly declaring to be hazardous and unprofitable.

Detectives appear in almost every scene of our story, and are as common in its plot as in any extravagant melodrama of the Bowery thirty years ago. To counteract the anonymous circulars the City Council sent a committee headed by Mayor Hamilton—the "War Mayor," one of the ablest lawyers of the city, upright and loyal at all times to Toledo—to visit the Eastern money-markets. The committee, in their official report, state that they were assured by responsible dealers in municipal securities in New York and Boston that they would bid for the entire amount to be sold. "We regret, however, to have to report that the powerful and influential parties who have on all occasions and in every way sought to obstruct and defeat the enterprise for which the proceeds of these bonds were to be used, in some way succeeded in inducing those who intended to purchase to withhold their bids—in fact, no matter how guarded our movements, we believe that every person or firm with whom we had interviews was reported to the agents of the Standard Oil Company, for in every instance where from our interviews we had encouragement that the bonds would be bid for, within a short time more or less influential agents of opponents interviewed these parties and succeeded in changing their minds."

What a picture of "high finance," of the "beneficent inter-play of the forces of supply and demand," of the "marvellous perfection" with which capital moves under "natural laws" to carry its fertilizing influences where they are most needed! The officials of this free city compelled to sneak around in the open money-market under cover with "guarded movements," seeking buyers for its bonds as if they were stolen goods! About them a cloud of spies and detectives reporting every movement as if it were a crime to the little handful of trust millionaires in their grand building on Broadway! "They have entered the —— Bank!" "They have just left ——'s office!" After each report the leash is slipped of a waiting sleuth, who flies away to run down the quarry.

The gas trustees made public a letter and telegram they received from a prominent New York bank:

"NEW YORK, November 27, 1889.

"DEAR SIR,—A gentleman named" (naming a man who signs the certificates of the Standard Oil Trust as treasurer),[1] "introduced by the card of Mr. ——" (one of the richest men in New York not otherwise known as connected with the trust), "called on us to-day and stated that understanding that our firm was on the point of bidding on the Toledo bonds, etc., he would caution against the purchase, as they were not legal. Mr. —— represented himself as coming from ——" (one of the companies of the oil combination), "and referred us to their lawyer for further information. Now as this may hurt the sale of the bonds we want to be cautious, and on Friday will make further inquiries, and will wire you accordingly. We may not care to hand in our bids on this account."

The telegram sent on Friday is as follows:

"NEW YORK, November 30th.

"Fearing sale of bonds has been injured, will not bid at present."

"That tells the story," said one of the trustees, "in a nut-shell."

A local bank bid for $500,000 of the bonds, but did not sustain its bid. A reputable citizen, an ex-mayor, wrote for publication in one of the leading journals that he had been

---

[1] Trusts, New York Senate, 1888, p. 659.

informed by a well-known banker there was reason to believe a banking firm which, in 1892, defaulted on its bid for bonds, had been indemnified by the opposition for the $5000 it thereby forfeited to the city, and for the profits it would have made from the sale of the bonds. With the city line crippled the gas company would pocket the profits on the sale of a million dollars' worth of gas a year. Five thousand dollars, or several times that, was a small insurance to pay for such a gain.

This was the game of hide-and-seek played in Wall Street by detectives and financial stilettos against "simple greens," who thought supply and demand still rule values. This was the reality which the officials of Toledo found behind the outward aspect of its magnificent buildings, the benevolent millionaires who look out through their plate-glass, the grandiloquent generalizations of professors about "the money-market."

The city was brought to the humiliation of seeing its officials meet in public session at an appointed hour to open bids it had invited from all the money centres for its bonds, only to have the news flashed all over the country that not a bid from abroad had been made. This opposition cost the city in one way and another not less than $1,000,000, according to the estimate of the city's natural-gas trustees. The feeling of the people was expressed in the following language in a circular sent out with the pamphlet report of the committee appointed in mass-meeting to make a statement of Toledo's case to the public:

"We have seen the modern aggregation of corporations—trusts—suppress other corporations in the same line of business. But this Toledo contest is believed to be the first instance where private corporations—creatures of the State—have assumed to exercise monarchical powers over a portion of the State—one of its leading municipalities; to dictate the policy of its people; to seek to control the legislation as to the laws that should be enacted for such portion of the State; to bribe and intimidate the votes of such city at the polls; to attempt to subsidize the press by the most liberal expenditure of money ; to at last purchase, out and out, a heretofore leading paper of the city, place its own managers and attorneys as directors, import one of its long-trained men as editor, and turn this paper into an engine of attack upon the city, an attack upon the city's honor and credit, characterized by the most unscrupulous misrepresentation and a perfect abandonment of all the amenities of civilized warfare."

The Toledo public felt no doubt as to who were attacking it under the convenient anonymity of the two gas corporations. At a public conference, January 16, 1889, between the presidents of the private natural-gas companies and the people assembled in mass-meeting, the representative of the former said the only condition on which the members of the oil trust had been induced to interest themselves in natural gas in Northwestern Ohio was that of absolute and unqualified control of the entire business through a majority of the stock of all the gas companies to be organized.

" The trust is interested in companies engaged in supplying natural gas ?" the president of the oil trust was asked by the New York Legislature about this time.

" To a limited extent, yes."

" Have they a majority interest in any of these companies ?"

" I think they have." [1]

This was identically the arrangement by which the nine trustees owned as their private property the control of the oil business. At several later conferences with the city's trustees and the Common Council the gas companies were represented by one of the principal members of the oil combination, the ingenious gentleman who had managed the negotiations with the railroads by which, under the *alias* of the American Transfer Company, the trust claimed and got a rebate of 20 to 35 cents a barrel,[2] not only on all oil it shipped, but on all shipped by its competitors. He was also its representative in the similar arrangement by which the Cleve-

<hr>

[1] Testimony, Trusts, New York Senate, 1888, p. 428.　　　[2] See p. 99.

22

land and Marietta Railroad agreed to carry its oil for 10
cents a barrel, to charge Rice 35 cents, and to pay it 25 out
of every 35 cents Rice paid.[1] He had acted in the same interest throughout the gas field as well as in oil, and his path-
way could be traced through one independent company after
another, whose wrecks, like those in oil, are milestones.

July 27, 1889, in an item originating in New York, in the
Tribune, a friendly paper, and given an extensive circulation
by news despatches sent to the leading papers in other cities,
it was said that the representatives of the oil trust "in this
city say emphatically that they will attack in the courts the
right of the city to issue them "—the bonds.

At the great meeting of the citizens, October 19, 1889, to
organize a popular subscription to take the bonds killed in the
money-market, the resolutions named the oil combination as
the power responsible for the attacks on the city, and appealed
to the people to observe that it, "no longer content with
destroying individuals and associations which stand in the
way of its moneyed interests, now rises to grapple with and
destroy the rights of cities and states; we therefore ask all
liberty-loving men to make common cause with us in the
defence of the community against the aggression of colossal
power."

The aldermen and the Common Council of Toledo unanimously adopted resolutions, September 15, 1890, requesting
the State and Federal courts to give decisions as promptly as
possible in the suits pending against the validity of the natural-gas bonds. These bodies in their official utterance declared that the oil combination, "through its officers and
agents in the city of Toledo and at many other points in the
United States, has circulated false and malicious statements
about the bonds of the city of Toledo issued for natural-gas
purposes." The natural-gas trustees of the city say in their
report for 1890: "These injunctions and circulars, although
fathered in the first instance by non-resident taxpayers, and

---

[1] See p. 206.

in the second by irresponsible or anonymous parties, were traced directly to the oil trust, a trust having a large number of corporations within its control, among which is the Northwestern Ohio Natural Gas Company, and to whom the city of Toledo may reasonably attribute a loss of more than a million of dollars already. What further financial embarrassment it may suffer in the future cannot be measured by the depravity and moral turpitude which its seeds have sown in our midst." [1]

When the warfare against Toledo became a scandal ringing throughout the country and beyond, the organ of the trust in Toledo attempted to make it appear that the oil trust was not the party in interest. But there was open confession on the record. Its connection and its control were admitted by two representatives in conference with a committee appointed by the mayor at their request to discuss the situation. [2] They described the circumstances under which the members of the oil trust had gone into the project of the Toledo line and the project of the natural-gas business. One of the two stated that he came into it as its "more direct representative." The pipe line of the private gas company was built, he went on to say, by one of the principal corporations in the oil trust. At the same interview it was admitted that the oil trust owned 60 per cent. of the natural-gas company's stock.

The people of Toledo did not surrender to this success of their enemies in the money-market. The bonds which calumny and espionage prevented them from selling at wholesale to the great capitalists of New York and Boston they took themselves at retail. The Legislature having given authority for such sales, a committee of one hundred had been appointed by the citizens' meeting, October 19, 1889, to canvass all the wards of the city for subscriptions to the gas bonds. "Gas Bond Pledges" were circulated, to which people subscribed according to their ability, in amounts ranging from $2 to $5000. The employés at the Wabash Railway's

---

[1] Annual Report of Natural Gas Trustees, 1890, p. 9.
[2] Toledo *Blade*, February 7 and 27, 1889.

car shops sent in a list signed by fifty names for a total of $1102, an average of $22 each. The labor of two hundred men for a week without pay was offered the gas trustees as an earnest of the good-will of the people. Piece by piece the city's pipe line was pushed through. At a critical moment a shrewd and patriotic contractor saved the enterprise by building a large part of the line, and taking for his pay the bonds the banks would not take. In June, 1890, the public were gratified by the announcement that their trustees had secured the means "for the construction of three miles more," making eight miles in all, or nearly one-fourth the entire line. In August a contract was made for five miles more, and so the work went on, step after step.

CHAPTER XXV

A SUNDAY IN JUNE

In the midst of the anxious discussion by the citizens of Toledo as to the character of the power which ruled them both by night and by day, the same question arose in the metropolitan religious press, but in its broader ethical aspects. After the petition of Toledo to be allowed to take the control of its light, heat, and power into its own hands had been laid before the Legislature, the *National Baptist* of Philadelphia, in an article on the trusts, criticised them as the prophet Nathan would have done. It gave to that in oil, "of course, the bad pre-eminence in all this matter." "This corporation has, by ability, by boldness, by utter unscrupulousness, by the use of vast capital, managed to control every producer, every carrier, to say nothing of the legislatures and courts." The *Examiner*, the leading religious weekly of the Baptist denomination in New York, rose against this. "We can readily understand how there should be differences of opinion in the matter of these trusts, and their influence is a proper subject of discussion; but to make it the occasion of so unjust and intemperate an attack on Christian men of the highest excellence of character is something that was not expected from a paper bearing such a name. The four most prominent men in the oil trust are eminent Baptists, who honor their religious obligations, and contribute without stint to the noblest Christian and philanthropic objects. . . . All of them illustrate in their daily lives their reverence for living Christianity."

The *National Baptist* did not submit to this attempt to cite men's creeds to prevent judgment on their deeds. It quoted the reply Macaulay makes Milton give to the similar pleas urged for King Charles: "For his private virtues they are beside the question. If he oppress and extort all day, shall he be held blameless because he prayeth at night and morning?" It held to its ground, and cited against the trust the recorded evidence, but it declared it was "a marked breach of propriety for the *Examiner* to bring their private character into the discussion." The *National Baptist*, going on to speak in praise of a series of lively cartoons in *Harper's Weekly* on the Forty Thieves of the Trusts and similar subjects, said, with some sadness: "It will be a sorry spectacle if the secular papers shall be ranged on the side of justice and the human race, while the defence of monopoly shall be left to the so-called representatives of the religious press."

Later, March 20, 1890, the *Examiner* returned again to its discussion of the religious performances of the chiefs of the oil trust as a matter of public importance. Of one of them it said: "The prayer-meetings of the Fifth Avenue Church are on Wednesday evening, and no business man in the church is less likely to be absent from one of them than he. His wife and children, when they are in the city, come with him, and it is by no means an unusual thing for the whole family to take part, each of them occupying one or two minutes of time. He and they are at church every Sunday when in the city, and no husband and wife keep up the good old Baptist habit more faithfully of exchanging a kind word with the brethren and sisters after the regular services are over. He dresses plainly, and so do his family, and every one of them has a kind heart and a pleasant word for all. They are among the last to leave the church and the prayer-meeting. Now the question is, How is it, as things go, that a man possessing the great wealth imputed to him should have so warm a fraternity of feeling for the lowly in their temporal conditions? And is there not an example here that might well be imitated in all the churches of our Lord?"

In an address on Corporations the reverend secretary of the Church Edifice Department of the Home Missionary Department of the Baptist Church followed the example of the leading Church journal. "The oil trust was," he said, "begun and carried on by Christian men.[1] They were Baptists, and, so far as the speaker knew, both the objects and the methods of the oil trust were praiseworthy." A clergyman of another denomination once called upon one of the great men of the trust to seek a subscription.

"But," said the rich man, "I am not of your Church."

"That does not matter," said the minister, "your money is orthodox."

The secular press followed the example of the religious press in treating their public faithfulness to Church ceremonies as news of the day, and part of the record of their social functions. The New York correspondent of the Philadelphia *Daily Record* wrote for the people of Philadelphia: "It is not often that a millionaire stands up to lead in prayer, but I heard the president of the oil combination make an excellent prayer the other evening. He is said to be worth $25,000,000, but he neither drinks nor uses tobacco, and he is a deacon in Dr. Armitage's church. He likes a fast horse, and has eleven horses in his stable here. Few men, however, lead plainer lives than he, and few put on less style. He gives liberally to unsectarian charities, but, he says, 'when it comes to Church work I always give to the Baptists—my own denomination— and to no other Church.'" A New York daily described the same trustee "as one of the few millionaires who devote much of their time to the improvement of the condition of others. When not called away by social or business engagements, you are pretty sure to find him at home evenings. Here, in his costly and well-equipped library, he receives his visitors, many of whom represent the various benevolent and religious undertakings in which he is interested. He has for years been a hearty supporter, financially and personally, of foreign-missionary work, and no layman, perhaps, is so well informed concerning the details of it. He has a personal acquaintance with many of the leading missionaries of the world, and his

---

[1] New York *Sun* of March 31, 1891.

residence is frequently the scene of a gathering of these workers among the heathen. He is now devoting considerable attention to home-missionary work, a field which, he is convinced, presents splendid opportunities for Christian endeavor."

Many descriptions have been given by the press, metropolitan and interior, of the success with which one of the trustees built up the largest Sunday-school in his city at the same time that he was building up the monopoly—leading the children of his competitors and customers to salvation with his left hand, while with his right he led their fathers in the opposite direction financially. The church where these men appear has had columns of admiring description in the leading daily papers of New York and other cities. "There are few wealthier congregations than this one," says a reporter of the New York *World*, though he adds, "the wealth is elsewhere more evenly divided." The trustee of the light of the world "is the magnate of the church, the centre around which all lesser millionaire lights revolve. Everybody stops to speak and shake hands with him. Everybody smiles upon him, this modest man of nearly $200,000,000." "It is amusing," says the Brooklyn *Eagle*, "to note the manner in which his neighbors watch him during the service. Quite a number of people loiter near the door to see him as he walks out of church." "They are worth a bit of careful study," says another paper of the trustees, "and no place is quite so convenient as when they are at church. Their interest in religion is as sincere as their belief in oil. From the moment they enter church until they leave they are examples that Christians of high and low degree might follow with profit." "They have made the most of both worlds," writes another journalist. The oil trust was criticised by the Rev. Washington Gladden at Chautauqua, in 1889. One of its prominent officials, as reported in a friendly journal, defended it as "a sound Christian institution; and all these communistic attacks are due entirely to the jealousy of those who cannot stand other people's prosperity."[1]

[1] New York *Tribune*, April 23, 1889

"In Anniversary week" in Boston, in May, 1889, at the meeting of the American Baptist Education Society, the secretary said he had an announcement to make. "It had been whispered about," says the New York *Examiner* of May 23, 1889, from whose friendly account we are quoting, "that something important was to occur at this meeting, and a breathless silence awaited the announcement. Holding up a letter, the secretary said that he had here a pledge from a princely giver to our educational causes, naming him (here he was interrupted by a tremendous cheer), of $600,000 for the proposed Chicago college. . . . This statement was followed by a perfect bedlam of applause, shouts, and waving of handkerchiefs. One brother on the platform was so excited that he flung his hat up into the air, and lost it among the audience." Eloquent speeches at once overflowed the lips of the leading men of the meeting, which was a delegate assembly. They sprang to their feet, one after the other, and mutually surpassed each other in praising God and the giver of this gift, which was equal to his income for a fortnight. "I scarcely dare trust myself to speak," said a doctor of divinity. "The coming to the front of such a princely giver—the man to lead. . . . It is the Lord's doing. . . . As an American, a Baptist, and a Christian I rejoice in this consummation. God has kept Chicago for us; I wonder at his patience." Another reverend doctor said: "The Lord hath done great things for us. . . . The man who has given this money is a godly man, who does God's will as far as he can find out what God's will is."

The audience rose spontaneously and sang the Doxology. On motion the following telegram was sent, signed by the president of the society:

"Boston, May 18, 1889.

"The Baptist denomination, assembled at the first anniversary of the Education Society, have received with unparalleled enthusiasm and gratitude the announcement of your princely gift, and pledge their heartiest co-operation in the accomplishment of this magnificent enterprise."

The name signed to this telegram happened to be the same as that of the divine with whom, when president of Brown

University in 1841, one of the most devoted of the laborers for the freedom of the negro had a discussion which is perhaps the most pungent in the literature of the antislavery movement.

On August 30, 1841, Henry C. Wright wrote to Edmund Quincy: "I once met the president of Brown University, in the presence of several friends, to converse on the subject of slavery. The conversation turned on the question: Can a slaveholder be a Christian? To bring it to a point, addressing myself to the doctor, I asked him, 'Can a man be a Christian and claim a right to sunder husbands and wives, parents and children, to compel men to work without wages, to forbid them to read the Bible, and buy and sell them, and who habitually does these things?' 'Yes,' answered the reverend doctor and president, 'provided he has the spirit of Christ.' 'Is it possible for a man to be governed by the spirit of Christ and claim a right to commit these atrocious deeds, and habitually commit them?' After some turning he answered, 'Yes, I believe he can.' 'Is there, then, one crime in all the catalogue of crimes which of itself would be evidence to you that a man had not the spirit of Christ?' I asked. 'Yes, thousands,' said the doctor. 'What?' I asked. 'Stealing,' said he. 'Stealing what, a sheep or a *man*?' I asked. The doctor took his hat and left the room, and appeared no more."[1]

The Sunday following a special service was held in the churches throughout the country in behalf of further help in "the new educational crisis." Many eulogistic sermons were preached that day by the leading clergymen of the denomination. "And so," one of them is reported to have said, "when a crisis came God had a man ready to meet it. . . . An institution was bound to come, and unless a God-fearing man established it it was likely to be materialistic, agnostic. . . . In this emergency, and in God's providence, society raised up a man with a colossal fortune, and a heart as large as his fort-

---

[1] From *Life of William Lloyd Garrison, Told by His Children*, vol. iii., ch. i., p. 12.

une." " God," said the Chicago *Standard*, a religious weekly, "has guided us and provided us a leader and a giver, and so brought us out into a large place."

Another of the trustees has poured into a Southern State hundreds of thousands of dollars for churches of various denominations, and millions for hotels of a more than Oriental magnificence. " There is no philanthropist," says an editor of that State, commenting on these expenditures, " who renders the world greater service than the man of enterprise." But " Western Pennsylvania," said the Pittsburg *Post*, " looks more with awe than pride at the liberal diffusion of its wealth in Florida improvements and Baptist universities." A daily paper of Richmond, Virginia, in an editorial commenting on a report that the hostlery glories of St. Augustine were to be repeated in Richmond, said : " We have naught to remark on the tyrant monopoly if some of its profits are to come in such a direction. We could forgive much that monopoly visits on the down-trodden, horny-handed son of toil if it would come with open pockets proclaiming the era of luxuriant accommodations for all those other millionaires whose money we want to see invested in Richmond."

The next year after the Boston meeting the Church celebrated its " Anniversary week " in the city which was to be the seat of the new college. And the anniversary closed with a jubilee meeting, which filled the largest assembly room in America. " All the church-going people of Chicago must have attended," one of the daily papers said. It was addressed by the principal clergymen of the denomination from all parts of the country. Again, as at Boston, the centre of interest was the gift of a fortnight's income to the university. A telegram making the gift conclusive, since the conditions on which it was promised had been complied with, was read. Cheer after cheer rose from the assembly, and oratory and music expressed the emotion of the audience. The divine who made the closing speech declared that he needed ice on his head on account of the joyful excitement of the occasion. The cheers and the hand-clapping closed again, as at Boston, with the spirited singing of the Doxology. Not only in the religious press of all denominations, but in the worldly press, the topic was the best of "copy." The great dailies gave columns, and even pages, to the incident, and to the subsequent gift from the same source of larger sums. "Conspicuously providential," "princely," "grand," "munificent contribution," "man of God," were the phrases of praise. A writer in the New York *Independent* said: "Your correspondent speaks from opportunities of personal observation in saying that pecuniary benefaction to a public cause seldom if ever, in his belief, flowed from a purer Christian source." The only recorded note of dissent came from a humbler source. Under the text, "I hate robbery as a burnt-offering," a weekly business journal said: "The endowment of an educational institution where the studies shall be limited to a single course, and that a primary course in commercial integrity, would be a still more advantageous outlet for superabundant capital. Such an institution would fill a crying want."

It was the last Thursday in May, 1890, when this great representative convention of the Church from all parts of the United States celebrated the acceptance of this endowment. Even while the roll of the Doxology was still rising to the roof of the auditorium the plans were preparing for a performance at Fostoria the next Sunday, three days later, which had a profound effect upon Toledo, though just the opposite of what was expected.

Fostoria, Ohio, is the home of the president of the principal natural-gas company in Ohio controlled by the oil trust and leader in the vendetta against Toledo. A wealthy miller erected in Fostoria in 1886 a flouring-mill, with a capacity of 1000 barrels a day. One of the inducements was a contract made with this manufacturer by the gas company, by which it bound itself to supply him with natural gas at a price which would be one-fifth what coal would cost him, and to continue to supply him as long as it supplied any one. The manufacturer carried out his agreement by the expenditure of $150,000 for the erection of the mill, and by running it continually to its full capacity. His bills for gas he paid promptly every month. Relying upon the contract with the gas company, the mill was built for natural gas, and could use no other fuel. In February, 1890, the gas company, dissatisfied with the bargain it had made, demanded better terms. The milling company refused. On a Sunday morning in June, "when, if ever, come perfect days," a gang of men appeared, led by an officer of the gas company, and dug up and tore out the pipes supplying the mill with gas.

Church bells of different denominations were scattering their sweet jangle of invitations to the sanctuary as the tramp of these banded men, issuing on their errand of force, mixed with the patter on the sidewalks of devout feet. Private grounds were unlawfully entered, property was destroyed, the peace broken, a day of love changed to one of hate, all the bonds of community cut asunder, and the people turned from the contemplation of divine goodness to gaze at shapes of greed and rage. Sunday is chosen for such deeds, since the help with which the pagan law, gift of heathen Rome, would interpose, cannot be invoked by the victims on Sunday, and because on Sunday Christian people go to church, and leave their property undefended. The peace-officers were summoned to arrest the invaders for violating the Sunday law, but before they could get on the ground the mischief was done. The pipes had all been excavated, the connections wrenched off, and the trench nearly filled up. The milling company began suit for $100,000 damages against the gas company,[1] but a private settlement was made, and the case has never been pressed to trial. The laborers who did the work of the Captains of Industry in this matter were tried and convicted at the County Court in July, but by no process did the law, which is "no respecter of persons," reach out towards the principals.

This Fostoria incident occurred during the heat of the Toledo contest—June, 1890—while the city was pushing the

[1] Petition of the Isaac Harter •Company *vs.* the Northwestern Ohio Natural Gas Company, Court of Common Pleas, Seneca County, Ohio, June 16, 1890.

sale of bonds for its emancipating pipe line by popular subscription and in odd lots. Notice had been already served on
the people of Toledo at public conference, that despite contracts, charters, franchises, the private companies would not
take any less price from Toledo than they demanded. In
pursuance of this, after the council had fixed the price in
accordance with its admitted right, a circular was sent out
containing this significant threat: "If it"—the legally declared price—"is approved by our customers we will know
what course to pursue."

Even before the occurrence at Fostoria it had been defi-
nitely suggested to the people of Toledo that in case the
council failed to accept the demand as to rates in making the
new ordinance (July, 1890) the pipes would be so far removed
as to cut off the supply on some Sunday when no legal help
could be invoked. The possibility of this Sunday cut-off of
the fuel supply of 15,000 consumers became a living topic of
discussion, public and private, and was considered in all its
bearings by the Toledo press. Calculations were made and
published of the number of men it would require to take up
the hundred miles or so of pipe in the streets of Toledo between dark and dark some holy Sabbath day. It was confessed, hopelessly, that they would be more than the police
could handle. "Of course," as was said in the Toledo *Blade*
by a leading citizen, "such enterprise would involve a very
remarkable degree of both lawlessness and desperation on the
part of the managers. It would be a mode of withdrawal
from trade quite unknown among sound business men. But
then their processes have been peculiar from the start."

It was nothing less than startling to Toledo, almost before
the print on the types of these words was dry, to hear the
news from Fostoria of the Sunday raid there. There were
those who declared that the Sunday violence at Fostoria was
deliberately done as a warning to Toledo. If it were a warning to them not to insist on the legal and equitable and contract right of their Common Council to fix the rates of gas,
it was a failure. The council went forward and did its duty.

If it were a warning to the people to redouble their labors to free themselves forever from the possibility of such thraldom as that in which Fostoria and other cities were enchained, it was a success. The people heard and heeded, and in ten months thereafter gas began to flow into the city through its own pipes.

CHAPTER XXVI

It was remarkable to see the revival of the passion of freedom of 1776 and 1861 in the editorials, speeches, resolutions of public meetings, and the talk of the common people in Toledo as in Columbus. The example of "the heroic liberty-loving people of Boston" was held up in every aspect to fire the heart of Toledo not to be frightened into subjection to the foreign power that threatened them. To resist "the domination of an economic monarchy" was the appeal made in posters with which the town was placarded.

"During all the time George III.'s soldiers were quartered in Boston that monarch did not spend as much money to bring the city to terms as has been been spent in this effort to subjugate the city of Toledo," said Alderman Macomber.

"A people like those of Toledo," said one of them in the press, "when once united and determined as they now are, cannot be subjugated by any combination of mercenaries yet known."

"It is evident," the Toledo *Sunday Gazette* said, "that the people of Toledo have come to a full realization of the truth that the money saved by the independent pipe line, though great, is a matter of little importance compared with the social and political issues involved. It would be a thousand times better," it continued, "to utterly bankrupt the city than permit the oil combination to win. The fight was not for the present alone, but it was for the present and future, and for all time to come. It was not for the people of Toledo alone, but it was for the whole Union, though God had chosen the people of Toledo for the struggle."

The Cincinnati *Commercial-Gazette* said, in its editorial columns: " In itself the Toledo enterprise is not a big one, but
it will prove an object-lesson for the whole country.   It will
show the open door through which people may pass from under the yoke of a most gigantic, unscrupulous, and odious monopoly.   And it will be surprising if this does not extend beyond gas and ultimately cover oil.   We are only on the verge
of a revolution that is as sure to come as that which followed
the throwing overboard of a lot of tea in Boston Harbor.
Neither the power nor the vulgarity of capital can long rule
the people."

Numerous letters of sympathy, congratulation, and indignation were received by the Toledo committee appointed by
the citizens' mass-meeting to make a statement of their case
to the people of the United States.   There were letters from
chairs of political economy in the universities, from scholars
and students in history and politics, and from men in affairs
and finance.

The completion of the line to the city was not the completion of the enterprise.   Mains had still to be laid in the
streets, and house connections made.   At every step, now as
before, unrelenting opposition did all that could be conceived
of—in the courts, the Legislature, the city government, the
money-market—to block municipal self-help.   Great numbers
of the citizens desired to change from the private companies
to the city.   Over 7500 consumers were at one time, in 1891,
calling upon the city to supply them.[1]   The litigation which
was kept up, and the defeat of the attempt of the city to sell
its natural-gas bonds in the open market, had exhausted the
funds at the disposal of the city trustees. · But they showed a
readiness of resource equal, with the help of the people, to all
these emergencies, and proving that public enterprise can
more than hold its own in the competition with private enterprise.   Contractors were got to pipe the streets by sections,
and take for pay the pledge of the income earned by the pipes

---

[1] Annual Report of the Toledo Natural Gas Trustees, 1891, p. 6.

23

so laid. In other cases people wanting the gas were willing to advance a part of the cost. The same contractor who had faith enough in the city to build the main line from the gas-fields and take the bonds while they were under fire volunteered in the same way to build the submerged lines across the Maumee River, and ten miles of mains within the city. This was done at a moment when otherwise the enterprise must have come to a stop, and the name of this patriotic contractor is given to the public by the trustees in their annual report with words of gratitude.

The amount of bonds originally authorized was $750,000. The trustees, in consequence of the delays and enhanced cost caused by lawsuits and other tactics of opposition, had to incur a floating debt of $300,000. The council by ordinance directed the issue of bonds by the city to the amount of $120,000 to pay off part of this floating debt. The State Circuit Court refused to sustain this action of the council, but pointed out that all the city lacked was the authorization of the Legislature. This was the only decision against the city in all the litigations, and in this the State Court was afterwards overruled by the United States Circuit Court. A bill was accordingly introduced, giving the city the right to issue $300,000 in bonds for the floating debt, and $100,000 for the extension of the gas plant: wells, pipes, pumps—whatever was needed. A strong lobby immediately appeared in the State Capitol to defeat the bill. As part of its ammunition a pamphlet was circulated among the legislators, giving " Facts and Reasons " why the Legislature should not authorize the new issue of bonds. This pamphlet illustrates the easy virtue with which some lawyers dispose of themselves to those who have the money to pay them. Two of its strongest points were that the contracts for which the floating debt had been incurred were let without proper competition, and that the trustees had no power to make the contracts. This pamphlet was signed by two lawyers, one of whom, before these contracts were let, had given the trustees his written opinion supporting such contracts unqualifiedly. The representatives of the people were able to exhibit to the Legislature his written opinion stating that the trustees had the power to make the contracts, and had let them in compliance with the requirements of the statute as to bids. The pamphlet declared that the court, in granting the injunction against the issue of the $120,000 of bonds by the Common Council, had declared the claims which were to be paid by the proceeds of the bonds to be "illegal and invalid." This was untrue. The court had held only that the city had not the power to issue the bonds, and pointed out that the remedy was in new legislation by the State to remedy the want of power.

Pursuing the tactics of defamation of the city and its authorities which had been used throughout this contest, the pamphlet said: "We are prepared to prove . . . that the contractors put in their bids substantially as gambling transactions, at such excessive price that they thought they could take the risk of the illegality of the natural-gas proceedings, trusting that these illegal transactions would be permitted to pass without question, or that subsequent legislation would ratify these illegal acts; all, or nearly all, of the contracts were taken at prices more than double the fair cash value for all the work and material provided for; and all the work and materials, the claims for which now aggregate about $350,000, could have been obtained in the open market, under valid laws, upon proper terms of payment, for less than $250,000. We have the evidence within our control to establish that the work under some of these contracts was actually done for less than 40 per cent. of the amount named in the contract. In addition to these facts, we can establish, if permitted to offer evidence, that the certificates issued by the natural-gas trustees were, immediately after the conclusion of the contracts and before any litigation was had upon them, hawked about the streets of Toledo at from 60 to 75 cents on the dollar; and that the great majority of these certificates are now in the hands of speculators, who bought them at not to exceed 65 per cent. of their face value."

The authors of these statements were at once challenged

by the city's gas trustees to prove them. "We assert," the gas trustees said, in a formal challenge, "that you cannot establish the truth of those statements. We deny that the facts are as you state them to be, either in substance or in detail." This was signed by John E. Parsons, W. W. Jones, Reynold Voit, J. W. Greene, gas trustees, and Clarence Brown and Thomas H. Tracy, ex-gas-trustees. The city's trustees proposed that they and their accusers deposit $1000 on each side as a forfeit to abide the result of an inquiry by the three judges of the Court of Common Pleas, or any other disinterested arbitrators. They placed at the service of the accusers and the arbiters all the books, records, and employés of the city's gas department.

The challenge was not accepted, and the authors of these attacks made no attempt to prove them. The Legislature disregarded them, and granted the city and the gas trustees all the additional power to issue bonds asked for. In a subsequent proceeding in the Federal courts—the issue involving the validity of these certificates—it was admitted, contrary to these allegations, that the prices were fair, and that the contracts were entered into in good faith, and the court held the certificates valid.

The most serious crisis in the contest was still to come. In 1892 the gas wells of the city began to do what the people of the city will never do—surrender to the enemy. When the oil trust found, after years of opposition in the Legislature, the courts, and the gas-fields, that it had been helpless to prevent Toledo from getting ample tracts of excellent gas territory, with some of the largest gas wells in the field, and equal to the supply of the entire consumption, domestic and manufacturing, it turned to other tactics.

All about this territory secured by Toledo and found so productive the private companies of the trust proceeded to buy or lease and to sink wells. The trust shut off all its own wells, except those adjacent to the city territory, and for two years drew exclusively from the wells nearest those of the city. When the city's line was completed to the wells the volume of gas was found to be largely reduced. It had been drawn off into the wells of the opposition. In the spring of 1892 the private companies resolved to put in pumps to strengthen the diminished natural pressure, but to prevent the city from doing the same thing. Then, with their pumps alone at work, the pressure could be so much further reduced as to render the Toledo pipe line valueless. To this end all efforts were directed. The newspapers were kept full of matter showing how impossible it was to pump gas, that all the money expended in pumps would be just so much wasted, and that the companies had canvassed the matter fully, but abandoned the idea. Column after column of inspired interviews filled the papers, all admonishing the city of Toledo not to commit such an act of folly as to put in gas pumps. Then application was made to enjoin the sale of the bonds authorized by the council and the Legislature for pumps. So month after month dragged along. The bonds remained unsold, and the pumps unobtainable.

The injunction was refused both by the Court of Common Pleas and by the Circuit Court. But there was a right of appeal to the Ohio Supreme Court until the beginning of 1892. Boston bankers had subscribed for a large block of the bonds, but withdrew upon learning these facts. "It is possible for the contestants," the lawyers advised them, "to carry the matter to the Supreme Court. This, we understand, they propose to do." The simple assertion of a purpose to continue the litigation was enough to defeat the sale of the bonds. The payment of costs and lawyers' fees would be a very moderate price to pay for compelling the city's gas plant to go past mid-winter without the pumps indispensable for its operation. One of the employés of the private pipe line, according to an account in one of the Toledo papers, declared to a reporter that "if we could not prevent the city from putting in a [pumping] plant any other way, we would blow it up with dynamite."[1]

[1] See p. 250 and ch. xxxi.

Any faithful employé familiar with the blowing up of derricks in the shut-down of 1887,[1] the explosion in the independent refinery at Buffalo,[2] and the "chemical war" waged by the whiskey trust against the "outsiders" in Chicago[3] might almost be pardoned for thinking this was "only good, reasonable talk." The oil monopoly is evangelical at one end and explosive at the other, and it has made both ends meet.

The people of Toledo were thus prevented from getting the pumping facilities ready during the summer of 1892 for the work of the winter. Meanwhile its rival had been secretly pushing pumps for itself to completion, in the hope that it alone would be ready when cold weather came. This would mean a gain to it, at the city's expense, of hundreds of thousands of dollars. Late in August, 1892, the representatives of the city found that two powerful duplex gas pumps had been shipped to the gas-field, and were being put in place by the very opponents who had declared pumps impracticable. Public sentiment became aroused to the need for the immediate purchase of pumps to protect their wells. The city attempted to use its income from the sales of gas to buy pumps. An injunction was applied for and granted. This emergency was finally met by having the gas trustees hand over to the city authorities the accumulated earnings they were forbidden by the court to spend themselves. The city thereupon turned around and invested this money in the gas bonds. In this way the identical money the gas trustees could not use while it remained in their hands was made available to them by passing through the hands of the Sinking Fund Trustees, and coming back to them. Thus the natural-gas trustees were enabled to make a contract in September, 1892, for pumps to assist the flow of gas to the city.

The gas pumps are a patented device. The private companies, wanting all the profit of everything, had had their pumps made at their own factory. The city made its contract directly with the owner of the patents. The result was

---

[1] See p. 154.   [2] See p. 250.   [3] See p. 21.

that the city got its pumps in place in time to save the city pipe line, while its opponents were delayed by the inexperience of their own pump-makers. This was the most critical period in our history. Greed had again defeated itself. Had the opposition gone to the owner of the patents he would have been unable afterwards to take the city's contract and complete it in time, and the effort to make the city line valueless would have succeeded—for the time being, at least. The bonds in question were afterwards held valid by the Supreme Court.

Toledo knew it was building wisely, and every day brought new proof that it had builded better than it knew. Its saving was great, but that was the least of its gains. It escaped tyranny and extortion and other wrongs which fell upon communities in plain sight, which had not the wit and virtue to establish their independence. When the city pipe line was opened in 1891 the city began supplying gas to its citizens at 8 cents a thousand for houses. The private companies were charging 12 cents a thousand, or 50 per cent. more. Profits were such at this charge of 12 cents a thousand feet that in some tracts single wells would repay the cost of the land every four days and two hours, or eighty-nine times a year. Since then the private corporations have raised their rate to 25 cents. The city continued the rates at 8 cents until December, 1892, when the rate was advanced to 15 cents. This advance would have been unnecessary but for the losses arising from the obstructions placed in the way of the city plant.

The people of Toledo got their gas lands, pipe line, and street mains for an outlay of $1,181,743 up to the end of 1891,[1] and $1,294,467 up to the end of 1892. In the canvass before the election in 1889 their opponents declared that $4,000,000 would be required.

Private enterprise cannot find rhetoric strong enough to express its contempt for the inefficiency, costliness, and des-

---

[1] Annual Report of the Natural Gas Trustees of Toledo, 1891, p. 4.

potisms of public enterprise. Private enterprise put at $6,-
000,000 — twelve times the amount of the property they
reported for taxation—the "capital" stock invested by the
two natural-gas companies. The city pipe line was capitalized (bonded) at just what it cost—a little more than a million. The city trustees built a better pipe line than private
enterprise had laid. The private line was of cheap iron of
14-feet lengths, while Toledo's was in 24-feet pieces. One of
the private lines was laid with rubber joints and in shallow
trenches, in many places of not more than plough depth. It
leaked at almost every joint; its course could be traced across
the fields by the smell of gas and the blighted line of vegeta-
tion. There were frequent explosions from the escaping gas;
lives and property were much endangered. The city line
was laid with lead joints, and had every device that engineering experience could suggest for its success, and was so constructed that it could be cleaned or repaired, and freed from
liquids interfering with the flow of gas, without shutting off
the supply—features the other pipe had not. The action of
the city trustees had to endure the microscopic scrutiny of
friend and foe. No one was able to show as to a single acre
that the title was defective, or that it could have been bought
for less, or to find any taint of a job in the construction of
the pipe. A committee of the city council sat and probed
for six weeks, but failed to find any evidence whatever to
confirm the reported "irregularities."

What Toledo will save in one year by the difference between the actual cost at which its people can supply themselves and the price the private companies would have
charged, to pay dividends on $6,000,000 of "capital," is only
part of the story. The profit of the city enterprise is to be
estimated by its competitive effect upon the charge of the
private companies. These have been kept down in Toledo
much below the average of other towns, where they have been
as high as 35 cents a thousand. If the city had not supplied
a foot of gas this check on the private companies would make
its pipe line still a good investment. The people, when it is

in full operation, can pay the cost of the system complete out of the savings of a few years, then pay off the entire city debt, and have a large income left for public buildings, roads, parks. Or by reduction of price they can keep this sum in their pockets, where it will do quite as much for the general welfare as if it had been transferred to the bank accounts of non-residents.

The city, at the end of 1891, had 3299¾ acres of gas land. In March, 1892, forty-five wells were giving over 50,000,000 cubic feet of gas, equal to 3500 tons of anthracite coal. Its income from the sale of gas was at the rate of $20,032 a month in winter, and $10,221 in summer. An investigation made in March, 1892, by a committee appointed by the mayor at the request of the city's gas trustees, showed that an income could be counted on ($180,000) ample to pay all expenses ($128,120), including interest, rentals, and the cost of drilling new wells, and provide a small fund annually ($51,880) for the extinction of the bonded debt. The committee said: "We believe that if the gas plant is properly managed upon prudent business principles and methods, that it can be made a profitable investment for the city and her people; that the class who will derive the greatest benefit is the laboring class, who pay rent or taxes upon their little homes, and to whom the matter of cheap fuel is quite an item in the total amount of annual expenses; and we believe it to be the duty of every good citizen to aid and encourage this class."

These were the results with a charge of 8 cents a thousand. Gas to the amount of $167,899 had been sold up to August 1, 1892. Between November, 1891, and August, 1892, the city earned on the million invested the sum of $150,000, or nearly one-ninth of the cost of the plant, and this at the low price of 8 cents a thousand feet. Unobstructed by its enemies and at the price charged by the private companies, 20 cents a thousand, the city would pay for its entire plant in less than three years.

To discourage the public from going forward with its pipe line the private companies "talked poor." In an interview in the public press the president of the principal company said it had paid but 9 per cent. in dividends in two and a half years. The net earnings were stated to be "about 4 per cent. per annum on the capital," $4,000,000;[1] for the smaller company they were figured out to be at the rate of a fraction less than 1 per cent. a year on its capital of $2,000,-000.[2] "We feel sore and hurt about it," said the "direct representative" of the oil combination to the citizens' committee; "we have seen no good return from our money." "It has pretty nearly swamped us," said the president of the company. The citizens of Toledo were shrewd enough to ask themselves how long their antagonists would have been likely to remain in a business which paid only 3 per cent., and was as "hazardous" and "shortlived" as they pictured it to be. Careful estimates made by close students of the question calculated that of the $6,000,000 of paper capital "invested" in the two companies which supplied Toledo and other cities, $1,125,000 was the proportion of actual cash devoted to Toledo. The receipts upon this Toledo investment in the two and three-quarters years between the opening of the business and the date at which, by the contract with the city, the council was to make new rates (June 30, 1890), were, as nearly as can be calculated from the figures of their report, $1,300,000 greater than the expenses of the Toledo business. This is a profit of 115 per cent. In less than three years the total investment had been repaid by the profits, and, in addition, enough to have paid dividends of 5 per cent. a year. This was an estimate, but it was an estimate publicly made from the companies' figures, and by a responsible man. It remained unchallenged at a time when every cranny of fact and fiction was being rummaged for missiles to fling at the people.

When the citizens' committee sought a reduction in price, the companies pointed to the small dividend their stockholders had had. In the face of the fact that they had received but a 3-per-cent. dividend the previous year, no business man,

---

[1] Report to Stockholders, Northwestern Natural Gas Company, January 7, 1889.
[2] Report to Stockholders, Toledo Natural Gas Company, January, 1889.

their spokesman said, could ask them to reduce their price. It is for such uses that shrewd men "water" stock. The surface of the capital is broadened, so that even large dividends can cover it only by being spread out very thin. This 3 per cent. a year was on $6,000,000 of dilution, representing a solid, at the most, of only $1,500,000. The balance sheets of the companies showed that the companies had paid small dividends for the additional reason that a large part of their receipts had been reinvested in lands, wells, and extensions of the pipes and plants.

The people are often assured that these false figures of capitalization are merely romantic and do them no harm, because charges must be governed by the "laws of trade." One of the "laws of trade" that regulates the "market price" of such commodities as transportation, light, water, gas, furnished by the help of the public franchises, is the power of the public to regulate. This public power depends upon the public knowledge and the public disposition. To make the public believe that the profit of serving it has been only 3 per cent. a year, when it has been nearer 50 per cent., is to manipulate public opinion, the most potent of all the "laws of trade," for a competing supply cannot be got easily, often not at all.

A committee of citizens were invited by the representatives of the gas companies to meet them to verify the statements of the companies as to the unprofitableness of the business, and the inexpediency of municipal self-supply. But when the committee wanted to know what had been the real cost of the private pipe lines, on the $6,000,000 nominal capital of which the people were expected to pay dividends, they could not get any satisfaction. The companies would only give an estimate. To the request for more definite information, the reply of both companies was, "We have not got the books of the contractors; we have never had them. We have no means of knowing the actual cost of the Toledo plant, or any books to show it.[1] We have no papers or documents in

[1] See ch. xxxii.

regard to the construction of this line." It came to light later that one of the companies in the oil trust had constructed the pipe line for the gas company, and at a price approximating the large figures claimed. The company that built this pipe line is a ring within the oil and gas ring, always on hand for such contracts and at like margins of profit, and it is owned almost wholly by the principals of the combination.[1] The people—mostly Ohioans—who took the minority 40 per cent. of stock of the gas company were really the "simple greens." All that was paid for this construction by those who were members both of the inside ring and the gas company came back to them; their associates in the minority paid, but got nothing back. It was from the latter came the profits of this contract to the insiders.

The people of Dayton had a similar experience. Their natural-gas company demanded an advance to 25 cents a thousand, and met a committee of the people to prove that the demand was proper. But it would not let the people know what the actual investment was to make which good it sought to tax the people. The books containing the construction account were "not accessible." "The actual cost to construct the plant is what we most desired to know," the committee reported. As at Toledo, so at Dayton; all private enterprise would let its customer-subjects know was what it wanted them to pay; information to show what they ought to pay "was not accessible." What the profits were elsewhere can be guessed at from the fact that in Pennsylvania $36 a year was charged in most of the towns for cooking-stoves. In Toledo the charge was $19.50 a year.

Almost every day after the pipe line had been decided on the people saw something done, showing how well founded their apprehensions had been. The power to discriminate in rates the people saw used by the private companies for selfish and anti-public purposes, precisely as they had foreseen it would be. When the fight for and against the city

---

[1] See p. 113.

pipe line was on, one of the gas companies sought to enlist the strong men in their support by making them special rates, pursuing the tactics of divide and conquer. Manufact-urers with influence useful in controlling public sentiment were conceded special rates. Others were given to under-stand that any lack of "loyalty" would be followed by pun-ishment. So effective were these alternating methods of boodling and bulldozing that the council committee on gas, in a subsequent investigation, found it almost impossible to obtain any information from manufacturers as to their use of natural gas for fuel. What little they did secure was under injunctions of secrecy. The committee found that some were made to pay twice, some three, and some even four times as much as was paid by neighbors for like service. The only rule for charging seemed to be to favor those who had "influ-ence." This was using municipal franchise just as the fran-chise of the highways had been used in their behalf by the railways. An assembly of divines could not be trusted with such power over their fellows.

After the Fostoria incident the people of Toledo had an-other illustration given them of how wisely they had build-ed. The gas supply of the people of Columbus, Ohio, was shut off arbitrarily and suddenly in midwinter — January, 1891—and they were informed that the company would sup-ply them with no more gas unless the City Council would raise the price to 25 cents a thousand feet from 10 cents. The gas had not failed. The caverns that discharge gas at 25 cents a thousand will let it come just as freely at 10 cents. The council had fixed the price at 10 cents, and the company had accepted it. The demand for a higher price was close upon an increase in the capital stock of the Columbus com-pany from $1,000,000 to $1,750,000. More stock called for more dividends, and this was one way to get it—to strike this sudden blow, and then to say, after the manner of Silas Wegg, "Undone for double the money!" It was for the power to do this at Toledo, to preserve the power of doing it every-where else, that hell and earth were being moved in Toledo to prevent the people from serving themselves and setting an example to the rest of America. In the same way the gas was turned off at Sidney, Ohio, and not turned on again until, upon the application of the mayor, the company was ordered to do it by the courts. "There is a great deal of suffering here," the press reported, "and it is feared that several deaths will result from exposure."

The people did not fail to comprehend the significance of criticisms in the Toledo organ on the municipal water supply. Monopoly must go on conquering and to conquer, or be overborne by the ever-recuperating resentment which rises against it, freshened with each new day. Nature hates monopoly, says Emerson. The studied attack on the city water works was believed to be meant to prepare the people to intrust that as well as the gas supply to the trust's "sound business men" and "private enterprise."

Finding that the council would not bend to the demands as to rates, and that the people were too resolute to be in any way diverted from their pipe line, Toledo was given some such doses as could be ventured upon of the Fostoria and Columbus medicine. The company shut gas off from those who would not pay the increased rate. It deprived public institutions of their fuel. It refused to supply gas to a new public school whose building was planned for natural gas. As the city's pipe line was not completed, the children had to go cold. The winter of 1891–2 was the first winter the city's pipe line was in operation. With the first cold snap, at the end of November, great distress and danger were brought upon the people by a lawless act, done secretly by some unknown person to the city's pipe line. One of the main pipes in the gas-field, through which flowed the product of two of the largest gas wells, was disconnected, so that its gas could no longer reach Toledo. Who did this was never discovered.[1]

Defeat, final and irrevocable, crowned the unvarying series of defeat which the private companies had suffered every-

---

[1] See chs. ix. and xxxi.

where and in everything—in public meetings, in the Legislature, in the gas-fields, at the polls, in the courts, in the sale of the bonds, and in the competition with the city. The City Council of Toledo, advised by its lawyers that it could recover damages from those responsible for the losses brought upon the city by the opposition to its pipe line, has had suit brought for that purpose. April 14, 1893, City Solicitor Read began proceedings to recover $1,000,000 damages from members of the oil combination and the various individuals who had been used as stalking-horses in the campaign. At the next meeting of the Common Council several citizens of the "influential" persuasion assisted the mayor in trying to coax and bully the council to abandon the suit, but without success. The council were threatened with a financial boycott to prevent the sale in future of any of the bonds of the city, but it refused to be terrorized.

April 8, 1893, the natural-gas trustees of Toledo had the happiness of being able to give formal notice to the city auditor that no taxes need be levied to pay the interest on the gas bonds, as it "can easily be met from the revenues derived from the sale of natural gas." The city pipe line was on a paying basis at last. Toledo had vindicated its claim to be a free city. The completion of the enterprise had been delayed three years. A loss of not less than two million dollars had been laid on the city, but its victory was worth many times that. Toledo's victory showed the country, in full and successful detail, a plan of campaign of which Columbus had merely given a hint. It was not a local affair, but one of even more than national importance, for the oil combination has invaded four continents. This struggle and its results of good omen will pass into duly recorded history as a warning and an encouragement to people everywhere who wish to lead the life of the commonwealth.

NOTE.—For the year ending December 31, 1893, the city trustees report that they sold gas to the amount of $139,066. The city owns 5433 acres of gas territory, and has 85 wells, 73 miles of pipe outside the city, and 91 miles in the city. Since the gas began to flow the sales have amounted to

$388,540.   Out of the receipts the debt has been reduced $60,000, besides refunding $67,000 to those who advanced the money for piping the streets. While doing this the plant has been considerably enlarged.   The city accomplished this while charging the people but 15 cents a thousand, while the gas companies of the trust charged 25 cents a thousand.   Had the city been permitted to act without obstruction, the cost of the gas plant would have been long since fully paid, and the price of gas made still lower.[1]

[1] See ch. xxx.

CHAPTER XXVII

"YOU ARE A—SENATOR"

How to control the men who control the highways?

The railroads have become the main rivers of trade and travel, and to control them has become one of our hardest problems in the field where politics and industry meet. The Duke of Wellington exhorted Parliament "not to forget, in legislating upon this subject, the old idea of the King's Highway." But here, as well as there, the little respect paid by the Legislature at first to this idea soon vanished. In England, as well as in America, the State, in giving some citizens the right, for their private profit, to take the property of others by force, legally, for railways, began by limiting strictly the power so acquired. Then, passing under the control of that which it had created, the State abandoned its attempts to control. Now the State is retracing its way, and for many years has been struggling painfully to recover its lost authority. In the first English charters there were the minutest regulations as to freight and passenger charges, and the right of citizens generally to put their own cars on the tracks was sacredly guarded.

The railroads became too strong to submit to this, and the success with which the teachings of Adam Smith were applied to the abolition of the old-fashioned restraints on trade bred a furor against any social control of industry. These limitations were left out of new charters, and for fair play were revised out of the old charters. After a brief dream of this *laissez faire*, England began, in 1844, investigating and legislating and, after nearly thirty years of experiments and failures, established the railway commission in 1873. This

24

was a step forward, but has not proved the solvent it was expected to be. The expense of getting a decision from the commission and the courts to which the road can appeal from the commission has frightened people from making complaints. "A complainant," says Hadley, "is a marked man, and the commission cannot protect him against the vengeance of the railroads. A town fares no better . . . even the [British] War Department is afraid. It has grievances, but it dares not make them public for fear of reprisals."[1]

The course of events in the United States was much the same. The first railroad powers were carefully limited. The early charters regulated the charges, limited the profits, gave citizens the right to put their private carriages on the road, and reserved to the State the right to take possession of the railroad upon proper payment. But as early as 1846 the railroads had grown strong enough—in the revision of the Constitution of New York, for example—to secure an almost complete surrender of these public safeguards.[2]

But it was seen immediately in America, as in England, that the new institution could not be left in the uncontrolled hands of individuals. It created simultaneously two revolutions, each one of the most momentous in modern civilization. It made the steam-engine master in transportation, as it had already become in manufacturing. It made the public highways the private property of a few citizens. An agitation arose among the people—to-day stronger because more necessary than ever—and they began to seek what they have not yet found : means of regulating the relations between new rich and new poor, and protecting the private interests of all from the private interests of the few who had this double sovereignty. As early as 1857 New York established a commission for the regulation of the railways. But the railroads within a year procured a law abolishing it, bribing the leading commissioner to make no opposition in consideration of

[1] *Railroad Transportation*, by Arthur T. Hadley.   G. P. Putnam's Sons, 1886.
[2] Speech of Simon Sterne, New York Assembly "Hepburn" Report, 1879, pp. 98–118.

receiving from them $25,000, the whole amount of his salary
for five years. "I was the attorney of the Erie Railway at
that time; I specially used to attend to legislation that they
desired to effect or oppose. . . . I remember the appointment
of that commission. . . . We agreed that if they" (the leading
railroad commissioner) "would not oppose the repeal of the
law we would pay $25,000, and have done with the commis-
sion; it was embarrassing. . . . The law was repealed, and we
paid the money, I think." "If the commission had been a
useless one," said the counsel of the New York Chamber of
Commerce before the Legislative Committee, "the railroads
would not have parted with their money to get rid of it." [1]

Thirty of the States and Territories of the Union had established commissions or passed laws to regulate the railroads
before Congress, in 1887, used its power under the Constitution to regulate commerce among the States, and passed the Interstate Commerce law, establishing the National Interstate
Commerce Commission, in the hope that it might protect the
people. Congress did not act until 1887, although for years
different sections of the public, in their efforts to find a cure
for the new evils which had come with the new good, had
sought to set in action their representatives in Washington.
The "Granger movement" of 1871, 1872, and 1873, with its
"Granger legislation" by the States against the railroads, is
one of the never-to-be-forgotten waves of public commotion
over this problem which took on its acutest form in the oil
regions. Illinois, California, Michigan, Minnesota, Missouri,
Rhode Island, Wisconsin, and Iowa established railway commissions, or put stringent regulations on the statute-books at
this time. Public opinion did not cease to demand action by
the national government under the constitutional power of
Congress to regulate interstate commerce, and became clam-
orous. Petitions poured in by the hundreds, public meetings
were held, chambers of commerce and boards of trade and
anti-monopoly conventions passed resolutions of urgency.

---

[1] Testimony, New York Assembly "Hepburn" Report, 1879, pp. 2723–24 and
p. 3900.

This was one of the main issues in the election of the 44th Congress.

Representative Hopkins, of Pennsylvania, rose in his place in the House of Representatives on May 16, 1876, and asked unanimous consent to offer a resolution for the appointment of a committee of five to investigate the charges that " many industries are crippled and threatened with extreme prostration " by the discrimination of the railroads, and to report a bill for the regulation of interstate commerce. This was the first move to reopen in Congress the great question, first on the order of the day both in England and in America, which had been smothered by the Committee of Commerce of 1872. It required unanimous consent to bring the resolution before the House.

"Instantly," said Representative Hopkins, in describing the occurrence afterwards,[1] " I heard the fatal words ' I object.' The objector was Mr. Henry B. Payne, of Cleveland." Other members appealed to Mr. Payne to withdraw his objection.

The Speaker of the House: "Does the gentleman from Ohio withdraw his objection?"

Mr. Payne: "I do not."

In a private conference which followed between Representative Payne and Representative Hopkins, the former said, as Mr. Hopkins relates: " What he objected to in my resolution was the creation of a special committee; but if I would again offer it and ask that it be referred to the Committee of Commerce he would not object. I thought perhaps there was something reasonable in his objection. A special committee would probably require a clerk, which would be an expense. He looked to me so like a frugal Democrat, who had great confidence in the regular order of established committees and did not want the country to be taxed for clerks attending to the business of special committees—I say that he so impressed me that, as the record will show, I adopted his suggestion."

When the Committee of Commerce to which the investi-

---

[1] New York *Herald*, January 19, 1884.

gation was accordingly referred began its investigation, a member of the oil combination, not then, as later, a member of the Senate, took his seat by the ear of the chairman, who was from his State, "presiding," as the oil producers said in a public appeal, "behind the seat of the chairman."[1] The financial officer of the oil combination was called as a witness, but refused to answer the questions of the committee as to the operations of the company or its relations with the railroads. The vice-president of the Pennsylvania Railroad also refused to answer questions. On the plea of needing time to decide how to compel these witnesses to answer, the committee let the railroad vice-president go until he should be recalled. But the committee never decided, and the witnesses were never recalled. The committee never reported to Congress, made no complaint of the contempt of its witnesses, and the investigation of 1876, like that of 1872, came to a mute and inglorious end.

When Representative Hopkins applied to the clerk of the committee for the testimony, he was told, to his amazement, that it could not be found. "Judge Reagan," he relates,[2] "who was a stanch friend of the bill"—for the regulation of the railroads—"and very earnest for the investigation, and who at the time was a member of the committee, told me that it had been stolen."[3]

Eight years after "I object" the people of Ohio were a suppliant before the Senate of the United States. They believed that their dearest rights had been violated, and they prayed for redress to the only body which had power to give it. Officially by the voice of both Houses of the State Legislature and the governor, unofficially by the press, by the public appeals of leading men, by the petitions of citizens, press, leaders, and people, regardless of party, the commonwealth asserted that the greatest wrong possible in a republic had been done their members, and sued for restitution. They declared it to

---

[1] Appeal to the Executive of Pennsylvania by the Petroleum Producers' Union, 1878. Trusts, Congress, 1888, p. 354.

[2] New York *Herald*, January 19, 1884.   [3] See ch. vii.

be their belief that against their will, as the result of violation of the laws, a man had taken their seat in the Senate of the United States who was not their senator, that they had been denied representation by the senator of their choice; and they demanded that, in accordance with immemorial usage, the evidence they had to offer should be examined, and their right of representation in the Senate of the United States restored to them, if it should be found to have been taken from them. After the Legislature had examined sixty-four witnesses, the Ohio House of Representatives resolved that "ample testimony was adduced to warrant the belief that . . . the seat of Henry B. Payne in the United States Senate was purchased by the corrupt use of money." The Ohio Senate charged that "the election of Henry B. Payne as Senator of the United States from Ohio . . . was procured and brought about by the corrupt use of money, . . . and by other corrupt means and practices."

Both Houses passed with these resolutions an urgent request for investigation by the Senate of the United States.[1]

Mr. Payne's election by the Legislature was a thunder-clap to the people of Ohio. They did not know he was a candidate. Who was to be United States Senator was of course one of the issues in the election of the Ohio Legislature of 1884, and the Democratic voters who elected the majority of that Legislature had sent them to the State Capitol to make George H. Pendleton or Durbin Ward senator. One of the leading newspaper men of the State testified: "I went over the entire State during the campaign. . . . Out of the eighty-eight counties I attended fifty-four Democratic conventions and wrote them up, giving the sentiment of the people as nearly as I could, and during that entire canvass I never heard a candidate for the Legislature say that he was for Henry B. Payne for United States Senator; but every man I ever talked with was either for George H. Pendleton or General Ward. I think out of the Democratic candidates throughout the State

---

[1] Report No. 1490, United States Senate, 49th Congress, 1886, p. 1.

I conversed with at least two-thirds of them."[1] As was afterwards stated before the Senate of the United States by the representatives of the people of Ohio, "He was in no wise publicly connected with the canvass for the Senate, nor had the most active, honorable, and best-posted politicians in the State heard his name in connection with the senatorial office until subsequent to the October election [of the Legislature]. He was absolutely without following."[2]

The Democratic constituencies sent their legislators to vote for Pendleton and Ward, but between the receipt and the execution of this trust from the people a secret charm was put to work of such a potency that the people woke up to find that the representative who had betrayed them in Congress in 1876 was their senator, instead of one of their real leaders. The people had been digging oil wells for twenty years that all the value might flow into the bank accounts of a few interceptors; they had been building railroads and pipe lines that their business and property might be transported into the same hands; they had organized agitation and conducted a national anti-monopoly campaign all over the country, only to see the men who were to have been investigated take command of the inquiry. The people had had enough such experience not to be surprised that when they started to make a beloved leader senator it was their enemy who came out of the voting mill with the senatorial toga upon his shoulders. But terrible was the moral storm that broke forth out of the hearts of the people of Ohio. The votes they had thrown, like roses to garland the head of a hero, had been transformed as they went, by a black magic, into missiles of destruction, and had fallen upon him like the stones that slew Stephen.

The press, without regard to party, gave voice to the popular wrath. Scores of the Democratic newspapers of Ohio went into mourning. One of them said: "The whole Democratic Legislature was made rotten by the money that was

[1] Testimony, Appendix to the Journal of the House of Representatives of the State of Ohio, 67th General Assembly, 1886, vol. lxxxii., p. 499.

[2] Report No. 1490, United States Senate, 49th Congress, 1886, p. 60.

used to buy and sell the members like so many sheep." Many representative Democrats of the State privately and publicly declared their belief in the charges of corruption. Allen G. Thurman, who had been a senator and representative at Washington, said: "There is something that shocks me in the idea of crushing men like Pendleton and Ward, who have devoted the best portion of their lives to the maintenance of Democracy, by a combination against them of personal hatred and overgrown wealth. . . . I want to see all the Democrats have a fair chance according to their merits, and do not want to see a political cutthroat bossism inaugurated for the benefit of a close party corporation or syndicate." Again he said: "Syndicates purchase the people's agents, and honest men stand aghast."[1]

It was the "irony of fate" that this Legislature, like the 44th Congress, had been specially elected to represent opposition to monopolies. Of course the Legislature that had done this thing was not to be persuaded, bullied, or shamed into any step towards exposure or reparation. But the people, usually so forgetful, nursed their wrath. They made the scandal the issue of the next State election, and put the Legislature into other hands. The new Legislature then forwarded formal charges to the Senate of the United States, and a demand for an investigation. The State of Ohio made its solemn accusation and prayer for an investigation through all the organs of utterance it had: the press of both parties; honored men, both Republican and Democratic; both Houses of the State Legislature and its senator whose seat was unchallenged—an aggregate representing a vast majority of the people of the State. The Hon. John Little and the Hon. Benjamin Butterworth, former Attorney-General of Ohio, both members of Congress, had been delegated to present the case of the State. They made formal charges, based on evidence given under oath or communicated in writing by reputable citizens, who were willing to testify under oath. None of the

---

[1] Report No. 1490, United States Senate, 49th Congress, 1886, pp. 77, 78.

matter was presented on mere hearsay or rumor.[1] No charge was made to connect Senator Payne personally with the corruption. His denials and those of his friends of any participation by him were therefore mere evasions of the actual charge — that his election had been corruptly procured for him, not by him. The substance of their accusation, as contained in their statement and the papers forwarded by the Legislature, was as follows:[2]

That among the chief managers of Mr. Payne's canvass, and those who controlled its financial operations, were four of the principal members in Ohio of the oil trust: its treasurer, the vice-president of one of its most important subordinate companies, its Cincinnati representative, and another—all of whom were named.

That one of these four, naming him, who was given the financial management of the Payne campaign at Columbus, carried $65,000 with him, "next to his skin," to Columbus to use in the election, as he had stated to an intimate friend whose name would be given.

That the cashier of the bank in Cleveland, where the treasurer of the oil combination kept one of his bank accounts, would testify that this money was procured on a check given by this treasurer of the oil trust to another of its officials, and passed over by him to its Cincinnati agent, who drew out the cash.

That the back room used by the Payne manager at Columbus as his office displayed such large amounts of money in plain view that it looked like a bank, and that the employé who acted there as his clerk stated upon his return home that he had never seen so much money handled together in his life.

That a prominent gentleman, going to the room used by the Payne managers for a "converter," had said that he saw "canvas bags and coin bags and cases for greenbacks littered and

---

[1] Report No. 1490, United States Senate, 49th Congress, 1886, p. 58.

[2] Same, pp. 37, 40, 66; Miscellaneous Document No. 106, United States Senate, 49th Congress, 1886, pp. 32, 46, 214, and *passim.*

scattered around the room and on the table and on the floor
. . . with something green sticking out," which he found to
be money.

That members who had been earnest supporters of Pendleton were taken one by one by certain guides to this room
which looked like a bank, and came out with an intense and
suddenly developed dislike of civil-service reform (Mr. Pendleton's measure), and proceeded to vote for Mr. Payne; and
that these conversions were uniformly attended with thrift,
sudden, extensive, and so irreconcilable with their known
means of making money as to be a matter of remark among
their neighbors; and that "the reasons for the change (of
vote) were kept mainly in this room, passed by delivery, and
could be used to buy real estate."

That this use of money in large amounts to procure the
sudden conversions of Pendleton legislators to Payne would
be shown by numerous witnesses, generally Democrats, several
of them lawyers of great distinction and high ability.

That the editor and proprietor of the principal Democratic
journal in Ohio had stated, as was sworn to, that he had spent
$100,000 to elect Payne, and that it cost a great deal of
money to get those representatives and senators to vote for
Payne, and they had to be bought. "It took money, and a
good deal of it, to satisfy them," and he complained that the
oil trust had not reciprocated in kind. This statement was
made by one of his editorial writers, who after making it was
discharged. The latter subsequently put it into the form of
an affidavit.

That Senator Pendleton would testify that more than
enough of the legislators to give him the election had been
pledged to him.

That the number of members of the Ohio Senate and
House of Representatives who had been paid money to vote
for Mr. Payne was so great that without their votes and influence his nomination would have been out of the question.

That a legislator who had been violently opposed to Payne,
then changed and became violently rich, had acknowledged

that the treasurer of the oil trust, out of gratitude for what he had done, had "loaned" him several thousand dollars—"a case," said the representative of Ohio before the United States Senate, "of a man becoming well-to-do by borrowing money."

That legislators who were so poor before the election that everything they had was mortgaged, and they had to beg or borrow funds for their election expenses, became so prosperous after their sudden conversion to Payne that they paid off their debts, rebuilt their houses, furnished them handsomely, deposited large amounts in the banks, or opened new bank accounts, bought more property, and that the reasons they gave for this new wealth were demonstrably untrue—or impossible.

That a member of the Legislature, a State senator, had himself stated that he had received $5000 to vote for Payne,[1] and had offered the same amount to an associate if he would do the same; and that after the election this member opened a new bank account, depositing $2500 in his wife's name, who immediately transferred it to him.

That another member of the Legislature, who changed suddenly after his election to the Legislature, and just before the caucus, from a warm advocacy of one of the recognized candidates to the support of Payne, when directly charged with having taken a bribe, did not deny it, but "became exceedingly sick, white as a sheet, and answered not. He went away, and laid in bed two days."

That, contrary to all the precedents of Ohio politics, the caucus of the majority party was not held until the night before election, so as to leave no time between the caucus and the election.

That, also contrary to the precedents, the nomination was made, not, as usual, by open vote, but by secret ballot and without debate, on the demand of the Payne managers and contrary to the protests of the opponents, so that it could not be known to the public who the Payne men were.

That this knowledge was made sure to the Payne managers,

---

[1] Report No. 1490, United States Senate, 49th Congress, 1886, p. 50.

who were to pay for the votes, by the ingenious device of requiring each purchased legislator to use a coupon ballot furnished by them, the corresponding stub of which they kept.
These legislators were not paid for their votes unless the torn
edges of the coupon ballot voted by them corresponded with
the edge of the stub in the possession of the managers.

That responsible men would testify that they had received
confessions from members of the Legislature that they had
been bribed with money to vote for Mr. Payne.

That two members of the Legislature who had been elected
as anti-monopolists became supporters of Mr. Payne, and
were heard discussing together the amount of money they
had received, and quarrelling because one had received more
than the other.

That a member of the Legislature which was corrupted,
standing on the floor of the Ohio House of Representatives,
pointed out members who had been purchased to vote for
Payne, saying: "These members were paid to vote in the
senatorial fight," holding a little book in his hand in which
he had the names and amounts; but although he made the
charges openly and defiantly, and although the same charges
were made in Republican and Democratic papers, no investigation was ordered. Three attempts to have an investigation
made by the Legislature in which the bribery occurred failed.

That a correspondent of a leading Cincinnati daily, sitting
on the floor of the House, daily charged that the election was
procured by bribery, talked about it generally, and dared the
House to investigate or the accused to sue for libel, and that
no such step was taken by either.

That a memorandum of the names of the legislators who
sold themselves, and the amounts they received, had been
furnished from a responsible source.

That on the eve of the election money was sent by draft to
twenty-four of the Democratic candidates for the Legislature,
with the promise of more the next day, and with the statement that thanks for both remittances were due to one of the
prominent members of the oil trust, who was named, and two

others of Payne's managers, "they paying most of it themselves."

That before the election of the Legislature one of the Payne managers sent large sums of money amounting to $10,000, or $12,000, perhaps $13,500—the treasurer of the oil trust "and other wealthy Democrats contributed it — . . . into different parts of the State."

That the managers of the election absented themselves from the State during the legislative investigation, and remained out of reach until it closed.

That during the two and a half years which had passed since these specific charges of bribery had been put into circulation, there had been no demand for investigation on the part of those whose reputation and honor were concerned, but there had been a manifest effort to prevent investigation.

That in addition to these offers of evidence the case against Mr. Payne would be greatly strengthened by new and additional testimony from responsible sources.

Testimony was taken by the Legislature that an ex-Lieutenant-Governor of Ohio, afterwards Consul-General of the United States at Frankfort, Germany, had been in the room of Payne's manager, had seen that he was using money to procure the election, and had so told Mr. Payne before the election, and that Mr. Payne's reply—"You don't suppose I would endorse anything of that kind, do you?"—showed that he had understood the use of money referred to to be an improper use, thereby fastening upon Mr. Payne, if true, the knowledge that his agents were corrupting the Legislature.

During this deluge of charges Mr. Payne made no denial.

After the investigation had been ordered by the State Legislature, Senator Payne made an offer to the committee to submit all his private papers and books of accounts to their examination—an empty offer, because it was not charged that the corruption had been done by him, but for him by others. These latter made no such offer, but fled from the jurisdiction of the Legislature. When the representatives of the people of Ohio appeared before the committee of the United

States Senate on elections, with the offer to prove under oath the foregoing charges, he remained voiceless. He did not rise in his place in the Senate to deny these accusations, as every other senator since the Senate began had done. He did not go before the committee, nor send before them any witness, or make any explanation. When the Senate committee decided to recommend the Senate not to investigate, and the representatives of Ohio begged the committee to reconsider, Senator Sherman declared that he heartily agreed with every word of the appeal, but Senator Payne still kept silent. The records of Congress show that his sole utterance or appearance in this matter in Congress was to make the motion that the papers forwarded by the Ohio Legislature should be sent, as was the routine, to the Committee on Elections. In doing this he did more than abstain from the utterance of a word which could be in any way construed as a demand for investigation. He delivered what was, in effect, an appeal to his fellow-senators not to investigate. He attacked the Legislature for sending the report of its investigation to Congress, characterizing "this proceeding—the transmission of the testimony here—as an attempt to circulate and give currency to baseless gossip and scandal, after everything substantial in the way of a charge had been discredited and disproved." In conclusion he left the matter to the committee "for such disposition of it as they may find to be in accordance with dignity and justice."

The Legislature which made the investigation selected as the reason for ordering it the fact that a well-known citizen had just repeated in an open letter in the public prints the charges of bribery which had been made already hundreds of times. When this citizen was called upon to testify before the Legislature he stated that, as his information was derived from others, he had no personal proof to offer of his own knowledge that bribery had been committed. Referring to this, Mr. Payne said to his colleagues of the Senate:

"Thus fell all that the investigation was originally based upon."[1]

---

[1] Miscellaneous Document 106, United States Senate, 49th Congress, 1886, p. 18.

This was not true. The witness furnished the committee with the names of the men on whose authority he had spoken, and through whom evidence based on personal knowledge could be procured as to the truth of the charges.[1] Therefore the statement, " Thus fell all that the investigation was originally based upon," so far as it was believed by the senators, deceived them. The State Legislature could not compel the witnesses to testify. Only the United States Senate could do this, and it was deterred from doing so by this concealment of the fact that the investigation, instead of falling because of no basis, had struck firmer ground. The proffer of evidence was of such a character that, as has been well said, none of the lawyers of the Senate committee who voted against recommending investigation " would have failed to recommend thorough investigation of such an incident if it had been relevant to an alleged title set up against a private client." [2] But the Senate Committee on Privileges and Elections—Senators Pugh, Saulsbury, Vance, and Eustis voting against Hoar and Frye—recommended the Senate not to investigate, and the Senate adopted this report.

No one had expected this. The unbroken precedents of the Senate had made it a matter of course in public expectation that the investigation would be made. A convention of Ohio editors, sending a memorial for a reconsideration, said: " No instance has yet arisen in the history of the Senate where specific and well-supported charges of bribery in a senatorial election, preferred by the Legislature of a State, have not been promptly investigated by the Senate. In fact, so jealous has the Senate been of its own integrity and honor that it has heretofore promptly ordered investigations upon the memorials of citizens, and in other cases upon the memorial of individual members of a Legislature charging fraud in senatorial elections." In so doing the Senate, to adopt the language used by the chairman of the Committee on Elections,

[1] Miscellaneous Document 106, United States Senate, 49th Congress, 1886, pp. 81–82.

[2] *The Payne Bribery Case and the United States Senate*, by Albert H. Walker.

Senator Hoar, declared that "it is indifferent to the question
whether its seats are to be in the future the subject of bargain
and sale, or may be presented by a few millionaires as a com-
pliment to a friend." [1] "This matter never can be quieted,"
said Senator Sherman in the debate in the Senate. "There
are six or seven men who are known—I could name them—
who, if they were brought before this Committee on Privileges and Elections, would settle this matter forever one way
or the other in my judgment."

The Senate decided that such a charge, accompanied by
such offers of proof, did not deserve its attention. The trial
of "even a criminal accusation," said the minority of the committee, "requires only the oath of the accuser who is justified if he have probable cause." The minority, Senators
Hoar and Frye, further said: "It will not be questioned that
in every one of these cases there is abundant probable cause
which would justify a complaint, and compel a grand-jury or
magistrate to issue process and make an investigation. Is
the Senate to deny to the people of a great State, speaking
through their Legislature and their representative citizens,
the only opportunity for a hearing of this momentous case
which can exist under the Constitution? The question now is
not whether the case is proved—it is only whether it shall be
inquired into. That has never yet been done. It cannot be
done until the Senate issues its process. No unwilling witness
has ever yet been compelled to testify; no process has gone
out which should cross State lines. The Senate is now to determine, as the law of the present case, and as the precedent
for all future cases, as to the great crime of bribery—a crime
which poisons the waters of republican liberty in the fountain
—that the circumstances which here appear are not enough to
demand its attention. It will hardly be doubted that cases of
purchase of seats in the Senate will multiply rapidly under
the decision proposed by the majority of the committee." [2]

[1] Minority Report of Senators Hoar and Frye, 49th Congress, 1st Session,
Senate, No. 1490, p. 34.   [2] Same, pp. 38, 39.

The debate upon the recommendation of the committee not to investigate was impassioned. Senator Hoar said: " The adoption of this majority report . . . will be the most unfortunate fact in the history of the Senate." When the vote of the Senate not to investigate was announced, Senator Edmunds turned to his neighbor in the Senate and summed up the verdict of posterity in these words: " This is a day of infamy for the Senate of the United States."

The same Legislature which sent Senator Payne to the Senate defeated the bill to allow the Cleveland independent refiners to build a pipe line to furnish themselves with oil. The defeat of the bill was accomplished by a lobby whose work was so openly shameless that it was characterized by the Ohio press " as an indelible disgrace to the State." The bill was one of many attempts which have been made by the people of Ohio and Pennsylvania, without success, to get from their Legislature the right to build pipe lines. It has been tried to get laws to regulate the charges of the existing lines, but without success. The history of the pipe-line bills in these legislatures for the past ten years has been a monotonous record of an unavailing struggle of a majority of millions to apply legal and constitutional restraints to a minority of a few dozens. The means employed in the Ohio Legislature of 1885 to defeat a bill giving equality in pipe-line transportation to refiners in competition with the oil trust, which owned the existing pipe lines, were of such a sort that that body has gone into the history of the State as the " Coal-oil Legislature." It is stated by Hudson, in his *Railways and the Republic*, that the Democratic agent of the bribery openly threatened to publish the list he had of the members of the Legislature he had purchased, and that in consequence of this threat proceedings which had been begun against him for outraging the House by appearing on the floor in a state of gross intoxication were abandoned.[1]

In a debate about combinations in trade and industry—

---

[1] Hudson's *Railways and the Republic*, p. 467.

25

trusts—in the United States Senate in 1888, the sore scandal
of this senatorial election of 1884 was disinterred.

"If there be such a trust," said Senator Hoar, referring to
the oil trust, "is it represented in the cabinet at this moment?
Is it represented in the Senate? I want to know the facts
about these five or six great trusts which are sufficient in their
power to overthrow any government in Europe, if they existed
in those nations, that should set itself against them—the coal,
the sugar, the whiskey, the cotton, the fruit, the railroad transportation of this country, controlled by these giant chieftains."

Senator Payne defended the oil trust and himself. "Even
at this date," he said, "it seems that that company is represented as being guilty of all sorts of unlawful and improper
things. Such allegations without proof to sustain them I regard as unworthy of an honorable man or an honorable senator. . . . The Standard Oil Company," he continued, "is a very
remarkable and wonderful institution. It has accomplished
within the last twenty years, as a commercial enterprise, what
no other company or association of modern times has accomplished." He went on to declare that he "never had a dollar's
interest in the company." But the charge which he and it
would never allow to be investigated was that the company
had a great many dollars' interest in him. "The majority of
the stockholders are very liberal in their philanthropic contributions to charity and benevolent works," he pleaded; "but
it contributed," he said, "not one dollar or one cent directly
or indirectly to my election to this body." During the demand for investigation he uttered no such denial to be taken
as a challenge.

The senator made what Senator Hoar properly called a
"very remarkable admission" concerning the part taken in
elections by the oil combination. "When a candidate for the
other House in 1871," Senator Payne said, "no association,
no combination in my district did more to bring about my
defeat, and went to so large an expense in money to accomplish it, as the Standard Oil Company."

The oil trust, then, does take part in elections, and as a

company spends larger sums of money than any other "institution, association, combination . . . to accomplish the defeat" of candidates for Congress!

Then Mr. Payne said: "There never has been a national election at which those two gentlemen—one of them was my own son—have not contributed very liberally." He named the two men who were, as Senator Hoar showed, among the most influential and important managers of his election to the Senate.

Senator Hoar closed the debate with these unanswered and unanswerable words: "A senator who, when the governor of his State, when both branches of the Legislature of his State, complained to us that a seat in the United States Senate had been bought; when the other senator from the State rose and told us that that was the belief of a very large majority of the people of Ohio, without distinction of party, failed to rise in his place and ask for the investigation which would have put an end to those charges, if they had been unfounded, sheltering himself behind the technicalities which were found by some gentlemen on both sides of this chamber, that the investigation ought not to be made, but who could have had it by the slightest request on his part, and then remained dumb, I think should forever after hold his peace." [1]

The election of this senator was meant to be only the prelude to his nomination and election as President of the United States. This was publicly and authoritatively declared by the men who were charged with having spent money to buy the Legislature for him. One of these was the proprietor of the most influential Democratic daily in Ohio, and that journal in a leading editorial, double leaded to make it more prominent, declared this to be the purpose of Payne's friends. The New York *Sun* of May 27, 1884, followed, also in double-leaded editorials, under the caption in staring black type of the name of the Senator, and said: "Henry B. Payne is looming up grandly in the character of a possible and not altogether improbable successor to Mr. Tilden as the Democratic

---

[1] *Congressional Globe*, September 12, 1888, pp. 8520-8604.

candidate for the Presidency. The fact that the Ohio delegation at Chicago in July is sure to be solid for Payne is of peculiar importance and significancy. Everybody can see what it may amount to."

Concurrently with these formal announcements came the news from all parts of Ohio that the Payne party were hard at work to control the election of the delegates who were to represent Ohio in the National Democratic Convention at Chicago in July. But the managers of this Presidential campaign found that they had gone too far. The election for senator had excited so fierce an anger over the whole country that it had become perfectly plain that Senator Payne was not "available." The education of the American public was still incomplete. It could see senatorships bought and endure it, but the Presidency—"not yet."

The use this senator made of his seat throws light where none is needed. Again, in 1887, the great question of 1876 of the control of the highways came up before Congress. The agitation of nearly twenty years had come to a point. Thirty of the States and Territories of the Union had established commissions or passed laws to regulate the railroads. Congress had before it the Interstate Commerce bill forbidding discriminations, and creating the Interstate Commerce Commission as a special tribunal to prevent and punish the crime. There had been investigation, debates, amendments, meetings of conference committees of both Houses. It was proposed to "recommit" the bill to prevent its passage for an indefinite time. Mr. Payne voted "Yes." Then the question before the Senate is, Shall the bill become a law? Senator Payne's name is called. He votes :

"No."

It is the same question as in 1876, and the same vote. Against the investigation, first, and then the legislation, his word is :

"I object."

IN 1891 Congress passed the Postal Subsidy law for paying a higher than the market rate of compensation to capitalists who would carry the mails in vessels built in America, of American materials, and manned by Americans. No contracts were made by the Post-office Department under the law for the mails between Europe and America, for there were no such capitalists and no such boats in that quarter.

In May of the next year, 1892, a bill was whizzed through Congress almost without debate, in which the forms of the principal beneficiaries-to-be of the law of 1891 loomed into view. The subsidy law gave its bonus only to vessels that could fly the American flag because American built and manned. This new act exempted from these conditions the two principal steamers of the Inman, now the International, line—the *City of New York* and the *City of Paris*—provided the company built two other steamers that fulfilled the requirements of the subsidy law. The sequel disclosed that their owners had a well-laid plan to build more than two other steamers to get the rich rewards of the subsidy law. The steamers and the company were not named. That was not needed. The bill was drawn with such limitations as to size, speed, ownership, etc., that these were the only two vessels which could come under its provisions. The bill was introduced in the House by a prominent Democrat, and in the Senate by a prominent Republican. It was passed by both Houses regardless of party distinctions. The Secretary of the Navy urged the bill upon the naval committees of Congress. He had begun to do so in his first report to Congress and subsequent communications, in which he referred by name to the vessels which were masked in this legislation. The head of the line and other owners were members of the oil combination. The president of the steamship company has been the president of the pipe-line branch of the oil trust—its largest single interest—from the time of its organization in 1881.[1] This exemption from the law was engineered through the Senate by one who had hitherto always been conspicuously strenuous in refusing to abate his opposition to admitting to American registry any ship not built in America, of American materials, by American labor, but who now had suffered some sea change.

Ordinary citizens who want to get the profits of carrying the American mails must build their boats in American shipyards; but the syndicate got members of Congress to grant them by law that which all others must earn.

The enactment of the Postal Subsidy law and the exemption of these steamers by special law were the first two parts of a progressive programme. The third step was the negotiation of contracts with the Postmaster-General for the prizes of subsidy. Immediately upon the passage of this special legislation the Postmaster-General went through the necessary but empty parade of advertising for bids for a service for which there could be only one possible bidder. The awarding of contracts to the steamship company so "fortunate in competing" was announced in the press in October, 1892.

The Postmaster-General dated the contracts 1895—three years ahead. They run for ten years from that time. An iron-clad, or, better than iron-clad, law-clad contract was thus secured, giving a complete monopoly of the mail business between America and Europe until A.D. 1905, five years into the twentieth century. The legislation of May contemplated the construction of two new boats. The contracts secured from the Postmaster-General showed that the line intended to build five, and obligated the government to pay subsidies to all of

---

[1] Testimony, Trusts, Congress, 1888, p. 395.

them, as well as to the two foreign-built steamers given by special legislation the right to fly the American flag. By these contracts the company, after the completion of its new steamers in about three years, will exclusively carry every bag of mail that leaves America for Europe. Meanwhile the mails are to be given to its two steamers now running, the *Paris* and the *New York*, whenever they are in port. This has been frequently done in the past on account of their speed, but the compensation for this, under the law and the new contracts, has been made much greater than the price hitherto paid. With but one or two exceptions the mails on all the routes where subsidy is given—to South America, Havana, China, Europe — were carried before the subsidy law on the same ships as now. Except a very trifling saving in time, the only change the law has made here is that the gains of the carriers have been swelled at the cost of the taxpayers. The American shippers carrying the mails at the regular weight rates were making a profit. The Post-office, under the new deal, gets only what it has been getting—the carriage of the mails; but the steamship company gets a great deal more. This is the "pleasure of making it cheap" applied to the postal service.

By this procession of moves the company secured profitable contracts ten years ahead on present ships, the *Paris* and the *New York*—although these had not yet done as much as fly the American flag in compliance with the special legislation in their behalf—and on future ships that were not yet built or contracted for. All was in the future—the American registry for the *Paris* and the *New York*, the building of the new steamers required by the special legislation. But one thing was got in hand, and was not in the future tense—the contract with the American Post-office, binding it to pay millions a year. The privileges conferred by this legislation were so valuable that, as Senator Frye stated in debate, its recipients to gain them were to forfeit $105,000 due them from the British Government.

The American registry would be a capital advertisement to

catch the American tourist. Travelling, says Emerson, is a fool's paradise, and the shifting population of that paradise would never stop to think out the fraud in the appeal to their patriotism. Much was made in the sentimental Senate of the privilege the law would give Americans of going abroad in their own ships under their own flag. The press was used shrewdly and widely to gain the favor of the public for these incursions into their Treasury. Pages of advertising, in the dress of news-matter, were put into prominent journals, telling in glowing phrases what a great thing Congress, the Postmaster - General, and the steamship company were doing for the people. The same editorial on the promised restoration of American maritime supremacy would appear as original in journals thousands of miles apart. As the panorama of journalism moved along with its daily shift any observer could see the methodical and business-like way in which the syndicate "inspired" the press. Articles about the "great steamship line" appeared on the same date in the papers of different cities, giving the same facts in the same order, and nearly the same words, following "copy" evidently supplied from a common source. One day these chimes all sing the immeasurable superiority of Southampton over Liverpool as a port for Americans; another day the unspeakable sagacity of the Postmaster-General in giving this company the mails is the tune; and again the ding-dong tells how, but for the syndicate and its subsidy, the American flag—"Old Glory"—would be seen no more on the seas. The average citizen who reads "his" paper is no doubt duly impressed.

"Old Glory on the seas!" cried the excitable metropolitan editors. "The dear old flag!" "America again Queen of the seas!" "A new era is about to dawn on our long-neglected commerce!" Our long-absent flag is about to reappear, but not, as in the old days, as the symbol of a people's commerce. It signalizes the commerce of syndicates. The democratic idea of a chance for all has been abandoned for the aristocratic idea of the favored few. "Poor indeed in spirit must be the

American," said the New York *Tribune*, " who will not hail with satisfaction and pride the early prospect of the reappearance of the flag in English, French, and Belgian ports." Poor, fortunately, it was replied, are many Americans in the spirit which taxes all the people out of an industry in which they once led the world, and then taxes them to give that same industry as an exclusive privilege to a syndicate—and such a syndicate !

There was a rapturous chorus from the press because American materials and American labor are to be employed in the construction and use of the new vessels to be built for subsidies. When American labor was free to employ itself and American materials with no subsidies, American boats did absolutely the whole packet business between England and America.[1]

Now American seamanship must remain content to be employed to such an extent and on such terms as may suit the interests of a few men, under whose captainship the once glorious expansion of our commerce on the seas is replaced by a system limited on every side. Limited by the expensiveness of entering the occupation : a special bill has to be passed through Congress in each case to confer the right to fly the American flag on ships bought abroad, and for this the merely legitimate expenses are heavy—trips to Washington, appearances before committees and departments, with expert representatives. Limited by their small number : instead of thousands building and running new ships, a score. Limited by their capital : great, it is still much less than the aggregate, if all had a chance. Limited by the narrowness of view and enterprise inevitable with a few, however capable : everybody knows more than anybody. Limited by the lack of diversity in opinion and interests : with many men of many minds, of varying forecasts and moods and gaits, the currents of industry are kept fuller and steadier than is possible under a clique rule. Limited by selfishness : the few will inevitably come to regard the ocean-carrying business as " belonging to

[1] Speech of John M. Forbes, Boston, April 30, 1889.

us," like oil, and with their crushing wealth will treat as
"blackmailers" intruders with new ships and new methods.
Limited by the impossibility the subsidy system imposes upon
the average citizen of competing against the government—
against himself multiplied by all his fellow-citizens. Limited
by corruption: when this subsidy bill was under discussion,
Representative Blount, of Georgia,[1] called attention to the
methods by which previous legislation of the same sort, "to
build up the American merchant marine and increase the
commerce of the country," had been sought from Congress.
Quoting from the report made to Congress in 1874–75 by
Representative Kasson, of Iowa, he showed that the Pacific
Mail Company, to get a subsidy, had disbursed $703,000
among the members and officers of Congress and other persons influential in legislation. "Yankee maritime enterprise,"
this is called. The great captains, Bursley, Anthony, De-
lano, Dumaresq, Comstock, Eldridge, Nye, Marshall, Hol-
dredge, Morgan, and other sturdy Americans who led the nau-
tical world wherever speed, safety, and courage were called
for, outsailing competition even from the land where "Blake
and mighty Nelson fell"[2]—they had a manlier idea of enterprise than being supported at the public expense in floating
poor-houses miscalled floating hotels.

The few men who are the beneficiaries of taxes paid by the
many will be powerful and shrewd enough to get other dis-
pensations or benefits, post-office contracts, naval contracts, or
modifications of the strict terms of their agreement, and with
this help from the taxpayer they can do business at a figure
which, though very remunerative to themselves, will drive
the unaided citizen competitor out of the business. Honest
citizens cannot ask for such favors. Poor men could not get
them.

It was the old spirit of rebate which sought and gave the
preference. Nothing could make such legislation respectable
but the extension of its benefits to all Americans owning such

[1] Congress Record, 51st Congress, 2d Session, p. 3651.
[2] Mr. John M. Forbes, in *Fossils, Free Ships, and Reform.*

ships. But no such extension was contemplated. The law gave a privilege not to the American flag, but to the owners of the American flags of these two steamers. " There is little probability," Senator Frye was reported as saying, December 22, 1892, in the New York *Tribune,* friendly to him and to the policy of subsidy, " of the passage of any more laws giving the privilege of an American registry to vessels upon the building of which no American labor has been expended. The twin steamers *City of New York* and *City of Paris* have set a fashion of which they will be the only exponents."

There is a pool of the steamers between America and Europe called the North Atlantic Steamship Association. At its meeting in December, 1892, this association discussed plans for reducing the number of trips, increasing passenger rates, withdrawing excursion rates to the World's Fair, and discontinuing the steerage traffic. This was duly followed by the announcement in March, 1893, for which it was presumably a preparation, that steerage traffic was renewed, but at an increase of rates. Passenger rates of the higher class have also been raised. Agreements to restrict the number of ships; pools to put up rates; steamship wars to destroy competitors; the use of "pull" to procure from the admiralty, sanitary, naval, immigration, and other governmental bureaus, here and abroad, regulations ostensibly for public convenience, really to make business, as nearly as can be, impossible for others; lobbies to buy legislation for private interests—all these may be expected to replace the magnificent and manly rivalries of the days when the unbribed flag floated on its own breath in every sea.

Under the policy of subsidy—the policy of aristocracy, exclusion, scarcity, corruption, war, and loss of liberty—the contest for maritime and commercial supremacy becomes a contest between the subsidy lobbies in Washington and at Westminster, Paris, and Berlin. If the duke who is at the head of one of the great English steamship lines obtains an increase of subsidy, the maritime dukes in America will call on Congress not to shame itself by doing less for Americans than Parliament has done for Englishmen. If all the English and American lines pass under one ducal yoke—following the internationalization of other syndicated businesses of Great Britain and America—one hidden hand will manage for one purse the make-believe duel between Parliament and Congress, while the uninitiated people glare across the ocean at each other, and each inspired press calls on its government not to allow its commercial supremacy to be destroyed by vulgar and unpatriotic economy. In advocacy of subsidy—breeder of sea-dogs, naval contractors, of war, and of treasury-suckled syndicates to fan its flames—the Secretary of the Navy wrote to the Chairman of the Senate Committee on Commerce in this case, "A fleet of such cruisers would sweep an enemy's commerce from the ocean." All through the press, from New York to Texas and the Pacific coast, every possible change of phrase is rung to fire the American heart with "jingo" exhortations to subsidize private steamers so as to increase our fighting kennel.

The "American idea" is that individuals as well as corporations, poor men as well as rich ones, small towns as well as large ones, one maritime State as well as another, should be encouraged to follow the sea. The old woman who thanked God, upon her first sight of the sea, that at last she had seen something there was enough of, lived before subsidies were invented and the sea shrank to be too small for all the people.

The contracts made with the International Company bind the government to pay it $4.00 a mile for fifty-two trips a year (3162 miles each) between New York and Southampton for the ten years (1895–1905)—$657,696 a year, and $6,576,960 for the ten years; and the same rate a mile for the same number of trips a year (of 3350 miles each) between New York and Antwerp for ten years—$696,800 a year, and $6,968,-000 for the ten years. This makes an income from the mails alone of $1,354,496 a year on the not-to-exceed $10,-000,000 which the company will have invested. At the end of the ten years it will have received from these government contracts alone its whole investment, and more than one-third in addition. The American taxpayer will receive for his share the profit and pleasure of being forbidden to send his letters to Europe by faster and cheaper boats, when these appear, as they have already begun to do. The trial trips of new steamers of other lines show them to be faster than the vessels we have bound ourselves to. "The American principle" used to be to send all mails by the fastest ships. Now, to develop the "American merchant marine," we relieve it from all necessity of competing in speed, or anything else, with the foreign marine.

With such legislation and contracts in hand, any syndicate could go to the banks and borrow at the lowest rates every cent of the millions it needed to carry out its plans. It need not invest a dollar of its own. Good enough "collateral" for borrowing would be this privilege—practically a capital of millions got from the government for nothing. Done for favored citizens, this is "the development of our national resources"; done for the whole people, it would be "socialism" or something more dreadful. Thus guaranteed dividends by the forced contributions of the American people, this company, if threatened with competition by other lines, old or new, can lower freights and fares to rates at which others cannot live. The subsidies are a reserve fund on which it can subsist while doing other business below cost. The vision of this will deter other capitalists from building vessels, as they have been frightened out of building tank-cars. The company can, by a war of rates, force the sale to it of such vessels as it wants out of the present Atlantic fleet. The scheme, which has progressed so smoothly through the various stages of the Postal Subsidy law—the exemption by special legislation of the two steamers from their foreign disabilities, the negotiation of the contracts for subsidies until A.D. 1905 for steamers yet unborn—is an entering wedge, the broad end of which may easily grow to be a monopoly of the transatlantic —and why not transpacific?—traffic and travel.

And in future legislation, tariffs, and contracts, what bulwark of the people would avail against the Washington lobby of these combined syndicates of oil, natural gas, illuminating gas, coal, lead, linseed-oil, railroads, street-railroads, banks, ocean and lake steamships and whalebacks, iron and copper mines, steel mills, etc.? These beggars on horseback — the poor we will always have with us as long as we give such alms —are forever at the elbows of the secretaries, representatives, senators. The people who pay are at work in their fields, out of sight, scattered over thousands of miles.

Having evaded, by the complaisance of Congress, the requirements of the subsidy law in the case of its two non-American steamers, the company sought to be relieved by the Secretary of the Treasury from the necessity of manning its boats with Americans, as stipulated by the law. It was unwilling to sacrifice the foreign captains in its employ, as the despatches said, "for the untried men of American citizenship," regardless that one of the strongest promises of the subsidy givers and takers was to recall to the sea the American citizenship banished thence. The company had already driven its foreign-built boats through the law, why not its foreign captains? It applied to the Treasury Department for permission to retain them. To furnish a ground for such a ruling, the foreign captains had given notice of their "intention" to become citizens. They could not become citizens for five years, and the courts hold that such a declaration does not meet the requirements of the law that the officers of United States vessels shall be citizens of the United States. The ruling asked for was refused by Assistant Secretary of the Treasury Nettleton. The question was not dropped. Some months later (December 2, 1892) the Washington despatches of the Philadelphia *Ledger* and the New York *Herald* reported that "Secretary Foster of the Treasury is disposed to accede to the wishes of the company, if it can possibly be done within the law," and in the New York *Tribune* we read that "he is inclined to the view that an exception might safely be made in this case."

The raising of the American flag on these steamers—one at New York and the other at Southampton—in the spring of

1893, was made a state ceremony in both countries. The President of the United States came on specially from the capital to honor the occasion, though this had never been done before when the American flag was raised on vessels admitted to foreign registry. The American minister left the embassy at London to officiate at Southampton. The vessels were announced to be under American captains transferred from other ships owned by the same men. But the Society of American Marine Engineers and the Brotherhood of Steamboat Pilots discovered that other officers—the foreign engineers of the vessels—had been retained, though they were foreigners. The former began an agitation for the protection of their legal rights. Remonstrances from every important branch of the two societies from San Francisco to New York were forwarded to the President of the United States and the Secretary of the Treasury of the new administration which had just gone into office. Counsel were employed to present their case. It was found that one of the last official acts of the outgoing Secretary of the Treasury had been the order authorizing the issue of licenses to foreign engineers. Attempts to procure a copy of this order from the department have failed. Engineers have always been considered to be officers. If they are such, this exemption was a violation of the statutes of the United States which require that officers shall be American. It reversed all the decisions which hold that declaration of an intention to become a citizen does not make one legally a citizen, for that would give foreigners, as in this case, the advantages of citizenship without its duties; and indefinitely, for the intention might never be executed. The order of the Secretary makes a precedent upon which foreign captains may be employed—the objection being the same in either case—and their reappearance may therefore be confidently looked for. The appropriation once got, "Old Glory" is hauled down.

An "American Seaman" wrote the New York *World* that when he offered himself for employment on the boat which had just replaced with so much pomp the British flag with

the American he was almost laughed at, and was told there
had been ninety men on board that morning on the same
errand.   All got the same answer, "We don't want you.   We
employ all our hands on the other side."   The articles circulated throughout the country to create public opinion in favor
of these subsidies dwell much on the "glory" and advantage
of having Americans in command of these vessels with a full
American force under them.   But the subsidy secured, we see
these American vessels, which may be called upon to take
part in a war with Great Britain, are manned by British engineers and British seamen.   The lower compensation they
are accustomed to will help keep down the cost of manning
the other vessels to be built for the line.

The secretary by whom this was done was he who, as president of a subordinate corporation of the oil combination, had
been the commanding officer at the front in the great battle
with Toledo.[1]   When he was nominated for Secretary of the
Treasury, Senator Payne made himself conspicuous by soliciting support among the Democrats for the confirmation
of this Republican.   "He could not be chosen to the Toledo
Council from any ward to-day," said the New York *Times*,
February 23, 1891, "so bitter is the feeling against him,"
and the same paper declared that his defeat in Ohio as a candidate for Congress in 1890 was entirely due to his connection with the oil combination.   But though of so little political power that he could not command a majority of the votes
in his own Congressional district, there was influence behind
him which could get the head of his party and the government to put him in the seat illustrious with the memory of
such men as Alexander Hamilton and Salmon P. Chase.   "The
objection to Governor Foster as Secretary of the Treasury,
that he was an associate in business of the members of the
great oil trust," said the New York *Press*, "President Har-
rison did not regard as serious enough to have any weight."
It was pointed out by the Buffalo *Courier* editorially, Febru-

[1] See p. 307.

ary 23, 1891, and other papers, that the oil trust, which Mr. Foster had been serving, " is not only a heavy exporter but a heavy importer, especially of tin plate, and is an extensive claimant for rebates of duty on the tin of cans in which oil is exported."

An item of Associated Press news in December, 1892, says that the Secretary of the Treasury has just decided that the oil combination shall be paid by the Treasury a drawback of the duties it has paid on imported steel hoops for barrels in which it exports oil. "It isn't pleasant," said the New York *World*, editorially, February 23, 1891, "to have a Secretary of the Treasury who holds intimate relations with the oil trust." It is through the Secretary of the Treasury that the company receives the mail subsidies of millions a year. All the statistics and official publications with regard to the "decline of American shipping" and "foreign competition with American oil," and about the tariff, as on oil, coal, steel, tin, etc., and many other financial and commercial matters of pecuniary concern to them, are under the charge of the Secretary of the Treasury. The Treasury Department's Commissioner of Navigation, in 1892, sends circulars to the boards of trade and chambers of commerce all over the country, calling attention to the small amount of money paid by our government to American steamers for the mails, and advocating the establishment of a merchant marine and naval reserve on the principle adopted by Great Britain—*i.e.*, the payment of subsidies.

When Senator Hoar, speaking of the oil combination in the debate on the Payne case,[1] asked, sharply: "Is it represented in the Cabinet at this moment?" he referred to the Secretary of the Navy. Subsidy had not then insinuated itself into the policy of the government; but when that came, the uses of a Secretary of the Navy were clear enough. It was by the influence of the Secretary of the Navy that the subsidies for these steamships of the oil trust were got through Congress.

[1] See p. 386.

26

It is the Secretary of the Navy who passes upon the speed of the ships receiving subsidies; and his findings are binding upon the Post-office Department which awards the contracts and upon the Treasury Department which pays. In the rush of the closing hours of the session of 1889–90 of the Fifty-first Congress, upon the urgent recommendation, made in person to the Naval Committee, of the same Secretary of the Navy who had pushed through the subsidy special legislation we have described, $1,000,000 was appropriated for the purchase of nickel ore. It is an emergency, said the senator who spoke for the Naval Committee to the Senate. The nickel was to be bought by the Secretary of the Navy; when and where was at his discretion. The ore was to be used for alloying steel in the manufacture of armor plate. The same Congress took off the duty of hundreds of dollars a ton on nickel imported. The only nickel mine of importance in America was then at Sudbury, Canada. In pressing the appropriation through Congress it was stated that the mine, like the steamship company subsidized later, was owned by "our citizens." After investigation in Cleveland, New York, Washington, and Canada, the *Daily News* of Chicago declared that the appropriation of $1,000,000 and the abolition of the duty were done in the interest of members of the oil combination; that they were "our citizens" who were the owners of the nickel mine at Sudbury; that they had sent an able lobbyist to Washington to secure the legislation; and that, in anticipation of his success, the product of the mine had been withheld for a year from the market, until ore to the value of millions had accumulated. It was said that by April 1, 1890, there were 5000 tons on the dump, the duty on which, at the old rate, would have been $1,500,000. Whether these statements were correct or not—and in the absence of official investigation it is impossible to tell—the narrative answers fully the purpose of giving the uninitiated public an idea of the relations that may exist between public departments and private syndicates with great profit—but not to the department. The appropriation was passed September 29, 1890. The books of the Navy Department show that the Secretary thereupon made contracts with the Canadian Copper Company, by which, up to June 15th following, it sold the government $321,321.86 worth of nickel. A litigation arising among its stockholders in the spring of 1893 disclosed among them no less close a connection of the oil trust than the senator from Ohio who had served it in Congress from 1876 to 1891.

The message of a Republican President in 1892 commended the special legislation in favor of the two steamers, and urged Congress not to fail to appropriate money to pay them their subsidies. The Democratic Postmaster-General, who now stands between the United States and these carriers of the foreign mails, is one of the firm of distinguished counsel who defended the interests of some of the owners of this steamship line in the conspiracy trial at Buffalo.[1] He is to give them the vouchers upon which the millions a year of subsidies are to be paid, and he may be called upon to consider new contracts. In the Presidential campaign of 1892 the head of the oil trust was prominent on one side figuring among the officers of great political mass-meetings in New York, while the associate referred to by Senator Hoar was the active manager of the political fortunes of the other party. This is not a solitary instance. The great man who testified twenty-one years ago that he was a Republican in Republican districts, a Democrat in Democratic districts, but everywhere an Erie man, has now an army of imitators. The people had this authoritatively explained to them while they were dazedly watching the speculation in sugar-trust stock in Wall Street and the Senate rise and fall with the manipulation of the sugar tariff in committee. The president of the sugar trust, before a special committee of the United States Senate, testified that this "politics of business" was the custom of "every individual and corporation and firm, trust, or whatever you call it."[2] Asked if he contributed to the State campaign funds, he said: "We always do that. . . . In the State of New

[1] See chs. xviii.–xxi.
[2] Senate Report No. 485, 53d Congress, 2d Session, June 21, 1894.

York, where the Democratic majority is between 40,000 and 50,000, we throw it their way. In the State of Massachusetts, where the Republican party is doubtful, they probably have the call. . . . Wherever there is a dominant party, wherever the majority is very large, that is the party that gets the contribution, because that is the party which controls the local matters"—which include the elections to Congress and the Presidential election.[1] Federal judges find the sugar trust not subject to the anti-trust law.[2] The Attorney-General has not got decisions in the suits against it for refusal to answer Census questions. Congress forces the people to buy sugar of it only, and at its price. The Secretary of the Treasury drafts for a committee of Congress a tariff like that the trust needs. Our President is the head of the "dominant party that gets the contribution," and he joins the sugar lobby by recommending, unofficially, legislation in its favor.[3]

By what law gives it, and by what law does not take from it, the sugar trust can issue $85,000,000 of securities on $10,000,000 of property, and collect $28,000,000[4] a year of profits. Control of government, with its Presidents, Congress, Federal Judges, Attorney-Generals, and Cabinet Secretaries, would be a great prize. Probably none of the trust's "raw material" would be so cheaply bought as this if it could be purchased by campaign contributions of a few hundred thousand dollars. In an interview in the New York *Herald* of March 25, 1894, the debonair president of the trust, to shame the objections of picayune souls, cries, "Who cares for a quarter of a cent a pound?" The answer is not far to seek. He does.

[1] Supplemental Report of Senator W. V. Allen, of the Senate Special Committee (ordered May 17, 1894) to Investigate Alleged Attempts at Bribery by the Sugar Trust.

[2] United States *vs.* E. C. Knight & Co., *et al.* United States Circuit Court of Appeals, Third Circuit, March 26, 1894, 60 *Federal Reporter*, p. 34.

[3] Letter of President Cleveland to Hon. W. L. Wilson, Chairman House Committee of Ways and Means, July 2, 1894, read to the House of Representatives July 18, 1894.

[4] New York *Journal of Commerce and Commercial Bulletin*, Sept. 21, 1893.

CHAPTER XXIX

"THE COMMODITY IS NOT SO GOOD AS BEFORE"
—*Lord Coke.*

THREE hundred years ago Lord Coke, in the "Case of the Monopolies,"[1] declared these to be the inevitable result of monopoly: the price of the commodity will be raised; the commodity is not so good as before; it tends to the impoverishment of artisans, artificers, and others.

In 1878 and 1879, when railway presidents were saying "No" to every application of the few remaining independents for passage along the road to market,[2] and the oil combination was supreme from the well to the lamp, a concerted protest was made against its oil by commercial bodies representing trade all over Europe. An international congress was held specially to consider means for the protection of the European consumer, by the interposition of the governments of Europe and America, or by commercial measures. In the archives of the State Department at Washington are the documents in which this episode can be read.[3] At this moment of triumph over all rivals, "even what was classed as superior brands was a poor article."[4] The English trade met in London, in January, 1879, and remonstrated. One of the delegates stated that a small dealer who bought of him had written, threatening to commit suicide on account of the trouble this poor oil was giving him.[5] The American consul at Antwerp, under date of February 19, 1879, called the attention of the State Department to the congress about to be held to consider the serious complaints which had been made of late

---

[1] II. Coke, 84.   [2] See ch. viii.
[3] New York Assembly "Hepburn" Report, Exhibits, pp. 614–19.
[4] Testimony, New York Assembly "Hepburn" Report, 1879, p. 3678.
[5] Same, p. 3683.

against American refined petroleums. He gave the warning that unless there was an improvement the Belgian government would interfere for the protection of the people with regulations which would greatly embarrass the export trade from America. A bill was introduced into the German Reichstag to protect the people of Germany against the flood of bad oil from America. Against those dealing in oil dangerous to human safety it provided penalties from fines to loss of citizenship and penal servitude.

At the congress which met at Bremen in February were represented all the European nations of any importance except France, which imports only crude, and does all its refining at home. It was an indignation meeting. The consul at Bremen wrote the State Department, under date of February 27, 1879, an account of it. It was "very important," he said. "Delegates were present from the chambers of commerce of Antwerp, Amsterdam, Berlin, Breslau, Christiania, Copenhagen, Danzig, Frankfort-on-Main, Hamburg, Königsberg, Lubeck, Mannheim, Nürnberg, Rostock, Rotterdam, Stettin, Trieste, Moscow, and Vienna."

The "united refiners," to explain away the faults of their oil, sent a representative to the congress who was one of the inspectors of the State of New York, in the pay of the people, but using his official prestige in behalf of a private interest. The consul at Bremen names the two chief points made in the defence: First, that the refined oil was bad because half the crude then produced in America was from the Bradford field, "and is so different in quality from the so-called Parker oil that the same quality of refined oil cannot be made—at any rate, by the ordinary processes hitherto in use." Second, that the wicks in common use were poor. That the inferior quality of the Bradford oil was not the real reason was proved by the fact that the refined oil manufactured and exported by the refineries of the combination from the crude of the other fields deteriorated at the same time and as much.[1] The

---

[1] Testimony, New York Assembly "Hepburn" Report, 1879, p. 3684.

Bremen congress knew this. It was at this precise moment —though this the Bremen congress did not know—that the combination was tying up a great inventor and hauling his apparatus to the junk-yard to prevent the test of a new method for making better and cheaper oil.[1] Its members would have had the benefit of it if successful, but with the spirit which men who seek exclusive control always exhibit, they did not want to change.

The congress declined to treat with any respect the excuses that were offered. It declared "that the complaints regarding the inferior quality of much of the petroleum recently received from America, and especially of the different brands of the" oil combination, were "fully justified." It consequently demanded from the American refiners, and especially from the oil combination, "First, that they give greater care to the refining of crude oil than they have recently done, in order that the petroleum may in the future be again as free as it formerly was from acids and heavy oils, that inferior qualities may no longer be shipped to Europe, and that the consumer may again receive the former customary good quality."

The superiority of its barrels was specially mentioned by the head of the oil combination to explain why all competitors failed. "All its advantages," he said in court in Cleveland, "are legitimate business advantages, due to the very large volume of supplies which it purchases, its long continuance in the business, the experience it has thereby acquired, the knowledge of all the avenues of trade, the skill of experienced employés, the possession and use of all the latest and most valuable mechanical improvements, appliances, and processes for the distillation of crude oil, and in the manufacture of its own barrels, glue, etc., by reason of which it is enabled to put the oil on the market at a cost of manufacture much less than by others not having equal advantages." But the Bremen congress made a special attack on the "barrels" and

[1] See ch. xiv., "I Want to Make Oil."

"glue." It complained that "the continental petroleum trade has suffered heavy losses on account of inferior barrels," and demanded that the oil combination should "only use barrels of well-seasoned, air-dried, split (not sawed) white oak staves and heads." It even particularized that the barrels should be "painted with blue linseed-oil paint, and supplied with double, strong head-hoops," and "more carefully glued, and not filled until the glue is thoroughly dry."

"They were substantially without competition," was said in explanation of the poor quality of the product sent to Europe, and also "to all parts of this country. The quality of the oil which they sent was not a matter of first-class importance for them to retain their business." It was "a negligence which came in a great measure from the absence of competition." This witness was asked by the lawyer of the combination if he meant the committee to understand that it "was committing suicide by furnishing a continuously deteriorating article of oil to the consumer."

"They were not committing suicide, because they had the business in their own hands almost exclusively at that time."[1]

This was in 1879, and the complaints of the quality of American oil sent abroad continue to this day. Export oil, the Interstate Commerce Commission say, in 1892, "is an inferior oil."[2]

One of the means by which a market was found for American oil in Scotland was the lowering of the British requirements in 1879 as to quality, from a flash-test of 100° to one of 73°, so that the more explosive American oil, until then debarred, could be legally sold to the people of Great Britain. The oil made in Scotland was "a very superior article—very good indeed."[3] There were two ways of getting the market: to meet the Scotch manufacturer with as good an oil, or to induce the government to permit the sale of

---

[1] Testimony, New York Assembly "Hepburn" Report, pp. 3683–94.

[2] Titusville and Oil City Independents' cases. Interstate Commerce Commission Reports, vol. v., p. 415.

[3] Testimony, New York Assembly, 1879, p. 3678.

something inferior. The latter policy was adopted. The government was induced to permit the sale to private consumers of oil that would give off an inflammable gas at a temperature of 73°—a lower temperature than often exists in living-rooms. Meanwhile the government continued to insist upon oil that would stand a test of 105° for its own use in the navy and 145° in its light-houses. The absurdity of this legal test was proved by Mr. T. Graham Young, son of Mr. James Young, founder of the Scotch oil industry, in a letter to the Glasgow *Herald* of May 12, 1894. He showed by the records that the year before there had been sixty days in London in which the temperature had gone above 73°. The government, that is, gave its sanction to the sale of oil which might explode at a heat below that ordinarily reached in an English summer! Commenting on the strange fact that the Scotch oil companies did not move against the change of test which had put them and the British consumer at the mercy of this explosive American oil, Mr. Young said: "It is generally understood that they are precluded from doing so by an agreement with the foreign producers. I hold a letter from one of the interested parties . . . stating that for the above reason he could not discuss the matter." In discussing this matter, the Glasgow *Herald* notes that even patient and poverty-struck India complains of the "very poor quality" of the oil sent there.

The Scotch papers are continually printing indignant comments on this action of the British government, and wondering inquiries as to the influence by which so injurious a change in the regulations for public protection could have been effected. The Scotch manufacturers are continually agitating to have the coroners in England and Ireland, and the procurators-fiscal in Scotland, make particular inquiry in all cases of fatal lamp explosions into the flash-point of the oil and its origin—whether American or Scotch. At the December, 1892, meeting of the Society of Chemical Industry of Great Britain it was declared that about three hundred deaths a year occurred in England and Wales from lamp accidents, due to the explosiveness of the American oil sold under this reduction of the test.

The agitation against this dangerous oil has been increasing in Great Britain year by year. The subject has been investigated by the Glasgow Chamber of Commerce, which found that many serious accidents to life and property had resulted from the use of this oil, and at its meeting of May 14, 1894, the chamber voted to petition the government to raise the test again to 100°. The Manchester and Edinburgh chambers of commerce took similar action. A number of other bodies have taken the subject up, and the government has had to promise to make an inquiry.

The statistics show that last year nearly one in five (19.3 per cent.) of the fires in London and more than one in eight (13.24 per cent.) of the fires in Liverpool came from kerosene. The oil used in those cities is principally the cheap American article sold under the lowered test of the English law. But in Glasgow, where most of the oil burned is that of the Scotch manufacturers, who, by agreement, sell no lower quality than 100° test, the number of fires from kerosene is less than two in a hundred (1.7 per cent.). At a meeting of representatives of the leading insurance companies of Edinburgh and Glasgow, June 20, 1894, experiments were made with the American, Russian, and Scotch oils. The American was found to be the most explosive, and some of it flashed at 69°. A lighted match thrown into this oil heated to 88° started an instantaneous blaze; thrown into Scotch oil it was extinguished. Experts testified that the cost of making the oil safe would be about a farthing a gallon, and that if the Americans, whose "self-interest" and "private enterprise" are not equal to a voluntary effort, were compelled by law to furnish a better illuminant, their profits would be greater, not less.

A rich field for investigation is concealed beneath the elaborate system of State inspection, by which the people have sought to protect themselves from being tempted by deceptive prices to buy a sure death. We have seen in several places how the State inspectors are in the employ, at the same time, of the State and the seller, whom it is their duty to watch for the State.[1] Evidence abounds at every turn of the use of inspectors and inspection laws to embarrass and even suppress the smaller refiners. One of the latest instances is a new law in Tennessee, which puts special difficulties in the way of oil reaching the State by river, the avenue to which independent refiners are forced by the discriminations of the railroad. We saw an inspector of the State of New York appear at the Bremen congress as the avowed representative of the "united refineries," complaints of whose bad oils occasioned the congress.

By one of those coincidences in which the world of cause and effect abounds, the Fire Marshal of Boston, in the same year in which Joshua Merrill described his fruitless efforts to continue the manufacture of a first-class oil,[2] found it necessary to warn the people against the dangerous stuff they were burning in their lamps. In his report in 1888 he called attention to the fact that one-tenth, nearly, of all the fires in Boston the preceding year had been caused by the explosion of kerosene or by its accidental combustion. He got samples of the oil used in a number of the places where fires had occurred from explosion, and had them analyzed by professors of the Institute of Technology in Boston and of the School of Mines of Columbia College in New York. They found them to be below the quality required by the State. Singularly enough, one of the State oil inspectors, examining similar samples, declared them to be above the standard of the State. The Boston *Herald*, discussing the matter, pointed out that the oil inspectors were paid by the owner of the oil. This, it said, placed inspectors practically under the oil combination, which has ways, it continued, of making things unpleasant for inspectors who make reports unsatisfactory to it. The fire marshal's conclusion in all the cases he investigated of these fires by explosion was: " I have felt warranted in

[1] See pp. 216, 320.   [2] See p. 188.

every instance in attributing the blame to the inferior quality of kerosene used." [1]

The European protest of 1879 followed close upon the success of the comprehensive campaign of 1878 [2] "to overcome competition." The warning from the Fire Marshal of Boston in 1888 and the success of the movement, begun in 1885,[3] to shut the independents of Oil City and Titusville out of Boston and New England came close together. These are not coincidences merely. They are cause and effect.

It is known that a practice has grown up among the oil inspectors of the States of allowing certain refiners to brand their own oil as they please, or letting it go to market unbranded. This permits the sale of unbranded and therefore illicit and presumably dangerous oil. Charges that inspectors in Iowa loaned their stencils to the oil combination to do its own branding were made formally in writing, in 1890, by one of the deputy inspectors, in the form required by law, to the governor of the State. The law provides that charges so made shall be investigated by the governor. No investigation was made, but the inspector was removed just as he was about to lay before a grand-jury documentary evidence of this and other violations of the law. This inspector declared publicly that inspectors were in the habit of leaving their official stencils with companies in the oil combination, and allowing them to put any brand they chose on any oil. He refused to continue this practice, nor would he brand barrels until they were filled. The representative of the combination in that State used every device except force, the inspector says, to induce him to conform to the practice. "Don't you know," this representative said, "that if you leave us your brand and get into trouble you will have the oil combination back of you? You will be taken care of." In his formal complaint to the governor, this inspector declared that this representative said in substance to him: "You are the only fool among the inspectors. We have the

---

[1] Second Annual Report, Fire Marshal of Boston, May, 1888, p. 9.
[2] See p. 84.   [3] See ch. xi.

stencils of the inspectors at every other point where we want them."

The law put upon the governor the duty to investigate upon receiving written complaint. But when written complaint was formally made, and that not by an ordinary citizen, but by one of the sworn officials of the State, the governor demanded that the inspector back up his charges with the affidavits of witnesses—that is, the governor demanded that the inspector, who had no power, should make the investigation. This put an end to the whole matter. The inspector could not make the investigation, and the governor would not. The same governor refused to allow the written charges to be seen, although they are public documents, and they remained invisible as long as he held office. Only a few weeks after the removal of this inspector, the State oil inspector was sued for heavy damages by the owner of a barn which had been burned down through the explosion of bad oil. The ground of the suit was that the inspector, having failed to inspect and condemn this oil, as he should have done, was liable on his bond to the State. The press of Iowa commented freely on the probable connection between destructive fires, like this one, and the custom of allowing the oil ring to inspect itself, by which it was given the opportunity to put inferior and dangerous oils on the market with the brand of the State on them as good. As far as the case has been carried, up to date, the Iowa courts have sustained the claim and held the inspector in damages.

That which is an uninvestigated charge in Iowa is an officially ascertained fact in Minnesota. The demonstration in the latter case amounts practically to confirmation for the former, since the parties in interest, the motive, and the opportunity are identical. An investigation was made of the conduct of the State oil inspector by the Committee on Illuminating Oils of the Minnesota Senate, in 1891. The committee say in their report, which was adopted by the Senate:

"The testimony further shows that stencils were left with different oil companies by the State inspector or his deputy, by which the companies caused their barrels containing oil to be branded by their own employés, without the supervision of any State official. It appears that after the arrangement for the payment of the inspectors' and deputies' salaries by the oil companies was made, the attitude of the inspector towards his duties may be summed up in a few words of his testimony: 'I am under no obligation to the State of Minnesota. The Standard Oil Company paid me.'"[1]

The methods covered by the general phrases of the Minnesota Senate Committee were described in detail by a "commissioner" of the Omaha *Daily Bee*, which found the same things being done in Nebraska. The *Bee* in 1891 made an elaborate investigation of the manner in which the oil inspection of Nebraska was executed. Its reporter passed incognito by the guardians of the portals of the warehouse of companies belonging to the oil trust in Omaha, and stood by while barrels were filled with uninspected oil and loaded on the cars for shipment to various points. That the people who bought the oil might know their lives were safe, each barrel bore the brand of approval provided by law, as follows:

Approved. Flash Test 105°.

....
State Inspector of Nebraska.

By ....
Deputy.

But there was no inspector present, and the barrels were all branded beforehand and while empty, in defiance of the law and public safety. The reporter stayed until the cars were loaded, the doors closed, and saw the trains pull out. It is from this warehouse that the greater part of the barrelled oil consumed in Nebraska is forwarded. At the warehouse of the same company in Nebraska City the reporter found the same thing going on, and there, too, he found the official stencil-plates of several of the State oil inspectors lying at hand on the tanks, waiting to be used at the pleasure of the

---

[1] Journal of the Senate of Minnesota, March, 1891, p. 716.

employés of the company to brand the desired government guarantee on any oil, regardless of what it was. The Illinois *State Journal* found the same practice permitted in Springfield by the oil inspector in February, 1894. The *Bee* reporter describes how tanks, once branded, came and went, were filled and emptied and filled again for months, with no inspection of the oil in them. Often the tanks were not even branded.

The Omaha *Daily Bee* of November 24, 1891, gives a careful analysis of the recently amended inspection law of Nebraska. It shows that in many important points the law has been changed so as to put the safety of the people in the power of the combination which supplies almost all the oil used in the State. The standard required has been lowered. The liability to a charge of manslaughter for death resulting from bad oil has been changed to a liability for damages. The method of making the tests has been changed for the worse. No provision has been made for the protection of travellers by the inspection of oil used by the railroads, although accidents, and serious ones, from the use of dangerous oil were frequent in the trains and at stations.[1] The *Bee* said editorially of the oil combination that it had " managed, by its shrewdness in enacting this law, to make Nebraska the refuse tank for its rejected Eastern oil, and at the same time to crowd out of the State about all opposition." By means of this lowering of the test, oil that was too poor to pass in Iowa could be sent on to Nebraska and sold there. The *Bee* gives instances where this was done.

The *Bee* continued its investigations in 1893. It declared, December 5, 1893, that the inspection law, imperfect at best, was "being still further annulled by the open defiance of the leading oil companies." It declared "the leading violator" to be one of the principal companies in the oil combination. In a later issue the *Bee* printed the result of tests made for it of oils purchased in the principal towns of the State. In al-

[1] Omaha *Daily Bee*, November 24, 27; December 5, 13, 21, 1891.

most every such case these showed that oils which were below the test were being sold to the people as good under the guarantee of the State. Some of them were "as safe for household use as dynamite," the *Bee* stated. It said editorially, December 15, 1893, that it had in its possession a letter from the secretary of the Iowa State Board of Health affirming that oil condemned by the State of Iowa is shipped to Nebraska. The oil inspector of the State made a vigorous denial, but the *Bee* refused to withdraw its statements. Its tests, it said, had been made by competent chemists. A suit is now pending in San Francisco, brought by the New Zealand Fire Insurance Company against the oil combination. It is charged that it sold low-test oil, that its inflammability caused fire and destruction of a dwelling insured by the insurance company, which was compelled to pay the loss. Some power, certainly not originating among the people, has for years, in States where the inspection laws required a high quality of oil, been at work procuring a reduction of the test. In some cases this has been accomplished only after persistent lobbying for years, as in Michigan. The test in Michigan has been lowered by legislation, as in Nebraska, and with similar results. The reports of the Michigan State Board of Health show that as the standard was lowered, fires and deaths from explosions increased. The Detroit *Tribune* of December 27, 1891, says that the reduction of the test in Michigan and Nebraska is due to the avarice of the producers (refiners) and nothing less than criminal carelessness of the legislators. The dangerous constituents of petroleum, such as naphtha and gasolene, are indistinguishable by the eye of the buyer from kerosene. They can be as easily mixed with it as hot and warm water with cold. These reductions of the test in various States permit mixtures more hazardous than dynamite to be sold to the people, lulled into reliance upon the State inspectors. "The advantage to the oil company," says the Detroit (Michigan) *Times* of April 30, 1891, "is obvious. Naphtha and gasolene are worth, perhaps, three cents a gallon. Kerosene is worth three times as much. A test which allows

one quart of kerosene and three quarts of gasolene to constitute a gallon of merchantable illuminating oil will enable a
few more colleges to be endowed, though increasing the death-
roll in a notable degree."

One of the demands of those who are conducting the agitation, noticed elsewhere, for the admission of American oils
free into Canada is that the standard of Canadian oil inspection be lowered. This, says the Hamilton (Ontario) *Spectator*,
will open the Canadian market to the low-test and dangerous
oils made by the American combination, and "restore the old
order of lamp explosions, with the consequent loss of life and
property."

An unwritten chapter of this story is the experience of the
Ohio oil producers, and the use of the inferior oil of the Ohio
field to adulterate oils made from Pennsylvania petroleums.

Lord Coke's dictum about the decrease of quality never had
a more spectacular illustration than was given at Oil City and
Titusville on Sunday, June 5, 1892. Oil Creek was high with
rains. A dam burst and made the creek a flood. Its waters
ate away the insufficient foundations of tanks, and rivers of
naphtha and gasolene and kerosene overran the river of water
for miles. A spark did the rest. Oil refineries took fire, tanks
exploded. There were two raging seas — water beneath, fire
above. Men, women, children, animals, property were swept
along in their intermingled waves. From every overturned
tank and blazing refinery fresh streams of oil flowed into the
sea of flame, which climbed the hills for the victims the other
sea could not reach. Those who escaped drowning breathed in
a more dreadful death. It was a volcano and deluge in one.
It was one of the most terrible catastrophes of our times.
Even the scare-heads of the newspapers could not exaggerate
its horrors. The governor of the State made a public appeal
for help. The coroner's jury held an inquest at Oil City upon
fifty-five bodies at one sitting. It declared the cause of the
calamity to have been the gross carelessness of the owners and
custodians of a tank of naphtha, in permitting it, while filled
with 15,000 barrels of naphtha, to stand without proper pro-

27

tection from fire and water. The tank was shown, by the testimony, to have stood on sand within a few feet of the creek and without safeguard. It was shown that complaints had been made to the managers of the refinery, which was one of the subsidiary companies of the oil trust, about this tank and others before the disaster, but without avail. The coroner's jury laid the blame where it belonged — upon the company whose tank gave way. Its verdict said: " The naphtha which caused this awful destruction of life and property . . . was stored in a tank located on the bank of Oil Creek, on the Cornplanter Farm, near McClintockville, where it was built about four years previous to this time. At the time of its construction the tank was from twenty to thirty feet from ordinary high-water mark in the creek, but this distance has been gradually reduced by the action of the water prior to this flood to between six and ten feet, and this flood further washed away the ground up to and under the tank, a distance of from fifteen to twenty feet. A part of the tank bottom, thus being left without support, tore out, allowing the naphtha to escape into the creek. The evidence of the watchman, James Marsh, shows that he realized danger from the undermining of the tank, for he made a feeble effort previous to this flood to protect it by throwing loose stones between the tank and the creek. The jury find from the evidence that all persons owning and having in custody this tank and its contents were guilty of gross carelessness in permitting it, while filled with naphtha, to stand without proper protection from fire and water."

The company which owned this tank belonged to the oil combination. It was, strange to say, one of the tanks of the Keystone refinery, to which Matthews, the Buffalo independent, had turned for a supply of crude oil when all other sources failed,[1] and which had been thereupon bankrupted and taken into the combination seven years before. Here was one fruit of that victory over competition. The coroner's

---

[1] See p. 291.

jury at Titusville reprobated in the strongest terms the folly of storing oil in tanks within reach of high-water. It called upon "citizens and officials, . . . for the common good of all," to do what it said was " entirely practicable : to so locate and guard and construct oil-tanks and other receptacles of inflammable petroleum products that they cannot be floated away, or the contents floated out of them by water," and that " in case of flood and fire lives and private property cannot be endangered by them." Although here and all over the oil regions the business was under the control of one combination, and had been so since early in the seventies, the Titusville jury, less courageous than that of Oil City, declared that it could " attach no blame to any one in particular for the present loss of life," because this " custom of storing and manufacturing oil and its products, regardless of endangering the lives and property of others, had been allowed to grow up here as well as all over the oil regions." These verdicts have been followed by suits now pending in the Pennsylvania courts, claiming heavy damages from the oil combination as responsible for the disaster and the loss of life and property.

The Oil City and Titusville disaster is but a provincial affair compared with the metropolitan avalanche of ruin which is all ready to move upon the cities on New York Bay from the refineries and tanks along its shores. Several condensed oceans of unignited fire are waiting for such accident as happens almost every day to some gas-works or refinery or tank-car. On creeks running into the East River, on bays opening from the New Jersey shore into the greater bay, in tanks whose contents would overlay the whole sheet of water from the Narrows to Hell Gate and Spuyten Duyvil, these volcanoes are dozing, and they are light sleepers.

CHAPTER XXX

"TO GET ALL WE CAN"

ARE the combinations, trusts, syndicates of modern industry organized scarcity or organized plenty? Dearness or cheapness? "They are doing their work cheaper," said one of the oil combination of himself and his associates, "than any rival organization can afford to do it, and that is their policy, and by that only will they survive."[1]

"We think our American petroleum is a very cheap light. It is our pleasure to try to make it so," said its head.[2]

"Our object has always been to reduce rates, and cheapen the product, and increase its consumption by making the lowest price possible to the consumer," said another.[3]

Even if this were true— But is it true?

The then president of the United Pipe Lines of the oil combination, who was also president of a subordinate corporation, was a witness in 1879 in the suit brought by the Commonwealth of Pennsylvania. His refinery, he stated, did nothing but make the oil. "It is taken and sold by another organization"—the oil combination. "We agree to take the same prices that they take for their oil. It is kind of pooled—the sale of the oil." The "agreement," he said, is "simply to hold up the price of refined oil, . . . to get all we can for it . . . under some arrangement by which they keep the price up to make a profit." Not only was the price fixed under the agreement "to get all we can," but the combination, as at Cleveland,[4] fixed the amount to be produced. The subordinate company was allowed to have nothing to do with the business—except to do the work, and to do

---

[1] Testimony, Corners, New York Senate, 1883, p. 670.
[2] Testimony, Trusts, Congress, 1888, p. 389. [3] Same, p. 317. [4] See p. 62.

only as much as its superior chose to permit. Other refiners, in the same investigation, were shown to be sufferers from the same kind of "grip." Asked what other concerns besides his of Oil City were in this arrangement, he named the principal ones of Titusville, Pittsburg, Philadelphia, and New York.

"These companies were all acting in concert, were they?"

"So far as sales of refined oil were concerned, I think they were."

Capitalists are usually supposed to be hard of heart and head, suspicious, great sticklers for "black and white," and careful to have all that is due them "nominated in the bond." This arrangement, by which this witness and his associates put themselves entirely at the disposal of others—as to how much they should manufacture, what freight they should pay, what price they should receive, etc.—was not in writing.

"It is a verbal one." [1]

The purchase of the refineries at Baltimore by the oil combination in 1877, under the name of the Baltimore United Oil Company, was immediately followed by an advance in price. The Baltimore *Sun*, in December, 1877, said: "The combination has already begun to exert its influence on the market. Oil for home consumption was yesterday quoted at 14 cents, having raised from $11\frac{1}{2}$ cents, the quotation on Wednesday. The combination will not make contracts ahead, which might be interpreted to mean an intended advance in price." In Buffalo the manager of one of the properties of the oil combination said in evidence: "My son is on a committee, he told me, that regulates the price of oil." [2] While the trust had the trade of Buffalo to itself, it held the price of oil at a high rate. "In Buffalo there were then no rival works," said State's Attorney Quinby to the jury who were trying its representatives for conspiracy against a competing refinery, "and we were paying for kerosene 18 cents a

[1] Testimony, Commonwealth of Pennsylvania *vs.* Pennsylvania Railroad *et al.*, 1879, pp. 369–85, 435, 534–35.

[2] Buffalo Lubricating Oil Company *vs.* Everest *et al.* Supreme Court Erie Co., N. Y., 1886.

gallon. To-day, with the little Buffalo company in the market making kerosene, you can get it for 6 cents a gallon."

This Buffalo competitor was a very modest affair, insignificant in capital and resources, but it cut down the price of oil as far away as Boston. It established there an agent who "went around" and "cut the prices down," and then the agent of the combination "went around and cut the prices further," as its Boston employé described it. He was instructed, he said, "to follow them down, . . . only not to sell at a loss." Before this competitor came he had been selling oil as high as 20 cents a gallon. "We got the price down to 18 cents, and got down then, I believe, to 8 cents, so that I have been selling them since then at 8 cents."[1] Eight cents, then, was not at a loss—since he had been told "not to sell at a loss"—and yet these passionate pilgrims of cheapness had been making the Boston buyer pay 20 cents! "I have been selling since at 8 cents," he says. This testimony was given in 1886; the reduction to 8 cents from 20 was made in 1882. Four years' consumption of this oil had been given to the buyer in Boston at 8 cents a gallon instead of 20, in consequence of the entrance of so insignificant a competitor.

When a member of the trust was testifying before the New York courts, he referred to the competition of the independent of Marietta as "his power for evil." Asked to define what he meant by his phrase "power for evil," he said, "It was to make prices that would be vexatious and harassing." He was asked if it harassed the oil trust, and the corporations connected with it, to have prices in any part of the country lower than they fixed.

"Lower than a reasonable basis."

"What they consider a reasonable basis?"

"Yes."[2]

That we can understand. But we cannot understand what the president of the trust meant when he said, "We like com-

---

[1] Testimony, Trusts, Congress, 1888, pp. 846–47.

[2] Testimony in the case of George Rice *vs.* Trustees of the Standard Oil Trust, New York Court of Appeals, 1888.

petition," for that would imply a natural proclivity for fellow-ship with the power of evil.

"Who fixes the price of oil in New York?" was asked of one of the witnesses before the Interstate Commerce Commission at Washington. That was done, he said, by the selling agent of the oil combination. He "has the price marked in the New York Produce Exchange daily — the price at which they will sell oil."[1] When the vice-president of the company representing the trust in St. Louis and the Southwest was on the stand before the Interstate Commerce Commission, he was asked what was the price of oil in the territory in which he was operating. The price of oil in tank-cars, in Arkansas, he said, "is now and has been during about three years or more—since Mr. Rice commenced shipping by water to Little Rock—10 cents per gallon. The average price, independent of competition, which I suppose is what you want, in the State of Texas is about 13 cents per gallon in bulk, covering the whole State of Texas. The average price per barrel would be about 17 cents, and the average price in cases about 20 cents."[2]

"Since Mr. Rice commenced shipping by water to Little Rock;" "the average price independent of competition in Texas"—these are telltale phrases. Where the combination was "independent of competition" the price was one-third greater.

The committee of Congress which investigated trusts in 1889 gathered a great deal of sworn evidence—the details of which remained uncontradicted, and which were met only by general statements like those quoted at the head of this chapter—showing how extortionate prices had been charged until competition appeared, that in all cases a war of extermination had been made upon those competitors, and that when their business was destroyed prices were put up again. Losses in

---

[1] Testimony, Independent Refiners' Associations *vs.* Western New York and Pennsylvania Railroad Company *et al.*, p. 401.

[2] Testimony, George Rice *vs.* Louisville and Nashville Railroad *et al.*, cases 51–60, p. 425.

competitive wars were merely investments from which to draw dividends in perpetuity. The "cheapness" of the combination followed the cheapness of competitors, and was merely a feint, one of the approaches in a siege to overcome the inner citadel of cheapness, a strategic cheapness to-day on which to build dearness forever. This battle of prices is shown in a table covering fifty towns in Texas, Mississippi, Louisiana, Alabama, Tennessee, Georgia, Kentucky, for three to five years. The appearance of competitive oil, for instance, cut the prices of oil from 15 cents a gallon down to 10 in Paris, Texas; from 25 to 15 in Calvert, Texas; from 22 cents to 10 in Austin, Texas; from 16 to 5 in Little Rock, Arkansas—evidently a war price; from 16 to $8\frac{1}{2}$ in Huntsville, Alabama; from 16 to 8 in Memphis, Tennessee, and so on.[1] The committee of Congress submit pages of evidence of the reimposition of high prices the moment competition was killed off. If the combination found a rival dealer out of oil for only a day it "popped the prices up $3\frac{1}{2}$ cents."[2] "One day," wrote one of the dealers, "oil is up to 20 cents and over, and when any person attempts to import here, other than the vassals 'of the oil combination,' it is put down to 7 cents a gallon."[3]

Prices were frequently put higher after the war than before. In the debate in the Canadian Parliament last year on the proposal to reduce the Canadian tariff, supported by a strong lobby from the American oil trust, it was shown by affidavits that at Selma, Alabama, oil was reduced during the "war" against outside refiners to 8 from 15 cents. After "competition was overcome," in the language of the South Improvement Company contract, the price was put up, not to 15 cents where it had been, but to 25 cents. In the same debate a large number of affidavits were exhibited showing how the price charged by the oil trust in America varied in places near each other in arbitrary and extraordinary ways, as 7 cents a gallon at Port Huron, Michigan, and $14\frac{1}{2}$ cents at Bay City,

---

[1] Testimony, Trusts, Congress, 1888, pp. 609–10. [2] Same, p. 732.
[3] Same, p. 735.

only a few miles distant. Under the rule of the trust prices are on a mechanical basis everywhere, from the retail markets to the seaboard, where the refined, the manufactured article, is quoted at a lower price than the crude, its raw material.[1]

In the report of the tenth United States census in 1886, on the necessaries of life, the retail price of kerosene is given for thirty-five places. At a few of these there was competition; there the price was 12½ to 15 cents a gallon. At all other points it ranged from 20 to 25 cents. Such a tax on the 400,000,000 gallons of oil consumed in this country is the only kind of income-tax that is "American."

Application was made in May, 1894, by the Central Labor Union of New York City to the Attorney-General of the State to vacate the charter of the principal corporation in the oil trust. In the argument to support it, it was shown that New York consumers were then paying twice as much for their lamp-oil as the people of Philadelphia, and three times as much as the foreign consumer buying in New York for export.

The trust, notwithstanding its powers of "producing the very best oil at the lowest possible price," compels dealers to sign away their rights to buy oil where they can buy it the cheapest or best. When opposition is encountered from any of the retailers in a town the plan of campaign of its "war" is very simple. Some one is found who is willing for hire to sell his oils at a cut price until the rest are made sick enough to surrender. Then contracts are made with all the dealers, binding them to buy of no one else, and prices are put up to a point at which a handsome profit is assured. After this competitors can find no dealer through whom to sell, and the consumer can get no oil but that of the monopoly. Price and quality are both thenceforth such as the combination chooses to make them. There are bargains in oil, but one party makes both sides of them. "We do not wish to ruin you without giving you another chance," said an agent of the combination

---

[1] See chs. xii. and xxxi.

gently to a merchant who persisted in selling opposition oil.
"Look at this map; we have the country divided into districts.
If you insist on war we will cut the prices in your territory
to any necessary extent to destroy you, but we lose nothing.
We simply make a corresponding advance in some other district. You lose everything. We cannot by any possibility
lose anything."

Only by thus contracting themselves out of their rights
could these "free" merchants get oil with which to supply
their customers. "Their agent," wrote a dealer of Hot
Springs, Arkansas, "has made threats to some of our merchants that they must or shall buy oil from them and no one
else, or if otherwise they would come here and ruin them—by
fair means if they could, by underhand ways if necessary."
Another firm in Pine Bluff, Arkansas, wrote that the agent
of the combination had called upon them and several of the
other large dealers to make a "contract, . . . and, failing to do
so, in a short time he threatens opening a retail house," as at
Columbus.[1]   Another wrote, December 13, 1886, from Nava-
sota that the monopoly "will not sell unless you sign an obligation to buy from them and them only." [2]

This maintenance of prices until some "power for evil"
appears with lower rates, then wars to kill, and raising of
prices if the war ends in victory—these phenomena of cheapness continue to date. Many chapters could be filled with
accounts of these wars of which record has been kept. To
merely name the battle-fields would require pages. When the
combination, through its agents, attacked Toledo in the courts
for undertaking the municipal supply of natural gas, it
"urged," as it is quoted in the language of the decision, "that
the main object and primary purpose of the act is to enable
the city to supply its individual inhabitants with fuel for private use and consumption at a cheaper rate than they can obtain it from other sources." The act of the Legislature gave
Toledo "a power for evil." At Denver oil was sold at 25

---

[1] See ch. xxii.   [2] Testimony, Trusts, Congress, 1888, pp. 734, 745.

cents a gallon until an independent company began refining the petroleum which abounds in the Rocky Mountain basin. During the Colorado war of 1892 all the familiar tactics—cut rates, espionage, and all—were employed. This continued after the dissolution of the trust as before, showing that its change of name and form meant no real change. In Pueblo and Colorado Springs the price was put down to 5 cents a gallon from 25 cents. In Denver the price was made 7 cents. Spotters followed the wagons of the independent company to spy out its customers, and get them, by threats or bribes, to sign away their right to buy where they could buy cheapest. The comments of the local press did credit to the inspiriting mountain air of the American Switzerland. The complaint recently filed with the Interstate Commerce Commission by a dealer of the Pacific coast charges that, among other discriminations injurious to the public, the rates between the Pacific coast and Colorado were so manipulated that the oil found in the Rocky Mountains and refined in Colorado could not be shipped to California and the other Pacific states. Consumers there had to buy the oil of the trust hauled all the way from Cleveland or Chicago. When an independent refiner ran the blockade into New York, in 1892, and began selling to the people from tank wagons, the price fell in New York, Brooklyn, and Jersey City from 8 and 8½ to 4 and 4½ cents. The St. Louis *Chronicle* of May 19, 1892, reports a reduction of the price of the best grade of oil to 5 cents a gallon—"the fortieth reduction," it says, made since an independent company "entered the field three years ago, at which time the price was 14½ cents," as it would be still but for competition.

War has been made on poor men, paralytics, boys, cripples, widows, any one who had the "business that belongs to us." An instance taken from abroad will be the last. The combination between the American and the Scotch refiners, formed several years ago, fixed the price of the principal product, scale, at threepence a pound in 1892. The break-up in that year was followed at once by a decline from threepence to twopence. This is a saving to the public of $1,000,000 a year.

"All the relative products," says the London *Economist*, November 12, 1892, "have practically collapsed in value." Candles, for instance, declined 20 cents a dozen, "and the finer qualities were sold at the same rate as the commoner sorts."

These are the facts, to fit the phrase of one of the monopoly who described to Congress how it "bridges it to the consumer at the lowest reasonable rate." The "bridge to the consumer" spans 1872 to 1894 and Europe and America, but it is not a bridge of cheapness.[1]

To prove that oil is cheaper than it was is not to prove that it is cheap.

Anything begins to be dear the moment the power to fix the price has been allowed to vest in one. The question whether our monopolies have made things cheap or dear in the past pales before the exciting query, What will they do in the future, when their power has become still greater, or has passed by death, descent, or sale into hands less shrewd and greedier? Such power never moves backward. Says President Andrews, of Brown University, in the article quoted below: "When a commodity is turned out under such conditions, cost no longer regulates the price. This is done quite arbitrarily for a time, the seller's whim being perhaps sobered a little by his memory of old competitive rates. Slowly caprice gives way to law; but it is a new law—that of man's need. Prices go higher and higher till demand, and hence profit, begins to fall off; and they then play about the line of what the market will bear, just as they used to about that of cost. The producer can be more or less exacting, according to the nature of the product. If it is a luxury, the new law may not greatly elevate prices above the old notch. If it is a necessity, he may bleed people to death."

"At any reasonable price, say three or four times the present selling price of refined oil, it is the cheapest light in the world, and if the prices were advanced to 20 cents a gallon the sales would be as large as they are now at 7½ cents," wrote Vice-

---

[1] Testimony, Trusts, Congress, 1888, p. 372.

president Cassatt, of the Pennsylvania Railroad, to the Pennsylvania Legislature, in 1881, opposing the Free Pipe Line bill. The possibilities here were touched upon by the New York committee of 1888: "What the trust's course would have been if, instead of increased production, it had been required to deal with the problem of a constantly diminishing or stationary volume of oil, is an interesting subject for speculation. Certain it is that the trust has the power to put up prices, even if it fails to exercise it. If, in the future, the field producing the commodity manufactured and sold by this combination of corporations shall fail to increase its present product, or shall return a diminished quantity, the oil trust will be able to fix the price of the product of its refineries in this country, if not in the world." [1]

It was not great capital which put this industry in the possession of these enthusiasts for "all the little economies." The same universal forces of cheapness which have been at work everywhere have been at work upon the cost of the instrumentalities of production, and put machinery, transportation, raw material, and market agencies within reach of moderate capital. Such great capital is wasteful capital. It operates through agents at great distances, attenuating incentives to energy and care. Many practical men, real refiners, who have been forced to give up their business to refiners of railroad privileges, have testified to the same effect as the manufacturer who said to Congress in 1872: "I believe a refinery of 100 barrels can be run cheaper than the larger establishments." [2]

If production on a natural scale, directed by the eye of the owner, were not more economical than production mobilized from the metropolis by salaried men hundreds of miles away, the independent refiners and producers of Pennsylvania, New York, and Ohio would not have been able to survive at all. It was said in one of the Buffalo papers by one of these independent refiners: "There are several well-equipped independent refineries in operation at the present time in Pennsylvania

---

[1] Report, Trusts, New York Senate, 1888, p. 12. [2] See ch. xi.

and Ohio oil-fields where the refiner has his own crude oil, his own pipe line, and produces his own natural gas for fuel purposes. It is needless to say that an experienced and skilful refiner operating under such favorable conditions can manufacture at less cost per barrel than any trust with a long list of pensioners and burdened with the control of two political parties and the maintenance of numerous city mansions, stock farms, and theological seminaries."

NOTE.—The claims of the oil combination to the credit of having cheapened oil have been subjected by competent men to statistical tests. President Andrews, of Brown University, shows that from 1861 to 1872, inclusive—*i.e.*, before any combination whatever existed—the net annual percentage of decrease in the price of refining oil and carrying it to tidewater—that is, the difference between the cost of the petroleum at the wells and of the refined at New York—was $10\frac{4332}{10000}$ cents; from 1873 to 1881, inclusive, the trust's infirm and formative period, the decrease was $7\frac{3597}{10000}$ cents; from 1882 to 1887, inclusive, the years of its full maturity and vigor, the decrease was only $2\frac{2879}{10000}$ cents.[1]

The New York *Daily Commercial Bulletin* (April 4, 1892) made a similar study with similar results. It finds that under competition in the refining of oil the difference between crude at the wells and refined oil at New York was reduced from 13.45 cents per gallon in 1872 to 6.02 cents per gallon in 1881; under the reign of the trust the difference was 5.84 in 1891—greater than in 1882, when the trust began operations, when it was only 5.77. It concludes: " It has been claimed that the oil trust has been a benefit to this country; that the economies which it has introduced in the transportation and refining of oil have been shared with the consumer, and that the enormous wealth which it has accumulated during the past ten years has been widely distributed. Not one of these claims has any substantial basis in fact."

The comparisons of cheapness are made on the wholesale price at New York of "export oil"—an inferior, almost a refuse product. Its price must meet that made by the Russians. These comparisons, therefore, really shed no light on the price movements of oil going into consumption throughout the country. But the trust really gets the retail price on all its domestic output. A full statistical statement of the price movement in retail markets cannot be had; nor even of the wholesale, for the combination has lately adopted a policy of suppressing the wholesale quotations of the higher grades of oil for domestic consumption. Comparisons, therefore, built on the export price of this poor oil at New York, though good as far as they go, are of oils of a low illuminating power.

[1] President E. Benjamin Andrews, of Brown University, "Trusts According to Official Investigation," *Quarterly Journal of Economics*, January, 1889, p. 146.

Comparisons that would really show the part played by the combination as a true merchant—one who discovers and distributes abundance for all at a fair price for his service—can only be made by such illustrations as we have been giving from its utterances, plans, and actions. But for monopoly an average price of 5 cents a gallon could prevail throughout the United States, with a saving of hundreds of millions to the people.

Trust prices are artificial prices, independent of supply and demand, and in their perfection superior even to panic. This is illustrated by the comparison below, made by Mr. Byron W. Holt :

COMPARATIVE PRICES OF STAPLES DURING THE CURRENT DEPRESSION

	April 28, 1893	July 20, 1894	Per cent. of Decline since April 28, 1893
Wheat, No. 2, red............	$ 0.76¾	$ 0.56½	26
Corn, No. 2, mixed...........	.50	.47⅓	5
Cotton, middling upland......	.07¹³⁄₁₆	.07¹⁄₁₆	10
Wool, Ohio and Pennsylvania, X.	.28	.18	36
Pork, mess, new.............	21.00	14.00@14.25	33
Butter, creamery............	.30@33	.17	45
Sugar, raw, 96°.............	.03¹⁵⁄₁₆@4	.03³⁄₁₆	18
Sugar, granulated...........	.05¹⁄₁₆	.04⁵⁄₁₆	15
Petroleum, refined, gal.......	.0555	.0515	7
Pig Iron, Bessemer, Chicago....	14.50@15.00	11.25@11.50	23
Steel Rails, Chicago..........	30.00@32.00	25.00@27.00	16
Steel Beams, Chicago.........	.02	.01½	25
	June 30, 1892	June 30, 1894	June 30, 1892
Coal, Bituminous, Pittsburg....	$ 1.07	$ 0.86	20
Coal, Anthracite, New York....	4.15	4.15	00

The prices of four of these products—granulated sugar, petroleum, steel rails, and anthracite coal—are controlled by strong trusts. These prices have declined, since the beginning of the depression—about May 1, 1893—not quite 10 per cent. Prices of the other ten products have declined 24 per cent.

Under free conditions prices of manufactured articles would decline faster than prices of farm products. Cost of production can be lowered faster in machine or factory products than in farm products. Under the influence of trusts the natural order is not only reversed, but prices of farm products have declined more than twice as fast as prices of factory or trust products. Trust influence is conspicuous in the cases of sugar and coal. The price of raw sugar, in which there is no trust, has declined 5 per cent. since June 30, 1891. The price of granulated has advanced 4 per cent. The president of the trust admitted to Congress in 1894 that it had advanced the price ⅔ of a cent a pound. Cost of refining has declined since 1891. There being no well-defined trust in bituminous coal, its price has declined 30 per cent. since 1891. The price of anthracite coal has advanced 2 per cent. in the same time, because the producers have "regulated" production.

CHAPTER XXXI

ALL THE WORLD UNDER ONE HAT

"THIS business belongs to us." This was the reply the president of the oil combination made to a neighbor who was begging to be allowed to continue the refinery which he had successfully established before his tardier but more fortunate competitors had left their produce stores, lumber-yards, and book-keepers' stools. He could remember, the neighbor told the New York Legislature, before there was any such company as theirs, and when the president of the poor man's light was still in the commission business opposite him and his refinery. He described how the president left this commission business, and "commenced to build a refinery there of a small capacity. . . . He used to say to me, 'What is a good time to sell?' and 'What is a good time to hold?' as he said he thought I knew." The day came when the neighbor who had been first found that the last was to be first. He was making $21,000 to $22,000 a year, but he had "to sell or squeeze." He had several conversations with the new-comer who had been so successful in learning when it was "a good time to hold." To save his livelihood, "I did almost condescend to tease him," he testifies. But the only reply he could get was: We have freighting facilities no one else can get.[1] This business belongs to us. Any concern that starts in this business we have sufficient money to lay aside a fund to wipe it out. "They went on just as if it did belong to them, and there were others started before he did in it which I thought it belonged to quite as much as it did to

[1] See ch. xiv.

him. . . . I am wiped out and made a poor man. . . . I think they are making a profit out of my ruin."

His refinery had been giving him a profit of $21,000 to $22,000 a year. It had cost him $41,000, but he had to sell it for $15,000. This purchase of $41,000 for $15,000 was one of "the little economies" to which the trust ascribes its success. It was not a "good time to sell," but he sold. Part of the "squeeze" put upon him was the rebate given to the buyer. He could not have got the rebate if he had applied for it, but he would not apply for it. "I made application for lower freights, but not for any drawbacks; I did not suppose that was the right way to do business." [1]

"This business belongs to us." This remark was not prophecy, but history. It was in 1878, and the claim had been already made good. The New York Legislature, in 1879, reported that the speaker and his associates had control of 90 or 95 per cent. of the industry. "It has absorbed and monopolized this great traffic, which ranks second on the list of exports of our country." [2] This conclusion was based on the evidence of officers and stockholders. [3] Their shadow grew no less. The Interstate Commerce Commission found in 1890 that they "manufacture nearly 90 per cent. of the petroleum and its products in the United States." [4]

"Trifles make perfection, and perfection is no trifle." For the perfection of this triumph no trifle has been disdained, from the well in the mountain to the peddler's cart in the city. The bargemen of the Alleghany, the coasters of the sea-shore, and the stern-wheelers of the Western rivers all had to go one way. "We drove out the shipments in the schooners from Baltimore and Washington, and we stopped almost the shipments by river down the Mississippi by boat," said one of the successful men. His plan

---

[1] Testimony, New York Assembly "Hepburn" Report, 1879, pp. 2623–40.

[2] Same, Report, p. 44.

[3] Testimony, same, pp. 2615, 2696.

[4] George Rice *vs.* Atchison, Topeka and Santa Fé Railroad *et al.* Interstate Commerce Commission Reports, vol. iv., p. 228.

28

had been so thorough as even to seek to "drive off the river schooners." [1]

The last stage in their economic development — that in which the people of the oil region lose the ownership of the oil lands and become hired men—is already far along. Although at first the oil combination owned no oil lands to speak of—"It does not own any oil wells or land producing oil, and never did," its president said, in 1880; "an infinitesimal amount," he said later [2]—it has of late years, through corporations organized for that purpose, been a heavy buyer and leaser of the best oil lands in Pennsylvania, New York, Ohio, Kentucky, and the West.

Monopoly anywhere must be monopoly everywhere. At the beginning it was enough to control the railways; by these the pipe lines, refineries, and markets were got. These were secured, only to find that it was vital to control the source of supply. The producers once gave an illustration of what it would be for the sole buyer to come to the market and find that the oil he must have was not on sale at his price. [3] "We have during the past year," one of the combination said, in 1891, before a committee of the Pennsylvania Legislature, "invested a very large amount of money, and have induced our friends to come forward with new capital to engage in the business of producing oil." [4] By the policy of becoming producers the combination has changed its position from that of mere intermediary—though one as irresistible as a toll-gate keeper—to that of absolute owner. The spectre it has seen rise before it, of the producers organized as one seller to meet it as the only buyer, has been laid to rest.

"We are pushing into every part of the world, and have been doing so," the president told the New York Legislature in 1888. [5] Their tank-steamers go to all the ports of Europe and

---

[1] Testimony, Trusts, Congress, 1888, pp. 528–29.

[2] Testimony, Trusts, New York Senate, 1888, pp. 386, 425.   [3] See pp. 56–57.

[4] Before the Pennsylvania Legislature, Harrisburg, February 19, 1891. Harrisburg *Daily Patriot*, February 25, 1891.

[5] Testimony, Trusts, New York Senate, 1888, p. 422.

Asia, and their tank-wagons are as familiarly seen in the cities of Great Britain and the Continent as of America. An agitation of extensive proportions was begun in 1893 in the press of Canada and in the Dominion Parliament to admit American oil at a lower duty. There was no popular demand for such a step. No general reduction of the tariff was proposed. The movement was simultaneous in the press of different parts of Canada, and it was promoted by papers as important as the Toronto *Globe* and Montreal *Star*. It was resisted with desperation by the 20,000 persons who are employed in the Canadian oil industries, the growth of thirty - two years—"not a rich, gay, bloated population, rioting with the plunderings of the farmers, revelling in all kinds of luxuries, making merry with their friends," says a newspaper correspondent, who visited them in December, 1892, "but a hard-working community, in which all live comfortably; few are rich."

This opposition was successful with the Dominion Parliament in that year, and it refused to admit American oil at a lower tax. But the finance minister then, by executive action, did in part what the Legislature had refused to do. By lowering the inspection duty and changing custom-house conditions he made a considerable reduction in the tax. The agitation to reduce the tariff was not relaxed, and was finally successful in 1894, when Parliament lowered the duties on oil, and to that extent surrendered the Canada producers and refiners to their American competitors.

The Scotch refiners, some of whom have been in business forty years, have become as loyal subjects of an American ruler as of their own queen. They make only as much as he allows, and sell at the price he fixes. He has demanded year by year a greater proportion of their business.[1] In 1892 they were notified that they must reduce their output by 10 per cent.[2] The Scotch, anxious for the accelerating future, begged that the "arrangement" might be made for three years instead of one. But this was denied them. The agent

---

[1] *Scotsman*, October 7, 1892. [2] *Pall Mall Gazette*, January 27, 1892.

from America who brought them their orders would promise no more than " to place the matter in a favorable light before his colleagues in America."[1] By October of that year the capital of the Scotch companies, held mainly by small investors, had shrunk $5,000,000 in value. But to this item the London *Economist* adds the consolation that "that powerful organization"—the American—"has for years professed the kindliest feelings for the Scotch producers." Dr. Johnson said that much may be made of a Scotchman if caught young. The American caught him old.

The disturbance fell heaviest, as always, on the workingmen. "Reduction in wages is now being effected," writes the managing director of the oldest and largest of the Scotch companies in the *Economist*. "Another 10 per cent. reduction in miners' wages has been resolved upon," the *Economist* announces in its issue of October 8, 1892.

One of the causes that contributed to the downfall of the Scotch refiners was the fact that the British government reduced the test required for illuminating oil. This new regulation opened the British markets to a flood of cheap oil from America.[2] The Scotch oil is better made and more expensive. "We cannot tell," said a correspondent of the Glasgow *Herald*, "what powerful interest the American oil combination did not bring to bear on our government. The public had then no champion, and as a rule never have on these occasions."

The unkindest cut of all is that it was from the Scotch manufacturers themselves that their American rival and ruler learned the secrets of the industry it is now absorbing on the instalment plan. In one of its publications it has told how its "experts visited the great shale works in Scotland, and studied their methods," and how "the consequence was that extensive works were erected."[3]

The economic development of Germany is not so much behind that of Great Britain and America as to seem uninviting

[1] *Standard*, Shoe Lane, January 26, 1892.   [2] See p. 408.
[3] *Combinations*, by S. C. T. Dodd, 1888, p. 31.

to the unhasting but unresting American. Some years ago
enterprising German importers invested a large amount of
capital in tank-steamers, because they thought these solved the
problem of the transportation of petroleum. When the Americans refused to supply them any longer with oil for their
steamers to carry, they saw that there was more in this problem than they had guessed. Importers who had no steamers
found one day that American enterprise had secured practically all of them, and had very decided notions as to whom
cargoes should be taken. The heads of two or three of the
largest houses boarded a steamer for New York, and came
back stockholders in a German-American company which controls most of the German business, as the Anglo-American company controls that of Great Britain. "If the great company
with unlimited capital cares to lose money, it can drive us
from the field," was the explanation of the head of one of the
largest German concerns, as quoted in the Weser *Zeitung*.

At the beginning of the next year some Holland firms were
invited into the same shelter, and became the "fittest"; and
then followed the Belgian and the Scandinavian countries. The
Berlin *Vossische Zeitung* of June 18, 1891, described the line
of march : " One group of business men after another is thus
made superfluous and pushed aside. First the wells, pumps,
and refineries in America, then the American export trade,
then the private freight vessels adapted for transportation of
petroleum, then the European import trade, then the export
trade from European ports, and, finally, this over-powerful
company threatens to seize the entire retail trade in petroleum. It is a world monopoly." Hundreds of boatmen engaged in a flourishing river trade in Germany were driven out
by tank-boats. If they had changed to tanks, they would have
been dependent on their opponent for the oil to fill them. Importers in barrels were cut off by a change which the German
government made in the tariff on barrels. The Americans
were also helped by an increase in the German tariff on Russian oil of 50 per cent., which made it so much the more
difficult for it to compete with American oil. As one way

to kill competition where it still existed, all statistics were suddenly withheld by the German - American member of the trust. Neither exports nor imports were known except to the ruling company; all others were kept in the dark.

This success in Germany has not been due to favoritism on the highways. The extraordinary discrimination on railroads in America would be impossible in Germany. With hardly an exception the railroads are under the supervision of the State, and are very carefully controlled. Even the private roads would not dare to give any but the open rates. In Austria-Hungary, formerly, secret rates were in full swing, but the system is now said to be destroyed.

Prices have declined in Germany, and the people at large make few complaints except about the quality of the American oil. It has become more sooty than formerly. In the beginning it burns well, but it ends with giving a very poor light. This has been conjectured to be due to a mixture of the inferior Ohio oil with that of Pennsylvania; but "it cannot be proved," the German chronicler reports.[1] "The working people," says one of the Berlin papers, " will have to foot the bill, and the working people only. The well-to-do and rich of to-day can have other fuel and light, but to the oppressed working-man petroleum is as great a necessity as his potatoes." The German papers, in casting about for means of checkmating the increase of prices which they believe will result from the consummation of this monopoly, advocate the use of water-power and also wind-power to create electricity.

The attention that has been attracted to the growth of this power does not come from the public at large, but from those directly interested and the sympathy and interest of the German "national economists." The latter point out that the present cheap prices are "war prices." They predict that as soon as the world monopoly is established and all territory is under complete control a rise of prices will take place. They are advocates of State monopoly as better than private mo-

---

[1] *Die Monopolisirung des Petroleum Handels und der Petroleum Industrie,* by E. F. Seemann. L. Simeon, Berlin.

nopoly. If State monopolies prevent free competition, at least they are able, they say, to give some compensation to those who are hurt. In the tobacco monopoly hundreds of millions were set aside by the German government for this purpose, but even that was not considered sufficient. But this monopoly is a private affair. It swallows the profits of all those whom it destroys. Numerous industries have been ruined—importers, ship-owners, brokers, local dealers, export-ers, retailers, river boatmen, and numerous other trades—but no one receives indemnity. The public opinion of the gov-ernment, the Reichstag, the national economists, the philan-thropists, is active in support of the middle class, but in spite of all this a whole department of industry has been torn away from it.

There are one or two "independents" in Germany whom, like the independents in America, the trust has not yet been able to crush, though it is turning the markets topsy-turvy for that purpose. The *Pall Mall Gazette* of June 18, 1894, notes that the trust is selling refined oil in Europe at prices lower than those at which crude oil can be delivered from America.

The Austrian journals have been chronicling the absorption of the principal refineries of Austria and Hungary by a com-bination, of which the Rothschilds are the most important members, as they are of that in Russia. This combination, which first appears in 1892, has by 1894 accumulated a re-serve of 3,000,000 gulden on a capital of 1,000,000 gulden, and its profits for 1894 are expected to be 100 per cent. The *Prager Lloyd* of April 26, 1894, giving these and other facts, adds that "the government of Austria as well as of Hungary takes the ground that if a petroleum monopoly is to be formed it should be in the hands of the State, not of a corporation, certainly not of a foreign corporation, least of all an Ameri-can one."

This remedy of a State monopoly as an alternative to pri-vate monopoly, as suggested in Austria and Germany, has as yet had few advocates in America. Our public opinion, so

far as there is any public opinion, restricts itself to favoring recourse to anti-trust laws and to boycotting the monopoly and buying the oil of its competitors. But there
are too few of these to go around, and they are shut out
of most of the markets. The shrewd monopoly is itself the
most diligent caterer to such American demand as there is for
the "anti-monopoly" product. It does business under hundreds of assumed names, and employs salesmen at large salaries to push the sale of "opposition oil" in our disaffected
provinces.

With the news from Germany came the announcement that
similar control had been obtained of the business of the firm
at Venice which did most of the oil business of Italy, and
a new company had been formed, of which the American
"trustees" own a majority. In a letter sent to Minister
Phelps, at Berlin, a resident representative of the American
oil combination says, as quoted in the New York *Tribune*,
October 5, 1891: "For the furtherance of our programme
and as participators in the large European investment which
this programme involves, we have sought and been fortunate
enough to secure the co-operation of a coterie of well-known
merchants, who have been long and prominently identified
with the petroleum commerce of the Continent." The So-
cietà Italo-Americana del Petrolio (the Italian-American Oil
Company) is in Italy what the concerns just described are in
the countries to the north of it. The head of the oil combination was quoted by the New York *Tribune* of July 1,
1891, as saying: "The cable despatches are substantially
correct as regards our interest in the German and Italian
companies."

The French government a year ago lowered the tariff on
petroleum one-half. This was followed, the French press reports, by the erection of a refinery by the American trust at
Rouen, and the purchase by it of land in Marseilles, Cette,
Bordeaux, and Havre for other refineries. The machinery
needed was shipped from America. Large offices were opened
at Paris by the American combination for the administration

of the industry in France, which was to be concentrated into its hands like that of the rest of Europe. The sequel, if the *Frankfurter Zeitung*, a prominent German commercial paper, is correctly informed, is that the French refiners, as the Scotch did before them, have come to terms with the American trust. It has agreed not to start up its refineries in France, not to sell any refined oil in America for shipments to France, and not to allow any American outsiders to compete with the French refiners.

There was a report in June, 1892, that a Dutch company had succeeded in refining petroleum in Sumatra, one of the possessions of the Netherlands' East India colonies, and selling it in India. The solicitor of the trust, asked about it by the New York *Times*, June 5, 1892, said, "It cannot be true." The oil combination, he continued, "has agents in the Netherlands' East India colonies and at Sumatra, and it would certainly have heard of this corporation and its competition if there was anything worth hearing."

There are great oil-fields in Peru. Since the close of the war with Chili there has been an active development of them, and the commercial reports of San Francisco say that fuel oil is now being supplied from this source to our Pacific States. This has not been done by the Peruvians. It was an American who organized the oil industry of Peru. The principal company was formed by the same expert who went years ago from Pennsylvania to Russia to Americanize the oil interests of the Caucasus. After he had succeeded in that task he went to Peru. He died in the spring of 1894. At about the time of his death the newspapers, by a coincidence that arrests attention, chronicled the departure from New York of a well-known man who was going to Peru, as he stated in an interview, to look after the interests of the members of the oil trust. But there is no official information that they have any ownership or control there.

When one of the officers of the combination was before Congress, in 1888, he was asked if there had been any negotiations by his associates with the Russian oil men.

"We have never had any serious negotiations,"[1] he replied.

The word "serious" was a slip. He withdrew it. "We have never had any" was his revision. Three years later the same official, in a speech to persuade the Pennsylvania Legislature that the pipe-line interests of the oil country did not need the regulation by the State then under debate, but were abundantly safeguarded by him and his associates, said: "It may not be amiss for me to say that we have had, at different times during the last several years, most flattering propositions from people who are identified with the Russian petroleum industry, to come there and join them in the development and introduction of that industry. We have declined these offers, gentlemen, always and to this day, and have held loyal to our relations to the American petroleum."[2]

There had been negotiations, after all!

The reports of the United States consul-general at Berlin, in 1891, transmitted many interesting articles from the German papers concerning the alliance which it was believed had been made between the Rothschilds and the American oil combination. A company managed by the great bankers has obtained a commanding position in the Russian oil business, and the American and the Russian were even then said to have divided the world between them. The Berlin *Vossische Zeitung* said: "Heretofore the two petroleum speculators have marched apart, in order to get into their hands the two largest petroleum districts in the world. After this has been accomplished they unite to fight in unison, and to fix as they please the selling price for the whole world, which they divide between themselves. So an international speculating ring stands before the door, such as in like might and capital power has never before existed, and everywhere the intelligible fear prevails that within a short time the price of an article of use indispensable to all classes of people will rise

---

[1] Testimony, Trusts, Congress, 1888, p. 792.
[2] Harrisburg *Patriot*, February 25, 1891.

with a bound, without its being possible for national legislation or control to raise any obstacles."[1]

But some of the closest European observers have seen reasons from the beginning to believe that the Rothschilds are in the Russian oil business only as the agents of the American combination. This is freely asserted by the Continental press. The policy of the Rothschilds has been never to engage in commercial enterprise on their own account. The tactics used by the Rothschilds in oil have been an almost exact reproduction of those of the combination in America. From the first they gave the subject of freights their special attention. They showed no ability for new or independent undertakings, but they tried, to use the words of an Austrian-Hungarian consular report from Batoum in 1889, "following the example of the combination in the United States, to get the bulk of the Russian petroleum trade into their hands"; using the large money power at their command for speculation, freely advancing money for leases and delivery contracts, and specially acquiring all the available means of transportation. The experience of the people of Parker[2] is recalled by the statement that the Rothschild company would leave hundreds of cars loaded with petroleum on the tracks for weeks to prevent competitors from shipping and from filling their contracts. When the city of Batoum, in 1888, refused to allow it to lay pipes over the city lands to the harbor, it was with the enthusiastic approbation of the agitated citizens. The authorities gave as their reason that through large establishments of this kind the capitalists gained a monopoly, crushing out smaller producers to the disadvantage of all classes of the population. In the absence of official investigations, a free press, and civilized courts—that knowledge which is not only power but freedom—it is impossible for any one in Russia, or out of it, to know the truth as to the relations of the Rothschilds to the American monopoly. The latest news in the summer of 1894 is of a

---

[1] Translation from the Berlin *Vossische Zeitung*, June 12, 1891. Report of Consul-General Edwards, of Berlin.

[2] See p. 106.

great combination of Russian and American oil interests, under the direction of the Russian Minister of Finance, for a division of territory, regulation of prices, and the like. Information of this was given to the world by that minister's official organ in November, 1893. Thus says the Hanover (Germany) *Courier* of November 11th: "With the direct sanction of the Russian government the management of the enormous wealth that lies in the yearly production of Russian petroleum will be concentrated in the hands of a few firms. . . . The Russian government lends its hand for the formation of a trust that reaches over the ocean—a trust, under State protection, against the large mass of consumers. This is the newest acquisition of our departing century."

It was announced that, in pursuance of this plan, the Russians were to be given exclusive control of certain Asiatic markets. The officers of the American combination are not easily reached by newspaper men. But when this news came long interviews with them were circulated in the press of the leading cities, dwelling upon the "Waterloo" defeat they had suffered, and reassuring the people with this evidence that there was, after all, "no monopoly." The Russian interests are dominated by the Rothschilds, and if the Rothschilds are, as these European observers declare, merely the agents of the Americans, even unsophisticated people can understand the cheerfulness with which the trustees in New York dilate on their Waterloo at the hands of their other self. Only this could make credible the report that the world has been divided with the Russians by our American "trustees," who never divide with anybody. In dividing with the Russians they are dividing with themselves.

Though it is reported that discriminations by the government railroads of Russia were used to force the Russian producers into this international trust, still, at worst, every Russian producer was given by his government the right to enter the pool. But no similar right for the American producer is recognized by our trust. It admits only its own members. The others must "sell or squeeze." There is something in the world more cruel than Russian despotism—American " private enterprise."

One of the conditions said to have been made by the Russian government is the natural one that the American trust, as it has agreed to do for the French, must protect its Russian allies from any competition from America. Extinction of the " independents" has therefore become more important than ever to the trust. The prize of victory over them is not only supremacy in this country, but on four other continents. This will explain the new zeal with which the suppression of the last vestige of American independence in this industry has been sought the last few months of 1893 and in 1894. Especially strenuous has been the renewal of the attack on the pipe line the independents are seeking to lay to tide-water, and which they have carried as far as Wilkesbarre.[1]

That pipe line, as it is the last hope of the people, is the greatest menace to the monopoly. The independents, as they have shown by the fact of surviving, although they have to pay extraordinary freights and other charges from which the trust is free, can produce more cheaply than the would-be Lords of Industry, as free men always do.[2] By means of this pipe line, suspended though it is at Wilkesbarre, are now made the only independent exports of oil that go from America to Europe. Once let the " outsiders" with their line reach the sea-shore and its open roads to the coast of America and Europe, and it will be a long chase they will give their pursuers. Everything that can be brought to bear by market manipulation, litigation, and other means is now being done to prevent the extension of this line, and to bankrupt the men who are building it through much tribulation. The mechanical fixation of values, by which the refiners who use this line to export oil are compelled to meet a lower price for the refined in New York than can be got for the crude out of which it is made, has been already referred to, and, as shown above, the same prestidigitation of prices is

[1] See ch. xii.   [2] See chs. xi. and xxx.

being resorted to in Europe against the independents of Germany.

Early in 1894 the independent refiners and producers resolved to consolidate with this pipe line some other lines owned by them in order to strengthen and perfect the system, and put it in better shape to be extended to tide-water. This consolidation was voted by a large majority both of stock and stockholders. But a formidable opposition to it was at once begun in the courts by injunction proceedings in behalf of one man, a subordinate stockholder in a corporation of which the control is owned, as he admitted in court, by members of the oil trust.[1] The real litigant behind him, the independents stated to the court, was the same that we have seen appear in almost every chapter of our story, with its brigades of lawyers. "An unlawful organization," the independents described it to the court, "exercising great and illegal powers, . . . and bitterly and vindictively hostile to our business interests." They came into court one after the other and described the ruin which had been wrought among them, telling the story the reader has found in these pages.

"It is our hope," they said, "when we once reach the salt-water that there will be no power there controlling the winds and the waves, the tides and the sun and moon, except the Power that controls everything. When we once are there the same forces that guide the ships of this monopoly to the farther shore will guide ours. The same winds that waft them will waft ours. There is freedom, there is hope, and there is the only chance of relief to this country. . . . Through three years of suffering and agony we have attempted to carry on our purpose. . . . You could have seen the blood-marks in the snow of the blood of the people who are working out their subscription as daily laborers on that line with nothing else to offer."

The injunctions asked for by this opposition were granted

---

[1] Testimony of J. J. Carter in the case of J. J. Carter *vs.* Producers and Refiners' Oil Company, Limited. Court of Common Pleas, Crawford County, Pa., May Term, 1894.

by the lower court, but the independents took an appeal
to the Supreme Court of Pennsylvania. They first placed
their petition for the rehearing in the hands of the chief-
justice on Thursday, May 24th; on Monday, May 28th,
the petition was renewed before the full court; on Thursday, May 31st, the court adjourned for the summer without taking any action upon the petition. The court in July
agreed to hear the case at the opening of its next term,
the first Monday of October. Section II. of Article I. of
the Constitution of Pennsylvania says : " All courts shall be
open, and every man, for an injury done him in his lands,
goods, person, or reputation, shall have remedy by due course
of law, and right and justice administered, without sale, denial, or delay." To guard against the injustice which might
arise by the granting of special injunctions by the lower
courts — like that granted in this case — which might remain
for months without remedy, the Legislature, in 1866, enacted
a law which reads as follows: "In all cases in equity, in which
a special injunction has been or shall be granted by any Court
of Common Pleas, an appeal to the Supreme Court for the
proper district shall be allowed, and all such appeals shall be
heard by the Supreme Court in any district in which it may
be in session."

As if there had not been enough to try these men, misfort-
une marked them in other ways. The Bradford refinery
of the president of their pipe line was visited by a destructive
fire during these proceedings in court. The Associated Press
despatches attributed the fire to "spontaneous combustion,"
whatever that may be. But in another newspaper an eye-
witness described how he saw a man running about the works
in a mysterious way just before the flames broke out. On the
same day, by a coincidence, the main pipe of the independent
line was cut, and the oil, which spouted out to the tree-tops,
was set on fire at a point in a valley where the greatest possible
damage would result, and the telegraph wires were simultaneously cut, so that prompt repairs or salvage of oil were impossible. The Almighty is said to favor the heaviest battalions,

and accident, if there is such a thing, seems to have the same preference, as has been shown in many incidents in our history, such as the mishaps to the Tidewater pipe line, and the Toledo municipal gas line.[1]

An intimation is given in the Continental press as to one of the motives under which the Russian government acted in promoting the alliance between the Russian and American oil men. It desired, it is said, to secure the influence of the powerful members of the oil combination in favor of certain plans for which Russia needed co-operation in America. There has been nothing for which the Russian government has so much needed "sympathetical co-operation" in America as for the ratification of the Extradition Treaty. The Russian government has obtained this ratification, and obtained it in a way which indicated that some irresistible but carefully concealed American influence was behind it. The New York *World*, in its editorial columns of May 25, 1894, made the suggestion that the power behind this treaty of shame was that of the oil trust, earning from the czar the last link in its chain of world monopoly. It asked if it was the influence of the oil combination that induced the Senate's consent to this "outrageous treaty." "Was this one of the conditions upon which that monopoly was permitted to secure its present concessions from Russia? Did it wield an influence in the Senate like that which the sugar trust has since exercised, though for an advantage of a different kind?" The Philadelphia *Press* points out that the Russian government had long and unsuccessfully sought to obtain the ratification of this treaty, but at last got it quickly and quietly. Did the oil combination, it asks, "succeed in bartering the character of this country as a political sanctuary for the monopoly of the world's markets?" Seldom has any public measure been so universally and so indignantly condemned in America as was this proposal to use the powers of Anglo-Saxon justice to return men who were accused only, and were, therefore, legally

---

[1] See pp. 111, 366.

innocent, to be tried without jury, counsel, publicity, or appeal. Never has public opinion availed less. The Federal executive refused even to delay the ratification in deference to the sentiment against it. Those who were active in the agitation against the treaty found something inexplicable in the unresting and unlistening relentlessness with which it was pushed through. Napoleon said that in fifty years Europe would be all Russian or all republican. Even he did not dream that republican America would become Russianized before Europe. The San Francisco *Call* of March 3, 1894, discussing the report that a commercial treaty with China was under consideration at Washington, says the negotiation is in the interest of the oil combination. It warns the public that the trust is willing to reopen the opium trade in reciprocity to China for better terms for the admission of American petroleum. This free trade with China and Russia in the souls and bodies of Russians, Chinese, and Americans would add only another instance of the many manipulations of government which this combination has successfully attempted in all parts of the world — in the tariffs of France, Germany, Cuba, Canada, and our own country; in the raising or lowering of the governmental requirements as to explosiveness of oil sold the people in England and the United States, and in the subsidy legislation by which it got from Congress for its ocean steamers a privilege rigorously denied by law to all other citizens.

In this the oil trust is but an illustration. What it has done scores of other combinations have accomplished, though not with equal genius. The Hon. John De Witt Warner, member of Congress from New York, has published a list of one hundred trusts which have been able to influence the tariff legislation of the country in their favor. The orgy of the sugar trust and Congress, out of which the tariff bill of 1894 was born, was in the plain view of all the people. "The appalling fact already disclosed," the New York *Daily Commercial Bulletin*, the most important commercial and financial daily in the United States, said in its editorial columns of June 4,

29

1894, "is that for some months past the sugar trust has been the government of the United States." The *Bulletin* estimates that the profit to the trust of one detail of the tariff bill postponing the duty on raw sugar for six months will be $34,620,000. In all this our country is not singular. The governments of Europe are used as the instruments of profit for private enterprise to an extent which the people endure only because they do not understand it. The latest instance is one of the best. The *Investor's Review* of London, England, in May, 1894, calls attention to the fact that upon the accession of Lord Rosebery to the Premiership of England the hitherto outspoken opposition of the War Office to the Maxim gun had become entirely silent, and the gun had been put into use in the army without competitive trial with other machine-guns, some of them its superiors. "This is an unfortunate fact for Lord Rosebery," says the *Investor's Review*, "because of his relationship to the Rothschilds." This great house, the *Review* says, has "a strong pecuniary interest in the Maxim-Nordenfeldt Company," and his lordship's affinities to the house "have not in the past been confined to those of family relationship alone, but extend to community of interests on the stock exchange." The *Review* therefore appeals to Lord Rosebery, for his own sake and the sake of the government "to prove by his deeds that he not only has had nothing to do with it, but will peremptorily stop this crime." If not, the *Review* hopes enough may be made of the scandal to overthrow Lord Rosebery's government, for it desires "to see a beginning made of the endeavor to purge Parliament of the guinea-pig director, the stock-gambler and punter, and the whole unclean brood of City 'bulls' and 'bears,' jobbers in patents, bribers and bribed, who help to degrade public life."

We of America are most sovereign when we sit in Constitutional Convention by our representatives, and change the fundamental law as we will. The Constitutional Convention gives us the unique power of peaceful and perpetual revolution, to make bloody and spasmodic revolutions unnecessary. Of all the inventions of that ablest group of statesmen the world has seen — the founders of this government — this is the greatest. The people of the State of New York are holding a Constitutional Convention in 1894 to enlarge the garment of 1846 to fit the growth of half a century. In that half-century the revolution in society and industry which had been getting under headway ever since the steam-engine and competition were invented has come to its consummation. But the basic law of the Empire State has faced this new world as changeless as the sphinx. Nearly half the other states have made new constitutions, or amended the old ones to bring law into line with life. Pennsylvania forbids the common carrier to become the owner of coal-mines, or to consolidate with competing carriers, or to give preference to any citizen. Michigan, Illinois, Nebraska, Colorado, and many other states have framed provisions to control the abuse of industrial and highway power. The State of Washington in its Constitution declares that "monopolies and trusts shall never be allowed in this State," and it forbids any association "for the purpose of fixing the price or limiting the production, or regulating the transportation of any product or commodity." The manual of the constitutions of the world prepared for the use of the New York convention shows that fifteen of the states of the Union have in one way or another recognized the revolution which has taken place in the industrial economy of the people, and sought to meet it with the necessary political safeguards.

When the delegates of the citizens of New York State meet in May, 1894, at Albany, in such a time to face such problems, the press notes that a large proportion of them are corporation lawyers. The place of president of the convention is secured by the chief counsel of the oil trust. He is in Albany to resist the application to the Attorney-General of the State to move for the forfeiture of the charter of the principal corporation in the trust, and on his way he plucks the presidency of the Constitutional Convention. "It is truly a momentous event," he says in his opening speech, "when the delegates of many millions of people gather together after an interval of fifty years almost, for the purpose of revising and amending the fundamental law of the State." The delegates thus momentously assembled, when they came to choose the officer who was to wield over them a power as great as that of the Speaker over the Federal House of Representatives, momentously selected the most conspicuous attorney of the most conspicuous embodiment of the forces with which the people are in conflict. The president found words of kindly reference for many great questions—of education, suffrage, city government, and the like—but for the great questions of social power which fifteen states have found serious enough for constitutional cognizance he had not a syllable. No plan or even suggestion, great or little, for the new Constitution can reach the convention direct. All must go to the appropriate committee, to be smothered or reported, as the case may be. There are thirty of these committees, and they are made up by the president of the convention, who also designates their chairmen. Each committee has its subject, and the subjects cover the bill of rights, the regulation of suffrage, the control of corporations, the election of judges, future amendments of the Constitution, and every other part of the organic law. Practically the work of the convention will be the work of the committees, and the committees are the work of one who is not only the attorney of the oil trust, but is a part of the trust, a member of the organization. "I happen to own one hundred shares in the Standard Oil Trust," he said in his argument in Albany before the Attorney-General in behalf of the trust. The trust has given formal notice that out of deference to public opinion and the decision of the Supreme Court of Ohio, and in pursuance of an agreement with the late Attorney-General of New York,[1] it had dissolved itself. But this distinguished member disregards the dissolution, for reasons of personal convenience, as he tells the Attorney-General. "I have never gone forward and claimed my aliquot

---

[1] Affidavit of the President of the Standard Oil Company of New York before the Attorney-General, May, 1894.

share." The character of this trust, of which the president and organizer of the Constitutional Convention persists in being a member to the extent of refusing to be "dissolved" out of it, has been adjudicated. It was, the Supreme Court of Ohio said,[1] "organized for a purpose contrary to the policy of our laws. Its object was to establish a virtual monopoly . . . throughout the entire country, and by which it might not merely control the production but the price at its pleasure. All such associations are contrary to the policy of our State and void." A similar judgment has been passed upon the trust by the judiciary of the State of which this president of the Constitutional Convention, besides being an officer of the courts, is a citizen. It was entered into, the Supreme Court of New York has said,[2] "for the purpose of forming a combination whose object was to restrict production, control prices, and suppress competition, and the agreement was therefore opposed to public policy and void." And a higher court, the highest in the State, the Court of Appeals, decided in the sugar-trust case that a trust was in avoidance and disregard of the laws of the State.

To the monopoly of oil, which was the starting-point, are being added by its proprietors, one after the other, as we have shown, a progressive series of other monopolies, from natural gas to iron. To these assets is now to be added our bill of rights. The long fingers of this power of mortmain reincarnate are long enough to reach from its counting-room to the Constitutional Convention. The new Magna Charta, to which the people look for help against void and unlawful combinations, is to be drafted by committees made up by the attorney of the chief of these void and unlawful combinations. The instrument which is to protect the people against monopoly will come to them only after every section has been exposed

---

[1] State of Ohio *ex rel.* David K. Watson, Attorney-General, *vs.* Standard Oil Company of Ohio. 49 Ohio State Reports, p. 317.

[2] Rice *vs.* Trustees of the Standard Oil Trust. Supreme Court, Special Term, Part I. Andrews, Judge. Reported in the New York *Law Journal*, April 26, 1894.

to the moulding touch of the greatest monopoly in history.
" This business belongs to us," and theirs is the first and the
last hand on the reins of the convention. The people can vote
on the Constitution after it is made, but the trust will see it
made. If the new Constitution is made so obnoxious that it
is rejected, as that of 1867 was, the old Constitution will do for
the next fifty years as for the last fifty. It is not monopoly
that needs the revision.

Is this the end ? When before the Interstate Commerce
Commission, the head of the combination was asked :

" The properties included in your trust are distributed all
over the United States, are they not ?"

" Oh, not all over the United States. They are distributed."

" Are they not distributed, and are they not sufficiently
numerous to meet the requirements of your business from the
Atlantic to the Pacific, and from the Gulf to the northern
boundary ?"

" Not yet." [1]

The reply came in a tone and with a smile so significant
that it was answered by a comprehending laugh from the
whole room—judges, lawyers, reporters, spectators, and all.

" Not yet !"

---

[1] Testimony, Rice *vs.* Louisville and Nashville Railroad *et al.*, before Interstate Commerce Committee, p. 366.

CHAPTER XXXII

"NOT BUSINESS"

THIS "business success" is the greatest commercial and financial achievement of history. Its broad foundation was laid in the years from 1872 to 1879, the severest time of panic for others the world has known. A universal jaundice of ill-fortune has given its sallow complexion to every one else. From the Alleghanies to the Caucasus thousands of men have been somehow thrown out of work because so much new work has come to the world. "At the flash of a telegraphic message from Cleveland, Ohio," said the people of the oil regions in their appeal to the Governor of Pennsylvania in 1878, "hundreds of men have been thrown out of employment at a few hours' notice, and kept for weeks in a state of semi-starvation." These men filled up many of the insurrectionary ranks of the great railway strike of 1877, as the employés of the Pennsylvania Railway declared in a public communication at that time. The eight oil-producing counties of Pennsylvania were said by the general council of the petroleum producers, in a public address in 1879, to be "fast sinking beneath such financial distress that resistance to threatened bankruptcy or servitude could not long be made." They grew too poor to pay the counsel they employed to help them in the courts, the legislatures, and before the executive of Pennsylvania and Congress. "The universal complaint we find is the poverty of the people, not their unwillingness to give." "I am ashamed," said one of them in court, "to see our counsel every day on account of the beggarly amounts I have paid them. A large number of producers have sub-scribed that have not paid." [1]

Men who were "frozen out" of their occupation in trans-porting or refining oil took to digging wells. "That is the only thing they have been allowed to do. They went on in a wild way, hunting new oil, and when they found it they would develop it rapidly." This made oil fall in price, and the more they produced the more they had to produce. The wages of labor kept going down. They were lower in 1888 than they were twenty-four years before. "A well-digger that I paid $6 a day and his expenses twenty-four years ago is now work-ing for $40 a month. That is true of every department of the oil business so far as the wages of workmen are concerned." "We were $10,000,000 poorer at the end of 1887 than at the beginning," said the association of oil producers of Pennsyl-vania. Their executive committee the next year said the people were on "the verge of bankruptcy." [2]

The railroads were no happier than the laborers, the pro-ducers, the manufacturers, or the merchants. As early as 1879 Vanderbilt II. declared that the oil business of the rail-roads—worth $30,000,000 a year—had been destroyed.

"I think the business is gone." [3]

In 1892 a number of refiners and producers of Pennsyl-vania, in a formal appeal to Governor Pattison, asked him to investigate the causes which were working "to the injurious depression if not the ultimate destruction of a great industry." In the same year mutterings of a turbulent discontent and threats of violence and the destruction of property, repeating those of 1872, were heard again in Pennsylvania and in Ohio, which had become an oil-producing State. "Many of the oil producers," a member of their protective association in Ohio said, in the spring of 1892, "are in a bad way. They are at

[1] Testimony, Commonwealth of Pennsylvania *vs.* Pennsylvania Railroad *et al.*, 1879, p. 577.

[2] Testimony, Trusts, Congress, 1888, pp. 18, 38, 65, 89, 111.

[3] W. H. Vanderbilt, New York Assembly "Hepburn" Report, 1879, pp. 1597, 1669. Testimony, Trusts, Congress, 1888, p. 218.

that point that they don't know just where their next sack of flour is coming from, and I am not surprised at anything they may do."

This area of low pressure, following the habit of American storms, made itself felt abroad in bankruptcies and falling wages from Scotland to Baku and beyond. Meanwhile the little nest-egg of nothing of the group which came into the field in 1862 grew to $1,000,000 in 1870; to $2,500,000 in 1872; to $3,500,000 in 1875; to $70,000,000 in 1882; and in 1887 to a capital of $90,000,000, which the New York Legislature reported in 1888, "according to the testimony of the trust's president," to be worth "not less than $148,000,000." [1] Before the trust was dissolved in name, in 1892, and the "trustees" betook themselves to the greater seclusion of separate corporations, acting in concert, its stock sold as high as 185, a valuation of $166,500,000 for the whole.

Its dividends had been $10,800,000 a year for several years. These ducal incomes and the vaster sums accumulated as undivided profits made themselves visible in the progressive *embonpoint* of the capitalization. In the six years (1876–81) preceding their taking the veil as trustees their net earnings added up the total of $55,000,000. In the next six years (to 1888) the dividends alone—not the net earnings—were more than $50,000,000.[2] These did not absorb their profits. In one year they spent $8,000,000 out of their profits for construction, besides making the regular payments to stockholders.[3]

"All this vast wealth," the New York Legislature said, "is the growth of about twenty years; this property has more than doubled in value in six years, and with this increase the trust has made aggregate dividends during that period of over $50,-000,000. It is one of the most active," the report continued, "and possibly the most formidable moneyed power on this continent." [4]

---

[1] Report, Trusts, New York Senate, 1888, p. 9.   [2] Same, pp. 9, 10.

[3] Testimony, Corners, New York Senate, 1883, p. 679.

[4] Report, Trusts, New York Senate, 1888, pp. 9, 10.

"This is an immense property," says the Interstate Commerce Commission, "... and it gives an immense power which is capable of being so employed as to put all competitors at a great and perhaps ruinous disadvantage." [1]

For the first time the New York investigation of 1888 revealed that it was only the beginning of the truth that these hundreds of millions were controlled by "trustees." It now became known that some one or more of the trustees owned personally more than half of every concern in the trust, and of the best ones owned all.

"These eight trustees control all these ninety millions of property scattered over the United States?" the president of the trust was asked.

"They have as trustees, and they have as individual owners both." [2]

In corroboration of this testimony the trust furnished the New York Senate Committee of 1888 a "list of corporations, the stocks of which are wholly or partially held by the trustees of the Standard Oil Trust." In this list, under the head of "New York State," appears this: "Capital stock, $5,000,-000. Standard Oil Company of New York, manufacturers of petroleum products. Standard Oil Trust ownership, entire." [3] But when the company was threatened with the forfeiture of its charter by the proceedings before the Attorney-General in May, 1894, its president made oath as follows: "The Standard Oil Company of New York never permitted its stock to be transferred to trustees." [4]

Even this ownership by eight men is not the whole of the truth. The eight trustees have a ruling power within themselves. An examination of the personnel of the board at the

[1] Interstate Commerce Commission Reports, vol. i., p. 722.

[2] Testimony, Trusts, New York Senate, 1888, pp. 398, 407, 411, 412, 415, 419–43, 594. [3] Same, p. 571.

[4] Before the Attorney-General of New York. In the matter of the application of the Central Labor Union and others to the Attorney-General to have him apply to the Supreme Court for leave to begin action against the Standard Oil Company of New York to vacate the charter thereof. Affidavit, president Standard Oil Company, May, 1894.

beginning, middle, and end of its career as a board shows four men always there. This agrees with the remark reported in the press to have been made by the solicitor of the trust upon its ostensible dissolution in 1892: "A majority of the stock being held by four men."

A friendly journal, the New York *Sun*, of April 25, 1889, in an editorial paragraph concerning the wealth of one of the trustees, said: "His regular income is twenty millions of dollars a year. That makes him the richest man in the United States—perhaps the very richest in the world." This is nearly three times the dividends paid in 1892 to all its stockholders by the Bank of England. The Bank of England has built up this earning power by two hundred years' work at the head of the finances of the greatest empire of history. This American wins thrice its dividend capability in less than a generation by contriving and managing an institution which he says does not do any business. Another entirely friendly paper, with sources of information of the very best, put his income two years later at $30,000,000 a year.[1] No denial of the *Sun's* statement was attempted, and the *Sun* never withdrew or modified its figures. Shortly after the secretary of the trust gave, in a public interview, a statement of the income of its principal members. That of one of them he put at $9,000,000 a year; his own at $3,000,000.

This wealth is as much too vast for the average arithmetical comprehension as the size of the dog-star, 400 times larger than the sun. These incomes are sums which their fortunate owners could not count as they received them. If they did nothing but stand all day at the printing-presses of the Treasury Department while the millions came uncrinkled out in crisp one-dollar greenbacks, or worked only at catching the new dollars as they rolled out from the dies of the Mint, they could not count them. If they worked eight hours a day, and six days a week, and fifty-two weeks in the year, they could not count their money. The dollars would come faster than

---

[1] New York *Mail and Express*, November 12, 1890.

their fingers could catch them; the dollars would slip out of their clutch and fall to the floor, and, piling up and up, would reach their knees, their middle, their arms, their mouth, and Midas would be snuffed out in his own gold.

Commodore Vanderbilt, Parton tells us, was forty-four years old before he was worth $400,000. In the next thirty years he increased this to over $100,000,000—perhaps twice that; no one knows. Vanderbilt had to multiply this nest-egg of his forty-fourth year 250 times, but one of these "trustees" will be a billionaire when he has turned himself over only ten times. Poor's *Railroad Manual* shows these men and their associates to be presidents or directors in thousands of miles of railroads, valued at hundreds of millions. Their names were prominent in the railroad "deal" of 1892 and 1893, which had for its end to put the whole of New England under one hand, controlling both its land and water connections with the rest of the country. They stand at the receipt of custom at the railroad gates to the oil regions; to the coal-fields of Pennsylvania, Ohio, Kentucky, West Virginia, Illinois; the copper, gold, and silver mines of the West; the iron mines of the West and South; the turpentine forests and the lumber regions and cotton fields; the food-producing areas of the Mississippi basin; the grazing lands of the plains. They are owners in the principal steamship line between America and Europe, and in the "whalebacks," which appear destined to drive other models out of the freight traffic of the lakes, and have begun to appear on the Eastern and Western oceans, to capture the carrying business of the world. Every dollar for the construction of a State building at the World's Fair was advanced by one of them, as the principal journal of the State announced, and it referred to him as "the man who breathes life into its East coast towns, and the lifting of his pen by his hand is like turning upsidedown the horn of plenty." They are "in" the best things—telegraphs, the gas supply of our large cities, street-railways, steel mills, ship-yards, Canadian and American iron mines, town sites. Ore dug out of their own iron mines at the head of Lake Superior is carried over their own railroad to their own furnaces and mills. It rolls along until that which began to move as ore lies at the docks of their ship-yards as a finished vessel, cut out of the mountains, as it were, at one cheap stroke, or is loaded in the cars in some perfected shape of steel, as steam radiators or what not. They feed entire mountain ranges into their mills with one hand, and with the other despatch the product in their own cars and ships to all markets. Betrayal, bankruptcy, broken hearts, and death have kept quick step with the march of the conquerors in iron as in oil. They are in the combination in anthracite coal, with which the acquisition by an American syndicate of the Nova Scotia coal deposits is closely connected. Theirs is the largest share in the natural-gas business in Pennsylvania, Ohio, New York, Indiana, Illinois. They are in the combination which controls lead, from pig to white lead, and turpentine and linseed-oil and paints.

"Its members," it was said in the application to the Attorney-General of New York, in 1894, for a forfeiture of one of their charters, "are now presidents and directors in 33,000 miles of road, one-fifth of the total mileage in the United States. Its surplus is invested in banking, in natural and manufacturing gas companies, in iron ore beds and coal beds and crude-oil production, in lead and zinc, in turpentine and cotton-seed oil, in steel, in jute manufacture, in ocean steamships, in palatial hotels, in street-railroads."

Most of their interests are in public functions, railroads, pipe lines, telegraphs, postal contracts, steamers, municipal franchises, and the like; but it is impossible to know their full extent with our present crude means for enforcing the truth that property is power and that civilization endures no irresponsible anonymous power. The corporation is an agency by which the capitalist can do business in ambuscade. "They are all in our company," said the manager of a very important public agency, "but their names do not appear." It is not out of deference to the obsolete idea that such matters are private business that all the details of their possessions are not given, but only because they are not known.

"There is no such thing as extemporaneous acquisition," Daniel Webster said; but he spoke of eloquence, not of the perfected modern commerce. Selligue, the French genius to whose discoveries nothing of equal importance has been added, is not dignified with an entry in the encyclopædias or biographical dictionaries. For "Colonel" Drake, who struck oil, a pension had to be provided by his friends in the regions which he had filled with fountains of wealth. Mr. Van Syckel, who first proved the pipe line to be practicable, died in Buffalo, paralytic, helpless, and poor.

The "age of oil" could not have come without the oil well and the drill and derrick, and these in America are the lineal descendants of the first salt well, drilled and whittled out of the rocks by the Ruffner brothers, in 1806, in the "Great Buffalo Lick" of the Kanawha. Their first "drill" was a great sycamore-tree, four feet through, hollowed out, set on end on the ground in the lick, and gradually lowered as the earth and stone within were dug away by a man inside. When they came to the rock, which they could not blast because it was under water, they hung a roughly-made iron drill by a rope to a spring pole and went inch by inch through the rock, "kicking down" the well. Metal tubes were not to be had, but the Yankee whittler solved the problem of tubing the well. Two slender strips of wood were whittled into two long, thin, half tubes, and tied together. This is the genesis of the bored "well" and the "drill and derrick." [1] It took eighteen months to accomplish this, but the wonder is that it was done at all "without preliminary study, previous experience or training, without precedent, in a newly-settled country without steam-power, machine-shop, skilled mechanics, suitable tools or materials."

These almost-forgotten men, shrewd, patient, undauntable,

[1] Dr. J. P. Hale, of Charleston, West Virginia, in the volume prepared by Prof. M. L. Maury, and issued by the State Centennial Board, on the resources of the State. Quoted by S. F. Peckham, United States Census, 1885, p. 6.

were the pioneers of the skilful well-borers who have gone forth from the Kanawha wells all over the country to bore wells for irrigation on the Western plains, for cities, factories, and private use, for salt, for gas, for geological and minera- logical explorations, and for oil. "Billy Morris," of the Ka- nawha borings, invented a tool simple enough, but not so sim- ple as to be described here, called the "slips" or "jars," which has done more for deep boring than anything except the steam-engine, and for which, considering the part played in the life of man by oil, gas, water, brine, and other wells, we are told he "deserves to be ranked with the inventors of the sewing-machine, reaper, and cotton-gin."[1] But "Uncle Billy" made a free gift to the well-diggers of the world of his invaluable "slips," and slipped into poverty and an un- known grave. To Joshua Merrill, more than to any one else, belongs the honor of bringing the manufacture of oil in America to its perfection.[2] He made better oil than any one else, and he loved his work. "I was thirty-two years in the oil business. It was the business of my life."[3] But he had to dismantle his refinery, and join the melancholy procession of two thousand years of scouts, inventors, pioneers, capital- ists, and toilers who march behind the successful men.

Yet, strange to say, these successful men did not discover the oil, nor how to "strike" it. They were not the lucky owners of oil lands. As late as 1888 they produced only 200 barrels a day—about 1 in every 3000—"an infinitesimal amount," their president said.[4] They did not invent any of the processes of refining. They did not devise the pipe line, and they did all they could to prevent the building[5] of the first pipe line to the seaboard, and to cripple the successful experi- ment of piping refined oil.[6] They own all the important re-

---

[1] *Petroleum and Its Products*, by S. F. Peckham, U. S. Census, 1885, p. 7.

[2] S. Dana Hayes, quoted in Henry's *Early and Later History of Petroleum*, p. 186.

[3] Testimony, Joshua Merrill, Trusts, Congress, 1888, p. 570.

[4] Testimony, Trusts, New York Senate, 1888, pp. 386, 425.

[5] Testimony, Trusts, Congress, 1888, p. 82. [6] See p. 165.

fineries, and yet they have built very few. They did not project the tank-car system, which came before them,[1] and have used their irresistible power to prevent its general use on the railroads, and successfully.[2] They were not the first to enter the field in any department. They did not have as great capital or skill as their competitors.[3] They began their career in the wrong place — at Cleveland — out of the way of the wells and the principal markets, necessitating several hundred miles more of transportation for all of their product that was marketed in the East or Europe.[4] They had no process of refining oil which others had not, and no legitimate advantages over others.[5] They did not even invent the rebate. They made oil poor[6] and scarce[7] and dear.[8]

The power to chalk down daily on the black-board of the New York Produce Exchange the price at which people in two hemispheres shall buy their light has followed these strokes of "cheapness":

1. Freight rates to the general public have been increased, often to double and more what is paid by a favored few.[9]

2. The construction has been resisted of new lines of transportation by rail,[10]

3. And pipe.[11] This has been done by litigation,[12] by influence, by violence,[13] even to the threatened use of cannon,[14] and by legislation, as in Ohio and Pennsylvania, to prevent the right of eminent domain from being given by "free pipe-line bills" to the people generally.

4. The cost of pipeage has been raised.[15]

5. Rivers and canals have been closed.[16]

---

[1] Testimony, Trusts, Congress, 1888, p. 258.   [2] See chs. xi. and xvii.

[3] New York Assembly "Hepburn" Report, 1879, p. 44. Testimony, same, pp. 2623, 2645. Testimony, Trusts, Congress, 1888, pp. 223–26, 542, 543, 548.

[4] New York Assembly "Hepburn" Report, 1879, p. 43. Testimony, Trusts, Congress, 1888, p. 213.

[5] New York Assembly "Hepburn" Report, 1879, p. 712. Testimony, Commonwealth of Pennsylvania *vs.* Pennsylvania Railroad *et al.*, 1879, p. 302.

[6] See p. 405.   [7] See pp. 61, 153.   [8] See p. 420.   [9] See pp. 49, 217.

[10] See p. 306.   [11] See p. 108.   [12] See pp. 111, 291, 446.

[13] See p. 291.   [14] See p. 162.   [15] See pp. 118–27.   [16] See pp. 97, 224.

6. Oil has been made to run to waste on the ground.[1]

7. The outflow of oil from the earth has been shut down.[2]

8. The outflow of human energy that sought to turn it to human use has been shut down by restricting the manufacture by the combination and by others, by contract,[3] dismantling,[4] and explosion.[5]

9. High fees have been maintained for inspection,[6] and the inspectors have been brought into equivocal relations with the monopoly.[7]

10. The general use of tank-cars and tank-steamers has been prevented.[8]

11. The people have been excluded from the free and equal use of the docks, storehouses, and other terminal facilities of the railroads in the great harbors of export.[9]

12. Inventors and their better processes have been smothered.[10]

13. Men have been paid more for spying than they could earn by working.[11]

14. "Killing delay" has been created in the administration of justice.[12]

All are poorer—oil-producers, land-owners, all labor, all the railroads, all the refiners, merchants, all the consumers of oil—the whole people. Less oil has flowed, less light shone, and there has been less happiness and virtue. In every one of the few intervals, says Hudson, during which oil could flow freely to Pittsburg, all the businesses connected with it were active and expanding.[13]

When the trust's secretary was asked for the proper name of the combination, his reply was: "The Lord only knows; I don't." "An indescribable thing," he said again.[14]

"Do you understand the practical work of refining as a refiner?" he was asked.

---

[1] See pp. 106, 164. [2] See pp. 107, 154. [3] See pp. 62, 79.
[4] See pp. 42, 72, 188. [5] See p. 251. [6] See p. 216.
[7] See pp. 216, 413. [8] See pp. 189, 228, 437. [9] See pp. 102, 140.
[10] See pp. 182–98. [11] See p. 298. [12] See pp. 149, 447.
[13] *Railways and the Republic*, by J. F. Hudson, p. 77.
[14] Testimony, Corners, New York Senate, 1883, pp. 637–42.

30

"I do not. . . . I have not been inside a refinery in ten years."[1]

"Two mills a ton a mile for five hundred miles would be a dollar a ton?"

"I am not able to demonstrate that proposition."

"You have some arithmetical knowledge?"

"I cannot answer that question."[2]

He could not state what proportion of the oil trade is now controlled by the trust. He had never looked into that question. He did not know who knows these things.[3]

"You own the pipe line to New York?"

"Yes, sir."

"What does it cost you to do business on that pipe line?"

"I do not know anything about it. . . . I have never been in the oil regions but once in my life. . . . I am not a practical oil man. . . . For perhaps eight years I have given absolutely no attention to the details of our business."[4]

Asked upon another occasion, before the Pennsylvania Legislature, about the accounts of the company when he was its secretary, he said:

"I am not familiar with the accounts."[5]

"I am a clamorer for dividends. That is the only function I have," said another trustee.[6]

"When was your last rate given you, the rate at which you are now being carried (on the New York Central)?"

"I could not tell."[7]

The secretary had testified that this associate attended to getting the rates of freight; but the latter avowed that he could not remember "any rate" that he had paid "at any time." But a little later he who could not remember any rate he had ever paid was able to tell the committee, off-hand, the exact rate of freight on oil by steamer from Batoum in Russia to

---

[1] Testimony, Trusts, Congress, 1888, p. 298.　　[2] Same, p. 784.

[3] Same, p. 295.　　[4] Same, pp. 295, 778–80.

[5] Investigation of Relations of Standard Oil Company to the State, 1883, p. 473.

[6] Testimony, New York Assembly "Hepburn" Report, 1879, p. 2665.

[7] Same, p. 2667.

Liverpool, and knew the rate from the wells at Baku by rail to the sea at Batoum ! [1]

"Had you ever been interested in the refinery of oil in any manner when you first became connected with the oil business?" another trustee was asked.

"Never."

"Or the production of oil?"

"Never."

He was a railroad man, and had been taken into the combination for his value as such; but when he was asked if he could tell any of the rates of freight his company had paid, he said :

"I cannot." [2]

"What is your business and where do you reside?" another of the trustees was asked by the State of New York.

"I decline to answer any question until I can consult counsel." [3]

"What is the capital stock?" was asked of another.

"I do not know."

"How much has the capital been increased since?"

"I don't know."

"Where are the meetings of the Standard Oil Company held?"

"I don't know."

"How many directors are there?"

"I don't know."

"Do they own any pipe lines?"

"I don't know."

"I don't know anything about the rates of transportation." [4]

"What quantity of oil was exported by the different concerns with which you were connected from the port of New York in 1881?" the president was asked.

"I do not know."

---

[1] Testimony, Trusts, Congress, 1888, pp. 296, 322, 787, 788.   [2] Same, p. 365.
[3] Testimony, New York Assembly "Hepburn" Report, 1879, p. 2603.
[4] Same, pp. 2604–14.

"How many millions of barrels of oil were refined by such concerns in the vicinity of New York in 1881?"

"I don't know how much was refined."

"Did not the concern with which you were so connected purchase over 8,000,000 barrels of crude petroleum in 1881?"

"I am unable to state."

He was asked to give the name of one refinery in this country, running at the time (1883), not owned or substantially controlled by his concern. "I decline to answer." [1]

He was asked if he would say the total profits of his trust's companies for the last year (1887) were not as much as $20,000,000.

"I haven't the least knowledge on that subject." [2]

Phrenologists are right. Memory is not to be ranked with the mental attributes of the highest importance. The head of the New York Central could not tell when a stock dividend of something like $46,000,000 had been declared on one of his railroads—and a $46,000,000 dividend is something worth remembering. "I don't know. . . . I don't remember." [3] It is lucky for the rest of us that these great men forget something.

One of the chiefs of the oil combination was a witness in Cleveland in 1887 in a suit by the State of Ohio against certain railroads.

"What business in connection with the oil business is done in the building in which the oil trust has its office in New York?"

"I do not think I could state just what business is done in that building, I am sure."

Asked on the witness-stand in the Buffalo explosion case when it was he formed the "trust" with $70,000,000 of capital, the president replied: "I am unable to state," and he could not say where its articles of agreement were, nor who

---

[1] Testimony, Corners, New York Senate, 1883, pp. 929, 931, 932.

[2] Testimony, Trusts, New York Senate, 1888, p. 417.

[3] Testimony, New York Assembly "Hepburn" Report, 1879, p. 1636.

has control of it. When questioned before the Interstate Commission he could not tell within $25,000,000 how much business they were doing a year.[1]

These men keep no books. The whole arrangement is just a happy family, like Barnum's monkeys, birds, cats, dogs, and mice in the same cage. " It is a business of faith," one of the ruling four puts it. Another was asked about the by-laws under which he and his associates transacted their business. " I don't know that I have seen a copy," he replied, and as to where it was he was able only to " suppose." [2]

When the committee of the Legislature called for the books recording the transactions of the trust and its attorneys and committees, there were practically none to produce. All there was in the way of a record of transactions of a magnitude beyond those of any other commercial institution in this country or the world were a few pages of formal entries from which nothing could be learned. The executive committee received and passed upon the disbursements of money by the treasurer, and the reports of sub-committees and of members, who had sweeping powers of attorney, by which these countless millions were kept rolling themselves up into more, but it never kept any records.

" I have no knowledge of any formal record having been made," one of them said. The reports were " either verbal or on pieces of paper. . . . I think it was memorandums," he continued, and the memorandums were " undoubtedly destroyed." They were transcribed into the records of the trustees, he said, but the search of the committee showed that the transcription was a " skeleton," consisting mainly of the mere phrase, " Minutes of the executive committee approved." " The real minutes do not appear upon the book," Senator Ives, of the committee, said.

" There is no book to produce ?"

" There is no book."

[1] Testimony, Rice cases, 51–60, Interstate Commerce Commission, 1887, pp. 366, 368.   [2] Testimony, Trusts, New York Senate, 1888, pp. 455, 577.

" And there is no memorandum ?"

" There is no memorandum." [1]

" Does the trust keep books?" the " president" was asked by Congress.

" No, we have no system of book-keeping."

On further pressure he said that the treasurer had " a record to know what money comes in."

" You have never seen those books ?"

" I do not think I have ever seen those books."

" Has any member of the nine" (trustees) " ever seen those books ?"

" I do not know that they have." [2]

Simplicity is said to be always a characteristic of greatness. What could be simpler, and so greater, than this ? The elements of success are only—

1. Not to know anything about the business.

2. To keep no books.

3. To have " a record to know what money comes in," and

4. Never to look at it.

Finally, the operations of these men have, in their own language, not been "business." Its secretary told Congress that the " trust" was " not a business corporation," [3] and an associate declared in court that it " cannot do business." The report of the New York Legislature shows that on October 3, 1883, the president had by a formal instrument been made the attorney of the trust to sign and execute all the contracts made by it. The same instrument in express terms confirmed the execution of contracts heretofore signed by him, showing that he had been making contracts. [4]

"Those gentlemen" (the members of the trust who hold its power of attorney) " do actually execute contracts involving pretty large amounts, sometimes without a formal resolution of the Board of Trustees, do they not?" one of them was asked.

[1] Testimony, Trusts, New York Senate, 1888, pp. 576–89.

[2] Testimony, Trusts, Congress, 1888, pp. 391, 392.   [3] Same, p. 294.

[4] Trusts, New York Senate, 1888, p. 658.

"Undoubtedly they do."[1]

Following their employers, the lawyers in the Pennsylvania Tax case for the oil combination argued that its operations were not business within the meaning of the tax law. If the "no money" of 1862 has become the control, in one industry alone, of $160,000,000 in 1892 by methods that are not "business," what are they?

NOTE.—The principal members of the oil combination were heard at great length in its defence before the committee of Congress investigating trusts in 1888.[2] Their testimony has been frequently used in our pages. But they felt that their case needed further elucidation, and asked the committee to hear them again. The committee declined to hear them again "explain or contradict," as they offered to do, but by printing their communication gave them the benefit of their denials and explanations.[3] Their offer was mainly to go again over the ground that the "South Improvement Company never did any business," that the combination "obtained no preferences" on the railroads, that they had cheapened transportation, improved machinery, made better oil at less cost, and so on. The chief officers and owners had been heard on all these points to the extent of hundreds of pages of testimony. But though it did not recall them to the witness-stand, the committee, in addition to printing their communication, printed most of the documentary evidence they desired to submit. This covered nearly two hundred pages more.[4]

The examination, which any one can make, of this record discloses an interesting fact concerning the proof, and the trust's offer to prove, which can best be shown in parallel columns:

THE TRUST'S OFFER TO PROVE.	THE PROOF.
It offered the evidence of the third vice-president of the Pennsylvania Railroad to "show the South Improvement Company never did any business, and its charter was repealed in 1872."	But the testimony of this witness states that his connection with the oil business of the Pennsylvania Railroad—the principal railroad in that scheme—did not begin until 1873.[5]

[1] Testimony, Trusts, New York Senate, 1888, p. 580.

[2] Testimony, Trusts, Congress, 1888, pp. 266, 287, 314, 365, 387, 395, 526, 537, 565, 627, 768, 790, 799.

[3] House of Representatives, 50th Congress, 2d Session. Report No. 4165, Part II., Appendix C, p. 33.

[4] Trusts, Congress, 1888, pp. 174–210, 801–951.

[5] Testimony, Commonwealth of Pennsylvania *vs.* Pennsylvania Railroad *et al.*, 1879, printed in Trusts, Congress, 1888, p. 195.

It offered the same evidence to prove that the same rebates granted it by the contract of October 17, 1877, "were also granted to every shipper who contracted to do *all* his business over the Pennsylvania Railroad."

But this witness stated that his road would give other shippers as low rates as to the oil combination, "if they would guarantee the same quantity—not otherwise—under that contract";[1] and the contract itself states that no other shipper should have the same rebate — "commission," it is called—unless his business gave the road "the same amount of profit you realized from our trade."[2] No shipper could get the same rates by giving "all his business." He must give "the same quantity"—a totally different proposition.

It offered the evidence taken in the Buffalo Explosion case, to show that "C. B. Matthews testified falsely" in testifying that it was sworn to that the members of the oil combination on trial employed detectives in Matthews' refineries, and that the detective was some time in Matthews' employ, and made his report to the lawyer of the trust, and he got his pay from this lawyer.

The evidence shows that this was what was sworn to: "I have now a detective agency here" (Buffalo). "I employed L—— B——. At the time he was in my employ he was employed at the works of the Buffalo Lubricating Company" (Matthews' company). "He made reports to me. . . . I forwarded copies—one to New York, one to Rochester. . . . The one forwarded to New York was addressed to" (the lawyer of the oil trust). "I met" (this lawyer, naming him) "at New York City, at No. 44 Broadway, which is the office of the" (oil trust). "I received my pay from" (him). "My instructions from" (him) "were in writing."[3]

It offered "to prove that C. B. Matthews testified falsely in saying that it was proved by a witness" that the Rochester representative of the oil combination said that the principal company in it "would sue

This was what "was proved by a witness," and referred to by Matthews. "He" (the Rochester representative of the oil combination) "said he thought they" (Matthews' company) "would not survive.... By

---

[1] Testimony, Commonwealth of Pennsylvania *vs.* Pennsylvania Railroad *et al.*, 1879, printed in Trusts, Congress, 1888, p. 206.   [2] Same, p. 208.

[3] Testimony in Buffalo Explosion case, printed in Trusts, Congress, 1888, p. 894.

Matthews once a month, or once a week, if necessary, to squeeze him out."

the time they got through with all the suits that they " (the oil combination) " would bring, the Buffalo Lubricating Company would be pretty much used up. . . . He didn't know as they would gain anything really, but they would embarrass them by bringing these suits, and if it was necessary they would bring them once a month—yes, they would bring them once a week." [1]

Similarly, throughout, the trust's offer to prove falls when confronted with its own proof. Many more instances could be given, but more than one instance is not needed.

[1] Deposition of Albert N. Reynolds, Buffalo Lubricating Oil Company, Limited, *vs.* Everest & Everest. Supreme Court, New York, Erie County, City of Buffalo, August 29, 1884.

CHAPTER XXXIII

THE SMOKELESS REBATE

With searching intelligence, indomitable will, and a conscience which makes religion, patriotism, and the domestic virtues but subordinate paragraphs in a ritual of money worship, the mercantile mind flies its air-line to business supremacy. That entirely modern social arrangement—the private ownership of public highways—has introduced a new weapon into business warfare which means universal dominion to him who will use it with an iron hand.

This weapon is the rebate, smokeless, noiseless, invisible, of extraordinary range, and the deadliest gun known to commercial warfare. It is not a lawful weapon. Like the explosive bullet, it is not recognized by the laws of war. It has to be used secretly. All the rates he got were a secret between himself and the railroads. "It has never been otherwise," testified one of the oil combination.[1] The Chevalier Bayard declared proudly, as he lay on his death-bed, that he had never given quarter to any one so degraded and unknightly as to use gunpowder. Every one would close in at once to destroy a market combatant who avowed that he employed this wicked projectile.

The apparatus of the rebate is so simple that it looks less like a destroying angel than any weapon of offence ever known. The whole battery consists only of a pen and ink and some paper. The discharge is but the making of an entry—but the signing of a check. But when the man who commands this simple enginery directs it against a business

[1] Testimony, New York Assembly "Hepburn" Report, 1879, p. 2668.

competitor you can follow the track of wreckage like the path of a cyclone, by the ruins which lie bleaching in the air for years. The gentlemen who employ it give no evidence of being otherwise engaged than in their ordinary pursuits. They go about sedate and smiling, with seemingly friendly hands empty of all tools of death. But all about them as they will, as if it were only by wish of theirs which attendant spirits hastened to execute, rivals are blown out of the highways, busy mills and refineries turn to dust, hearts break, and strong men go mad or commit suicide or surrender their persons and their property to the skilful artillerists.

"And in the actual practice of daily life," says Ruskin, "you will find that wherever there is secrecy, there is either guilt or danger." "When did you discover the fact that these rebates had been paid?" one of the victims was asked.

"We never discovered it as a fact until the testimony was taken in 1879. . . . We always suspected it; but we never knew of it of our personal knowledge, and never would really have known it of our personal knowledge. . . . I had no idea of the iniquity that was going on." [1]

Nothing so demolishing was ever so delicate and intangible as this, for its essence is but a union of the minds of a railroad official and some business friend, perhaps a silent partner, bent on business empire. The model merchant, fortunate in having a friend willing so to use a power sovereigns would not dare to use, walks the public way, strong in his secret, and smiles with triumph as all at whom he levels his invisible wand sicken and disappear. "He has the receipt of fernseed. He walks invisible."

Men who hunt their fellow-men with this concealed weapon always deny it, as they must. To use it has always been a sin, and has been made a crime in every civilized State. Under United States law it is, since 1887, an offence punishable with imprisonment in the penitentiary. [2] Moral ideals are not born in legislatures. When an act attains by a law the distinction of

---

[1] Testimony, Trusts, Congress, 1888, pp. 215, 223, 226.

[2] Interstate Commerce Law, sec. 10.

being made a crime, it is already well on its way to extinction. It is made infamous by law, because it has already become infamous before the conscience and honor of men. It was not the prohibition of highway privilege by the Constitution of Pennsylvania or the laws of the United States which made the rebate an iniquity. This legal volley is but a salute to the established conscience.

The question most often pressed before all the many legislative and judicial inquests held upon the dead bodies which strew every field of the oil industry has been whether the extraordinary powers which the invention of the locomotive and the transformation of public highways into private property had given railways over the livelihoods of the people had been used to make it impossible for any but a preferred few to live.

One of the successful men disposed of the evidence that these powers had been so used by styling it before the committee of Congress of 1888 as the "worst balderdash," and before the New York Legislative Committee of 1888 as "irresponsible newspaper statements," "a malignity and mendacity that is little short of devilishness." The secretary of the oil trust waved it away as "all this newspaper talk and flurry." The president knows nothing about the existence of such privileges, except that he has "heard much of it in the papers." And yet another of the trust in the *North American Review* of February, 1883, similarly describes the accusation as "uncontradicted calumny," to which, he regrets to say, "several respectable journals and magazines lent themselves."

After taking 3700 pages of evidence and sitting for months, the committee of 1879 of the New York Legislature said in their report: "The history of this corporation is a unique illustration of the possible outgrowth of the present system of railroad management in giving preferential rates, and also showing the colossal proportions to which monopoly can grow under the laws of this country.[1] . . . The

[1] New York Assembly "Hepburn" Report, 1879, pp. 40–41.

parties whom they have driven to the wall have had ample capital and equal ability in the prosecution of their business in all things save their ability to acquire facilities for transportation." [1]

The committee of the Ohio Legislature which took the evidence of the treatment of the Marietta independents by the railroads [2] is, so far as the author knows, the only body of all the legislative and judicial tribunals that have been investigating for the past thirty years which has found the relations of the railroads and the oil combination to be proper. It used the words " public," " uniform," " in accordance with law," " equitable," " no special discriminations or privileges " to describe the conduct of the common carriers in that case. But in doing so it had to except from these exculpations the railroad which originated the attack on the independent refiners, and the rates of which controlled the others, as it was the initial road. It had also to admit that the oil combination had received " better rates," but defended them on the ground that its shipments were larger. These two exceptions are doors wide enough to admit every possibility of the rebate. The Secretary of State for Internal Affairs of Pennsylvania made an investigation in 1878 on the complaint of citizens. He reported to the Attorney-General that no case had been made out " beyond the ordinary province of individual redress." He was hung in effigy by the citizens, and the evidence he took remains, like that of the Ohio Committee of 1879, a valuable repository of facts from which students can draw their own conclusions.

More than any others the wrongs of the oil industry provoked the investigations by Congress from 1872 to 1887, and caused the establishment of the Interstate Commerce Commission, and more than any others they have claimed the attention of the new law and the new court. The cases brought before it cover the oil business on practically every road of any importance in the United States—in New England, the

[1] New York Assembly "Hepburn" Report, 1879, p. 44.   [2] See p. 202.

Middle States, the West, the South, the Pacific coast; on the great East and West trunk roads—the Pennsylvania, the Erie, the Baltimore and Ohio, the New York Central, and all their allied lines; on the transcontinental lines—the Union Pacific, the Central Pacific, the Southern Pacific; on the steamship and railroad association controlling the South and Southwest. They show that from ocean to ocean, and from the Gulf of St. Lawrence to the Gulf of Mexico, wherever the American citizen seeks an opening in this industry, he finds it, like the deer forests and grouse moors of the old country, protected by game-keepers against him and the common herd. The terms in which the commission have described the preferences given the oil combination are not ambiguous: "Great difference in rates," "unjust discrimination," "intentional disregard of rights," "unexcused," "a vast discrepancy," "enormous," "illegal," "excessive,"[1] "extraordinary," "forbidden by the act to regulate commerce,"[2] "so obvious and palpable a discrimination that no discussion of it is necessary," "wholly indefensible," "patent and provoking discriminations for which no rational excuse is suggested," "obnoxious," "disparity . . . absurd and inexcusable," "gross disproportions and inequalities,"[3] "long practised," "the most unjust and injurious discrimination . . . and this discrimination inured mostly to the benefit of one powerful combination."[4]

This was what the Interstate Commerce Commission found all along the record from 1887 to 1893. When one of those who got the benefits so characterized was before the New York Legislature in 1888, he said:

"I know of no discrimination in the oil traffic of any kind since the passage of the Interstate Commerce Act."

[1] Rice *vs.* Louisville and Nashville Railroad *et al.* Interstate Commerce Commission Reports, vol. i., p. 722. Trusts, Congress, 1888, pp. 675–84.

[2] Scofield *vs.* Lake Shore and Michigan Southern Railroad. Interstate Commerce Commission Reports, vol. ii., p. 90.

[3] Rice, Robinson and Witherop *vs.* Western New York and Pennsylvania Railroad *et al.* Interstate Commerce Commission Reports, vol. iv., p. 131.

[4] Same.

"Do you use any means for the purpose of avoiding the effect of that new law?"

"None whatever." [1]

But the people have found that the explicit prohibitions of the Interstate Commerce law were of no more protection to them than the equally explicit prohibitions given long before by the State constitutions and laws, the common law of the court, and by the still older common law of right, which the statute was created to enforce. The "unjust," "enormous," "illegal" differences in freights by which the public was excluded were got from the railroads after, as before, Congress, obedient to an aroused and universal demand, had passed a special statute and created a special tribunal to prevent and punish this special sort of crime. This is the adjudicated fact.

This "uncontradicted calumny," "worst balderdash," "malignity and mendacity," "irresponsible newspaper statements" proves upon examination to be:

1. Testimony of unimpeached and in many cases uncontradicted witnesses, given under oath in legislative investigations and in court, subject to examination and cross-examination and rebuttal.

2. Reports of State legislative committees.

3. Copies of the contracts. [2]

4. Decision of courts, State and national. [3]

The South Improvement plan of 1872 is still in unrelenting operation, according to the latest news. A case is now pending before the Interstate Commerce Commission, [4] in which charges of highway abuse even more sensational than any of those we have seen judicially proved are made against the

[1] Testimony, Trusts, New York Senate, 1888, p. 597.

[2] South Improvement Company, p. 45; American Transfer Company, p. 99; Rutter Circular, p. 85; Contract with Pennsylvania Railroad in 1877, p. 89; Contract with New York Central and Lake Shore and Michigan Central Railroads, 1875 and 1876; New York Assembly "Hepburn" Report, 1879, Exhibits, p. 175; Contract with the Erie road, same, p. 573; Contract in the "Agreement for an Adventure" case, p. 62.

[3] See pp. 69, 130, 146, 149, 151, 208, 219, 224, 239.

[4] Wm. C. Bissel *vs.* Atchison, Topeka and Santa Fé Railroad Company *et al.*

thirty railroads by which the oil of Ohio, Pennsylvania, and New York reaches the Pacific coast. A San Francisco oil dealer is the petitioner for relief. He recites the discriminations given the oil combination on the Pacific coast before the Interstate Commerce law was enacted. These were admitted by the officials of the roads before the United States Pacific Railway Commission of 1887. The traffic managers of the Southern Pacific testified that the oil combination, "from the time it acquired the oil business on this coast, had lower rates than the general tariff provided, or than other shippers paid on coal oil." [1] The general freight agent of the Central Pacific Railroad admitted that his road had the same arrangement, and had accepted the business "at rates dictated" by the oil combination. [2] The general traffic manager of the Union Pacific Railroad said:

"We have paid them a good deal in rebates." It was a "pretty large" preference.

"What was the effect on the small dealer?"

"I should think it would be embarrassing to the small shipper!" [3]

When the Interstate Commerce law went into force the oil combination introduced a patented car for the transcontinental trade, which it claimed the sole right to use. Though the new car was to the disadvantage of the railroads, as it cost more to haul, the managers gave it lower rates than any other car and carried it back free, while they punished the shippers who gave them a lighter and better car by charging them $105 for carrying that back.

The San Francisco complainant goes on to charge that a plan was concocted and put in operation by which rates were lowered whenever the combination wanted to fill its warehouses on the Pacific coast, and as soon as they were full were put back again. This lowering and raising of rates was "to the public sudden and unexpected." [4] It was known in

---

[1] Testimony, United States Pacific Railway Commission Report, 1887, p. 3301.

[2] Same, p. 3581.

[3] Same, pp. 1132–33.   [4] See pp. 49, 200, 218.

advance only to the ring and the railroads. Before other shippers could take advantage of the low rates they would be raised again. The complaint recites that in pursuance of this plan, after the combination had transferred to the Pacific coast at the end of 1888 from its Eastern refineries all it needed for the next season's business, the railroads advanced the rates from 82½ cents a hundred pounds to $1.25. The next May the railroads made a similar seesaw, and, he says, in December, 1892, "are still making . . . such arbitrary and sudden reductions . . . to the undue advantage" of the oil combination "and to the detriment and injury of all other shippers." The San Francisco merchant also charges that in the interest of the Eastern refineries of the combination rates are made to prevent the large product of the oil-fields and independent refineries of Colorado and Wyoming from reaching the Pacific coast, "which needs them to furnish fuel for its manufactories, as well as for light for its residents." Similarly we find the Chicago and Northwestern Railroad charging $105 for a car-load of cattle from Wyoming to Chicago, while for a car of 75 barrels of oil the freight would be $348. In connection with these charges the press published the telegrams, filling columns, which were said to have passed between the officials of the railroads and the oil combination in the negotiation of this arrangement. In one of these telegrams the freight agent of the Southern Pacific explains the new deal. "He" (the agent of the oil combination) "would stock up at the low rate, then notify the association of railroads when to advance." The advance or decline was to be "made at certain seasons of the year in accordance with this supply on hand." When the negotiation was finished and the plan was agreed to, a San Francisco agent of the oil combination is said to have telegraphed to its officers in New York: "I think we have managed this freight business pretty well from this long distance, especially when you think that we have secured the 90-cent rate with which to stock up from time to time." His telegram also discloses that the arrangement extended to lead and linseed-oil, showing, what is well known,

31

that the combinations in these articles belong to the members of that in oil.   These charges are, it is to be remembered, still unadjudicated, this published evidence is not yet substantiated. But the arrangement which is charged is in exact pursuance of that part of the South Improvement Company contract which bound the railroads to " lower or raise the gross rates of transportation . . . for such times and to such extent as may be necessary to overcome . . . competition." [1]   And Attorney-General Olney has been publicly informed [2] that during the summer of 1894 oil rates between Pennsylvania and Colorado were put down from 75 cents a hundred to 25 cents, and a few weeks later raised again to the old rate.   Another increase made the rates to Denver higher, for oil, than to the Pacific coast.   He has been asked to ascertain, judicially, if this shuffling of rates was not made, like that complained of before the Interstate Commerce Commission, to allow the oil trust "to stock up at the old rate."   His informants suggest that the same powers with which he has brought railway employés to trial for infractions of the Interstate Commerce law can be used against the railways.

This is not all of the story.   This patented car spoken of was a mere aggregation of old elements, as the courts held, and the patent was void.   Advised by their lawyer that this would be the view the courts would have to take, competitors of the combination in the business of the Pacific coast, where they had been at the head until these new tricks of trade came in, introduced a car of their own of the same class.   They thus became entitled to the same low rates and the same free return of the car as their powerful rival. This put them again on an equality in transportation.   They had not been using these new cars long before two of them, shipped as usual from the East, failed to arrive.   Their search for the missing cars put them in possession of the interesting information that a litigation, of which they had had no notice or knowledge whatever, had for some time been in progress,

---

[1] See p. 48.   [2] Titusville *World*, July 12, 1894.

and was at that moment at the point of decision. As their interests had been entirely unrepresented, this decision would certainly have been against them, and would have forever made impossible the use of their cars on any railroad of the United States. This had been done by an apparently hostile litigation by the oil combination against the Southern Pacific Railroad. The former sued in the United States courts for an injunction to forbid the railroad from hauling the cars of the competitor, on the ground that they were an infringement on its own patented cars. No notice was given the persons most interested—the owners of the cars in question—whose business life was involved, and they were not at first made parties to the suit. The dummy defendant—the railroad—made no valid opposition, but with great condescension admitted that all the averments of its antagonist were true. The case was sent through the courts on a gallop to get a decision. After that the merchants whose cars were the object of the attack, as they had not been parties to the case, could not have it reopened, and it would stand against them without possibility of reversal. The firm found that a temporary injunction had been applied for and had been granted; that this had been followed by proceedings to make the injunction perpetual; that subpœnas had been issued, served, and returned, and an order had been obtained from the court for taking testimony. In place of the regular examiner of the court, a special examiner had been appointed; he had begun taking evidence the same day, and taking it privately. The testimony so taken had been sealed and filed. The railroad had made its answer December 2d, the testimony already taken was filed in court December 3d, making the case complete for decision by the judges. December 4th the firm heard for the first time of what was being done, and December 5th applied for the right to take part, which saved them. To get such cases ready for a hearing in the United States Circuit Court, where this was done, usually requires a year. But in this instance it was done in two weeks! Only just as the door of the court was closing irrevocably, as far as their

rights were concerned, did the firm get inside, and secure
leave to have their side represented. The whole fabric of
the litigation fell at the first touch. The temporary injunction against the use of their car was dissolved, the permanent injunction was refused, the patent of the oil trust's car
was declared worthless, and this decision was upheld by the
United States Circuit Court of Appeals in February, 1893.[1]

Meanwhile their oil, side-tracked in the Mojave Desert and
elsewhere, was being cooked to death, their customers were
going elsewhere, and they were being put to loss and damages which they are now suing to have made good to them.
" There are some equivocal circumstances in the case," said
Judge Hoffman, dissolving the injunctions in 1890. He
pointed out that the railroad made no objection to the injunction which deprived it of business. This "tends to
corroborate suspicions," he said, suggested by other features
of the case. The railroad persisted in remaining in the case
to the end, after the real parties in interest came in, and,
although codefendants with these parties, the road manœuvred
for the benefit of the other side in a way which the Court
again said " had an equivocal appearance." The counsel for
the firm, in his brief for the United States Circuit Court
of Appeals, pointed out more causes for " suspicion." He
showed the Court that the records of the case had been mu-
tilated in many places. All the mutilations were in favor of
the other side of the case. Who was the author of the mutilations was not shown, but it was shown that the record had
been intrusted by the lower court to a representative of one
of the oil trust, to be printed and delivered to the Court of
Appeals. "It would be a very easy matter for a vicious attorney," said the lawyer of the independents, " under such
circumstances, to make changes and alterations in the record
that might not be noticed, but would nevertheless greatly
prejudice the case."

When the victims of the smokeless rebate used the only prop-

[1] Standard Oil Company *vs.* Southern Pacific Railroad and Whittier, Fuller &
Co., 48 *Federal Reporter*, p. 109.

erty many of them had left—their right of appeal to courts
or Legislature or executive officials—they were showered with
abuse, as people with "private grievances," [1] "strikers and sore-
heads," "black-mailers," [2] "moss-backs," . . . "naturally left in
the lurch" . . . "people who came forward with envy and
jealousy of the success" of the oil combination, [3] "throttlers,"
"ravenous wolves" "hoary old reprobate," "senile old liar,"
"public till-tapper," "plunderers," "pestilence." [4] Such are a
few of the blossoms of rhetoric with which those who sought
their rights in courts or before the Legislature have been
crowned. These witnesses have come forward all through
the period between 1872 and 1892, and from every point of
importance in the industry—New York, Pittsburg, Cleveland, Oil City, San Francisco, Titusville, Philadelphia, Marietta, Buffalo, Boston, Cincinnati, Louisville, Memphis, New
Orleans. They have come from every province of the industry—the refineries, the oil fields, the pipe lines, railroads, the
wholesale and retail markets. Bound together by no common tie of organization or partnership, they have, each and
all, exactly the same kind of story to tell. The substance of
their complaint—that one selected knot of men, members of
one organization, were given, unlawfully, the control of the
highways, to the exclusion and ruin of the people—has been
sustained by the evidence taken by every official investigation, and by the decision of every court to which the facts
have been submitted.

As the counsel of the New York Chamber of Commerce
before the New York Legislative Committee of 1879 said:
"Such a power makes it possible to the freight agents of the
railways to constitute themselves special partners in every
line of business in the United States, contributing as their
share of capital to the business the ability to crush out
rivals." Men who can choose which merchants, manufactur-

---

[1] Testimony, New York Assembly "Hepburn" Report, 1879, p. 2753.
[2] Testimony, Trusts, Congress, 1888, pp. 333, 534.
[3] Testimony, New York Assembly "Hepburn" Report, 1879, pp. 2656-57.
[4] See pp. 145, 319, 320.

ers, producers shall go to market and which stay at home, •
have a key that will unlock the door of every business house
on the line; they know the combination of every safe.

In their appeal to the executive of Pennsylvania, the Petroleum Producers' Union refer to the conduct of the railroad officials as "inexplicable upon any ordinary hypothesis,
or under any known theory of railroad politics."[1] What the
railroad managers did, we know; why they did it, has never
been judicially demonstrated. One of the earliest intima-
tions of the kind of lubricant used was given by the anti-monopoly leader of the people in the Constitutional Convention
of Pennsylvania of 1872, who is now the legal leader of the
oil combination. He said: "I am told that discriminations
are now made to so great an extent as to be ruinous to certain companies unless the railroad companies' officers are
given a bonus. That is the evil under which we labor. I do
not know how to cure it, but it must be cured somehow."
Again he said: "It is charged—I do not make the charge
myself—but it is charged upon a railroad company running
through the oil regions that it will not, without delay, transport oil delivered to the railroad station by the various pipe
lines unless it is interested in the pipe line. . . . It is said
that whenever a new pipe line is built, it is necessary that
somebody connected with the particular railroad company
shall be presented with stock in the pipe line; otherwise, it
(the railroad company) will not furnish cars without tedious
and unnecessary delay. This is a discrimination which should
be stopped."[2]

It is plain that the purpose of the discrimination was something more than to shunt the control of the trade—more than
"to maintain the business" of the favorite. Ten cents a
barrel difference would have done that, for, as the Supreme
Court of Ohio pointed out, that alone amounted to a tax of
21 per cent. a year on the capital of the "outsiders."[3] When

---

[1] Trusts, Congress, 1888, p. 354.

[2] Debates, Constitutional Convention to amend the Constitution of Pennsylvania,
1872, vol. viii., pp. 261, 262.   [3] See p. 69.

10 cents was enough, why was the tax made 22½ cents, 25 cents, 64½ cents up to $1.10?

Some railroad men are known to have been stockholders in the oil combination. "I think I owned—I guess I had $100,000 in it. . . . I don't know anything at all about it"— the company—the head of the New York Central admitted.[1] Who were the owners of certain shares of their capital stock these men have always refused to divulge. In giving in court a list of stockholders of one of their corporations one of the officers uncovered only three-quarters of the stock. Who held the other fourth he avowed he could not say, although the stock-book was in his custody.[2] The dividends were paid to the vice-president, and by him handed over to these veiled prophets. There was a similar mystery about the owners of about $2,000,000 of the National Transit stock, the concern which owns and manages the pipe lines. Asked for the names of the owners of this portion, the "secretary" said:

"It is a private matter. . . . I decline to answer."[3]

The president of this pipe-line branch also refused to give Congress this information.[4] This secrecy will couple itself at once in the mind of the investigator with the charges just quoted, that railroad officials had to be given backsheesh of pipe-line stock before their roads would carry the oil of the pipe lines.

The United States Senate Committee which investigated the cattle and meat monopolies had a similar experience. Their report says: "The secretary of the Union Stockyards testified at Chicago that when the company was established the stock was subscribed by the railroads; but when asked to show his stock-books he declined, after consultation with the company's attorneys, and persisted in this refusal at Washington City. For the purposes of our investigation it was not considered necessary to ascertain in

---

[1] Testimony, New York Assembly "Hepburn" Report, 1879, pp. 1314–15.

[2] Testimony, Commonwealth of Pennsylvania *vs.* Pennsylvania Railroad *et al.*, 1879, p. 529.

[3] Testimony, Trusts, Congress, 1888, pp. 367–68.   [4] Same, p. 396.

whose names the stock now stands, for we were satisfied
that whatever the ownership it would not appear in the
names of the railroad presidents, directors, and stockholders,
who are the real owners. . . . The refusal of the secretary,
under direction of his employers, to make public the list
of stockholders must have been because of the fact that the
same men own the stockyards and the railroads running to
them, and they do not propose to submit their books to scrutiny because they dread the truth. . . . This extraordinary conduct on the part of the stockyards company is not alone in
the chain of evidence which shows complicity between the
stockyards and the railroads."[1]

The smokeless rebate makes the secret of success in business to be not manufacture, but manufracture—breaking down
with a strong hand the true makers of things. To those who
can get the rebate it makes no difference who does the digging, building, mining, making, producing the million forms
of the wealth they covet for themselves. They need only
get control of the roads. All that they want of the wealth
of others can be switched off the highways into their hands.
To succeed, ambitious men must make themselves refiners of
freight rates, distillers of discriminations, owners, not of lands,
mines, and forests—not in the first place, at least—but of the
railway officials through whose hands the produce must go
to market; builders, not of manufactories, but of privileges;
inventors only of schemes to keep for themselves the middle
of the road and both sides of it; contrivers, not of competition, but of ways to tax the property of their competitors
into their pockets. They need not make money; they can
take it from those who have made it.

In the United States the processes of business feudaliza-
tion are moving more rapidly to the end than in any other
country. In Chicago, the youngest of the great cities of the
youngest of the great nations, there are fewer wholesale dry-
goods stores in 1894 for a population of 1,600,000 than there

[1] Report of the United States Senate Committee on Meat Products, 51st Congress, 1st Session, 1890, No. 829, p. 18.

were in 1860 for 112,172. In almost every one of the mete-
oric careers by which a few men in each trade are rising to
supreme wealth, it will generally be found that to some privilege on the railed highways, accomplished by the rebate, is
due the part of their rise which is extraordinary. A few
cases of great wealth from the increased value of land, a few
from remarkable inventions like the sewing-machine, are only
exceptions.

From using railroad power to give better rates to the larger
man, it was an easy step to using it to make a favorite first a
larger man, then the largest man, and finally the only man in
the business. In meat and cattle we see men rising from
poverty to great wealth. From being competitors, like other
men, in the scramble, they get into the comfortable seat of
control of the prices at which the farmer must sell cattle, and
at which the people must buy meat.[1] Many other men had
thrift, sobriety, industry, but only these had the rebate, and
so only these are the "fittest in the struggle for existence."
We find a merchant prince of the last generation in New
York gathering into his hands a share of the dry-goods business of the country which appears entirely disproportionate
to his ability and energy, great though these be. Is his secret
a brain so much larger than his competitors' brains as his business is greater than theirs? The freight agent of the New
York Central testified that he gave this man a special rate
"to build up and develop their business."

"They were languishing and suffering?"

"To a great extent."[2]

"This," said the counsel for the Chamber of Commerce of
New York before the committee, "is deliberately making
the rich richer and the poor poorer, by taxing the poor for
the benefit of the rich through the instrumentality of the
freight charge."[3]

---

[1] Testimony, New York Assembly "Hepburn" Report, 1879, pp. 397, 781, 825,
924, 1383. United States Senate Report on Meat Products, p. 23.

[2] Testimony, New York Assembly "Hepburn" Report, 1879, pp. 808–9.

[3] Same, speech of Simon Sterne, p. 3996.

The officials of the Pennsylvania Railroad, by the use of rebates, handed over the State of Pennsylvania to three coal-dealers, each of whom had his territory, and was supreme in it, as would-be competitors found out when they undertook to ship coal into his market. They made a similar division of the iron and steel business. The rebate is the golden-rule of the "gospel of wealth." We have already seen that the secret of the few corporations which have become the owners of almost every acre of the anthracite coal of Pennsylvania was the rebate.[1]

Along one of the most important lines out of Chicago grain dealers who had been buying and selling in an open market, building elevators, investing capital and life, found five years ago market and railroad and livelihood suddenly closed to them, and the work of thirty years brought to an untimely end. The United States Interstate Commerce Commission, and the United States District Attorneys co-operating with it, broke down in the attempt to compel the railroad men who gave these privileges of transportation, or the business men who received them, to testify or to produce their books. The United States grand-jury in Chicago, in December, 1890, proceeded against the shippers and the railroad men. All of them refused to tell the rates given or received, or to produce their books.

Why do you refuse to answer? they were asked.

Because to do so would incriminate us.

Here, too, would-be successful men have gone gunning with the smokeless rebate for control of the wheat and corn and all the produce of the American farmer. Grain is fated to go the way that oil, hard coal, cattle, and meat have already gone. The farmer may remain the nominal owner of his farm under these circumstances, but he will be real owner of nothing but the piece of paper title.

First the product of the farm; then the farm. In America rises the shadow of a coming land-ownership more concen-

----

[1] See pp. 13, 19.

trated, more cruel, with the impersonal cruelty of corporate anonymity, than any the world has yet seen.

The grain broker who becomes, by favor of the general freight agent, the sole shipper and warehouseman of grain along a line of railroad, becomes thereby the sole buyer, and in the sole buyer of the produce we have the fast-growing germ of the future sole buyer of the land.

"Petroleum is the victim to-day," said the address, in 1872, of the Petroleum Producers' Union "to all newspapers and boards of trade opposing monopoly. . . . Coal, iron, cotton, breadstuffs, or live-stock may be in the grasp of the monopoly to-morrow." The prediction is more than half fulfilled.

"I ran away from home, and went to California," said a prominent grain merchant to the writer, "to escape being compelled to testify as to the freight rates I was paying. But these decisions that we cannot be forced to incriminate ourselves give me safe-conduct, and I am going home to take all the rebates I can get."

This is what is going on to-day in the "division of property" in America. Our society is woven together by the steam shuttle that moves between its farms and dinner-tables, its cotton-fields and factories, thousands of miles apart, and the shuttle is crooked. Out of $800,000,000 paid yearly in this country for the carriage of freight, it was estimated in 1888, by one who knew, that $50,000,000 to $100,000,000 goes to favored shippers.[1] As the result of personal examination made as an expert for stockholders, he declared that one of the great trunk lines had in the last twenty years thus diverted to favorites of the managers $100,000,000 of the money of the stockholders. Besides his yachts and trotters, every Captain of Industry worth talking about keeps his stud of railway presidents and general freight agents.

Public opinion, as yet only in the gristle in these new questions, turns upon first one and then another as the author of its troubles—the soulless corporation, the combination

---

[1] Franklin B. Gowen, before the United States Senate Interstate Commerce Committee, March, 1888.

of corporations, railroad oppression, or what not. But the corporation is merely a cover, the combination of corporations an advantage, the private ownership of public highways an opportunity, and the rebate its perfect tool. The real actors are men ; the real instrument, the control of their fellows by wealth, and the mainspring of the evil is the morals and economics which cipher that brothers produce wealth when they are only cheating each other out of birthrights.

The success of the same men in Europe shows that railroad discrimination is not the essence of their power, though it has in America been the chief instrument. By their wealth and their willingness to use it in their way they have become supreme. Supreme even where, as in England and Germany, they had no such unjust and crushing preference on the highways as in America. Back of highway privilege, back of money power, back of trade supremacy gained by these two means must be reckoned, as the essence of this phenomenon, the morality—our morality—which not only allows but encourages men to do each other to death, provided only the weapon be a bargain and the arena a market. "Everything shall not go to market," says Emerson ; but everything does go to market. The millionaire is the modern hero, says the New York *Evening Post*. The men who have found in the rebate the secret of business success—and there are more of them than the public guesses—have only extended a fiercer hand to the results all were aiming at. They have used the smokeless rebate because it was the best gun. But if that had not been ready to their hand, they would have taken the next best. The course of conquest might have been slower, but, unless checked by moral interventions, it would have reached the same end. If society is founded on the idea that property belongs to the strongest, these will sooner or later get all the property, by bargains or by battles according to "the spirit of the age."

The highest State and national courts and the Interstate Commerce Commission of the United States have sustained the people in the assertion of their rights, under the law, to come and go with free and equal rights on the highways. The judges have solemnly warned the guilty men that they must give up their "abhorrent" attempt to drive citizens out of the industries of their choice, and to add the property of the people to their vast estates. Although thus declared in the right by the highest judges of the law and the fact, the people are poor, defeated, and unsuccessful. Though thus warned by the authoritative voice of the ministers of right and justice that their purposes and practices are iniquitous and intolerable, the men who have determined that whole provinces of American industry shall be theirs, and theirs only, continue their warfare of extermination upon poor men with methods practically unchanged. They evade or defy the laws of the States and of the nation, and the decisions of the courts, State and national. Guided by the advice of the skilfullest lawyers, they persist in open violation, or make such changes in their procedure as will nullify statute and decision without danger to them. For thirty years the independents in the oil regions have had this reinforcement of the law, and for thirty years, in spite of it, their rights have been defiantly, continuously violated to the common ruin. The people spend their lives passing about from field or factory, or shop or office, to market, from market to court, from court to Legislature, from Legislature to printing-office. They are the type of the time, disturbed by the demand of the new tyranny of wealth for tribute from their daily labors, and forbidden to rest until out of their suffering a new liberty has been won—the industrial liberty, for which political and religious liberty wait for their full realization.

CHAPTER XXXIV

THE OLD SELF-INTEREST

THE corn of the coming harvest is growing so fast that, like the farmer standing at night in his fields, we can hear it snap and crackle. We have been fighting fire on the well-worn lines of old-fashioned politics and political economy, regulating corporations, and leaving competition to regulate itself. But the flames of a new economic evolution run around us, and we turn to find that competition has killed competition, that corporations are grown greater than the State and have bred individuals greater than themselves, and that the naked issue of our time is with property becoming master instead of servant, property in many necessaries of life becoming monopoly of the necessaries of life.

We are still, in part, as Emerson says, in the quadruped state. Our industry is a fight of every man for himself. The prize we give the fittest is monopoly of the necessaries of life, and we leave these winners of the powers of life and death to wield them over us by the same "self-interest" with which they took them from us. In all this we see at work a "principle" which will go into the records as one of the historic mistakes of humanity. Institutions stand or fall by their philosophy, and the main doctrine of industry since Adam Smith has been the fallacy that the self-interest of the individual was a sufficient guide to the welfare of the individual and society. Heralded as a final truth of "science" this proves to have been nothing higher than a temporary formula for a passing problem. It was a reflection in words of the policy of the day.

When the Middle Ages landed on the shores of the sixteenth century they broke ranks, and for three hundred years every one has been scurrying about to get what he could. Society was not highly developed enough to organize the exploration and subjugation of worlds of new things and ideas on any broader basis than private enterprise, personal adventure. People had to run away from each other and from the old ideas, nativities, guilds, to seize the prizes of the new sciences, the new land, the new liberties which make modern times. They did not go because the philosophers told them to. The philosophers saw them going and wrote it down in a book, and have believed themselves ever since to be the inventors of the division of labor and the discoverers of a new world of social science. But now we are touching elbows again, and the dream of these picnic centuries that the social can be made secondary to the individual is being chased out of our minds by the hard light of the crisis into which we are waking.

"It is a law of business for each proprietor to pursue his own interest," said the committee of Congress which in 1893 investigated the coal combinations. "There is no hope for any of us, but the weakest must go first," is the golden rule of business.[1] There is no other field of human associations in which any such rule of action is allowed. The man who should apply in his family or his citizenship this "survival of the fittest" theory as it is practically professed and operated in business would be a monster, and would be speedily made extinct, as we do with monsters. To divide the supply of food between himself and his children according to their relative powers of calculation, to follow his conception of his own self-interest in any matter which the self-interest of all has taken charge of, to deal as he thinks best for himself with foreigners with whom his country is at war, would be a short road to the penitentiary or the gallows. In trade men have not yet risen to the level of the family life of the animals. The true law of business is that all must pursue

[1] Testimony, Trusts, Congress, 1888, p. 215.

the interest of all. In the law, the highest product of civilization, this has long been a commonplace. The safety of the people is the supreme law. We are in travail to bring industry up to this. Our century of the caprice of the individual as the law-giver of the common toil, to employ or disemploy, to start or stop, to open or close, to compete or combine, has been the disorder of the school while the master slept. The happiness, self-interest, or individuality of the whole is not more sacred than that of each, but it is greater. They are equal in quality, but in quantity they are greater. In the ultimate which the mathematician, the poet, the reformer projects the two will coincide.

Our world, operated by individual motive, is the country of the Chinese fable, in which the inhabitants went on one leg. Yes, but an "enlightened self-interest"? The perfect self-interest of the perfect individual is an admirable conception, but it is still individual, and the world is social. The music of the spheres is not to be played on one string. Nature does nothing individually. All forces are paired like the sexes, and every particle of matter in the universe has to obey every other particle. When the individual has progressed to a perfect self-interest, there will be over against it, acting and reacting with it, a correspondingly perfect self-interest of the community. Meanwhile, we who are the creators of society have got the times out of joint, because, less experienced than the Creator of the balanced matter of earth, we have given the precedence to the powers on one side. As gods we are but half-grown. For a hundred years or so our economic theory has been one of industrial government by the self-interest of the individual. Political government by the self-interest of the individual we call anarchy. It is one of the paradoxes of public opinion that the people of America, least tolerant of this theory of anarchy in political government, lead in practising it in industry. Politically, we are civilized; industrially, not yet. Our century, given to this *laissez-faire*—"leave the individual alone; he will do what is best for himself, and what is best for him is best for all"—

has done one good : it has put society at the mercy of its own ideals, and has produced an actual anarchy in industry which is horrifying us into a change of doctrines.

We have not been able to see the people for the persons in it. But there is a people, and it is as different from a mere juxtaposition of persons as a globe of glass from the handful of sand out of which it was melted. It is becoming, socially, known to itself, with that self-consciousness which distinguishes the quick from the dead and the unborn. Every community, said Pascal, is a man, and every man, said Plato, is a community. There is a new self-interest—that of the " man called million," as Mazzini named him—and with this social motive the other, which has so long had its own way, has now to reckon. Mankind has gone astray following a truth seen only partially, but coronated as a whole truth. Many civilizations must worship good men as gods and follow the divinity of one and another before civilization sees that these are only single stars in a firmament of humanity. Our civilization has followed the self-interest of the individual to learn that it was but one of the complex forces of self-interest.

The true *laissez-faire* is, let the individual do what the individual can do best, and let the community do what the community can do best. The *laissez-faire* of social self-interest, if true, cannot conflict with the individual self-interest, if true, but it must outrank it always. What we have called "free competition" has not been free, only freer than what went before. The free is still to come. The pressure we feel is notice to prepare for it. Civilization—the process of making men citizens in their relations to each other, by exacting of each that he give to all that which he receives from all—has reached only those forms of common effort which, because most general and most vital, first demanded its harmonizing touch. Men joining in the labors of the family, the mutual sacrifices of the club or the church in the union of forces for self-defence and for the gains of co-operation on the largest scale in labors of universal concern, like letter-carrying, have come to be so far civilized.

32

History is condensed in the catchwords of the people. In the phrases of individual self-interest which have been the shibboleths of the main activities of our last hundred years were prophesied: the filling up of the Mississippi by the forest-destroying, self-seeking lumber companies of the North; the disintegration of the American family—among the rich by too little poverty, and among the poor by too much; the embezzlement of public highways and public franchises into private property; the devolution of the American merchants and manufacturers into the business dependants—and social and political dependants, therefore—of a few men in each great department of trade, from dry-goods to whiskey; the devolution of the free farmer into a tenant, and of the working-man into a fixture of the locomotive or the factory, forbidden to leave except by permission of his employer or the public; and that mêlée of injunctions, bayonets, idle men and idle machinery, rich man's fear of poor man and poor man's fear of starvation, we call trade and industry.

Where the self-interest of the individual is allowed to be the rule both of social and personal action, the level of all is forced down to that of the lowest. Business excuses itself for the things it does—cuts in wages, exactions in hours, tricks of competition—on the plea that the merciful are compelled to follow the cruel. "It is pleaded as an excuse by those" (common carriers) "who desire to obey the" (Interstate Commerce) "law that self-preservation drives them to violate it because other carriers persist in doing so," says Senator Cullom. When the self-interest of society is made the standard the lowest must rise to the average. The one pulls down, the other up. That men's hearts are bad and that bad men will do bad things has a truth in it. But whatever the general average of morals, the anarchy which gives such individuals their head and leaves them to set the pace for all will produce infinitely worse results than a policy which applies mutual checks and inspirations. Bad kings make bad reigns, but monarchy is bad because it is arbitrary power, and that, whether it be political or industrial, makes even good men bad.

A partial truth universally applied as this of self-interest has been is a universal error. Everything goes to defeat. Highways are used to prevent travel and traffic. Ownership of the means of production is sought in order to "shut down" production, and the means of plenty make famine. All follow self-interest to find that though they have created marvellous wealth it is not theirs. We pledge "our lives, our fortunes, and our sacred honor" to establish the rule of the majority, and end by finding that the minority—a minority in morals, money, and men—are our masters whichever way we turn. We agonize over "economy," but sell all our grain and pork and oil and cotton at exchanges where we pay brokerage on a hundred or a thousand barrels or bushels or bales of wind to get one real one sold. These intolerabilities—sweat-shops where model merchants buy and sell the cast-off scarlet-fever skins of the poor, factory and mine where childhood is forbidden to become manhood and manhood is forbidden to die a natural death, mausoleums in which we bury the dead rich, slums in which we bury the living poor, coal pools with their manufacture of artificial winter—all these are the rule of private self-interest arrived at its destination.

A really human life is impossible in our cities, but they cannot be reconstructed under the old self-interest. Chicago was rebuilt wrong after the fire. Able men pointed out the avenues to a wider and better municipal life, but they could not be opened through the private interpositions that blocked the way. The slaughter of railway men coupling cars was shown, in a debate in the United States Senate, to be twice as great as it would be if the men were in active service in war. But under the scramble for private gain our society on its railway side cannot develop the energy to introduce the improved appliances ready to hand which would save these lives, all young and vigorous. The cost of the change would be repaid in 100-per-cent. dividends every year by the money value alone to us of the men now killed and wounded. But we shall have to wait for a nobler arithmetic to give us investments so good as that. The lean kine of self-interest devour the fat kine.

The railroad stockholder, idolater of self-interest, lets himself be robbed—like the stockholder of all the railroads in this story—either because he is too rich to mind, too feeble to make himself heard, or too much implicated elsewhere as principal in the same kind of depredation to care or dare to stir what he knows to be a universal scandal. He has become within himself the battle-ground of a troop of warring devils of selfishness; his selfishness as a stockholder clutched at the throat by his selfishness as a parasite, in some "inside deal," feeding on the stockholder; some rebate arrangement, fast-freight line, sleeping-car company, or what not. And, as like as not, upon this one's back is another devil of depredation from some inner ring within a ring. Torn at the vitals, the enlightened swinishness of our *leit-motif* is hastening to throw itself into the sea.

We are very poor. The striking feature of our economic condition is our poverty, not our wealth. We make ourselves "rich" by appropriating the property of others by methods which lessen the total property of all. Spain took such riches from America and grew poor. Modern wealth more and more resembles the winnings of speculators in bread during famine—worse, for to make the money it makes the famine. What we call cheapness shows itself to be unnatural fortunes for a very few, monstrous luxury for them and proportionate deprivation for the people, judges debauched, trustees dishonored, Congress and State legislatures insulted and defied, when not seduced, multitudes of honest men ruined and driven to despair, the common carrier made a mere instrument for the creation of a new baronage, an example set to hundreds of would-be commercial Cæsars to repeat this rapine in other industries and call it "business," a process set in operation all over the United States for the progressive extinction of the independence of laboring men, and all business men except the very rich, and their reduction to a state of vassalage to lords or squires in each department of trade and industry. All these—tears, ruin, dishonor, and treason—are the unmarked additions to the "price marked on the goods."

Shall we buy cheap of Captain Kidd, and shut our ears to the agony that rustles in his silks? Shall we believe that Captain Kidd, who kills commerce by the act which enables him to sell at half-price, is a cheapener? Shall we preach and practise doctrines which make the Black Flag the emblem of success on the high seas of human interchange of service, and complain when we see mankind's argosies of hope and plenty shrink into private hoards of treasure, buried in selfish sands to be lost forever, even to cupidity? If this be cheapness, it comes by the grace of the seller, and that is the first shape of dearness, as security in society by the grace of the ruler is the first form of insecurity.

The new wealth now administers estates of fabulous extent from metropolitan bureaus, and all the profits flow to men who know nothing of the real business out of which they are made. Red tape, complication, the hired man, conspiracy have taken the place of the watchful eye of the owner, the old-fashioned hand at the plough that must "hold or drive." We now have Captains of Industry, with a few aids, rearranging from office-chairs this or that industry, by mere contrivances of wit compelling the fruits of the labor of tens of thousands of their fellows, who never saw them, never heard of them, to be every day deposited unwilling and unwitting to their own credit at the bank; setting, as by necromancy, hundreds of properties, large and small, in a score of communities, to flying through invisible ways into their hands; sitting calm through all the hubbub raised in courts, legislatures, and public places, and by dictating letters and whispering words remaining the master magicians of the scene; defying, though private citizens, all the forces and authorities of a whole people; by the mere mastery of compelling brain, without putting hand to anything, opening or closing the earth's treasures of oil or coal or gas or copper or what not; pulling down or putting up great buildings, factories, towns themselves; moving men and their money this way and that; inserting their will as part of the law of life of the people— American, European, and Asiatic—and, against the protest of a whole civilization, making themselves, their methods and principles, its emblematic figures.

Syndicates, by one stroke, get the power of selling dear on one side, and producing cheap on the other. Thus they keep themselves happy, prices high, and the people hungry. What model merchant could ask more? The dream of the king who wished that all his people had but one neck that he might decapitate them at one blow is realized to-day in this industrial garrote. The syndicate has but to turn its screw, and every neck begins to break. Prices paid to such intercepters are not an exchange of service; they are ransom paid by the people for their lives. The ability of the citizen to pay may fluctuate; what he must pay remains fixed, or advances like the rent of the Irish tenant to the absentee landlord until the community interfered. Those who have this power to draw the money from the people—from every railroad station, every street-car, every fireplace, every salt-cellar, every bread-pan, wash-board, and coal-scuttle — to their own safes have the further incentive to make this money worth the most possible. By contracting the issue of currency and contracting it again by hoarding it in their banks, safe-deposit vaults, and the government treasury, they can depress the prices of all that belongs to the people. Their own prices are fixed. These are "regular prices," established by price-lists. Given, as a ruling motive, the principles of business—to get the most and give the least; given the legal and economic, physical and mechanical control, possible under our present social arrangements, to the few over the many, and the certain end of all this, if unarrested, unreversed, can be nothing less than a return to chattel slavery. There may be some finer name, but the fact will not be finer. Between our present tolerance and our completed subjection the distance is not so far as that from the equality and simplicity of our Pilgrim Fathers to ourselves.

Everything withers — even charity. Aristocratic benevolence spends a shrunken stream in comparison with democratic benevolence. In an address to the public, soliciting subscriptions, the Committee of the United Hospitals Association of New York said, in December, 1893: "The committee have found that, through the obliteration of old methods of individual competition by the establishment of large corporations and trusts in modern times, the income of such charitable institutions as are supported by the individual gifts of the benevolent has been seriously affected."

Franklin pricked the bubble of the lottery by showing that to buy all the tickets and win all the prizes was to be most surely the loser. Our nascent common-sense begins to see that the many must always lose where all spend their lives trying to get more than they give, and that all lose when any lose. The welfare of all is more than the welfare of the many, the few, or the one. If the few or the one are not fine enough to accept this truth from sentiment or conscience, they can find other reasons as convincing, though not as amiable. From the old régime of France, the slave-holders of the South, the death-rate of tyrants, the fear of their brothers which the rich and the great of to-day are printing on their faces, in fugitive-slave treaties with Russia, and in the frowning arsenals and armories building in our cities for "law and order," they can learn how to spell self-interest.

If all will sacrifice themselves, none need be sacrificed. But if one may sacrifice another, all are sacrificed. That is the difference between self-interest and other-self interest. In industry we have been substituting all the mean passions that can set man against man in place of the irresistible power of brotherhood. To tell us of the progressive sway of brotherhood in all human affairs is the sole message of history. "Love thy neighbor as thyself" is not the phrase of a ritual of sentiment for the unapplied emotion of pious hours; it is the exact formula of the force to-day operating the greatest institutions man has established. It is as secular as sacred. Only by each neighbor giving the other every right of free thought, free movement, free representation which he demands for himself; only by calling every neighbor a friend, and literally laying down his life for his friend against foreign invasion or domestic tumult; only by the equalization which gives the vote to all and denies kingship to all, however strong or "fittest"—only thus is man establishing the community, the republic, which, with all its failings, is the highest because the realest application of the spirit of human brotherhood. Wonderful are the dividends of this investment. You are but one, and can give only yourself to America. You give free speech, and 65,000,000 of your countrymen will guard the freedom of your lips. Your single offer of your right arm puts 65,000,000 of sheltering arms about you. Does "business" pay such profits? Wealth will remain a secret unguessed by business until it has reincorporated itself under the law which reckons as the property of each one the total of all the possessions of all his neighbors.

Society could not live a day, the Bishop of Peterborough said, if it put the principles of Christ into practice. There is no rarer gift than that of eyes to see what we see. Society is society, and lives its day solely by virtue of having put into actual routine and matter-of-fact application the principles of Christ and other bringers of the same message. Imperfect and faulty though the execution, it is these principles which are the family, the tribe, the sect, the club, the mutual-benefit society, the State, with their mutual services, forbearance, and guarantees. The principles of Christ are the cause and essence of society. They are not the ideal of which we dream; they are the applied means with which we are working out our real life in "the light of common day." They have not been so much revealed to us by our inspired ones as best seen and best said by them. Insurance for fire, accident, sickness, old age, death—the ills that flesh is heir to—has the same co-operation for its innermost forces. Limited now by the intervention of the selfishness of profit-seeking, it needs only to be freed from this, and added, as in New Zealand, to the growing list of the mutualities of the general welfare operated by the State to be seen as what it is. The golden rule is the original of every political constitution, written and unwritten, and all our reforms are but the pains with which we strive to improve the copy.

In the worst governments and societies that have existed one good can be seen—so good that the horrors of them fall back into secondary places as extrinsic, accidental. That good is the ability of men to lead the life together. The more perfect monopoly makes itself the more does it bring into strong lights the greatest fact of our industry, of far more permanent value than the greed which has for the moment made itself the cynosure of all eyes. It makes this fair world more fair to consider the loyalties, intelligences, do-cilities of the multitudes who are guarding, developing, op-erating with the faithfulness of brothers and the keen inter-est of owners properties and industries in which brotherhood is not known and their title is not more than a tenancy at will. One of the largest stones in the arch of "consolida-tion," perhaps the key-stone, is that men have become so in-telligent, so responsive and responsible, so co-operative that they can be intrusted in great masses with the care of vast properties owned entirely by others and with the operation of complicated processes, although but a slender cost of sub-sistence is awarded them out of fabulous profits. The spec-tacle of the million and more employés of the railroads of this country despatching trains, maintaining tracks, collecting fares and freights, and turning over hundreds of millions of net profits to the owners, not one in a thousand of whom would know how to do the simplest of these things for him-self, is possible only where civilization has reached a high average of morals and culture. More and more the mills and mines and stores, and even the farms and forests, are being administered by others than the owners. The virtue of the people is taking the place Poor Richard thought only the eye of the owner could fill. If mankind, driven by their fears and the greed of others, can do so well, what will be their productivity and cheer when the "interest of all" sings them to their work?

This new morality and new spring of wealth have been

seized first by the appropriating ones among us. But, as has been in government, their intervention of greed is but a passing phase. Mankind belongs to itself, not to kings or monopolists, and will supersede the one as surely as the other with the institutions of democracy. Yes, Callicles, said Socrates, the greatest are usually the bad, for they have the power. If power could continue paternal and benign, mankind would not be rising through one emancipation after another into a progressive communion of equalities. The individual and society will always be wrestling with each other in a composition of forces. But to just the extent to which civilization prevails, society will be held as inviolable as the individual; not subordinate—indeed inaudible—as now in the counting-room and corporation-office. We have overworked the self-interest of the individual. The line of conflict between individual and social is a progressive one of the discovery of point after point in which the two are identical. Society thus passes from conflict to harmony, and on to another conflict. Civilization is the unceasing accretion of these social solutions. We fight out to an equilibrium, as in the abolition of human slavery; then upon this new level thus built up we enter upon the struggle for a new equilibrium, as now in the labor movement. The man for himself destroys himself and all men ; only society can foster him and them.

The greatest happiness of the greatest number is only the doctrine of self-interest writ large and made more dangerous by multitude. It is the self-interest of the majority, and this has written some of the unloveliest chapters of history. There have never been slaves more miserable than those of Sparta, where the State was the owner. American democracy prepares to repeat these distresses of the selfishness of the many, and gives notice to its railway employés of a new divine right —"the convenience of the public"—to which they must forego every right of manhood. No better definition of slave could be found than one who must work at the convenience of another. This is the position into which recent legal decisions and acts of the Federal executive force railway men.

These speak in the name of Interstate Commerce, but their logic can be as easily applied by State judges to State commerce, and all working-men are manifestly as necessary, each in his function, to the convenience of the public as the men of the rail. The greatest happiness of all must be the formula. When Lamennais said, "I love my family more than myself, my village more than my family, my country more than my village, and mankind more than my country," he showed himself not only a good lover, but the only good arithmetician.

Children yet, we run everything we do—love or war, work or leisure, religion or liberty—to excess. Every possibility of body and mind must be played upon till it is torn to pieces, as toys by children. Priests, voluptuaries, tyrants, knights, ascetics—in the long procession of fanatics a new-comer takes his place; he is called "the model merchant"—the cruelest fanatic in history. He is the product of ages given to progressive devotion to "trading." He is the high-priest of the latest idolatry, the self-worship of self-interest. Whirling-dervish of the market, self, friends, and family, body and soul, loves, hopes, and faith, all are sacrificed to seeing how many "turns" he can make before he drops dead. Trade began, Sir Henry Sumner Maine tells us, not within the family or community, but without. Its first appearances are on the neutral borderland between hostile tribes. There, in times of peace, they meet to trade, and think it no sin that "the buyer must beware," since the buyer is an enemy. Trade has spread thence, carrying with itself into family and State the poison of enmity. From the fatherhood of the old patriarchal life, where father and brother sold each other nothing, the world has chaffered along to the anarchy of a "free" trade which sells everything. One thing after another has passed out from under the régime of brotherhood and passed in under that of bargainhood. The ground we move on, the bodies we work with, and the necessaries we live by are all being "exchanged," by "rules fetched with cupidity from heartless schools," into the ownership of the Jacobs of mankind. By these rules the cunning are the good, and the weak and the tender the bad, and the good are to have all the goods and the weak are to have nothing. These rules give one the power to supply or deny work to thousands, and to use the starvation terms of the men he disemploys as the measure of the cost of subsistence of all workmen. This must be near the end. The very churches have become mercantilized, and are markets in which "prophets" are paid fancy prices—"always called of God," as Milton said, "but always to a greater benefice"—and worshippers buy and sell knee-room.

Conceptions of duty take on a correspondingly unnatural complexion. The main exhortations the world gives beginners are how to "get on"—the getting on so ardently inculcated being to get, like the old-man-of-the-sea, on somebody's back. "If war fails you in the country where you are, you must go where there is war," said one of the successful men of the fourteenth century to a young knight who asked him for the Laws of Life. "I shall be perfectly satisfied with you," I heard one of the great business geniuses of America say to his son, "if you will only always go to bed at night worth more than when you got up in the morning." The system grows, as all systems do, more complicated, and gets further away from its first purposes of barter of real things and services. It goes more under the hands of men of apt selfishness, who push it further away from general comprehension and the general good. Tariffs, currencies, finances, freight-rate sheets, the laws, become instruments of privilege, and just in proportion become puzzles no people can decipher. "I have a right to buy my labor where I can buy it cheapest"—beginning as a protest against the selfish exclusions of antiquated trade-guilds outgrown by the new times—has at last come to mean, "I have a right to do anything to cheapen the labor I want to buy, even to destroying the family life of the people."

When steaming kettles grew into beasts of burden and public highways dwindled into private property administered by private motives for private ends, all previous tendencies were intensified into a sudden whirl redistributing wealth and labors. It appears to have been the destiny of the railroad to begin and of oil to lubricate to its finish the last stage of this crazy commercialism. Business colors the modern world as war reddened the ancient world. Out of such delirium monsters are bred, and their excesses destroy the system that brought them forth. There is a strong suggestion of moral insanity in the unrelieved sameness of mood and unvarying repetition of one act in the life of the model merchant. Sane minds by an irresistible law alternate one tension with another. Only a lunatic is always smiling or always weeping or always clamoring for dividends. Eras show their last stages by producing men who sum up individually the morbid characteristics of the mass. When the crisis comes in which the gathering tendencies of generations shoot forward in the avalanche, there is born some group of men perfect for their function—good be it or bad. They need to take time for no second thought, and will not delay the unhalting reparations of nature by so much as the time given to one tear over the battle-field or the bargain. With their birth their mission is given them, whether it be the mission of Lucifer or Gabriel. This mission becomes their conscience. The righteous indignation that other men feel against sin these men feel against that which withstands them. Sincere as rattlesnakes, they are selfish with the unconsciousness possible to only the entirely commonplace, without the curiosity to question their times or the imagination to conceive the pain they inflict, and their every ideal is satisfied by the conventionalities of church, parlor, and counting-room. These men are the touchstones to wither the cant of an age.

We preach " Do as you would be done by" in our churches, and "A fair exchange no robbery" in our counting-rooms, and "All citizens are equal as citizens" in courts and Congress. Just as we are in danger of believing that to say these things is to do them and be them, there come unto us these men, practical as granite and gravitation. Taking their cue not from our lips, but from our lives, they better the instruction, and, passing easily to the high seats at every table, prove that we are liars and hypocrites. Their only secret is that they do, better than we, the things we are all trying to do, but of which in our morning and evening prayers, seen of all men, we are continually making believe to pray: Good Lord, deliver us! When the hour strikes for such leaders, they come and pass as by a law of nature to the front. All follow them. It is their fate and ours that they must work out to the end the destiny interwoven of their own insatiate ambition and the false ideals of us who have created them and their opportunity.

If our civilization is destroyed, as Macaulay predicted, it will not be by his barbarians from below. Our barbarians come from above. Our great money-makers have sprung in one generation into seats of power kings do not know. The forces and the wealth are new, and have been the opportunity of new men. Without restraints of culture, experience, the pride, or even the inherited caution of class or rank, these men, intoxicated, think they are the wave instead of the float, and that they have created the business which has created them. To them science is but a never-ending répertoire of investments stored up by nature for the syndicates, government but a fountain of franchises, the nations but customers in squads, and a million the unit of a new arithmetic of wealth written for them. They claim a power without control, exercised through forms which make it secret, anonymous, and perpetual. The possibilities of its gratification have been widening before them without interruption since they began, and even at a thousand millions they will feel no satiation and will see no place to stop. They are gluttons of luxury and power, rough, unsocialized, believing that mankind must be kept terrorized. Powers of pity die out of them, because they work through agents and die in their agents, because what they do is not for themselves.

Of gods, friends, learnings, of the uncomprehended civilization they overrun, they ask but one question: How much? What is a good time to sell? What is a good time to buy? The Church and the Capitol, incarnating the sacrifices and triumphs of a procession of martyrs and patriots since the dawn of freedom, are good enough for a money-changer's shop for them, and a market and shambles. Their heathen eyes see in the law and its consecrated officers nothing but an intelligence-office and hired men to help them burglarize the treasures accumulated for thousands of years at the altars of liberty and justice, that they may burn their marbles for the lime of commerce.

By their windfall of new power they have been forced into the position of public enemies. Its new forms make them seem not to be within the jurisdiction of the social restraints which many ages of suffering have taught us to bind about the old powers of man over man. A fury of rule or ruin has always in the history of human affairs been a characteristic of the "strong men" whose fate it is to be in at the death of an expiring principle. The leaders who, two hundred years ago, would have been crazy with conquest, to-day are crazy with competition. To a dying era some man is always born to enfranchise it by revealing it to itself. Men repay such benefactors by turning to rend them. Most unhappy is the fate of him whose destiny it is to lead mankind too far in its own path. Such is the function of these men, such will be their lot, as that of those for whom they are building up these wizard wealths.

Poor thinking means poor doing. In casting about for the cause of our industrial evils, public opinion has successively found it in "competition," "combination," the "corporations," "conspiracies," "trusts." But competition has ended in combination, and our new wealth takes as it chooses the form of corporation or trust, or corporation again, and with every change grows greater and worse. Under these kaleidoscopic masks we begin at last to see progressing to its terminus a steady consolidation, the end of which is one-man power. The conspiracy ends in one, and one cannot conspire with himself. When this solidification of many into one has been reached, we shall be at last face to face with the naked truth that it is not only the form but the fact of arbitrary power, of control without consent, of rule without representation that concerns us.

Business motived by the self-interest of the individual runs into monopoly at every point it touches the social life—land monopoly, transportation monopoly, trade monopoly, political monopoly in all its forms, from contraction of the currency to corruption in office. The society in which in half a lifetime a man without a penny can become a hundred times a millionaire is as over-ripe, industrially, as was, politically, the Rome in which the most popular bully could lift himself from the ranks of the legion on to the throne of the Cæsars. Our rising issue is with business. Monopoly is business at the end of its journey. It has got there. The irrepressible conflict is now as distinctly with business as the issue so lately met was with slavery. Slavery went first only because it was the cruder form of business.

Against the principles, and the men embodying them and pushing them to extremes—by which the powers of government, given by all for all, are used as franchises for personal aggrandizement; by which, in the same line, the common toil of all and the common gifts of nature, lands, forces, mines, sites, are turned from service to selfishness, and are made by one and the same stroke to give gluts to a few and impoverishment to the many—we must plan our campaign. The yacht of the millionaire incorporates a million days' labor which might have been given to abolishing the slums, and every day it runs the labor of hundreds of men is withdrawn from the production of helpful things for humanity, and each of us is equally guilty who directs to his own pleasure the labor he should turn to the wants of others. Our fanatic of wealth reverses the rule that serving mankind is the end and wealth an incident, and has made wealth the end and the service an accident, until he can finally justify crime itself if it is a means to the end—wealth—which has come to be the supreme good; and we follow him.

It is an adjudicated fact of the business and social life of America that to receive the profits of crime and cherish the agents who commit it does not disqualify for fellowship in the most "solid" circles—financial, commercial, religious, or social. It illustrates what Ruskin calls the "morbid" character of modern business that the history of its most brilliant episodes must be studied in the vestibules of the penitentiary. The riches of the combinations are the winnings of a policy which, we have seen, has certain constant features. Property to the extent of uncounted millions has been changed from the possession of the many who owned it to the few who hold it:

1. Without the knowledge of the real owners.
2. Without their consent.
3. With no compensation to them for the value taken.
4. By falsehood, often under oath.
5. In violation of the law.

Our civilization is builded on competition, and competition evolves itself crime—to so acute an infatuation has the lunacy of self-interest carried our dominant opinion. We are hurried far beyond the point of not listening to the new conscience which, pioneering in moral exploration, declares that conduct we think right because called "trade" is really lying, stealing, murder. "The definite result," Ruskin preaches, "of all our modern haste to be rich is assuredly and constantly the murder of a certain number of persons by our hands every year." To be unawakened by this new voice is bad enough, but we shut our ears even against the old conscience.

We cannot deal with this unless we cleanse our hearts of all disordering rage. "The rarer action is in virtue rather than in vengeance." Our tyrants are our ideals incarnating themselves in men born to command. What these men are we have made them. All governments are representative governments; none of them more so than our government of industry. We go hopelessly astray if we seek the solution of our problems in the belief that our business rulers are worse men in kind than ourselves. Worse in degree; yes. It is a race to the bad, and the winners are the worst. A system in which the prizes go to meanness invariably marches with the meanest men at the head. But if any could be meaner than the meanest it would be they who run and fail and rail.

33

Every idea finds its especially susceptible souls. These men are our most susceptible souls to the idea of individual self - interest. They have believed implicitly what we have taught, and have been the most faithful in trying to make the talent given them grow into ten talents. They rise superior to our half-hearted social corrections : publicity, private competition, all devices of market-opposition, private litigation, public investigation, legislation, and criminal prosecution—all. Their power is greater to-day than it was yesterday, and will be greater to - morrow. The public does not withhold its favor, but deals with them, protects them, refuses to treat their crimes as it treats those of the poor, and admits them to the highest places. The predominant mood is the more or less concealed regret of the citizens that they have not been able to conceive and execute the same lucky stroke or some other as profitable. The conclusion is irresistible that men so given the lead are the representatives of the real "spirit of the age," and that the protestants against them are not representative of our times—are at the best but intimators of times which may be.

Two social energies have been in conflict, and the energy of reform has so far proved the weaker. We have chartered the self-interest of the individual as the rightful sovereign of conduct ; we have taught that the scramble for profit is the best method of administering the riches of earth and the exchange of services. Only those can attack this system who attack its central principle, that strength gives the strong in the market the right to destroy his neighbor. Only as we have denied that right to the strong elsewhere have we made ourselves as civilized as we are. And we cannot make a change as long as our songs, customs, catchwords, and public opinions tell all to do the same thing if they can. Society, in each person of its multitudes, must recognize that the same principles of the interest of all being the rule of all, of the strong serving the weak, of the first being the last—"I am among you as one that serves"—which have given us the home where the weakest is the one surest of his rights and of

the fullest service of the strongest, and have given us the republic in which all join their labor that the poorest may be
fed, the weakest defended, and all educated and prospered,
must be applied where men associate in common toil as
wherever they associate. Not until then can the forces be
reversed which generate those obnoxious persons—our fittest.

Our system, so fair in its theory and so fertile in its happiness and prosperity in its first century, is now, following the
fate of systems, becoming artificial, technical, corrupt; and, as
always happens in human institutions, after noon, power is
stealing from the many to the few. Believing wealth to be
good, the people believed the wealthy to be good. But, again
in history, power has intoxicated and hardened its possessors,
and Pharaohs are bred in counting-rooms as they were in palaces. Their furniture must be banished to the world-garret,
where lie the out-worn trappings of the guilds and slavery and
other old lumber of human institutions.

CHAPTER XXXV

AND THE NEW

WE have given the prize of power to the strong, the cunning, the arithmetical, and we must expect nothing else but that they will use it cunningly and arithmetically. For what else can they suppose we gave it to them? If the power really flows from the people, and should be used for them; if its best administration can be got, as in government, only by the participation in it of men of all views and interests; if in the collision of all these, as in democracy, the better policy is progressively preponderant; if this is a policy which, with whatever defects, is better than that which can be evolved by narrower or more selfish or less multitudinous influences of persons or classes, then this power should be taken up by the people. "The mere conflict of private interests will never produce a well-ordered commonwealth of labor," says the author of the article on political economy in the *Encyclopædia Britannica*. The failure of monarchy and feudalism and the visibly impending failure of our business system all reveal a law of nature. The harmony of things insists that that which is the source of power, wealth, and delight shall also be the ruler of it. That which is must also seem. It is the people from whom come the forces with which kings and millionaires ride the world, and until the people take their proper place in the seat of sovereignty, these pseudo owners—mere claimants and usurpers—will, by the very falsity and iniquity of their position, be pushed into deceit, tyranny, and cruelty, ending in downfall.

Thousands of years' experience has proved that government must begin where it ends — with the people; that the general welfare demands that they who exercise the powers and they upon whom these are exercised must be the same, and that higher political ideals can be realized only through higher political forms. Myriads of experiments to get the substance of liberty out of the forms of tyranny, to believe in princes, to trust good men to do good as kings, have taught the inexorable truth that, in the economy of nature, form and substance must move together, and are as inextricably inter-dependent as are, within our experience, what we call matter and spirit. Identical is the lesson we are learning with regard to industrial power and property. We are calling upon their owners, as mankind called upon kings in their day, to be good and kind, wise and sweet, and we are calling in vain. We are asking them not to be what we have made them to be. We put power into their hands and ask them not to use it as power. If this power is a trust for the people, the people betrayed it when they made private estates out of it for individuals. If the spirit of power is to change, institutions must change as much. Liberty recast the old forms of government into the Republic, and it must remould our institutions of wealth into the Commonwealth.

The question is not whether monopoly is to continue. The sun sets every night on a greater majority against it. We are face to face with the practical issue: Is it to go through ruin or reform? Can we forestall ruin by reform? If we wait to be forced by events we shall be astounded to find how much more radical they are than our utopias. Louis XVI. waited until 1793, and gave his head and all his investitures to the people who in 1789 asked only to sit at his feet and speak their mind. Unless we reform of our own free will, nature will reform us by force, as nature does. Our evil courses have already gone too far in producing misery, plagues, hatreds, national enervation. Already the leader is unable to lead, and has begun to drive with judges armed with bayonets and Gatling guns. History is the serial obituary of the men who thought they could drive men.

Reform is the science and conscience with which mankind

in its manhood overcomes temptations and escapes consequences by killing the germs. Ruin is already hard at work
among us. Our libraries are full of the official inquiries and
scientific interpretations which show how our master-motive
is working decay in all our parts. The family crumbles into
a competition between the father and the children whom he
breeds to take his place in the factory, to unfit themselves to
be fathers in their turn. A thorough, stalwart resimplification,
a life governed by simple needs and loves, is the imperative
want of the world. It will be accomplished : either self-con-
scious volition does it, or the slow wreck and decay of superfluous and unwholesome men and matters. The latter is the
method of brutes and brute civilizations. The other is the
method of man, so far as he is divine. Has not man, who
has in personal reform risen above the brute method, come
to the height at which he can achieve social reform in masses
and by nations? We must learn ; we can learn by reason.
Why wait for the crueler teacher?

We have a people like which none has ever existed before.
We have millions capable of conscious co-operation. The
time must come in social evolution when the people can organize the free-will to choose salvation which the individual
has been cultivating for 1900 years, and can adopt a policy
more dignified and more effective than leaving themselves to
be kicked along the path of reform by the recoil of their own
vices. We must bring the size of our morality up to the size
of our cities, corporations, and combinations, or these will be
brought down to fit our half-grown virtue.

Industry and monopoly cannot live together. Our modern perfection of exchange and division of labor cannot last
without equal perfection of morals and sympathy. Every
one is living at the mercy of every one else in a way entirely
peculiar to our times. Nothing is any longer made by a man ;
parts of things are made by parts of men, and become wholes
by the luck of a good-humor which so far keeps men from flying asunder. It takes a whole company to make a match. A
hundred men will easily produce a hundred million matches,

but not one of them could make one match. No farm gets its plough from the cross-roads blacksmith, and no one in the chilled-steel factory knows the whole of the plough. The life of Boston hangs on a procession of reciprocities which must move, as steadily and sweetly as the roll of the planets, between its bakeries, the Falls of St. Anthony, and the valley of the Red River. Never was there a social machinery so delicate. Only on terms of love and justice can men endure contact so close.

The break-down of all other civilizations has been a slow decay. It took the Northerners hundreds of years to march to the Tiber. They grew their way through the old society as the tree planting itself on a grave is found to have sent its roots along every fibre and muscle of the dead. Our world is not the simple thing theirs was, of little groups sufficient to themselves, if need be. New York would begin to die to-morrow if it were not for Illinois and Dakota. We cannot afford a revulsion in the hearts by whose union locomotives run, mills grind, factories make. Practical men are speculating to-day on the possibility that our civilization may some afternoon be flashed away by the tick of a telegraph. All these co-operations can be scattered by a word of hate too many, and we left, with no one who knows how to make a plough or a match, a civilization cut off as by the Roman curse from food and fire. Less sensitive civilizations than ours have burst apart.

Liberty and monopoly cannot live together. What chance have we against the persistent coming and the easy coalescence of the confederated cliques, which aspire to say of all business, "This belongs to us," and whose members, though moving among us as brothers, are using against us, through the corporate forms we have given them, powers of invisibility, of entail and accumulation, unprecedented because impersonal and immortal, and, most peculiar of all, power to act as persons, as in the commission of crimes, with exemption from punishment as persons? Two classes study and practise politics and government: place hunters and privilege hunters. In a world of relativities like ours size of area has a great deal to do with the truth of principles.   America has grown so big— and the tickets to be voted, and the powers of government, and the duties of citizens, and the profits of personal use of public functions have all grown so big—that the average citizen has broken down.   No man can half understand or half operate the fulness of this big citizenship, except by giving his whole time to it.   This the place hunter can do, and the privilege hunter.   Government, therefore—municipal, State, national—is passing into the hands of these two classes, specialized for the functions of power by their appetite for the fruits of power.   The power of citizenship is relinquished by those who do not and cannot know how to exercise it to those who can and do—by those who have a livelihood to make to those who make politics their livelihood.

These specialists of the ward club, the primary, the campaign, the election, and office unite, by a law as irresistible as that of the sexes, with those who want all the goods of government—charters, contracts, rulings, permits.   From this marriage it is easy to imagine that among some other people than ourselves, and in some other century than this, the off-spring might be the most formidable, elusive, unrestrained, impersonal, and cruel tyranny the world has yet seen.   There might come a time when the policeman and the railroad president would equally show that they cared nothing for the citizen, individually or collectively, because aware that they and not he were the government.   Certainly such an attempt to corner "the dear people" and the earth and the fulness thereof will break down.   It is for us to decide whether we will let it go on till it breaks down of itself, dragging down to die, as a savage dies of his vice, the civilization it has gripped with its hundred hands; or whether, while we are still young, still virtuous, we will break it down, self-consciously, as the civilized man, reforming, crushes down the evil.   If we cannot find a remedy, all that we love in the word America must die.   It will be an awful price to pay if this attempt at government of the people, by the people, for the people must perish from off the face of the earth to prove to mankind that political brotherhood cannot survive where industrial brotherhood is denied. But the demonstration is worth even that.

Aristotle's lost books of the Republics told the story of two hundred and fifty attempts at free government, and these were but some of the many that had to be melted down in the crucible of fate to teach Hamilton and Jefferson what they knew. Perhaps we must be melted by the same fierce flames to be a light to the feet of those who come after us. For as true as that a house divided against itself cannot stand, and that a nation half slave and half free cannot permanently endure, is it true that a people who are slaves to market-tyrants will surely come to be their slaves in all else, that all liberty begins to be lost when one liberty is lost, that a people half democratic and half plutocratic cannot permanently endure.

The secret of the history we are about to make is not that the world is poorer or worse. It is richer and better. Its new wealth is too great for the old forms. The success and beauties of our old mutualities have made us ready for new mutualities. The wonder of to-day is the modern multiplication of products by the union of forces; the marvel of to-morrow will be the greater product which will follow when that which is co-operatively produced is co-operatively enjoyed. It is the spectacle of its concentration in the private fortunes of our day which reveals this wealth to its real makers — the whole people — and summons them to extend the manners and institutions of civilization to this new tribal relation.

Whether the great change comes with peace or sword, freely through reform or by nature's involuntary forces, is a mere matter of detail, a question of convenience—not of the essence of the thing. The change will come. With reform, it may come to us. If with force, perhaps not to us. But it will come. The world is too full of amateurs who can play the golden rule as an aria with variations. All the runs and trills and transpositions have been done to death. All the "sayings" have been said. The only field for new effects is in epigrams of practice. Titillation of our sympathies has become a dissipation. We shed a daily tear over the misery of the slums as the toper takes his dram, and our liver becomes torpid with the floods of indignation and sentiment we have guzzled without converting them into their co-efficients of action.

"Regenerate the individual" is a half-truth; the reorganization of the society which he makes and which makes him is the other half. Man alone cannot be a Christian. Institutions are applied beliefs. The love of liberty became liberty in America by clothing itself in the complicated group of structures known as the government of the United States. Love is a half-truth, and kissing is a good deal less than half of that. We need not kiss all our fellow-men, but we must do for them all we ask them to do for us—nothing less than the fullest performance of every power. To love our neighbor is to submit to the discipline and arrangement which make his life reach its best, and so do we best love ourselves.

History has taught us nothing if not that men can continue to associate only by the laws of association. The golden rule is the first and last of these, but the first and last of the golden rule is that it can be operated only through laws, habits, forms, and institutions. The Constitution and laws of the United States are, however imperfectly, the translation into the language of politics of doing as you would be done by—the essence of equal rights and government by consent. To ask individuals to-day to lead by their single sacrifices the life of the brother in the world of business is as if the American colonist had been asked to lead by his individual enterprise the life of the citizen of a republic. That was made possible to him only by union with others. The business world is full of men who yearn to abandon its methods and live the love they feel; but to attempt to do so by themselves would be martyrdom, and that is "caviare to the general." "We admire martyrdom," Mazzini, the martyr, said, "but we do not recommend it." The change must be social, and its martyrdoms have already begun.

The new self-interest will remain unenforced in business until we invent the forms by which the vast multitudes who have been gathered together in modern production can organize themselves into a people there as in government. Nothing but this institutionalization will save them from being scattered away from each other again, and it can be achieved only by such averaging and concessions and co-operations as are the price of all union. These will be gains, not losses. Soldiers become partners in invincibility by the discipline which adopts an average rate of march instead of compelling all to keep step with the fastest and stay with the strongest. Moralists tell men to love each other and the right. How, by doing what things, by leaving what undone, shall men love each other? What have the ethicals to say upon the morality of putting public highways in private hands, and of allowing these private hands to make a private and privileged use of them? If bad, will a mere "change of heart," uninstitutionalized, change them?

New freedoms cannot be operated through the old forms of slavery. The ideals of Washington and Hamilton and Adams could not breathe under kingly rule. Idle to say they might. Under the mutual dependence of the inside and outside of things their change has all through history always been dual. Change of heart is no more redemption than hunger is dinner. We must have honesty, love, justice in the heart of the business world, but for these we must also have the forms which will fit them. These will be very different from those through which the intercourse of man with man in the exchange of services now moves to such ungracious ends. Forms of Asiatic and American government, of early institutions and to-day's, are not more different. The cardinal virtues cannot be established and kept at work in trade and on the highways with the old apparatus. In order that the spirit that gave rebates may go to stay, the rebate itself must go. If the private use of private ownership of highways is to go, the private ownership must go. There must be no private use of public power or public property.

These are created by the common sacrifices of all, and can
be rightfully used only for the common good of all—from
all, by all, for all. All the grants and franchises that have
been given to private hands for private profit are void in
morals and void in that higher law which sets the copy for
the laggard pens of legislatures and judges. "No private use
of public powers" is but a threshold truth. The universe,
says Emerson, is the property of every creature in it.

No home so low it may not hope that out of its fledglings
one may grow the hooked claw that will make him a millionaire. To any adventurer of spirit and prowess in the Italy of
the Renaissance might come the possibility of butchering or
poisoning his way to a castle or a throne. Such prizes of
power made the peninsula a menagerie of tyrants, murderers,
voluptuaries, and multitudes of misery. We got republican
liberty by agreeing each with the other never to seek to become kings or lords or dukes. We can get industrial and
economic liberty only by a like covenant never to let ourselves or any one else be millionaires.

There can be no public prosperity without public virtue,
and no public virtue without private virtue. But private cannot become public except by organization. Our attempts at
control, regulation, are but the agitations of the Gracchi, evi-
dencing the wrong, but not rising to the cure. We are waiting for some genius of good who will generalize into one body
of doctrine our partial truths of reform, and will help us live
the generalization. Never was mankind, across all lines of
race, creed, and institutions, more nearly one in discontent and
restless consciousness of new powers and a new hope and
purpose, never more widely agitated by influences leading in
one direction, never more nearly a committee of the whole on
the question of the day. Never before were the means for
flashing one thought into the minds of the million, and flashing that thought into action, what they are to-day. The good
word or good deed of Chicago in the morning may be the inspiration of Calcutta before nightfall. The crusades were but
an eddy in comparison with the universal tide waiting for an-

other Peter the Hermit to lead us where the Man who is to rise again lies in the hands of the infidel.

Our problem can be read from its good side or its bad, and must be read from both, as: Business has become a vice, and defeats us and itself; or, Humanity quickens its step to add to its fellowships the new brotherhood of labor. The next emancipation, like all emancipations, must destroy and build. The most constructive thinker in history said, Love one another; but he also drove the money-changers from the temple, and denounced the scribes and Pharisees, and has been busy for nineteen hundred years pulling down tenements unfit for the habitation of the soul. We see something new and something old. Old principles run into mania, a wicked old world bursting into suicidal explosion, as Carlyle said of the French Revolution. New loves, new capabilities, new institutions, created by the expansion of old ideals and new opportunities of human contact. Our love of those to whom we have been "introduced" is but unlocking a door through which all men will pass into our hearts. What makes men lovable is not the accident of our knowing them. It is that they are men. Before 1776 there were thirteen patriotisms in America.

The bishops of Boswell's day had no ear for the lamentations of the victims of the slave-trade, but there came a new sympathy which rose superior to their divine displeasure that this commerce of Christian merchants should be attacked. We are coming to sympathize with the animals, and Queen Victoria contributes money to a hospital for the succor of decayed old gentlemen and lady cats. By-and-by royal hearts may widen to include men and women evicted in Ireland, or —worse fate—not evicted from Whitechapel. The spirit that defended the slave-trade now finds its last ditch behind the text, The poor ye have with you always. But a new sympathy rises again, like that which declared that the poor should be free of the slave-trade and slavery, and declares that the poor shall be freed from starvation of body, mind, and soul. Slave-trade, slavery, poverty; the form varies, but against them all runs the refusal of the human heart to be made happy at the cost of the misery of others, and its mathematical knowledge that its quotient of satisfactions will increase with the sum of the happiness of all.

The word of the day is that we are about to civilize industry. Mankind is quivering with its purpose to make men fellow-citizens, brothers, lovers in industry, as it has done with them in government and family, which are also industry. We already have on our shelves the sciences—hygienic, industrial, political, ethical—to free the world almost at a stroke from war, accidents, disease, poverty, and their flowing vices and insanities. The men of these sciences are here at call praying for employment. The people, by the books they read, show themselves to be praying to have them put at work. If we who call ourselves civilization would for one average span devote to life-dealing the moneys, armies, and genius we now give to death-dealing, and would establish over the weaker peoples a protectorate of the United States of Europe and America, we would take a long step towards settling forever the vexed question of the site of the Garden of Eden.

"Human nature," "monotony," and "individuality" are the lions which the reformer is always told will stop the way to a better world. "You cannot change human nature." There are two human natures—the human nature of Christ and of Judas; and Christ prevails. There is the human nature which seeks anonymity, secrecy, the fruits of power without its duties; and there is the human nature which rises against these and, province by province, is abolishing them from human affairs. Men have always been willing to die for their faith. The bad have died as bravely as the good, Charles I. with as smooth a front as Sir Harry Vane. In this readiness to die lies folded every loyalty of life.

"You would make the world a dead level of monotony." Good society does not think it monotonous that all its women should at the same time dust the streets with long-tailed gowns, or that its men should meet every night in funereal black and identical cut, but it shrinks from the monotony of having all share in reforms which would equalize surfeit and starvation. "Good society" is still to come, and it will find some better definition of "monotony" than a fair share for all—a better definition of variety than too much for ourselves at the cost of too little for all others. Shall we choose the monotony of sharing with every one under George III. or Alexander II. the denial of all right to participate in the supreme power, or shall we choose the monotony of sharing with every fellow-citizen the right to become President?—the monotony of being forbidden to enter all the great livelihoods, some syndicate blocking each way with "This business belongs to us"? Or the monotony of a democracy, where every laborer has equal rights with all other citizens to decide upon the administration of the common toil for the common welfare, and an equal right with every other to rise to be a Captain of Industry? Such are the alternatives of "monotony." We have made an historic choice in one; now for the other.

And "individuality." "You are going to destroy individuality." We can become individual only by submitting to be bound to others. We extend our freedom only by finding new laws to obey. Life outside the law is slavery on as many sides as there are disregarded laws. The locomotive off its tracks is not free. The more relations, ties, duties, the more "individual." The isolated man is the mere rudiment of an individual. But he who has become citizen, neighbor, friend, brother, son, husband, father, fellow-member, in one, is just by so many times individualized. Men's expanding powers of co-operation bring them to the conscious ability to unite for new benefits; but this extension of individuality is forbidden in the name of individuality. There are two individualities: that of the dullard, who submits to take his railroad transportation, his light, his coal, his salt, his reaping-machine at such prices and of such quality as arbitrary power forces upon him, and that of the shrewder man who, by an alliance of the individualities of all, supplies himself at his own price.

Time carries us so easily we do not realize how fast we move. This social debate has gone far beyond the question whether change there must be. What shall the change be? is the subject all the world is discussing. Exposure of abuses no longer excites more than a languid interest. But every clear plan how things might be rearranged raises the people. Before every revolution marches a book—the *Contrat Social*, *Uncle Tom's Cabin*. "Every man nowadays," says Emerson, "carries a revolution in his vest-pocket." The book which sells more copies than any other of our day abroad and at home, debated by all down to the boot-blacks as they sit on the curb-stones, is one calling men to draw from their success in insur-ing each other some of the necessaries of life the courage to move on to insure each other all the necessaries of life, bid-ding them abandon the self-defeating anarchy which puts rail-road-wreckers at the head of railroads and famine-producers at the head of production, and inspiring them to share the common toil and the fruits of the toil under the ideals which make men Washingtons and Lincolns. You may question the importance of the plan ; you cannot question the importance of its welcome. It shows the people gath-ering-points for the new constitution they know they must make.

In nothing has liberty justified itself more thoroughly than in the resolute determination spreading among the American people to add industrial to political independence. It is the hope of the world that good has its effects as well as evil, and that on the whole, and in the long-run, the seed of the good will overgrow the evil. "Heaven has kindly given our blood a moral flow." Liberty breeds liberties, slavery breeds sla-veries, but the liberties will be the strongest stock. If the political and religious liberties which the people of this coun-try aspired to set up had in them the real sap and fibre of a better life than the world had yet known, it must certainly follow that they would quicken and strengthen the people for discovery and obedience in still higher realms. And just this has happened. Nowhere else has the new claim to tax with-out representation been so quickly detected, so intelligently scrutinized, and so bravely fought. Nowhere else has this spreading plague of selfishness and false doctrine found a people whose average and general life was pitched on so high a level that they instantly took the alarm at its claims over their lives and liberties. It has found a people so disciplined by the aspiration and achievement of political and religious rights that they are already possessed of a body of doctrine capable, by an easy extension, of refuting all the pretensions of the new absolutism. At the very beginning of this new democratic life among the nations it was understood that to be safe liberty must be complete on its industrial as well as on its political and religious sides. This is the American principle. "Give a man power over my subsistence," said Alexander Hamilton, "and he has power over the whole of my moral being." To submit to such a power gives only the alternative of death or degradation, and the high spirit of America preferred then, as it prefers now, the rule of right, which gives life.

The mania of business has reached an acuter and extremer development in America than elsewhere, because nowhere else have bounteous nature and free institutions produced birthrights and pottages so well worth "swapping." But the follies and wickedness of business have nowhere been so sharply challenged as in free America. "Betake yourself to America," said Carlyle to a friend beginning a literary career; "there you can utter your freest thoughts in ways impossible here." It is to this stern wakefulness of a free people that the world owes it that more light has been thrown in America than in any other country on the processes of modern money-making. A free press, organ of a free people, has done invaluable service. The legislatures have pushed investigation after investigation into the ways in which large masses of the people have been deprived, for the benefit of single men or groups of men, of rights of subsistence and government. Through the courts the free people have pursued their depredators by civil and criminal process, by public and private prosecutions. Imperfect and corrupt, these agencies of press, courts, legislatures have often been; they have still done a work which has either been left undone altogether in other

34

countries, or has been done with but a fraction of our thoroughness.

It is due to them that there exists in the reports of legislative investigations, State and national, in the proceedings of lawsuits and criminal trials, in the files of the newspapers, a mass of information which cannot be found in any other community in the world. There is in these archives an accumulation of the raw material of tragedy, comedy, romance, ravellings of the vicissitudes of human life, and social and personal fate, which will feed the fires of whole generations of literary men when once they awake to the existence of these precious rolls. In these pigeon-holes are to be found keys of the present and clews to the future. As America has the newest and widest liberty, it is the stage where play the newest and widest forces of evil as well as good. America is at the front of the forward line of evolution. It has taken the lead in developing competition to the extreme form in which it destroys competition, and in superfining the processes of exchange of services into those of the acquisition of the property of others without service.

The hope is that the old economic system we inherited has ripened so much more rapidly than the society and government we have created that the dead matter it deposits can be thrown off by our vigorous youth and health. "It is high time our bad wealth came to an end," says Emerson. It has grown into its monstrous forms so fast that the dullest eye can separate it from the Commonwealth, and the slowest mind comprehend its mischievousness. In making themselves free of arbitrary and corrupt power in government the Americans prepared themselves to be free in all else, and because foremost in political liberty they have the promise of being the first to realize industrial liberty—the trunk of a tree of which political liberty is the seed, and without which political liberty shrinks back into nothingness.

"The art of Italy will blossom over our graves," Mazzini said when, with true insight, he saw that the first artistic, first literary task before the Italians was to make their country free. Art, literature, culture, religion, in America, are already beginning to feel the restrictive pressure which results from the domination of a selfish, self-indulgent, luxurious, and anti-social power. This power, mastering the markets of a civilization which gives its main energies to markets, passes without difficulty to the mastery of all the other activities. When churches, political campaigns, the expounding of the law, maintenance of schools and colleges, and family life itself all depend on money, they must become servile to the money power. Song, picture, sermon, decrees of court, and the union of hearts must pass constantly under stronger control of those who give their lives to trade and encourage everybody else to trade, confident that the issue of it all will be that they will hold as property, in exclusive possession, to be doled out on their own terms, the matter by which alone man can live, either materially or spiritually.

In America, where the supreme political power and much of the government of church and college have been taken out of traditional hands and subjected to the changing determinations of popular will, it has inevitably resulted that the State, church, and school have passed under this mercantile aristocracy to a far greater extent than in other countries where stiffer régimes under other and older influences still stand. Our upper classes—elected, as always, by the equipoise of effort and opinion between them and the lower classes—are, under this commercial system, the men who trade best, who can control their features and their consciences so that they can always get more than they give, who can play with supply and demand so that at the end of the game all their brethren are their tributaries for life. It is the birthright-buying minds that, by the adoption of this ideal, we choose for our rulers. The progressive races have altered their ideals of kings with the indescribable advantage of being ruled by Washingtons and Lincolns and Gladstones instead of Caligulas and Pharaohs. We have now to make a similar step forward in another part of life. The previous changes expressed outwardly an inner change of heart. The reformer of to-day is simply he who, with quicker ear, detecting that another change of heart is going on, goes before.

Another great change is working in the inner mind of man, and will surely be followed by incorporation in institutions and morals and manners. The social head and heart are both being persuaded that too many are idle—rich and poor; too many are hurt in body and soul—rich and poor; too many children are "exposed," as in the old Greek and Roman market-places; too many are starving within reach of too much fertile waste; too many passions of envy, greed, and hate are raging among rich and poor. There is too much left undone that ought to be done along the whole scale of life, from the lowest physical to the highest spiritual needs, from better roads to sweeter music and nobler worship. It cannot be long, historically speaking, before all this new sense and sentiment will issue in acts. All will be as zealously protected against the oppression of the cruel in their daily labor as now against oppression from invader or rioter, and will be as warmly cheered in liberty to grow to their fullest capabilities as laborers—*i.e.*, users of matter for the purpose of the spirit—as they are now welcomed to the liberty of the citizen and the worshipper. Infinite is the fountain of our rights. We can have all the rights we will create. All the rights we will give we can have. The American people will save the liberties they have inherited by winning new ones to bequeath.

With this will come fruits of new faculty almost beyond calculation. A new liberty will put an end to pauperism and millionairism and the crimes and death-rate born of both wretchednesses, just as the liberty of politics and religion put an end to martyrs and tyrants. The new liberty is identical in principle and purpose with the other; it is made inevitable by them. Those who love the liberties already won must open the door to the new, unless they wish to see them all take flight together. There can be no single liberty. Liberties go in clusters like the Pleiades.

We must either regulate, or own, or destroy, perishing by

the sword we take. The possibility of regulation is a dream. As long as this control of the necessaries of life and this wealth remain private with individuals, it is they who will regulate, not we. The policy of regulation, disguise it as we may, is but moving to a compromise and equilibrium within the evil all complain of. It is to accept the principle of the sovereignty of the self-interest of the individual and apply constitutional checks to it. The unprogressive nations palter in this method with monarchy. But the wits of America are equal to seeing that as with kingship and slavery so with poverty—the weeding must be done at the roots. Sir Henry Sumner Maine says mankind moves from status to contract; from society ruled by inherited customs to one ruled by agreement, varied according to circumstances. Present experience suggests the addition that the movement, like all in nature, is pendulous, and that mankind moves progressively from status to contract, and from this stage of contract to another status. We march and rest and march again. If our society is settling down to an interval of inertia, perhaps ages long, we must before night comes establish all in as much equality and comfort as possible.

The aspirations are not new. We have had them since Plato. The knowledge of means for realizing them is not new. We have had it since Aristotle, and the history of civilization is but the record of the progressive embodiment of the ideals in institutions for the life together—sexual, social, spiritual. What is new in our moment is that mankind's accumulating forces are preparing for another step forward in this long processional realization of its best possible. Nothing so narrow as the mere governmentalizing of the means and processes of production. It is only the morally nerveless who ask government to do that which they will not rise to do. The conversion which is now working itself out within us, and perhaps is more nearly born than we suspect ("We shall not live to see slavery abolished," said Emerson, in 1859) is making itself felt on all sides of our life. In manners, in literature, in marriage, in church, in all, we see at work the saving ferment which is to make all things new by bringing them nearer to the old ideals. George Sand was revolted by the servile accent of the phrase of her day, "Madame est servie." Society has grown to the better fellowship her finer ear found wanting in these words, and is now told it is dinner, not madame or monsieur, that is served.

We are to have, of course, great political changes. We are to apply the co-operative methods of the post-office and the public school to many other common toils, to all toils in which private sovereignty has become through monopoly a despotism over the public, and to all in which the association of the people and the organization of processes have been so far developed that the profit - hunting Captain of Industry may be replaced by the public-serving Captain of Industry. But we are to have much more. We are to have a private life of a new beauty, of which these are to be merely the mechanical exhibitions on the side of politics. We are to move among each other, able, by the methodical and agreed adherence of all, to do what the words of Lamennais mean, instead of being able, as now, in most things, to afford only an indulgence in feeling them. We are to be commoners, travellers to Altruria.

We are to become fathers, mothers, for the spirit of the father and mother is not in us while we can say of any child it is not ours, and leave it in the grime. We are to become men, women, for to all about reinforcing us we shall insure full growth and thus insure it to ourselves. We are to become gentlemen, ladies, for we will not accept from another any service we are not willing to return in kind. We are to become honest, giving when we get, and getting with the knowledge and consent of all. We are to become rich, for we shall share in the wealth now latent in idle men and idle land, and in the fertility of work done by those who have ceased to withstand but stand with each other. As we walk our parks we already see that by saying "thine" to every neighbor we say "mine" of palaces, gardens, art, science, far beyond any possible to selfishness, even the selfishness of kings. We shall become patriots, for the heart will know why it thrills to the flag. Those folds wave the salute of a greater love than that of the man who will lay down his life for his friend. There floats the banner of the love of millions, who, though they do not know you and have never seen you, will die for you and are living for you, doing in a thousand services unto you as you would be done by. And the little patriotism, which is the love of the humanity fenced within our frontier will widen into the reciprocal service of all men. Generals were, merchants are, brothers will be, humanity's representative men.

There is to be a people in industry, as in government. The same rising genius of democracy which discovered that mankind did not co-operate in the State to provide a few with palaces and king's-evil, is disclosing that men do not co-operate in trade for any other purpose than to mobilize the labor of all for the benefit of all, and that the only true guidance comes from those who are led, and the only valid titles from those who create. Very wide must be the emancipation of this new self-interest. If we free America we shall still be not free, for the financial, commercial, possessory powers of modern industrial life are organized internationally. If we rose to the full execution of the first, simplest, and most pressing need of our times and put an end to all private use of public powers, we should still be confronted by monopolies existing simply as private property, as in coal-mines, oil lands.

It is not a verbal accident that science is the substance of the word conscience. We must know the right before we can do the right. When it comes to know the facts the human heart can no more endure monopoly than American slavery or Roman empire. The first step to a remedy is that the people care. If they know, they will care. To help them to know and care; to stimulate new hatred of evil, new love of the good, new sympathy for the victims of power, and, by enlarging its science, to quicken the old into a new conscience, this compilation of fact has been made. Democracy is not a lie. There live in the body of the commonalty the unexhausted virtue and the ever-refreshened strength which can rise equal to any problems of progress. In the hope of tapping some reserve of their powers of self-help this story is told to the people.

APPENDIX

PARTIAL LIST OF TRADE COMBINATIONS, OR TRUSTS, ACHIEVED OR ATTEMPTED, AND OF THE COMMODITIES COVERED BY THEM [1]

I.—LIGHT, HEAT, AND POWER

Boilers, for house heating.

Candle-makers, Great Britain, United States.

Coal: anthracite, bituminous.

Coke.

Electric: carbon points, 1885; candles, 1888; electric goods, national, 1887; lighting, United States, Great Britain, 1882; light-fixtures, national, 1889.

Gas: illuminating and fuel, local, sectional, national; fixtures, national; pipes, 1875; natural.

Gasoline stoves, 1894.

Governors of steam-boilers.

Hot-water heaters, 1892.

House furnaces, 1889.

Kerosene, 1874.

Kindling wood, Boston, 1891.

Matches: United States; Great Britain; Canada; Sweden; international, 1894.

Paraffine.

Petroleum and its products, 1874.

Radiators, steam and hot-water, Western, 1891.

Scotch mineral oil, 1888.

Steam and hot-water master fitters, national, 1889.

Stearine.

Stove-boards, zinc, national, 1890.

Stoves and ranges, 1872.

Stoves, vapor, national, 1884.

II.—CHEMICALS

Acids: acetic, citric, muriatic, nitric, sulphuric, American, 1889; oxalic, Great Britain, 1882.

Alkali Union, England, 1888.

Alkaloids, United States.

Alum, sectional, 1889.

Ammonia, 1889.

Bismuth salts, United States.

Bleaching-powder, England, 1888.

Boracic acid, United States.

Borax: United States; Great Britain, 1888.

Chemical Union, England, 1890.

Chloroform, United States.

Drug manufacturers: United States; Canada, 1884.

Iodine, England, 1890.

Iodoform, United States, 1880.

Lime, acetate of, 1891.

Mercurials: as calomel, corrosive sublimate, etc., United States.

Nitrates, Chili, 1884.

Paris-green, 1889.

Potash: bichromate of, Great Britain; bichloride of, United States; chlorate, prussiate, Great Britain, 1888.

Quinine, international, 1893.

Rochelle salts, United States.

Saltpetre.

Santonine, United States.

Soda, bichromate, United States; carbonate, caustic, England, 1888; nitrate of, Chili and England, 1884.

Strychnine.

Sulphur, Italy.

Ultramarine: United States; Germany, 1890.

Vitriol, 1889.

III.—METALS

Aluminum, national, 1888.

Barbed wire, 1881.

Brass: sectional, 1884; rolled and sheet, sheet German silver, copper rivets and burrs, copper and German-silver wire, kerosene-oil burners and lamp trimmings, and braised brass tubing.

Copper: cold, bolt, rolled, sheet, 1888; ore, Lake Superior, 1879; international, 1887; bath-tubs, boilers, sinks, and general ware, 1891; wire.

Iron: founders; galvanized, national, 1875; malleable, national, 1882; manufacturers, Germany, 1887; nuts, 1884; ore, Germany, 1884, Atlantic coast, 1886, Michigan, 1882, Southern, 1884, Northwestern, 1887, Lake Superior, 1893; pig, Eastern, Southern, 1883, national, 1889; pipes, steam and gas, 1884; wrought iron, 1887; sheet, enamelled, Germany, 1893; structural, national, 1881; tubes, 1884; wire-cloth, national, 1882; Russian, 1893.

Lead: pig, pipe; sheet-lead, 1888; white, national, 1884.

Mica, national, 1887.

Nickel.

Quicksilver, California.

Silver and lead smelters.

Steel: armor-plate, Bessemer beams (in existence nearly thirty years), castings, 1894; galvanized; rails (see traffic and travel); rods, United States and Germany, 1888; rolling-mills.

Tin: jobbers; American, national, 1883; English, 1889.

Zinc.

IV.—SOME OTHER INSTRUMENTS AND MATERIALS OF INDUSTRY

Alcohol.

Axes and axe-poles.

Belting, leather, rubber.

Blankets (press), American Paper-makers' Felt and Jacket Association.

Bobbins, spools, and shuttles, 1886, for cotton, woollen, silk, and linen mills.

Bolts, 1884.

Boxes, wooden, local, 1885; Western and Southern.

Bridge-builders: Eastern, 1886; Iowa, Nebraska, Kansas, Missouri, 1889.

Butchers' skewers and supplies, Western, 1889.

Carpet yarns, Eastern, 1889.

Cash-registers, national, 1890.

Celluloid, lythoid, zylonite, Eastern, 1890.

Chains, national, 1883.

Color trust, Great Britain, 1889.

Cordage: rope, twine, United States, 1875; England, 1892.

Corks.

Cotton duck, national, 1891.

Cotton-seed oil, national, 1884.

Creels, for cloth and woollen mills, national, 1893.

Damasks, Pennsylvania, 1886.

Emery wheels, national.

Felting.

Fibre, indurated, pails, bowls, measures, water-coolers, filters, etc., national, 1888.

Files, 1875.

Fire-brick, 1875.

Fish-oil, menhaden, New England, 1885.

Forge companies, national, 1889.

Glass bottles: beer, United States, 1884; green glass, English bottle manufacturers, 1889.

Glass: flint, Western, 1891; crown, cylinder, unpolished; plate, French, 1888; German, 1887; international, 1890; window, 1875; sectional, national, international, 1884.

Glass, plate, Underwriters, 1894.

Glue.

Gutta-percha.

Hardware manufacturers, 1884.

Label printers.

Leather: belting, national; board, national, 1891; hides, Northwestern, 1888; morocco, Eastern, 1886; patent, national, 1888; sole, 1893; Tanners' Association, 1882; Oak Harness Leather Tanners, national, 1890.

Linen mills, Eastern, Western, 1892.

Linseed oil: local, 1877; national, 1887; dealers, Canada, 1892.

Manilla, international, 1887.

Oil: lubricating, 1874; for curing leather; menhaden; safety burning oil for miners.

Onyx, Mexican, 1890.

Paper: local, sectional, national; bags, Eastern and Western, 1887; book and newspaper; boxes, national, 1883; card-board, 1890; flour sacks, 1887; straw; tissue, 1892; wrapping, Western, 1878, Eastern, 1881; writing, national, 1884. Papermakers' trust in Great Britain to check the operation of the Alkali trust, 1889; Papermakers' Felt and Jacket Association, national; rags, Eastern, 1883; wood-pulp, Western, 1890; New York, Canada, Eastern, 1891.

Pitch, national, 1887 or earlier.

Planes, carpenters'.

Pumps, national, 1871.

Rubber: belting, 1875; electric web goring (for shoes), national, 1893; gossamers, 1887; hose, 1875; importers, national, 1882; manufacturers, national, 1882; Brazil producers, 1890; stamps and stencils, national, 1893.

Sandpaper, emery and emery cloth, flint, garnet, ruby, sand cloth, national, 1887.

Saws, national, 1890.

Scales.

Screws: machine, 1887; wood, national, international.

Seed Crushers' Union, England, 1889.

Sewer pipe, 1875.

Sewing-machines, 1885.

Sewing-machine supplies, New York and New England, 1883.

Spirits.

Straw braid.

Straw-board, 1887.

Tacks, 1875.

Talc mills, New York, 1893.

Tar, national, 1886.

Teasel, national, 1892.

Textile manufacturers, Pennsylvania, 1886—embracing dress goods, ginghams, upholstery goods, woollens, yarns, chintzes, worsteds, damasks.

Tools, edge, American Axe and Edged Tool Company, national, 1890.

Turpentine, Southern, 1892.

Type founders, national, 1888.

Washers, 1884.

Watch-cases, 1886.

Well tools, for oil, gas, and artesian wells, 1889.

Wood, excelsior, shavings for packing, national, 1889.

Wooden-ware, 1883 or earlier.

Wood-working machines, 1891.

Wool felt.

Wrenches, 1875.

V.—TRAFFIC AND TRAVEL

The Road, Horse, and Wagon

Bicycles, United States, 1893. Board of Trade formed to regulate prices.

Bicycle tires.

Bridge-builders, 1886.

Buggy pails, fibre trust, national, 1888.

Carriage builders, national, 1884.

Carriage hardware, 1884.

Harness dealers, manufacturers, national, 1886.

Liverymen's Associations, local, 1884.

Paving: asphalt, 1886; brick, Western, 1892; pitch, national, 1887.

Road-making machines, Western, 1890.

Saddlery Association, national, 1891.

Saddle-trees, Indiana, Missouri, 1892.

Wagons, local, 1886.

Wheels, Western, 1889.
Whips, national, 1892.

Shipping

Ballast, Havana, 1882.
Canal-boats, 1884.
Cotton duck, sail-cloth, national, 1888.
Ferries, New York and Brooklyn.
Lake carriers, Hull pool, 1886.
Lake Dock Trust.
Marine insurance, 1883.
Naval stores.
Ocean steamers : European, Asiatic, and American ; German steamship companies, 1894.
Pilotage, New York, San Francisco.
Steamboats : in the Cincinnati and New Orleans trade, 1884 ; forwarding lines along the Hudson River, 1891.

Railroads

Car-axles, 1890.
Car-springs, steel, national, 1887.
Cars, freight and cattle.
Elevators, grain, local, Western, 1887.
Express companies.
Locomotives : national, 1892 ; boiler flues, 1875 ; tires, national, 1892.
Railroad : pools, freight and passenger, sectional, national ; Eastern Railroad Association, of 800 railroads, to fight patents.
Steel sleepers, 1885 ; steel rails, national.
Street railways, local, sectional.

VI.—BUILDING

Asbestos, for paints, roofing, steam-pipe and boiler coverings, 1891.
Beams and channels, iron and steel, national, 1875.
Blinds : Northwestern, 1885 ; national, 1888.
Brass, gas, plumbing, steam, water goods, 1884.
Brick : local, sectional, 1884 ; Chicago, New York, New Jersey, Washington (State) ; pressed brick, 1890.

Cement : Mississippi valley, 1883 ; Eastern, 1884 ; Northwestern, 1884.
Cornice-makers, national, 1884.
Doors : Northwestern, 1885 ; national, 1888.
Fire engines, including hook and ladder trucks, hose-carriages, heaters, carts, stationary pumps, and other supplies, United States and Canada, 1892.
Fire insurance.
Glue, national, 1894.
Gypsum stucco, Eastern, Northwestern, 1884.
Hinges, 1875.
Lime, Western, 1883.
Lumber : California pine, 1883 ; California redwood, 1883 ; Chicago ; Mississippi valley ; Northwestern, 1880 ; Pacific coast, 1883 ; poplar, 1889 ; Puget Sound, 1883 ; yellow pine, Southern, 1890, Eastern, 1891 ; dealers, national, 1878.
Nails : Pennsylvania, 1875 ; Western Association, 1882 ; Atlantic States Association, 1883.
Paint.
Plaster, national, 1891.
Roofing : felt ; iron ; pitch, Vermont, national, 1887.
Sanitary pottery.
Sash, doors, and blinds, national.
Sewer pipes, national, 1884.
Stone : brown stone, Lake Superior, 1890, New York, 1884 ; cut-stone quarry owners, Western, 1892 ; freestone ; granite, national, 1891 ; limestone, rubble, and flag, Illinois, 1884 ; marble, Western dealers, 1885, Vermont marble quarries, 1889 ; sandstone, New York, 1883.
Structural steel.
Stucco, 1883.
Varnish dealers, national, 1888.
Wall-paper : national, 1879 ; international, 1882.

VII.—FARM AND PLANTATION

Agricultural implements, manufacturers, dealers, 1891.

Binders, Harvester Trust, 1883.
Churns, 1884.
Corn-harvesters, national, 1892.
Cotton bagging, 1888.
Cotton presses, local, 1892.
Drain tile, Indiana, 1894.
Fencing, barbed wire, national, 1881.
Fertilizers : 1888 ; guano ; menhaden oil, New England, 1885 ; phosphate, South Carolina, 1887 ; Canada, 1890 ; Florida, 1891.
Forks, national, 1890.
Harrow manufacturers, national, 1890.
Harvesting-machines, national, 1883.
Hay-presses, national, 1889.
Hay tools, Western and Northwestern, 1884.
Hoes, national, 1890.
Horse-brushes, prison-made, 1889.
Jute grain bags, national, 1888.
Mowers, national, 1883.
Pails, fibre trust, national, 1888.
Paris green.
Ploughs, Northwestern, 1884.
Rakes, national, 1890.
Reapers, 1883.
Scythe-makers, national, 1884.
Shovels, national, 1890.
Snath manufacturers, national, 1891.
Threshing - machines, national, 1890, 1891.
Twine, binding, 1887.
Vehicles.

VIII.—SCHOOL, LIBRARY, AND COUNTING-ROOM

Blank-books, 1888.
Envelopes, 1888.
Lead-pencils, 1878.
Lithographic printers, national, 1892.
Novels (paper-covered "libraries "),1890.
School-books, national, 1884.
School-furniture, national, 1892.
Slates and slate-pencils, national, 1887.
Subscription - books, local, sectional, 1892.
Type-founders, national, 1888.
Type-writers.
Writing-paper, national, 1884.

IX.—" THE SHOT HEARD ROUND THE WORLD "

Ammunition, 1883.
Arms, 1883.
Cartridges, national, 1883.
Dynamite, Germany.
Fireworks, national, 1890.
Gunpowder, national, 1875.
Guns, 1883.
Shot-tower companies, national, 1873.

X.—FOR THE PERSON

Barbers, National Tonsorial Parlor Company, organized to establish barber-shops in all the large cities of the United States, 1890.
Buttons.
Calico, England, 1891.
Clothes-brushes, prison-made, 1889.
Coat and cloak manufacturers : New York, 1883 ; Chicago, 1893.
Collars and cuffs, New York, 1890.
Cotton : England, 1890 ; Fall River ; Southern mills, 1881 ; thread (spool-cotton), 1888.
Diamonds : mines in South Africa ; dealers in Europe, 1889.
Dress-goods, Pennsylvania, 1886.
Furs.
Ginghams, Pennsylvania, 1886.
Gloves, New York.
Hats : fur, 1885 ; woollen, national.
Knit goods : New York, 1884 ; Western, 1889.
Jewellers, national.
Laundries : Chicago ; Chinese Laundry Union, New York City, 1889 ; St. Louis, 1893.
Pocket-knives, national, 1892.
Ribbons, national, 1892.
Rubber boots and shoes, national, 1882.
Seal-skin, national, 1892.
Shirts : Troy, New York City, 1890.
Shoe : manufacturers, national, 1887 ; retailers, New England, 1885, national, 1886.
Silk : manufacturers, international. France , England, Italy, Germany,

1888; sewing, national, 1887; ribbon, 1884.

Trunks, national, 1892.

Umbrellas, Eastern, 1891.

Watch: manufacturers, makers and jewellers, national, 1886; National Association of Jobbers of American Watches and Cases, 1886.

Woollens: manufacturers, 1882; worsteds, yarns, Pennsylvania, 1886.

XI.—SMOKING AND DRINKING

Beer, United States Brewers' Association, 1861.

Champagne, New York City, 1889; France, 1891.

Meerschaum pipes, New Jersey, 1892.

Soda fountains, 1890.

Spittoons, fibre trust, national, 1888.

Tobacco and cigars, local, sectional, national, 1882; cigarettes, 1890.

Waters, mineral, national, 1889.

Whiskey and "domestic"— or artificial—brandy, rum, gin, and cordials made in imitation of the genuine.

Wine-growers, California, 1889.

XII.—"HOME, SWEET HOME"

In General

Candles, coal, furnaces, gas, oil, matches, ranges, stoves, etc. (see Light, Heat, and Power).

Carpets: Eastern, 1885; Brussels, ingrain, 1888.

Chairs: cane, 1889; manufacturers, Western, 1880; seats, perforated, national, 1888.

Furniture: national, 1883; Chicago manufacturers, 1886; retailers, New England, 1888; national, 1893.

Hair-cloth, Rhode Island, 1893.

Oil-cloth, table and stair, Oil-cloth Association, 1887.

Pails, fibre trust, national, 1888.

Soap, national, 1890.

Upholsterers' felt.

Upholstery goods, textile manufacturers, Pennsylvania, 1886.

Window-shades, 1888.

The Kitchen

Boilers.

Bottles.

Brooms, 1886.

Brushes, scrubbing, prison-made, 1889.

Chopping-bowls, wooden-ware, national, 1884.

Crockery, national, 1883.

Fruit-jars, 1891.

Glass-ware, 1883.

Hollow-ware, prison-made, 1888.

Keelers, fibre trust, national, 1888.

Kettles, prison-made, 1888.

Lamp-chimneys, 1883.

Measures, fibre trust, national, 1888.

Pans and pots, prison-made, 1888.

Potato-mashers, wooden-ware, national, 1884.

Pottery, yellow-ware, national, 1889.

Sinks, copper.

Stamped-ware, national, 1882.

Tin-ware: national, 1883; English, 1889.

Water-coolers, filters, pails, fibre trust, national, 1888.

Water-pails, wooden-ware, national, 1884.

Wooden-ware, national, 1884.

Laundry

Borax.

Clothes-pins, New York, 1888.

Clothes-wringers.

Soap, national, 1890.

Soda, 1884.

Starch: Western, 1882; national, 1890.

Washboards, New York, 1888.

Wash-tubs, wooden-ware, national, 1884.

Washing-machines, national, 1891.

Water-tubs, fibre trust, national, 1888.

Zinc, sheet, 1890.

Dining-room

Butter-dishes, 1886.

China, England, 1888.

Glass table-ware, 1889.

Plated-ware.
Silver-plated ware.
Silver-ware, national, 1892.
Table cutlery, national, 1881.
Table oil-cloth, national, 1888.
Tables, extension-tables, national, 1893.

Parlor

For carpets, furniture, upholstery, etc.,
  see under ",In General," above.
Mantel lambrequin, wool felt, 1888.
Music, books and instruments, Boston,
  New York, Chicago, Cincinnati, 1892.
Organs, local, sectional, 1889.
Parlor frame manufacturers.
Parlor furniture, Western Association,
  1886.
Pianos, local, sectional, 1889; national,
  1893.
Piano-covers, wool felt, 1888.
Picture-frames, 1890.
Rugs, Eastern, 1885.
Table-covers, wool felt, 1888.
Tapestries, Eastern, 1885.

Bath-room

Bath-tubs (see " Copper ").
Sanitary-ware, 1889.
Sponges, Florida, New York, 1892.

Bedroom

Chintzes, Pennsylvania, 1886.
Looking-glass: French silvered plate-
  glass, 1888; German, national, 1887;
  international, 1890.
Spring beds, national, 1890.
Wire mattress: Northwestern, 1886;
  national, 1890.

XIII.—"OUR DAILY BREAD"

Bread, biscuit, crackers, local, sec-
  tional, national.
Butter, local, 1889.
Candy, local, national, 1884.
Canned goods: Western, 1885; national,
  1889; California canned fruit, 1891.
Cider and vinegar, national, 1882.
Coffee, Arbuckle trust, 1888.
Corn-meal, Western, 1894.

Cotton-seed oil.
Dairy Association, national, 1893.
Eggs, local, in United States and Canada.
Fish: England, 1749 and before; New
  York and New England, 1892; salm-
  on, Alaska, 1891; salmon canners
  of the Pacific coast, 1893; sardines,
  Eastern, 1885; international, 1890;
  sardine canneries, Canada, 1893.
Flour: United States, National Millers'
  Association, 1883; winter wheat
  mills, national, 1888; spring wheat
  mills of the United States; millers of
  northeast England, 1889; rye flour,
  local, 1891; flour-mills of Utah and
  Colorado, 1892.
Food Manufacturers' Association, United
  States, 1891.
Fruit: bananas, Southern, 1888; California fruit-growers, 1892; cranber-
  ries, Cape Cod, 1888; England, 1884;
  Florida, 1889; foreign fruit, New
  York, 1884; Fruit-trade Association,
  New York, 1882; fruit-growers of
  the Eastern and Middle States against
  commission-merchants, 1887; pre-
  serves and jellies, Western, 1883;
  American Preservers' Company, 1889;
  prunes, California; strawberry-grow-
  ers, Wisconsin, 1892; watermelons,
  Indiana, South Carolina, 1889.
Grape-growers, northern Ohio, 1894.
Grocers: wholesale, retail; local, sec-
  tional, national.
Honey, local, 1888.
Ice: local, sectional, 1883; artificial,
  Southern, 1889.
Lard-refiners, Eastern, 1887.
Meat and cattle: beef, mutton, pork;
  Butchers' National Protective Association; Chicago packers; Inter-
  mountain Stock-growers' Associa-
  tion, Utah, 1893; International Cattle
  Range Association; Live-stock Asso-
  ciation, 1887; Northwest Texas Live-
  stock Association, 1878; Western
  Kansas Stock-growers' Association,
  1883; Wyoming Stock-growers' Association, 1874.

Milk: local, sectional, 1883; condensed milk, New York, Illinois, 1891.

Oatmeal, 1885; Canada, 1887.

Olive-oil.

Oysters, local, 1890.

Pea-nuts, 1888.

Pickles, national, 1891.

Produce: Produce Commission - merchants, eight large cities — North, South, East, West, 1883; West, 1888.

Raisins, California, 1894.

Rice-mills, Southern, 1888.

Salt: rock; English Salt Union, 1888; international, United States and Canada, 1889; Canada, 1891.

Sugar: Hawaii, 1876; United States, 1887. Glucose, national, 1883; international, 1891.

Wine, California, 1894.

XIV.—LIFE AND DEATH

Artificial teeth, United States, 1889.

Castor-oil, 1885.

Cocoa-nut oil, American importers, 1881.

Coffins, National Burial - case Association, 1884.

Dental machines and supplies, United States, 1889.

Drugs: importers; druggists, retail, sectional, national, 1883; wholesale, sectional, national, 1884; Canada, 1874; manufacturers, national, 1884.

Ergot, 1891.

Glycerine, New York, 1888.

Life insurance, 1883, national, 1891.

Patent medicines, national, 1884.

Peppermint, local, 1887.

Quinine, 1882.

Tombstones, local, Brooklyn, Chicago, 1891.

Vaseline.

XV.—MISCELLANEOUS

Athletic clubs, 1893, to reduce charges made by prize-fighters for exhibition.

Base-ball, national, 1876.

Billiard-tables and furniture, 1884.

Bill-posters, United States, Canada, 1872.

Dime museums, national, 1883.

Landlords' Union, London, England, 1890.

News-dealers, 1884; newspapers, Associated Press, United Press; sectional, national.

Photographers, national, 1889.

Playing-cards.

Printers, show and job, 1893.

Racing trust, jockey club, 1894.

Retailers, 1891. Small retail storekeepers of Kansas City protest against mammoth department stores.

Safes, national, 1892.

Theatrical trust, Interstate Amusement Company, Springfield, Ill., 1894.

Warehouses: Brooklyn, 1887; national, 1891.

INDEX

Abusive language, use of, 319, 485.
Acme Oil Company, Samuel Van Syckel
    vs., 187.
Adams, H. C., quoted on municipal mo-
    nopolies, 322.
Adulteration of liquors, 27.
Advice of counsel, 249.
Alcohol in industry and politics, 20.
Allen, W. V., supplemental report on
    sugar-trust bribery, 404.
American, early, refiners of petroleum,
    39.
American Transfer Company receives
    from 20 to 35 cents per barrel on all
    oil shipped by competitors, 99; the
    South Improvement Company reap-
    pears in, 100; false map of, before
    New York Legislature, 101.
Andrews, E. Benjamin, on prices under
    monopoly, 428; on oil-trust prices,
    430 *n*.
Anonymous circulars, in war against
    Toledo, 327.
Artificial liquors, 27.
Atchison, Topeka and Santa Fé Rail-
    road *et al.*, William C. Bissell *vs.*,
    479.
Atlantic and Great Western Railroad
    and South Improvement Company,
    48, 50; war of 1877, 88.
Attorney - General, of Pennsylvania,
    management of tax-case against
    Standard Oil Company by, 170–81;
    of United States, on monopoly, 37;
    report for 1893, 3, 6; cases against
    the sugar trust, 404.

35

Austria, refineries of, consolidated, 439.

Bad oil, 405–19.
Baltimore and Ohio, and railroad war
    of 1877, 88; closes Baltimore to inde-
    pendent shippers, 102; withdraws
    rates, 221; freight agent escapes from
    Congress, 222.
Baltimore closed to independent ship-
    pers by Baltimore and Ohio Railroad,
    102; sale of refineries at, 421.
Bank of England's income compared
    with an American millionaire's, 459.
Bankers indemnified for withdrawing
    bids on Toledo bonds, 336.
Bankruptcy of oil refineries in 1873,
    60; 1879–92, 455–70.
Baptist, the *National*, quoted, 341.
Barrel shipments better for railroads
    than tanks, 138, 231; destroyed by
    railroads, 138.
Barrett, Judge, defines monopoly, 3;
    on sugar trust, 3, 4.
Batoum refuses Rothschild permission
    to lay pipe line, 443.
Baxter, Judge, decision on rebates paid
    oil combination, 207.
Bee, Omaha *Daily*, investigates oil in-
    spection of Nebraska, 414.
Beef, combination of packers of, 33,
    36; price of, under combination, 35.
Belgium, 437.
Bernheimer, Simon, testimony as to
    abundance of capital for early refin-
    ers, 41.
"Big Four" combination, 35.

THE END

By the Same Author

A STRIKE OF MILLIONAIRES AGAINST MINERS

OR, THE

STORY OF SPRING VALLEY

AN OPEN LETTER TO THE MILLIONAIRES

Notices by the Press

The Springfield (Mass.) *Republican* (editorial).

Those who keep note of passing events will not have forgotten the lock-out of coal miners at Spring Valley, Illinois, in the early months of 1889, and the sufferings of the families of the workmen in consequence.

This sad story of corporate inhumanity has been effectively told by Henry D. Lloyd in a book entitled *A Strike of Millionaires against Miners.* It merits no less a volume than this. It is not an isolated case—an industrial phenomenon springing from conditions rarely repeated—but one of many similar cases, a part only of the whole story of coal mining in the United States. More than this, it is an aggravated illustration of the soullessness of the corporation in general, through the agency of which the bulk of the producing powers of the nation is working.

Behind this legal fiction men hide and do deeds of grasping cruelty that disgrace manhood, and are fast bringing the industrial organism into contempt. In the case of Spring Valley, the directors and stockholders of the Chicago and North-Western Railroad and the Spring Valley Coal Company—controlled by the same men—are as responsible for the sufferings and death from starvation of miners in Spring Valley in 1889 as if they had all been personally present and assisted in the business of bringing men from a distance to work in their mines on assurance of steady employment, and then of locking them out without warning, to starve them into submission to lower wages, for the sake of higher profits on their stock. This is the conclusion of Mr. Lloyd, and we see no escape from it.

If the corporation is to be considered an impersonality without moral responsibility, it will either have to go, or the industrial system which makes it an essential part will have to go. All the power of government, or wealth, or vested interests cannot maintain that system which, resting as our present system must on the charitable instincts of men, offers a way of escape from the responsibilities imposed thereby to the most powerful factors of the society. Against that system "the pulses of men will beat until they beat it down." What must be the condition of that society which allows the wealthy capitalists who starved these thousands of miners not only to go unpunished, but to move in the very highest circles of business power and social influence? And one of them in particular is to-day figuring upon representing the Democratic party of Pennsylvania in the United States Senate.

The New York *Commercial Advertiser* (editorial).

It is to be remembered that Mr. Lloyd's book does not profess to be a dispassionate review of the situation. It is an indictment. The corporation's side should be given a fair hearing. But it must be heard soon. Mr. Lloyd's charges are too important, his formulation of them too worthy of respect to be treated with silent contempt. To ignore them is to confess their truth. Should such a reply be made, the readers of this column will be informed of it. *A Strike of Millionaires against Miners* describes the poverty, the suffering, the utter misery among the miners in Spring Valley, Illinois, during the past year. In the simplicity and restraint of his style, and in the massing of his facts, Mr. Lloyd shows genuine literary power. There is no attempt at rhetoric in his narrative. He depends upon statements of facts, many of them incontrovertible, to rouse the hot indignation of his readers. If the story is true, and it bears every appearance of truth, the Spring Valley mine owners have been guilty of damnable treachery and cruelty to their fellow-men.

Chicago *Herald* (editorial).

The *Herald* commends to the attention of its readers the open letter in another column, from Henry D. Lloyd, addressed to various millionaires of New York, Chicago, and St. Paul. It contains what the *Herald* believes to be the truth as to the Spring Valley scandal, and while in most respects it is a plain statement of facts, it is nevertheless one of the most powerful appeals for justice, and one of the most eloquent denunciations of wrong, which has come under the public eye in many a day.

Mr. Lloyd's high character, his superb attainments, and his well-known philanthropy give force to the arraignment it might not otherwise possess. His letter is a history of a crime—a crime resulting, no doubt, from an infamous conspiracy—and the story leads naturally and inevitably to the conclusion which Mr. Lloyd avows, that there must be conspiracy laws for millionaires as well as for workingmen.

Civilization must be bottomed on justice, or it cannot endure. A society which permits such inhuman outrages as that at Spring Valley is either asleep or in an advanced stage of decay. The money god cannot crush out the lives of human beings with impunity. Let its devotees look well to the ground on which they stand. The wise and humane will be warned in time. The foolish and insatiate must be left to the stern judgment of their fellow-men, who must some day pass upon their act.

The *Labor World*, London, England.

What does Mr. Andrew Carnegie, who chants vulgar pæans to "Triumphant Democracy" say to such a book as this of Mr. Lloyd? This story of the robbery and betrayal of thousands of working miners in Illinois by a great millionaire corporation is one of the worst things we have read for a long time, and is a terribly scathing satire on American "democracy."

Let us hear no more trash about "free" America as compared with down-trodden Europe. Both continents are down-trodden by the rich men who own the raw material out of which wealth is created by human labor. When the land of the United States is all absorbed by private persons, as it will be in twenty years' time, there will not be a pin to choose between America and Europe, so far as wage-workers are concerned. Wages may be higher in America, but the increased cost of living there will nearly equalize the condition of the two continents; while for swindling, lying, and merciless oppression many American capitalists leave their European brethren far behind. Mr. Lloyd's book, which is the first of a new "Bad Wealth Series," ought to open men's eyes to the fact that true freedom is impossible when a few men have a right to appropriate to themselves the raw material of the globe.

Chicago *Daily Inter-Ocean*.

Mr. Lloyd's reputation as a writer on economic questions is sustained in the manner of handling the usually dry statistical matter which tells the story of strikes and lock-outs. He makes the story interesting and often graphic, while he gives the facts and figures relating to the intricacy of contracts in a way to be easily understood by the ordinary reader. The book is a valuable compilation of the facts gathered relating to this shameless abuse of corporative power in Spring Valley.

The *New Ideal*.

Mr. Lloyd has been until recently on the editorial staff of the Chicago *Tribune*, and is now devoting his time to first-hand investigations into labor troubles. This book gives an account of a lock-out in one of the mining districts of Illinois, and is the more forcible and eloquent an arraignment of the "millionaires," as the statements are throughout verifiable. As Mr. Lloyd in effect says, professors of political economy do not come near enough to realities to discover such details as he portrays, and the workingmen do not know how to bring them before public opinion. Hence the necessity of a mediator, who shall thoroughly investigate the facts and at the same time give them to the public, not in statistical reports, but in a form that compels its attention. Mr. Lloyd is a practised writer; no one can read this narrative without being profoundly moved, and for the directors and stockholders of the Spring Valley Coal Company (and, besides, of the Chicago and North - Western Railway, an aider and abettor of the nefarious business) the effect must be to set their blood on fire—so far as they are blessed (or unblessed) with any moral sensitiveness. Every thoughtful citizen—whether man or woman—should read this book, and have fully brought home to him or her the problems it suggests. It belongs to the literature both of fact and of power.

The *Religio-Philosophical Journal.*

Mr. Lloyd admits that Spring Valley and its miseries and wrongs were, at the beginning, but the conception and achievement of one or two of the leading owners of railroad and other companies who did the planning, secured the approval of the Board of Directors, and the active influence of the railroads through whom, by special freights, the business of competitors was stolen, coal land was bought, and the scheme was invented by which fortunes were to be made from workingmen's necessities and the misuse of the powers of the common carrier. But none of the directors, none of the stockholders, who received the profits of the scheme, protested against it; on the contrary, all accepted unprotestingly their "share of the guilt and gilt." Mr. Lloyd gives a mass of facts and figures which prove, on the part of corporations employing men at Spring Valley, an amount of greed and heartlessness which seems incredible in an enlightened country.

Mr. Lloyd is a literary artist as well as a man of deep feeling, and he combines felicity of diction with fervor and eloquence of expression, and writes with effectiveness and power. The book should be read by all who are interested in the labor question—the practical issue of the hour.

Chicago *Times.*

It is a pitiful story, a heart-breaking story, and Mr. Lloyd tells it with a great deal of force and earnestness.

The *Dawn.*

Can it be possible in these happier days among men who share the Christian civilization of the very eve of the twentieth century, that there can exist any analogy to this relentless war of savagery, this cruel and cowardly subjugation of a competitor, not in honest, open combat, but by taking advantage of a position to deny him food, shelter, and the very necessaries of life? For an answer, such as would bring indignant emotion to every heart not indurated by avarice of gold, and shame to every cheek not rendered incapable of blushing by hardened selfishness, we refer to the terrible facts, so calmly told with the severity of simple truth by Mr. Lloyd.

Starved Rock and Spring Valley are not isolated instances. The malady is constitutional, not local. "The whole head is sick and the whole heart faint," may be said of our modern system of business.

The *Nationalist.*

In this age of strikes it is not always the workers who strike, as is indicated by the title of Mr. Lloyd's book. That brilliant and great-hearted journalist and publicist several months ago, in the shape of an open letter of several columns, printed in the Chicago *Herald,* told the story of the criminal and cold-blooded conspiracy of a group of enormously rich men against a body of honest and industrious workingmen. That letter he has made the basis of the present volume, which deserves a wide circulation among patriotic citizens of the United States. The strong and truthful words here uttered ought to ring throughout the land and arouse the people to a realizing sense of the greatest danger that has ever threatened our republic—the danger of its conversion into the worst of despotisms, that of rule by an irresponsible plutocracy.

The Burlington *Hawkeye.*

Mr. Lloyd proves every charge he makes, the testimony he brings forward being so presented as to leave no question as to its absolute correctness. In all the dark record of tyranny, cruelty, and brutality made by the coal barons of this country there is not a blacker chapter than that which tells of their crimes against the miners of Spring Valley in the year 1889. This is not the verdict of the "labor crank" alone; the people of Chicago and the whole of northern Illinois, in the press and pulpit and on the platform, have denounced the outrage, and the cooler judgment of to-day, when the lock-out is about worn out and the majority of the old miners are scattered all over the country, is in accord with the denunciation made by Mr. Lloyd.

The *Rock Islander*, Rock Island, Ill.

A Strike of Millionaires against Miners, or the Story of Spring Valley. The above is the title of a beautifully printed volume of 264 pages, by Henry D. Lloyd. Its prelude is the story of the starved Indians of Starved Rock, and it proceeds to parallel that by the starvation of labor by the millionaires. The story of Spring Valley is given in detail, with official proof of its truthfulness, and is graphically told by Mr. Lloyd. Its exposure of the oppressors of labor is terrific. It shows who they are; who has done this thing; how the town was boomed; how it was doomed; how the ghost of Starved Rock walks abroad; and how people are bought and enslaved in this boasted free country. It gives Governor Fifer a deserved slap for not going in person to the scene of starvation, and it roasts his military toady of the rich (Adjutant-General Vance) who was sent there by the governor to investigate, and whose report is proven to be a tissue of sneers at the poor, and falsehoods in regard to them and their situation. He quotes freely and approvingly from the report of Judge Gould and Mr. Wines, proving all that was claimed for the suffering there. He shows (page 66) that the Chicago, Milwaukee and St. Paul Railroad Company generously acknowledged the necessity for help by hiring a physician for its miners at Braceville, and sending supplies of necessaries for sick women and children to be given out by its agent there. He shows up the campaign of slander against Spring Valley, which was carried on through capitalistic newspapers and corporation tools; says the Spring Valley case is only a preliminary skirmish of capital against labor, and, after showing the first fruits, asks what the last will be. He closes with a chapter giving part of the moral. An appendix is added, showing what the millionaires said of themselves, and the replies by the miners and the press. Everybody should read this most remarkable and ably prepared story of the crime of capital upon labor.

Seed-Time (London), the organ of the New Fellowship.

Perhaps the most striking of all the American object-lessons on the tendencies of capitalism has been given us by Mr. Henry D. Lloyd, of Chicago, who has recently published a book entitled, *A Strike of Millionaires against Miners, or the Story of Spring Valley.* A more complete exposure of the tyranny and cruelty of capitalism has never before been made. Its great importance for us, however, lies in the fact that all the tyranny and wrong he witnessed and describes are but the natural outcomes of the principles of commercialism when those principles are carried to their logical conclusion, and capitalism has unchecked sway. Such terrible scenes do not occur everywhere, simply because capitalism is held in check by other social forces, and has not everywhere attained that full and unfettered development which discloses the evils which in its more undeveloped stage lie concealed.

The *Twentieth Century*.

It is a mind-agitating and heart-rending tale, and unless I am much mistaken the publication of it will create an epoch in economic thinking and social regeneration. What is the remedy for such crimes as Mr. Lloyd has exposed? The remedy will be found if open-minded persons will read such books as Mr. Lloyd's, and keep themselves informed as to what is being done to reduce a people to servitude. This single book ought to produce such a revulsion of feeling against the monstrous millionaires who perpetrated this awful crime that they would be looked upon by all decent people with abhorrence.

If you will read Mr. Lloyd's book I think you will agree with me that if before long, as many persons believe, this country is to be deluged in the blood of revolution, the catastrophe will be brought on by condoning such crimes as that at Spring Valley; it will be brought on because you and I read such stories as this, and, knowing they are true, straightway forget all about them; it will be brought on because editors and preachers, and others who have the public ear, keep silent through negligence or fear of the rich who misrule the land. If people will not think, if they will not care, you may depend upon it that the price of their indifference will be slavery or war.

From a letter to the *Twentieth Century.*

Your article, and the extracts from Mr. Lloyd's book in your issue of June 12, portraying the outrageous injustice inflicted on the Spring Valley coal miners by the railway and coal-mining barons, was read before our club by Judge Frank T. Reid, of this city, a member of the club, at its regular weekly meeting, Monday, June 23. A resolution was unanimously passed and sent to the General Executive Board of the Nationalist clubs at Boston, requesting it to get up a memorial to the Government Bureau of Labor, petitioning that body to institute a special inquiry into the outrages; that this be done with a view of publishing these crimes to the whole country, under the proper authority, and also with the view of memorializing Congress for the government to work either all or part of the coal-mining industry on the same principle that it works the postal service, the government printing-office at Washington, and other industries, as the present method of running the coal mines by corporations has resulted, and will continue to result, in rioting and bloodshed, and imperils the very existence of society. We would suggest that copies of the memorial be sent to all the Nationalist clubs for signatures, and also to the Federated trades, Knights of Labor, and other organized bodies and to individuals. Might we also suggest that you kindly communicate with the Executive Board of Boston, and with our worthy and earnest brothers, Messrs. Bellamy, Bliss, and others?   Yours fraternally,

J. L. JOHNSON,
Secretary Nationalist Club.

TACOMA, Wash.

The *Open Court.*

The story of Spring Valley will make every American citizen of healthy morals uncomfortable and ashamed. . . . A story which must be read, and the lesson of it heeded, or worse things come.

The St. Louis *Republic.*

A stirring account of the great mining strike, lock-out, and consequent misery at Spring Valley, Illinois, in 1888–89, the main features of which are still familiar to the reading public. Mr. Lloyd lays the blame where it belongs, and shows how the whole transaction worked to the profit of the plutocrats at the expense of their dupes—the enterprising thousands who believed in the promises made in booming the location. The booming of the town was followed by the dooming, and, as the *Republic* and many other papers showed at the time, the action of the mine operators all through was "a cruel abuse of intellectual strength to use it to force weakness and ignorance into such a condition of helplessness." The author gives facts and figures, and his account of the matter is borne out by the news columns of the times. It is a sad story, and its truthfulness is a shameful comment upon the tendencies of our day.

The Pittsburg *Labor Tribune*.

A Strike of Millionaires against Miners, or the Story of Spring Valley, is a handsome edition of the important matter written by Henry D. Lloyd when the notable strike was on at the mines located at Spring Valley, Illinois. Our miner readers especially will read with satisfaction the vim and ability with which Mr. Lloyd handles the literary end of that eventful period, and will be pleased to know that he has issued the matter in consecutive form.

The *Democrat* (London).

Bad as the social and industrial condition of Great Britain is, that of the United States threatens to become as bad or even worse unless the power of landlordism there is subjected to popular control. A striking instance of the rapid growth of monopoly and its ruinous effect on industry, as well as its atrocious tyranny over labor, is recorded in a striking little book by Mr. Henry D. Lloyd, of Chicago, called *A Strike of Millionaires against Miners*.

Rights of Labor (Chicago).

This narrative of the rapacity and greed of our coal barons we most earnestly commend to all our readers as a plain, clear statement of facts, admirably put; it deserves the widest circulation.

New York *Herald*.

This is one of the saddest, most enraging stories ever put on paper; of course the corporations protested, as corporations always do in such cases, that they were not to blame, but the awful facts cannot be denied or explained away. The *Herald* expressed its mind editorially at the time. Now that the whole case is presented, the *Herald's* readers can see how easily a scheming gang of heartless scoundrels can quickly reduce thousands of families to a condition worse than old-fashioned African slavery.

Tacoma (Washington) *Globe*.

Among the many books recently published on the labor question and the relations between the rich and the poor, none has excited a deeper interest than *A Strike of Millionaires against Miners*. Before the atrocities perpetrated in Spring Valley by the coal mining company, composed of some of the wealthiest men in the United States, the wrongs inflicted on the peasants in Ireland fade into insignificance. This book should have a wide reading, that all may know whither the nation is drifting.

Boston *Herald.*

The story of the labor disturbances at Spring Valley, Illinois, caused by a shut-down of the mines in 1888, is told by H. D. Lloyd in a thrilling presentation. In perusing the whole history, from the first alluring advertisements of the mining companies to the editorial comments in Chicago papers after the lock-out took place, a dweller in happier laboring regions will hardly believe that so much injustice could have been done in free America.

The *Worker* (Brisbane, Queensland).

A simple but complete account of a terrible injustice.

The *Christian Union.*

Six or eight years ago there appeared in the *North American Review* an article entitled "The Lords of Industry," by Henry D. Lloyd, which set forth with such power the nature and extent of the combinations to diminish production and increase prices that its author may be said to have initiated the anti-trust agitation of the last few years. Since that time he has gone on in the work thus begun, putting heart and soul into it. The *Strike of Millionaires against Miners* carries perhaps less weight with our intellects than Mr. Lloyd's earlier work, but it appeals so strongly to our hearts that we are carried with him through the volume, and share with him his indignation over the wrongs he describes.

CONCORD, New Hampshire, *October* 22, 1892.

DEAR MR. LLOYD,—I am reading the *Study* you so kindly sent me. I have read most of it, including the "Word to Coal Miners," and what a "study!" What a lesson! What an apocalypse! Through it, "the voice of our brothers' blood cries to us from the ground," literally, and in tones scarcely ever heard before by human or heavenly ear!

Would that you could peal out all the seven thunders of Patmos. I wish your work might outsell in number *Uncle Tom's Cabin*, and *Robert Elsmere* combined, till its note filled the earth as the waters the seas. Print the whole of this hasty testimony over my name, if it will be of service to the working man and woman.

Faithfully and fraternally yours, for every good thought, word, and work,

PARKER PILLSBURY.

A BOOK FOR THE TIMES

THE RAILWAYS AND THE REPUBLIC.
By James F. Hudson.   8vo, Cloth, $2 00.

The author studies carefully the evils of the system, inquires into the power of legislation to cure them, and describes the remedies which will preserve the usefulness of the railways, and at the same time protect legitimate investors.—*N. Y. Evening Post.*

It is seldom the public is given a work at once so timely, so brave, and so able. . . . . Mr. Hudson writes with the most exhaustive knowledge of his subject, and with an unusual ability in setting forth his ideas so that they are easily and clearly understood.   There is hardly a more vigorous chapter in modern literature than that in which he discusses the rise and growth of the Standard Company. . . . The book is everywhere marked by unusual ability, accuracy, and fearlessness, which make it one of the most important contributions of the day to a subject which of necessity engages more and more attention every day. The political principles of the writer are thoroughly sound and practical.—*Boston Courier.*

The subject is of such vital importance that no man or woman in the country should be ignorant about it.—*N. Y. Times.*

Mr. Hudson writes in the interests of the people, calmly and without passion, as one who thoroughly understands his subject, and in harmony with many others who have dealt with the same problems.—*Critic*, N. Y.

Published by HARPER & BROTHERS, New York

☞ *For sale by all booksellers, or will be sent by the publishers, postage prepaid, to any part of the United States, Canada, or Mexico, on receipt of price.*